AMERICAN EMPOWER

TEACHER'S BOOK

WITH DIGITAL PACK

A2

ELEMENTARY

Tim Foster with Ruth Gairns, Stuart Redman, Wayne
Rimmer, Lynda Edwards and Julian Oakley

CAMBRIDGE
UNIVERSITY PRESS

University Printing House, Cambridge CB2 8BS, United Kingdom

One Liberty Plaza, 20th Floor, New York, NY 10006, USA

477 Williamstown Road, Port Melbourne, VIC 3207, Australia

314–321, 3rd Floor, Plot 3, Splendor Forum, Jasola District Centre, New Delhi – 110025, India

103 Penang Road, #05-06/07, Visioncrest Commercial, Singapore 238467

Cambridge University Press is part of the University of Cambridge.

It furthers the University's mission by disseminating knowledge in the pursuit of
education, learning and research at the highest international levels of excellence.

www.cambridge.org
Information on this title: www.cambridge.org/9781108797191

First published 2022

20 19 18 17 16 15 14 13 12 11 10 9 8 7 6 5 4 3 2 1

Printed in Great Britain by CPI Group (UK) Ltd, Croydon CR0 4YY

A catalogue record for this publication is available from the British Library

ISBN 978-1-108-81751-6 Elementary Student's Book with eBook
ISBN 978-1-108-79716-0 Elementary Student's Book A with eBook
ISBN 978-1-108-79717-7 Elementary Student's Book B with eBook
ISBN 978-1-108-85046-9 Elementary Student's Book with Digital Pack
ISBN 978-1-108-86244-8 Elementary Student's Book A with Digital Pack
ISBN 978-1-108-86247-9 Elementary Student's Book B with Digital Pack
ISBN 978-1-108-81755-4 Elementary Workbook with Answers
ISBN 978-1-108-81756-1 Elementary Workbook A with Answers
ISBN 978-1-108-81757-8 Elementary Workbook B with Answers
ISBN 978-1-108-81758-5 Elementary Workbook without Answers
ISBN 978-1-108-81759-2 Elementary Workbook A without Answers
ISBN 978-1-108-81760-8 Elementary Workbook B without Answers
ISBN 978-1-108-81761-5 Elementary Full Contact with eBook
ISBN 978-1-108-81762-2 Elementary Full Contact A with eBook
ISBN 978-1-108-81763-9 Elementary Full Contact B with eBook
ISBN 978-1-108-85051-3 Elementary Full Contact with Digital Pack
ISBN 978-1-108-85054-4 Elementary Full Contact A with Digital Pack
ISBN 978-1-108-86243-1 Elementary Full Contact B with Digital Pack
ISBN 978-1-108-79719-1 Elementary Teacher's Book with Digital Pack
ISBN 978-1-108-79723-8 Elementary Presentation Plus

Additional resources for this publication at www.cambridge.org/americanempower

Contents

Teaching Notes

CAMBRIDGE

AMERICAN EMPOWER is a six-level general English course for adult and young adult learners, taking students from beginner to advanced level (CEFR A1 to C1). *American Empower* combines course content from Cambridge University Press with validated assessment from the experts at Cambridge Assessment English.

American Empower's unique mix of engaging classroom materials and reliable assessment enables learners to make consistent and measurable progress.

Content you'll love.
Assessment you
can trust.

Better Learning with *American Empower*

Better Learning is our simple approach where **insights** we've gained from research have helped shape **content** that drives **results**.

Learner engagement

1 Content that informs and motivates

Insights
Sustained motivation is key to successful language learning and skills development.

Content
Clear learning goals, thought-provoking images, texts, and speaking activities, plus video content to arouse curiosity.

Results
Content that surprises, entertains, and provokes an emotional response, helping teachers to deliver motivating and memorable lessons.

2A SHE LOVES HER JOB

Learn to talk about jobs
G Simple present: affirmative and negative
V Jobs

1 READING

a 🔊 Look at the picture. Answer the questions.
1 Where is this woman?
  a in a park   c by a river
  b at home
2 Do you think … ?
  a she's a tourist   b she works here
3 What do you know about alligators?

b Read the article and check your answers.

c Choose the correct answers.
1 Most people like / don't like alligators.
2 Gabby Scampone likes / doesn't like alligators.
3 Alligators like / don't like people swimming near them.
4 It is / is not dangerous to give alligators food.
5 Gabby has one job / two jobs.

d Read the article again. Find two reasons why Gabby's work is interesting.

e 🔊 Talk about the questions.
1 Would you like Gabby's job? Why / Why not?
2 What other unusual jobs do you know?

GATORGIRL

Gabby Scampone with an alligator

Everglades Holiday Park is an animal park in the U.S. It's in Florida. It has birds, fish, and … alligators! Many tourists visit the park every year. They come to look at the alligators. Most people think alligators are interesting, but they don't really like them, and they don't go too close to them!

Gabby Scampone is different. She lives in Florida, and she works at the park. She loves her job – and she also loves alligators. In her work, she teaches visitors about alligators. She tells visitors that alligators are not always dangerous animals. Usually, alligators don't attack people, but they don't like when people swim in the water near them. Also, if people give food to alligators, sometimes the alligators get too close, and that can be dangerous.

Gabby doesn't always work at the park. She also has a second job: she catches wild alligators. If a wild alligator goes near a person's house, Gabby and some other people catch it. They take the alligators back to the park. Her parents and friends think she's crazy, but she really enjoys the job. Gabby thinks many people don't understand alligators very well, but that alligators are smart and amazing animals. And so far she still has all of her fingers!

20

2 VOCABULARY Jobs

a Match words 1–9 with pictures a–i.
1 ☐ nurse   4 ☐ dentist   7 ☐ janitor
2 ☐ salesperson   5 ☐ pilot   8 ☐ photographer
3 ☐ police officer   6 ☐ engineer   9 ☐ taxi driver

b ▶02.01 Pronunciation Listen to the words and underline the stressed syllable.
police officer   engineer   photographer   dentist

c 🔊 Complete the sentences with jobs from 2a. Talk about your answers.
1 A(n) _____ has a dangerous job.
2 A(n) _____ has an easy job.
3 A(n) _____ has an exciting job.
4 The pay for a(n) _____ isn't very good.

d ▶ Now go to Vocabulary Focus 2A on p. 163 for more jobs vocabulary.

3 GRAMMAR
Simple present: affirmative and negative

a ▶02.03 Look at the sentences from 1b and complete them with the verbs from the box. Listen and check.

catches   come   doesn't   don't (x2)   go   attack   think   work   works

	I / we / you / they	he / she / it
+	Tourists _____ to look at the alligators. Her parents _____ she's crazy.	She _____ at Everglades Holiday Park. She _____ wild alligators.
–	They _____ too close to them. Alligators _____ people.	Gabby _____ always _____ at the park.

b Underline more simple present verbs in the text in 1b. Make two lists: affirmative and negative forms.

c ▶ Now go to Grammar Focus 2A on p. 140.

d Underline the verbs in sentences 1–2.
1 She loves her job.
2 She catches wild alligators.

e ▶02.05 Pronunciation Which verb in 3d has an extra syllable when we add the letter -s? Listen and check.

f Underline the correct answers.
1 After the sounds /s/, /v/, /dʒ/ (spelled j), /ʃ/ (spelled sh), and /tʃ/ (spelled ch), we don't add / add an extra syllable.
2 We don't add / add an extra syllable after other sounds.

g ▶02.06 Listen to these verbs. Check (✓) the verbs that have an extra syllable.
☐ works   ☐ eats   ☐ teaches
☐ finishes   ☐ listens   ☐ stops
☐ catches   ☐ uses   ☐ watches

h ▶ Communication 2A Student A go to p. 130. Student B go to p. 133.

4 SPEAKING

a Think about your job or the job of someone you know. Write four sentences about the job: two affirmative (+) and two negative (–). Use the verbs in the box.

work   drive   have   like   study
speak   go   start   leave   know

+ I start work at 7:00 in the morning.
– I don't drive to work.

b 🔊 Tell your partner your sentences. Can they guess the job?

c Tell other students about your partner's job. Can they guess it?

> She starts work at …

UNIT 2   21

---

2 Personalized and relevant

Insights
Language learners benefit from frequent opportunities to personalize their responses.

Content
Personalization tasks in every unit make the target language more meaningful to the individual learner.

Results
Personal responses make learning more memorable and inclusive, with all students participating in spontaneous spoken interaction.

> "There are so many adjectives to describe such a wonderful series, but in my opinion it's very reliable, practical, and modern."
>
> **Zenaide Brianez, Director of Studies, Instituto da Língua Inglesa, Brazil**

Measurable progress

1 Assessment you can trust

Insights
Tests developed and validated by Cambridge Assessment English, the world leaders in language assessment, to ensure they are accurate and meaningful.

Content
End-of-unit tests, mid- and end-of-course competency tests, and personalized CEFR test report forms provide reliable information on progress with language skills.

Results
Teachers can see learners' progress at a glance, and learners can see measurable progress, which leads to greater motivation.

Results of an impact study showing % improvement of Reading levels, based on global *Empower* students' scores over one year.

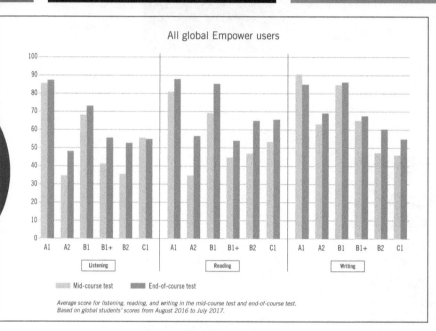

Average score for listening, reading, and writing in the mid-course test and end-of-course test.
Based on global students' scores from August 2016 to July 2017.

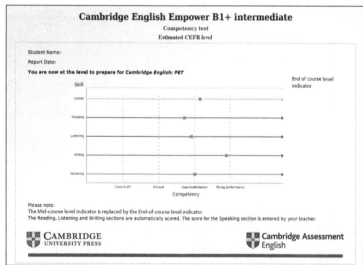

> **"** *We started using the tests provided with Empower and our students started showing better results from this point until now.* **"**
>
> **Kristina Ivanova, Director of Foreign Language Training Centre, ITMO University, Saint Petersburg, Russia**

2 Evidence of impact

Insights
Schools and colleges need to show that they are evaluating the effectiveness of their language programs.

Content
Empower (British English) impact studies have been carried out in various countries, including Russia, Brazil, Turkey, and the UK, to provide evidence of positive impact and progress.

Results
Colleges and universities have demonstrated a significant improvement in language level between the mid- and end-of-course tests, as well as a high level of teacher satisfaction with *Empower*.

Manageable learning

1 Mobile friendly

Insights
Learners expect online content to be mobile friendly but also flexible and easy to use on any digital device.

Content
American Empower provides easy access to Digital Workbook content that works on any device and includes practice activities with audio.

Results
Digital Workbook content is easy to access anywhere, and produces meaningful and actionable data so teachers can track their students' progress and adapt their lesson accordingly.

> *I had been studying English for 10 years before university, and I didn't succeed. But now with Empower I know my level of English has changed.*
>
> **Nikita, *Empower* Student, ITMO University, Saint Petersburg, Russia**

2 Corpus-informed

Insights
Corpora can provide valuable information about the language items learners are able to learn successfully at each CEFR level.

Content
Two powerful resources – Cambridge Corpus and English Profile – informed the development of the *Empower* course syllabus and the writing of the materials.

Results
Learners are presented with the target language they are able to incorporate and use at the right point in their learning journey. They are not overwhelmed with unrealistic learning expectations.

Rich in practice

1 Language in use

Insights
It is essential that learners are offered frequent and manageable opportunities to practice the language they have been focusing on.

Content
Throughout the *American Empower* Student's Book, learners are offered a wide variety of practice activities, plenty of controlled practice, and frequent opportunities for communicative spoken practice.

Results
Meaningful practice makes new language more memorable and leads to more efficient progress in language acquisition.

2 Beyond the classroom

There are plenty of opportunities for personalization.

Elena Pro,
Teacher, EOI
de San Fernando
de Henares,
Spain

Insights
Progress with language learning often requires work outside of the classroom, and different teaching models require different approaches.

Content
American Empower is available with a print workbook, online practice, documentary-style videos that expose learners to real-world English, plus additional resources with extra ideas and fun activities.

Results
This choice of additional resources helps teachers to find the most effective ways to motivate their students both inside and outside the classroom.

Unit overview

Unit Opener
Getting started page – Clear learning objectives to give an immediate sense of purpose.

Lessons A and B
Grammar and Vocabulary – Input and practice of core grammar and vocabulary, plus a mix of skills.

Digital Workbook (online, mobile): Grammar and Vocabulary

Lesson C
Everyday English – Functional language in common, everyday situations.

Digital Workbook (online, mobile): Listening and Speaking

Unit Progress Test

Lesson D
Integrated Skills – Practice of all four skills, with a special emphasis on writing.

Digital Workbook (online, mobile): Reading and Writing

Review
Extra practice of grammar, vocabulary, and pronunciation. Also a "Review your progress" section for students to reflect on the unit.

Mid- / End-of-course test

Additional practice
Further practice is available for outside of the class with these components.

Digital Workbook (online, mobile)

Workbook (printed)

Components

Resources – Available on cambridgeone.org

- Audio
- Video
- Unit Progress Tests (Print)
- Unit Progress Tests (Online)

- Mid- and end-of-course assessment (Print)
- Mid- and end-of-course assessment (Online)

- Digital Workbook (Online)
- Photocopiable Grammar, Vocabulary, and Pronunciation worksheets

Getting Started

Striking and unusual images arouse curiosity.

Clear learning objectives give an immediate sense of purpose.

CAN DO OBJECTIVES

- Talk about jobs
- Talk about study habits
- Ask for things and reply
- Complete a form

WORK AND STUDY

UNIT **2**

GETTING STARTED

a Look at the picture and answer the questions.

1 Where do you think the woman is?
2 What is she holding?
3 What's one good thing about her job and one bad thing?

b What kind of work do you think is interesting? Here are some ideas:

- working with people
- working with animals
- working with machines
- working on your own

Activities promote emotional engagement and a personal response.

19

Lessons A and B
Grammar and Vocabulary and a mix of skills

"Teach off the page"
A straightforward approach and clear lesson flow help to minimize preparation time.

Clear goals
Each lesson starts with a clear, practical, and achievable learning goal, creating an immediate sense of purpose.

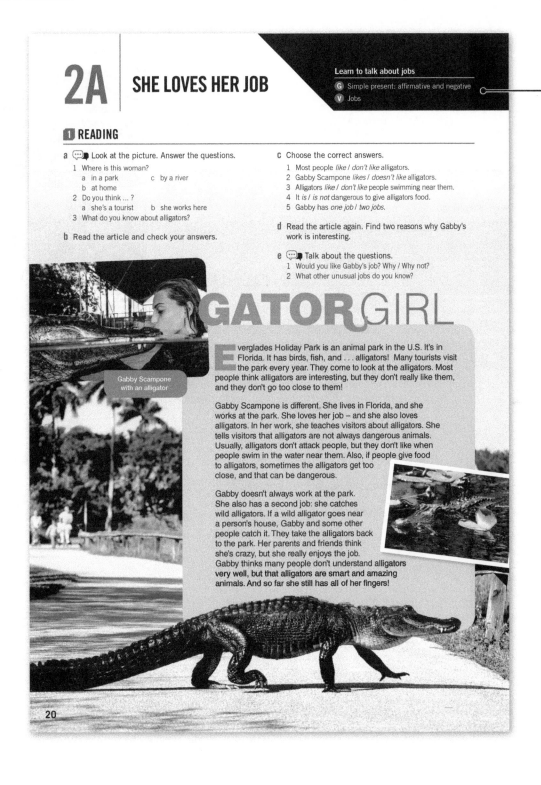

2A | SHE LOVES HER JOB

Learn to talk about jobs
G Simple present: affirmative and negative
V Jobs

1 READING

a 💬 Look at the picture. Answer the questions.
  1 Where is this woman?
    a in a park   c by a river
    b at home
  2 Do you think ... ?
    a she's a tourist   b she works here
  3 What do you know about alligators?

b Read the article and check your answers.

c Choose the correct answers.
  1 Most people *like / don't like* alligators.
  2 Gabby Scampone *likes / doesn't like* alligators.
  3 Alligators *like / don't like* people swimming near them.
  4 It *is / is not* dangerous to give alligators food.
  5 Gabby has *one job / two jobs*.

d Read the article again. Find two reasons why Gabby's work is interesting.

e 💬 Talk about the questions.
  1 Would you like Gabby's job? Why / Why not?
  2 What other unusual jobs do you know?

GATOR GIRL

Gabby Scampone with an alligator

Everglades Holiday Park is an animal park in the U.S. It's in Florida. It has birds, fish, and . . . alligators! Many tourists visit the park every year. They come to look at the alligators. Most people think alligators are interesting, but they don't really like them, and they don't go too close to them!

Gabby Scampone is different. She lives in Florida, and she works at the park. She loves her job – and she also loves alligators. In her work, she teaches visitors about alligators. She tells visitors that alligators are not always dangerous animals. Usually, alligators don't attack people, but they don't like when people swim in the water near them. Also, if people give food to alligators, sometimes the alligators get too close, and that can be dangerous.

Gabby doesn't always work at the park. She also has a second job: she catches wild alligators. If a wild alligator goes near a person's house, Gabby and some other people catch it. They take the alligators back to the park. Her parents and friends think she's crazy, but she really enjoys the job. Gabby thinks many people don't understand alligators very well, but that alligators are smart and amazing animals. And so far she still has all of her fingers!

20

Manageable learning

The syllabus is informed by English Profile and the Cambridge English Corpus. Students will learn the most relevant and useful language at the most appropriate point in their learning journey. The target language is benchmarked to the CEFR.

2 VOCABULARY Jobs

a Match words 1–9 with pictures a–i.

1 ☐ nurse   4 ☐ dentist   7 ☐ janitor
2 ☐ salesperson   5 ☐ pilot   8 ☐ photographer
3 ☐ police officer   6 ☐ engineer   9 ☐ taxi driver

b ▶ 02.01 **Pronunciation** Listen to the words and <u>underline</u> the stressed syllable.

po<u>lice</u> officer   engineer   photographer   dentist

c 💬 Complete the sentences with jobs from 2a. Talk about your answers.

1 A(n) _____ has a dangerous job.
2 A(n) _____ has an easy job.
3 A(n) _____ has an exciting job.
4 The pay for a(n) _____ isn't very good.

d ≫ Now go to Vocabulary Focus 2A on p. 163 for more jobs vocabulary.

Rich in practice

Clear signposts to **Grammar Focus** and **Vocabulary Focus** sections offer extra support and practice.

3 GRAMMAR
Simple present: affirmative and negative

a ▶ 02.03 Look at the sentences from 1b and complete them with the verbs from the box. Listen and check.

catches   come   doesn't   don't (x2)   go   attack   think   work   works

	I / we / you / they	he / she / it
+	Tourists _____ to look at the alligators. Her parents _____ she's crazy.	She _____ at Everglades Holiday Park. She _____ wild alligators.
–	They _____ _____ too close to them. Alligators _____ _____ people.	Gabby _____ always _____ at the park.

b <u>Underline</u> more simple present verbs in the text in 1b. Make two lists: affirmative and negative forms.

c ≫ Now go to Grammar Focus 2A on p. 140.

d <u>Underline</u> the verbs in sentences 1–2.

1 She loves her job.
2 She catches wild alligators.

e ▶ 02.05 **Pronunciation** Which verb in 3d has an extra syllable when we add the letter -s? Listen and check.

f <u>Underline</u> the correct answers.

1 After the sounds /z/, /s/, /dʒ/ (spelled j), /ʃ/ (spelled sh), and /tʃ/ (spelled ch), we *don't add / add* an extra syllable.
2 We *don't add / add* an extra syllable after other sounds.

g ▶ 02.06 Listen to these verbs. Check (✓) the verbs that have an extra syllable.

☐ works   ☐ eats   ☐ teaches
☐ finishes   ☐ listens   ☐ stops
☐ catches   ☐ uses   ☐ watches

h ≫ **Communication 2A** Student A go to p. 130. Student B go to p. 133.

4 SPEAKING

a Think about your job or the job of someone you know. Write four sentences about the job: two affirmative (+) and two negative (–). Use the verbs in the box.

work   drive   have   like   study
speak   go   start   leave   know

+ I start work at 7:00 in the morning.
– I don't drive to work.

b 💬 Tell your partner your sentences. Can they guess the job?

c Tell other students about your partner's job. Can they guess it?

She starts work at …

21

Regular speaking activities

Frequent speaking stages get students talking throughout the lesson.

Learner engagement
Engaging images and texts motivate students to respond personally. This makes learning more memorable and gives learners ownership of the language.

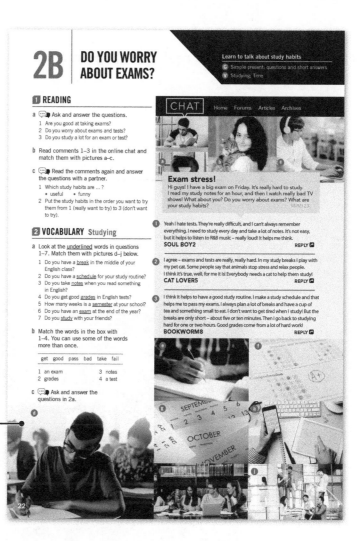

2B DO YOU WORRY ABOUT EXAMS?

Learn to talk about study habits
G Simple present: questions and short answers
V Studying; Time

1 READING

a Ask and answer the questions.
1 Are you good at taking exams?
2 Do you worry about exams and tests?
3 Do you study a lot for an exam or test?

b Read comments 1–3 in the online chat and match them with pictures a–c.

c Read the comments again and answer the questions with a partner.
1 Which study habits are … ?
• useful • funny
2 Put the study habits in the order you want to try them from 1 (really want to try) to 3 (don't want to try).

2 VOCABULARY Studying

a Look at the underlined words in questions 1–7. Match them with pictures d–j below.
1 Do you have a break in the middle of your English class?
2 Do you have a schedule for your study routine?
3 Do you take notes when you read something in English?
4 Do you get good grades in English tests?
5 How many weeks is a semester at your school?
6 Do you have an exam at the end of the year?
7 Do you study with your friends?

b Match the words in the box with 1–4. You can use some of the words more than once.

get good pass bad take fail

1 an exam   3 notes
2 grades   4 a test

c Ask and answer the questions in 2a.

CHAT Home Forums Articles Archives

Exam stress!
Hi guys! I have a big exam on Friday. It's really hard to study. I read my study notes for an hour, and then I watch really bad TV shows! What about you? Do you worry about exams? What are your study habits? MIMI123

① Yeah I hate tests. They're really difficult, and I can't always remember everything. I need to study every day and take a lot of notes. It's not easy, but it helps to listen to R&B music – really loud! It helps me think. **SOUL BOY2** REPLY

② I agree – exams and tests are really, really hard. In my study breaks I play with my pet cat. Some people say that animals stop stress and relax people. I think it's true, well, for me it is! Everybody needs a cat to help them study! **CAT LOVER5** REPLY

③ I think it helps to have a good study routine. I make a study schedule and that helps me to pass my exams. I always plan a lot of breaks and have a cup of tea and something small to eat. I don't want to get tired when I study! But the breaks are only short – about five or ten minutes. Then I go back to studying hard for one or two hours. Good grades come from a lot of hard work! **BOOKWORM8** REPLY

22

UNIT 2

Tania and Jack

3 LISTENING

a ▶02.07 Jack talks to Tania about her study habits. Listen and check (✓) the things they talk about.
1 ☐ places to study   3 ☐ exams
2 ☐ hours of study   4 ☐ free time

b ▶02.07 Listen again. Complete the information about Tania's studies.
• Part-time or full-time student?   • When?
• Hours a week?   • Where?

4 VOCABULARY Time

a Match the times that Tania talks about with the clocks.
1 Usually at **eight thirty**…
2 … last night at **a quarter after eleven**.

b Complete the sentences with the words in the box.

to after o'clock thirty

1 four _____   3 (a) quarter _____ four
2 four _____   4 (a) quarter _____ five

c ≫ Now go to Vocabulary Focus 2B on p. 164 for more practice with time vocabulary.

5 GRAMMAR Simple present: questions

a ▶02.09 Look at the questions. Which is correct? Listen and check.
1 You a full-time student or a part-time student?
2 Are you a full-time student or a part-time student?
3 You are a full-time student or a part-time student?

b Complete the questions with one word.
_____ … you study engineering?
_____ … they like tests?

c ▶02.10 Jack asks Tania about her daughter, Ellie. Listen and complete the information about Ellie's studies.
• Hours a week?
• When?
• Where?

d Read the question Jack asks Tania.
Does she study more before an exam?
Look at the questions in 5b. How are they different? Why?

e ≫ Now go to Grammar Focus 2B on p. 140.

f ▶02.12 Put the questions in the correct order. Listen and check.
1 a week / do you study / hours / how many?
2 study grammar / or vocabulary / do you?
3 you / when / study / do?
4 study / do / where / you?

g ▶02.12 Pronunciation Notice the pronunciation of *do you* in each question. Can you hear both words clearly?

6 SPEAKING

a Look at the questions in 5f. Write another question about studying.

b Ask and answer your questions in 6a.

c Do you have any new ideas about studying now?

> Natalia studies very early in the morning because she isn't very tired. I think it's a good idea, but I prefer to sleep!

23

Spoken outcome
Each A and B lesson ends with a practical spoken outcome, so learners can use language immediately.

xiii

Lesson C
Prepares learners for effective real-world spoken communication

Everyday English
Thorough coverage of functional language for common everyday situations helps learners to communicate effectively in the real world.

Comprehensive approach to speaking skills
A unique combination of language input, pronunciation, and speaking strategies offers a comprehensive approach to speaking skills.

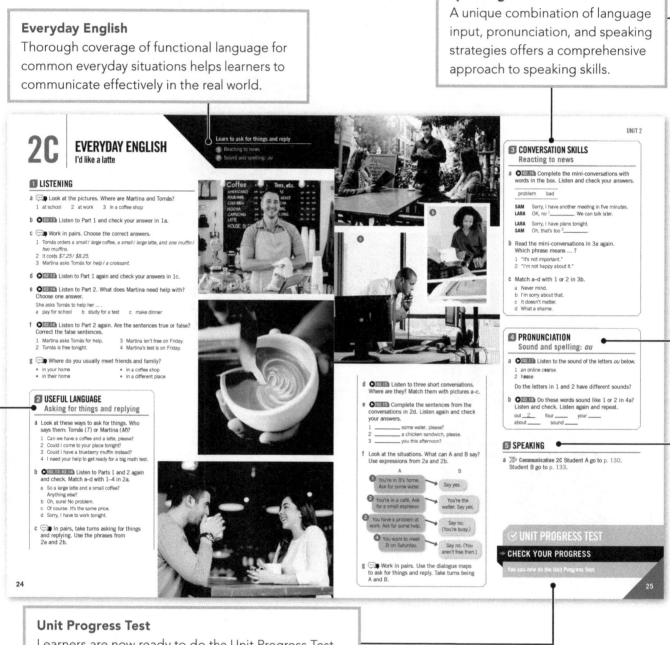

Unit Progress Test
Learners are now ready to do the Unit Progress Test, developed by Cambridge Assessment English.

Spoken outcome
Each C lesson ends with a practical spoken outcome.

Lesson D
Integrated skills with a special focus on writing

Skills for writing
The D lessons are highly communicative and cover all four skills, with a special focus on writing. They also recycle and consolidate the core language from the A, B, and C lessons.

Personal response
Clear model texts on which students can base their own writing are provided.

2D SKILLS FOR WRITING
I need English for my job

Learn to complete a form
W Spelling

1 SPEAKING AND LISTENING

a 💬 Why do you want to study English?
- to get a good job
- to meet new friends
- for travel and tourism
- to study something in English
- a different reason

b ▶ 02.19 Listen to three International College students talk about where they're from and their reasons for studying English. Underline the correct answers.

I'm from *Acapulco / Mexico City,* and I need English for my *job / studies.*

I'm from *Riyadh / Jeddah,* and I need English for my *job / studies.*

Said

I'm from *Tokyo / Osaka,* and I need English for my *job / studies.*

Daniela

Sakura

c ▶ 02.19 Listen again and complete the chart with the words in the box.

grammar   the classes   the teacher
reading and writing   listening   the schedule

	Likes at the college	Needs to improve
Daniela		
Said		
Sakura		

d 💬 Talk about the questions with other students.
1 What do you need to improve in English?
2 Why is this important for you?

e ▶ 02.20 Listen to Kate talk about a competition at International College. What can you win?

f ▶ 02.20 Listen again. Answer the questions.
1 Can students who don't go to International College enter the competition?
2 Is it OK to use a computer for the entry form?
3 Where can students get entry forms?

2 READING

a Look at the information about Daniela. Complete Part 1 of the form. Can you remember her nationality?

From: EIC Student Care
To: danielar@supermail.com

Dear Daniela,

We're looking forward to welcoming you to International College on July 6th.

You will be in class P1 and your teacher will be Kate Marks. We hope . . .

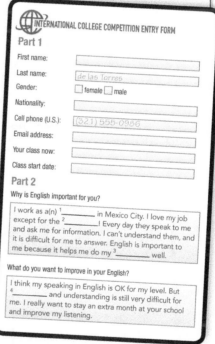

INTERNATIONAL COLLEGE COMPETITION ENTRY FORM

Part 1

First name:

Last name: *de las Torres*

Gender: ☐ female ☐ male

Nationality:

Cell phone (U.S.): *(321) 555-0986*

Email address:

Your class now:

Class start date:

Part 2
Why is English important for you?

I work as a(n) ¹ _____ in Mexico City. I love my job except for the ² _____! Every day they speak to me and ask me for information. I can't understand them, and it is difficult for me to answer. English is important to me because it helps me do my ³ _____ well.

What do you want to improve in your English?

I think my speaking in English is OK for my level. But ⁴ _____ and understanding is still very difficult for me. I really want to stay an extra month at your school and improve my listening.

b Read Part 2 of Daniela's form. Complete it.

c ▶ 02.21 Listen to Daniela again and check your answers.

26

Receptive skills development
Clearly staged tasks practice and develop listening and reading skills while supporting learners' understanding of texts.

Comprehensive approach to writing skills
A clear focus on key aspects of writing helps develop effective real-world writingskills.

Staged for success
Careful staging and scaffolding generate successful outcomes.

3 WRITING SKILLS Spelling

a Read Daniela's first draft of her entry form. Cover page 26. Look at the example spelling problem. Find eight more spelling problems.

b Check (✓) when it's important to have correct spelling.
   1 ☐ a first draft of a text
   2 ☐ a final draft of a text
   3 ☐ a text other people read
   4 ☐ a text only you read

c Find and correct a spelling mistake in each sentence.
   1 I really love swimming in the see.
   2 Can you please right your name on the form?
   3 I don't no the answer to this question.
   4 Can you speak up? I can't here you.
   5 Where can I bye bread?

d In what way are the incorrect and correct words in 3c the same?

4 WRITING

a Complete the form with your information.

b Use your ideas in 1d to write answers to the questions in Part 2.

c Switch forms with another student. Are your ideas in Part 2 the same?

INTERNATIONAL COLLEGE COMPETITION ENTRY FORM

Part 2

Why is English important for you?

> I work as a ~~trafic~~ traffic police offiser in Mexico City. I love my job except for the toorists! Every day they speak to me and ask me for informashion. I can't understand them, and it is dificult for me to anser. English is important for me becos it helps me do my job well.

What do you want to improve in your English?

> I think my speaking in English is OK for my level. I also find reading and writing pretty easy. But listning and understanding is still very hard for me. I really want to stay an extra month at your scool and improve my listening.

INTERNATIONAL COLLEGE COMPETITION ENTRY FORM

Part 1

First name: _____
Last name: _____
Gender: ☐ female ☐ male
Nationality: _____
Cell phone (U.S.): _____
Email address: _____
Your class now: _____
Class start date: _____

Part 2
Why is English important for you?
_____

What do you want to improve in your English?
_____

27

Written outcome
Each D lesson ends with a practical written outcome, so learners can put new language into practice right away.

Personal response
Frequent opportunities for personal response make learning more memorable.

UNIT 2
Review and extension

1 GRAMMAR

a Complete the text with the correct form of the verb in parentheses.

I'm a college student, but I ^{1}_____ (work) in a clothing store every weekend. On Saturday I ^{2}_____ (start) work at 9:00 a.m., but on Sunday I ^{3}_____ (not start) until 11:00 a.m. My sister's a nurse, so she ^{4}_____ (not have) a normal schedule. She sometimes ^{5}_____ (work) all night, but she ^{6}_____ (not like) it. My parents are both teachers, so they ^{7}_____ (work) from Monday to Friday.

b Write possible questions for the answers.

1 **A** What _____? **B** I'm a receptionist.
2 **A** Do _____? **B** No, I don't. I work in a hospital.
3 **A** Do _____? **B** Yes, I do. It's great.
4 **A** When _____? **B** I start at 9 o'clock in the morning.
5 **A** Does _____? **B** Yes, he does. My husband is a teacher.
6 **A** Where _____? **B** He works in a high school.
7 **A** Does _____? **B** Yes, he does. He loves it.

c 💬 Practice the conversation in 1b with a partner. Answer about your life.

2 VOCABULARY

a Put the letters in parentheses in the correct order to complete the job.

1 n_____ e (s r u)
2 d_____ t (t e i s n)
3 p_____ t (l o i)
4 e_____ r (n n i e g e)
5 j_____ r (i o t a n)
6 p_____ r (o o h e h p r a t g)

b Write the times in words.

10:15 – (a) quarter after ten or ten fifteen
1 11:30   3 6:00   5 2:40
2 12:45   4 8:15   6 5:20

c Match 1–5 with a–e to complete the sentences.

1 Read the text and take
2 I'm not worried because I usually get good
3 I hope we have
4 He is worried because he often fails
5 I need to study for the final

a a break soon because I'm tired.
b important exams.
c notes on a piece of paper.
d exam next week.
e grades on tests.

3 WORDPOWER work

a Match sentences 1–3 with pictures a–c.

1 I **work in** a hospital.
2 I **work for** Larkin Computers
3 I **work as** a receptionist.

b Look at the phrases in **bold** in 3a. Match them with 1–3.

1 the job I do
2 the place of work
3 the company

c Is *work* a verb or a noun in sentences 1–5?

1 I start **work** at 8:00 a.m. each day.
2 She leaves **work** at about 6:00 p.m.
3 I can't talk to you now – I'm at **work**.
4 I'm an actor, but I'm out of **work** at the moment.
5 They go to **work** very early in the morning.

d Which *work* phrase in 3c do we use when ... ?

a we don't have a job
b we are at the place we work

e Put the word in parentheses in the correct place in the sentence.

1 He works a nurse at night. (as)
2 We all work at 6:00 p.m. (start)
3 She'd like a job because now she's of work. (out)
4 She's a photographer and works *The Times*. (for)
5 When I'm work, I have no free time. (at)
6 We both work a large office downtown. (in)

f Write four sentences about people you know. Use *work* in different ways.

My brother works for a shoe store downtown.

⟳ REVIEW YOUR PROGRESS

How well did you do in this unit? Write 3, 2, or 1 for each objective.
3 = very well   2 = well   1 = not so well

I CAN ...	
talk about jobs	☐
talk about study habits	☐
ask for things and reply	☐
complete a form	☐

28

Each unit links to additional sections at the back of the book
for more grammar, vocabulary, and speaking practice.

Grammar Focus

Provides an explanation of the grammar presented in the unit,
along with exercises for students to practice.

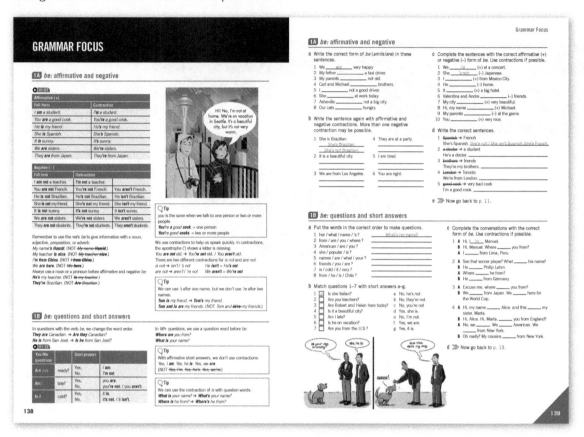

Communication Plus

Provides a series of communication activities
for each unit, providing additional opportunities
for students to practice their speaking.

Vocabulary Focus

Extends and consolidates the vocabulary.

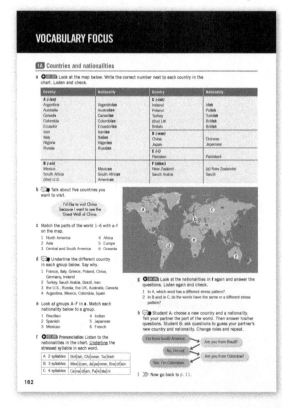

American Empower Methodology

A Learner-Centered Approach

American Empower, with its unique mix of learning and assessment, places students and their needs at the center of the learning process. This learner-centered approach also applies to the course methodology – the Student's Book and the additional resources provide a range of classroom materials that motivate learners, address their language needs, and facilitate the development of their skills. This wide range of materials also means different learning preferences are catered to in each unit of the course. It provides teachers with flexibility with different learner groups.

Meeting the Needs of Learners at Different Levels

Supporting the Teacher

American Empower also supports the teacher with classroom methodology that is familiar and easy to use, and at the same time is flexible and creative. A number of key methodological principles underpin the course, enhancing the interface between learners and their learning, and between students and teachers. *American Empower*:

1 encourages learner engagement
2 delivers manageable learning
3 is rich in practice
4 provides a comprehensive approach to productive skills.

Measurable Progress

American Empower includes a uniquely reliable assessment package developed by test experts at Cambridge Assessment English. This allows teachers and learners to measure progress and determine learners' strengths and needs. Not only do learners feel more motivated when they can see they are making progress, but they are then able to target and address specific learning needs.

Key Methodological Principles

1 Learner engagement

Getting Started

Each unit begins with a Getting Started page, designed to engage students from the very start of the unit – leading to greater motivation and more successful learning. It does this in the following ways:

- Striking images take an unusual perspective on the theme – this raises curiosity, prompts ideas and questions in the mind of the learner, and stimulates them to want to communicate.
- Speaking activities prompt a personal response – exploring beyond the surface of the image – while providing a cognitive and linguistic challenge for the student and a diagnostic opportunity for the teacher.

Remarkable texts, audio, and video

Throughout the course, learners encounter a range of **reading texts**, along with **audio and video**. The texts have been carefully selected to appeal to learners from a variety of cultural backgrounds. The topics will inform, amuse, surprise, entertain, raise questions, arouse curiosity and empathy, and provoke an emotional response. The texts, audio, and video in *American Empower* provide learners with new insights and perspectives on a variety of topics. By using a varied range of spoken and written contexts, students are consistently motivated to engage with the target grammar and vocabulary.

Frequent opportunities for personal and critical response

There are frequent opportunities to contribute personal views, experiences, and knowledge when discussing each lesson's themes. Every lesson includes regular activities that encourage learners to respond personally to the content of the texts and images. These include **personalization** tasks which make the target language in every unit meaningful to the individual learner. Many activities also involve some kind of critical response to the content of texts. This helps develop students' critical thinking skills as well as gives them further speaking practice.

Independent learning

In order to make progress, learners must build their language knowledge and their ability to use this knowledge in an active way. Reading and listening widely in English will help students to progress faster, as will the development of good study skills. In *American Empower*, **Learning Tips** support learners both in and outside the classroom. These features accompany the texts and audio and encourage learners to notice and systematically note useful language. The Teacher's Notes for each lesson include **Homework activities** which encourage students to put the Learning Tips into practice in their independent learning and motivate further reading and listening outside the classroom.

2 Manageable learning

A second core principle that informs *American Empower* is a recognition of the importance of manageable learning. This offers students (and their teachers) reassurance that the material is suitable for the level being taught: the language syllabus avoids overly complex language at any given level, and the reading, listening, and video materials are carefully chosen to be accessible while consistently acknowledging learners' linguistic competencies and challenging them. *American Empower* classroom materials reflect the concept of manageable learning in the following ways:

1 Syllabus planning and the selection of language

A key element in making learning material appropriate is the selection of target language. In *American Empower*, two powerful Cambridge English resources – the Cambridge Corpus and English Profile – have been used to inform the development of the course syllabus and the writing of the material. This means that learners using *American Empower* are presented with target language that includes:

Grammar

- a logically sequenced progression of grammar items and activities that focus clearly on both meaning and form
- systematic recycling of grammar within units and across each level
- a fresh approach to familiar language – accompanied by Cambridge Corpus–informed Tips, with notes on usage and typical errors – helps learners improve usage and tackle habitual mistakes

Vocabulary

- lexical sets that make vocabulary memorable and easier to learn
- an appropriate lexical load for each lesson so learners are not overwhelmed by too many vocabulary items
- activities that clarify different meanings of vocabulary
- Wordpower activities that aim to develop learners' vocabulary range.

Each level is carefully designed to offer measurable progress through the core syllabus while students develop toward each level's competency as independent individual learners.

2 Lesson flow

Teaching and learning are also made manageable through the careful staging and sequencing of activities, ensuring that each individual learner will be challenged and engaged while working together as a class. Every lesson is comprised of several sections, each with a clear focus on language and/or skills. Each section builds on the next, and activities within sections do likewise. Every section of language input ends in an output task, offering learners the opportunity to personalize the target language. At the end of each lesson, there is a substantial, freer speaking and/or writing activity that motivates learners to use new language in context.

3 Task and activity design

Tasks and activities have been designed to give students an appropriate balance between freedom and support. As an overall principle, the methodology throughout *American Empower* anticipates and mitigates potential problems that learners might encounter with language and tasks. While this clearly supports students, it also supports teachers because there are likely to be fewer unexpected challenges during the course of a lesson, which means that necessary preparation time is reduced to a minimum.

Students at all levels need to increase their language knowledge and their ability to use spoken and written language in a variety of situations. However, learners' needs can vary according to level. For example, at lower levels, students often need more encouragement to use language in an active way so they can put their language knowledge into immediate use. Conversely, at higher levels, learners need to be more accurate in the way they use language in order to refine their message and convey their ideas with more complexity and subtlety. *American Empower* responds to these varying needs in the following ways as the course progresses from level A1 to C1:

- **Topics, tasks, and texts with an appropriate level of cognitive and linguistic challenge at each level** motivate learners by providing new challenges.
- **Multiple communicative opportunities** in every lesson either encourage fluency or allow students to refine their message using a wider range of language.
- **Varied and stimulating texts** motivate learners to develop their reading and listening skills so that a wider range of texts becomes accessible as the course progresses.
- **Listening and video materials** expose students to a wide variety of voices and natural, colloquial speech, while giving a strong focus on the language that students need to produce themselves.
- **Learning Tips** support learners in developing a broad vocabulary both in and outside the classroom.

3 Rich in practice

It is essential that learners be offered frequent opportunities to practice the language they have been focusing on – they need to activate the language they have studied in a meaningful way within an appropriate context. *American Empower* is rich in practice activities and provides students and teachers with a wide variety of tasks that help learners to become confident users of new language.

Student's Book

Throughout each *American Empower* Student's Book, learners are presented with a wide variety of practice activities, appropriate to the stage of the lesson and real-world use of the language.

- There are frequent opportunities for spoken and written practice. Activities are clearly contextualized and carefully staged and scaffolded. Extended spoken and written practice is provided in the final activity in each lesson.
- Grammar Focus and Vocabulary Focus pages at the back of the Student's Book offer more opportunities for practicing the grammar and vocabulary, helping to consolidate learning.
- Review and Extension activities at the end of each unit provide more opportunities for both written and spoken practice of the target language.

Teacher's Book

- Many learners find practice activities that involve an element of fun to be particularly motivating. Such activities – seven per unit – are provided in the photocopiable activities in Cambridge One, providing fun, communicative practice of grammar, vocabulary, and pronunciation.
- The main teacher's notes also provide ideas for extra activities at various stages of the lesson.

Other components

- The Workbook provides practice of the target input in each A, B, and C lesson.
- The Digital Workbook component offers practice activities that can be completed on a mobile device or computer.
- Through Cambridge One, *American Empower* provides an extensive range of practice activities that learners can use to review and consolidate their learning outside the classroom.

4 A comprehensive approach to productive skills

Most learners study English because they want to use the language in some way. This means that speaking and writing – the productive skills – are more often a priority for learners. *American Empower* is systematic and comprehensive in its approach to developing both speaking and writing skills.

Speaking

The **C lesson** in each unit – Everyday English – takes a comprehensive approach to speaking skills, and particularly in developing learners to become flexible and effective users of spoken language for social and professional purposes. The target language is clearly contextualized by means of engaging audio that will be relevant and familiar to adult learners.

These Everyday English lessons focus on two key elements of spoken language:

- Useful and conversational language – focusing on functional language and speaking strategies that are most relevant to learners' needs
- Pronunciation – focusing on intelligibility and the characteristics of natural speech, from individual sounds to extended utterances, developing learners' ability to express meaning by varying intonation and stress

This comprehensive approach ensures that speaking skills are actively and appropriately developed, not just practiced.

Writing

In the *American Empower* Student's Book, learners receive guidance and practice in writing a wide range of text types. Writing lessons are not "heads-down." Instead, and in keeping with the overall course methodology, they are highly communicative, mixed-skills lessons with a special focus on writing. In *American Empower*, writing is dealt with in the following ways:

- **Writing is fully integrated into listening, reading, and speaking** – as it is in real life – and is not practiced in isolation.
- **There is an explicit focus on key linguistic features of written language** that encourage students to express themselves with greater clarity and accuracy.
- **A process writing methodology** is embedded in the instructions for writing activities, and learners are often encouraged to self-correct and seek peer feedback.
- **Communicative outcomes** – writing lessons lead to a final, communicative task, ensuring that learners are always writing for a purpose.

Assessment

Learning Oriented Assessment

What is Learning Oriented Assessment (LOA)?

Teachers are naturally interested in their students' progress. Every time they step into the classroom, teachers note if a learner is struggling with a language concept, is unable to read at a natural rate, or can understand a new grammar point but still can't produce it in a practice activity. This is often an intuitive and spontaneous process. By the end of a course or a cycle of learning, the teacher will know far more about a learner's ability than an end-of-course test alone can show.

An LOA approach to teaching and learning brings together this ongoing informal evaluation with a more formal or structured assessment, such as end-of-unit or end-of-course tests. LOA is an approach that allows the teacher to pull together all this information and knowledge in order to understand learners' achievements and progress and to identify and address their needs in a targeted and informed way. A range of insights into students and their progress feeds into total assessment of the learner. It also allows the teacher to use all of this information not just to produce a report on a learner's level of competence, but to plan and inform future learning.

How does *American Empower* support LOA?

American Empower supports LOA both informally and formally, and both in and outside the classroom:

1 **Assessment that informs teaching and learning**
- Reliable tests for both formative and summative assessment (Unit Progress Tests and skills-based Competency Tests)
- A clear record of learner performance through Cambridge One

2 **LOA classroom support**
- Clear learning objectives and activities that build toward those objectives
- Activities that offer opportunities for learner reflection and peer feedback
- A range of tips for teachers on how to incorporate LOA techniques, including informal assessment, into their lessons as part of normal classroom practice

1 Assessment that informs teaching and learning

American Empower offers two types of tests written and developed by teams of Cambridge Assessment English exam writers. The tests in the course have been piloted, involving thousands of candidates across all tests and levels, to ensure that test items are appropriate to the level. Cambridge Assessment English tests are underpinned by research and evaluation and by continuous monitoring and statistical analysis of performance of test questions.

American Empower tests are designed around the following essential principles:

- **Validity** – tests of real-world English and the language covered in the Student's Book
- **Reliability** – tasks are consistent and fair
- **Impact** – tests have a positive effect on teaching and learning, in and outside the classroom
- **Practicality** – tests are user-friendly and practical for teachers and students.

Unit Progress Tests

The course provides an online Unit Progress Test at the end of every unit that tests the target grammar, vocabulary, and functional language from the unit. The teacher and learner are provided with a score for each language area that has been tested, identifying the areas of mastery and where the learner has encountered difficulties and needs more support. Paper-based versions of the tests are also available.

Competency Tests

American Empower offers mid-course and end-of-course Competency Tests. These skills-based tests cover Reading, Writing, and Listening and Speaking and are calibrated to the Common European Framework of Reference (CEFR). They provide teachers and students with a digital record of achievement which indicates the students' performance in all language skills within the relevant course level.

Cambridge One provides teachers and students with a clear and comprehensive record of each learner's progress during the course, helping teachers and learners to recognize achievement and identify further learning needs. Cambridge One helps teachers to systematically collect and record evidence of learning and performance, and in doing so demonstrates to teachers and students how much progress has been made over time. Paper-based versions of the tests are also available.

2 LOA classroom support

Clear objectives

An LOA approach encourages learners to reflect and self-assess. In order to do this, learning objectives must be clear. In *American Empower*, each unit begins with a set of "can do" objectives so that learners feel an immediate sense of purpose. Each lesson starts with a clear "Learn to …" goal, and the activities all contribute toward that, leading to a significant practical outcome at the close of the lesson. At the end of each unit, there is a Review Your Progress feature that encourages learners to reflect on their success, relative to the "can do" objectives at the start of the unit. Within the lessons, there are also opportunities for reflection, collaborative learning, and peer feedback.

LOA classroom tips for teachers

In a typical lesson, teachers are likely to use some or perhaps all of the following teaching techniques:

- **monitor** learners during learner-centered stages of the lesson
- **elicit** information and language
- **concept check** new language
- **drill** new vocabulary or grammar
- encourage learners to **review and reflect** after they've worked on a task.

The chart below summarizes core and LOA-specific aims for each of the above techniques. All of these familiar teaching techniques are a natural fit for the kind of methodology that informally supports LOA. An LOA approach will emphasize those parts of a teacher's thinking that involve forming evaluations or judgments about learners' performance (and therefore what to do next to better assist the learner). The "LOA teacher" is constantly thinking things like:

- *Have they understood that word?*
- *How well are they pronouncing that phrase?*
- *Were they able to use that language in a freer activity?*
- *How many answers did they get right?*
- *How well did they understand that listening text?*
- *How many errors did I hear?*
- *What does that mean for the next step in the learning process?*

The *American Empower* Teacher's Book provides tips on how to use a number of these techniques within each lesson. This will help teachers to consider their learners with more of an evaluative eye. Of course, it also helps learners if teachers share their assessment with them and ensure they get plenty of feedback. It's important that teachers make sure feedback is well balanced so that learners know what they are doing well in and what needs a little more work.

Teaching techniques				
monitoring	**eliciting**	**concept checking**	**drilling**	**providing feedback**
Core aims • checking learners are on task • checking learners' progress • making yourself available to learners who are having problems	• checking what learners know about a topic in order to generate interest	• checking that learners understand the use and meaning of new language	• providing highly controlled practice of new language	• finding out what ideas learners generated when working on a task • praising learners' performance of a task • indicating where improvement can be made
LOA aims • listening to learners' oral language, and checking learners' written language, in order to: » diagnose potential needs » check if they can use new language correctly in context	• finding out if learners already know a vocabulary or grammar item • adapting the lesson to take into account students' individual starting points and interests	• checking what could be a potential problem with the use and meaning of new language for your learners • anticipating and preparing for challenges in understanding new language, both for the whole class and for individuals	• checking that learners have consolidated the form of new language • checking intelligible pronunciation of new language	• asking learners how well they feel they performed a task • giving feedback to learners on specific language strengths and needs • fostering 'learning how to learn' skills

LOA and learner motivation

The teaching and learning materials in *American Empower* ensure learners maintain motivation throughout the course. In addition, teachers can further amplify learner motivation by adopting LOA approaches in their lessons. Here are some core LOA motivation ideas:

- **Make learning aims explicit to learners** – teachers should point out the "can do" objectives and tell students how they will help their language development.
- **Modify learning objectives** on the basis of learner feedback – after learners complete an activity, teachers can get feedback on how they thought it went and respond to their suggestions (for example, learners may wish to repeat the activity because they feel they could do it better the second time).
- **Judge when to give feedback on learner language** – different learner groups and different activities require different types of feedback. Sometimes a teacher can give language feedback as learners are speaking, and sometimes it's better to wait until they have finished the activity; teachers should consider the most appropriate approach for each activity.
- **Balance developmental feedback with praise** – it's important to acknowledge what learners do well and praise their efforts, so teachers should give balanced feedback, but they should also make sure praise is targeted and not too general, otherwise it may sound insincere.

LOA and capturing learner language

One of the biggest challenges for teachers during the course of a lesson is being able to tune into learner language. This is particularly difficult with larger classes, when students are all speaking at the same time in pair or group work. If teachers want to adopt an LOA approach and capture language samples from a range of learners, they can consider some of the following techniques:

- **Listen only for the target language** that has just been taught and whether students are using it accurately – don't worry about the other mistakes learners might make.
- **Target specific learners for each activity** – sometimes it's not possible to listen to all learners for every activity, so if there are three speaking activities during the course of the lesson, the teacher can aim to tune into a different third of the class for each activity. By the end of the lesson, the teacher will have listened to all of the learners.
- **Ask learners to complete the speaking activities** located in each unit of the Digital Workbook – they can record their responses using a smartphone and submit the recordings in Cambridge One. The teacher can then give written feedback – it's not very different from giving feedback on written work that students have submitted.

Documentary videos

Expose your students to English via authentic, real-world contexts.

These high-interest supplementary Empower videos are thematically linked to the topics and language of each unit.

Each video comes with a downloadable and printable video worksheet.

Teachers can use the video and worksheet at any point in a unit.

Available on cambridgeone.org

eBooks

The *American Empower* eBook includes all of the content from the print Student's Book, and can also be used to:

Listen to audio

Highlight text

Make notes

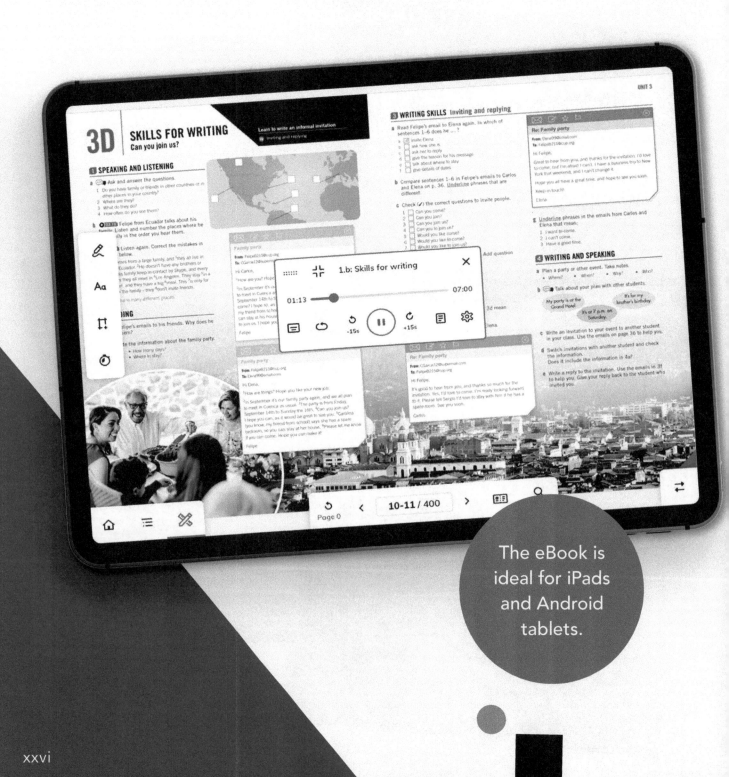

The eBook is ideal for iPads and Android tablets.

American Empower and the CEFR, English Profile

The CEFR and English Vocabulary Profile

The *American Empower* course syllabus is informed by English Profile and the Cambridge English Corpus and is carefully benchmarked to the Common European Framework of Reference (CEFR). This ensures that students encounter the most relevant and useful language at the right point in their learning.

The Cambridge English Corpus is a multi-billion word collection of texts taken from a huge variety of sources, including newspapers, the Internet, books, magazines, radio, schools, universities, the workplace, and even everyday conversation – and is constantly being updated.

Our language research features in most of our materials. In particular, we use it to:

- ensure that the language taught in our courses is natural, accurate, and up-to-date
- select the most useful, common words and phrases for a topic or level
- focus on certain groups of learners and see what they find easy or hard
- analyze spoken language so that we can teach effective speaking and listening strategies.

English Vocabulary Profile offers reliable information about which words (and which meanings of those words) and phrases are known and used by learners at each level of the CEFR.

For more information on English Profile and the Cambridge English Corpus, please use these links:

http://www.englishprofile.org

https://languageresearch.cambridge.org/cambridge-english-corpus

The CEFR is a standard guideline to recognize a learner's level of language fluency. Each level of *American Empower* is carefully mapped to the appropriate CEFR level in accordance with English Vocabulary Profile, guaranteeing that students encounter the right language at the right level.

Empower	CEFR Level
Starter	A1
Elementary	A2
Pre-Intermediate	B1
Intermediate	B1+
Upper Intermediate	B2
Advanced	C1

Resources – How to access

To access the online resources, go to cambridgeone.org and register.

Resource	For Teachers	For Students	
	Teacher's Book with Digital Pack	Student's Book with eBook	Student's Book with Digital Pack
Class Audio	cambridgeone.org	cambridgeone.org	cambridgeone.org
Class Video	cambridgeone.org	cambridgeone.org	cambridgeone.org
Video Activity Sheets	cambridgeone.org	cambridgeone.org	cambridgeone.org
Video Teaching Notes / Answer Keys	cambridgeone.org		
Digital Workbook	cambridgeone.org		cambridgeone.org
End-of-unit assessment (Online version)	A Unit Progress Test for every unit (automatically marked) covers grammar, vocabulary, and functional language. cambridgeone.org		A Unit Progress Test for every unit (automatically marked) covers grammar, vocabulary, and functional language. cambridgeone.org
Mid- and end-of-course assessment (Online version)	Mid-course and end-of-course competency tests cover all four skills and generate a CEFR report which reliably benchmarks learners to the target level. cambridgeone.org		Mid-course and end-of-course competency tests cover all four skills and generate a CEFR report, which reliably benchmarks learners to the target level. cambridgeone.org
End-of-unit assessment (Print version)	Unit Progress Tests with Teacher's answer key for every unit which covers grammar, vocabulary, and functional language. cambridgeone.org	Please ask your teacher for further information.	Please ask your teacher for further information.
Mid- and end-of-course assessment (Print version)	Mid-course and end-of-course competency Tests with Teacher's answer key for every unit which covers grammar, vocabulary, and functional language. cambridgeone.org	Please ask your teacher for further information.	Please ask your teacher for further information.
Workbook audio	cambridgeone.org	cambridgeone.org	cambridgeone.org
Workbook answers	In Workbook with Answers or cambridgeone.org		
Photocopiables	cambridgeone.org		
Presentation Plus	Displays all Student's Book material, plays all Class Audio and Video, shows answer keys and more. For access, contact your local Cambridge representative.		
Teaching with American Empower	An introduction to the American Empower online assessment and practice materials, via a short teacher training course. For access, contact your local Cambridge representative.		

American Empower components

The following American Empower components are available for 6 levels (A1–C1):

- Student's Book with eBook
- Student's Book with Digital Pack
- Full Contact with eBook
- Full Contact A with eBook
- Full Contact B with eBook
- Full Contact with Digital Pack
- Full Contact A with Digital Pack
- Full Contact B with Digital Pack

- Student's Book A with eBook
- Student's Book B with eBook
- Student's Book A with Digital Pack
- Student's Book B with Digital Pack
- Teacher's Book with Digital Pack
- Presentation Plus

Find out more:
cambridge.org/americanempower

Introduction to the Cambridge Life Competencies Framework (CLCF)

How can teachers prepare their students to succeed in a world that is rapidly changing? They need to help students develop transferable skills, to work with people from around the world, to think creatively, to analyze sources critically, and communicate their views effectively. How can they teach these skills alongside language? In response to these questions, Cambridge University Press has developed the Cambridge Life Competencies Framework. The Life Competencies are explored throughout the *American Empower* course.

The Cambridge Life Competency Framework

The Framework outlines core areas of competency that are important for development: creative thinking, critical thinking, learning to learn, communication, collaboration, social responsibilities.

Creative Thinking	Preparing for creativity	Generating ideas	Implementing ideas and solving problems	
Critical Thinking	Understanding and analysing ideas and arguments	Evaluating ideas and arguments	Solving problems and making decisions	
Learning to Learn	Developing skills and strategies for learning	Taking control of own learning	Reflecting on and evaluating own learning	
Communication	Using appropriate language and register for context	Facilitating interactions	Participating with appropriate confidence and clarity	
Collaboration	Taking personal responsibility for own contribution to a group task	Encouraging effective group interaction	Managing the sharing of tasks in a group activity	Working towards task completion
Social Responsibilities	Understanding personal responsibilities as part of a social group	Showing intercultural awareness	Understanding global issues	
Emotional Development	Identifying and understanding emotions	Managing own emotions	Empathy and relationship skills	

For more information about *American Empower* and the CLCF, scan the QR code. Or visit cambridge.org/americanempower/clcf

Lesson and objective	Grammar	Vocabulary	Pronunciation	Everyday English
Welcome!	Possessive adjectives; Question words; *a / an*; Regular plural forms	Numbers; The alphabet; Colors; Classroom objects and instructions	Noticing word stress	Saying hello and introducing people; Spelling words
Unit 1 People				
Getting started Talk about meeting people from other countries				
1A Talk about where you're from	*be*: affirmative and negative	Countries and nationalities	Syllables and word stress	
1B Talk about people you know	*be*: questions and short answers	Adjectives	Sound and spelling: /k/	
1C Ask for and give information			Intonation for checking; Consonant clusters	Asking for and giving information
1D Write an online profile				
Review and extension More practice		WORDPOWER *from*		
Unit 2 Work and study				
Getting started Talk about what kind of work you find interesting				
2A Talk about jobs	Simple present: affirmative and negative	Jobs	Word stress; *-s* endings	
2B Talk about study habits	Simple present: questions and short answers	Studying; Time	*do you*	
2C Ask for things and reply			Sound and spelling: *ou*	Asking for things and replying
2D Complete a form				
Review and extension More practice		WORDPOWER *work*		
Unit 3 Daily life				
Getting started Talk about what you do every day				
3A Talk about routines	Position of adverbs of frequency	Time expressions; Common verbs	Sentence stress; Sound and spelling: /aɪ/ and /eɪ/;	
3B Talk about technology in your life	*do, go, have*	Technology	Word stress; Sound and spelling: /ʌ/, /oʊ/, and /u/	
3C Make plans			Main stress; Thinking about what you want to say	Making plans
3D Write an informal invitation				
Review and extension More practice		WORDPOWER Prepositions of time		
Unit 4 Food				
Getting started Talk about eating with your family				
4A Talk about the food you want	Count and noncount nouns; *a / an, some, any*	Food	Sound and spelling: *ea*; Sound and spelling: /k/ and /g/	
4B Talk about the food you eat every day	Quantifiers: *much, many, a lot of*	Cooking		
4C Arrive at and order a meal at a restaurant			Word groups	Arriving at a restaurant; Ordering a meal in a restaurant
4D Write a blog post about something you know how to do				
Review and extension More practice		WORDPOWER *like*		
Unit 5 Places				
Getting started Talk about what a good home is				
5A Talk about towns	*there is / there are*	Places in a city	Sound and spelling: /s/ and /z/; Sound and spelling: /b/ and /p/	
5B Describe rooms and furniture in your house	Possessive pronouns and possessive *-'s*	Furniture	Sound and spelling: vowels before *r*	
5C Ask for and give directions			Sentence stress	Asking for and giving directions
5D Write a description of your neighborhood				
Review and extension More practice		WORDPOWER Prepositions of place		
Unit 6 Family				
Getting started Talk about a family you know				
6A Talk about your family and your family history	Simple past: *be*	Family; Years and dates	Sound and spelling: /ʌ/; Sentence stress	
6B Talk about past activities and hobbies	Simple past: affirmative	Simple past irregular verbs	*-ed* endings; Sound and spelling: *ea*	
6C Leave a voicemail message and ask for someone on the phone			Sound and spelling: *a*	Leaving a voicemail message
6D Write a life story				
Review and extension More practice		WORDPOWER *go*		

Listening	Reading	Speaking	Writing
Five conversations		Saying hello and introducing people	Names and addresses
A conversation about where you're from		Where you're from	Sentences about you
A conversation about people you know	Social media posts about people you know	People you know	Notes about people you know
Checking into a hotel		Asking for and giving information; Checking understanding	✓ Unit Progress Test
First day of an English class	Online profiles	Using social media sites	An online profile; Capital letters and punctuation
	An article about Gabby Scampone	Jobs	Sentences about jobs
A survey about study habits	An online forum about study habits	Studying; Study habits	Questions about study habits
Ordering in a café; Asking for help		Asking for things and replying; Reacting to news	✓ Unit Progress Test
Three monologues about studying English; A teacher addressing her class	A competition entry form	Studying English	A form; Spelling
A conversation about family routines	An article about an unusual workplace	Daily routines; Spending time with your family; Routines you share with others	A dialogue; Notes about routines you share with other people
Three conversations about gadgets	An interview about using the Internet	Technology in your life	Sentences about gadgets you have; Questions about gadgets you have
Making plans to go out		Making plans; Thinking about what you want to say	✓ Unit Progress Test
A monologue about someone's family	Two informal emails	Plan a party	An informal email invitation; Inviting and replying
A conversation about buying food	An article about world markets	Buying food; The food you like and don't like	
A conversation about cooking	A factfile about Aarón Sánchez; Two personal emails	Cooking shows; Cooking; The food you eat	Questions about food
At a restaurant		Arriving at a restaurant; Ordering a meal in a restaurant; Changing what you say	✓ Unit Progress Test
Four monologues about cooking	A cooking blog	Cooking; A good cook you know; Cooking for others	A blog post about something you know how to do; Making the order clear
	An article about an unusual town	Places you like; Describing a picture of a town; What there is in a town	Questions and sentences about what there is in a town
A conversation about a new home	An advertisement	Your home and furniture	Sentences about your home
On the street		Giving and following directions; Checking what other people say	✓ Unit Progress Test
Three monologues about neighborhoods	A website about neighborhoods around the world	What makes a good neighborhood; Your neighborhood	A description of your neighborhood; Linking ideas with *and*, *but*, and *so*
A conversation about a family tree		Your family	Notes about your family
A conversation about childhood hobbies	An article about Steve Jobs	Steve Jobs; What you did at different times; A childhood hobby	Notes about a childhood hobby
On the phone		Leaving a voicemail message; Asking for someone on the phone; Asking someone to wait	✓ Unit Progress Test
A monologue about someone's life story	A life story	Important years in your life	A life story about someone in your family; Linking ideas in the past

Lesson and objective	Grammar	Vocabulary	Pronunciation	Everyday English
Unit 7 Trips				
Getting started Talk about where you'd like to travel to				
7A Talk about past trips	Simple past: negative and questions	Transportation	*did you*; Sound and spelling: /ɔ/	
7B Talk about what you like and dislike about transportation	*love / like / don't mind / hate* + verb + *-ing*	Transportation adjectives	Word stress	
7C Say *excuse me* and *I'm sorry*			Intonation for saying *excuse me*; Emphasizing what we say	Saying *excuse me* and *I'm sorry*
7D Write an email about yourself				
Review and extension More practice		WORDPOWER *get*		
Unit 8 Healthy and in shape				
Getting started Talk about sports and exercise				
8A Talk about past and present abilities; Talk about sports and exercise	*can / can't; could / couldn't* for ability	Sports and exercise	*Can, can't, could,* and *couldn't*; Sound and spelling: /u/ and /ʊ/	
8B Talk about the body and getting in shape	*have to / don't have to*	Parts of the body; Appearance	*have to*; Word stress	
8C Talk about health and how you feel			Connecting words	Talking about health and how you feel
8D Write an article				
Review and extension More practice		WORDPOWER *tell / say*		
Unit 9 Clothes and shopping				
Getting started Talk about shopping in your town or city				
9A Say where you are and what you're doing	Present continuous	Shopping; Money and prices	Word stress in compound nouns; Sentence stress	
9B Talk about the clothes you wear at different times	Simple present or present continuous	Clothes	Sound and spelling: *o*; Syllables	
9C Shop for clothes			Connecting words	Choosing clothes; Paying for clothes
9D Write a thank-you email				
Review and extension More practice		WORDPOWER *time*		
Unit 10 Communication				
Getting started Talk about how you use your cell phone				
10A Compare and talk about things you have	Comparative adjectives	IT collocations	Sentence stress	
10B Talk about languages	Superlative adjectives	High numbers	Word stress; Main stress	
10C Ask for help			Main stress and intonation	Asking for help
10D Write a post expressing an opinion				
Review and extension More practice		WORDPOWER *most*		
Unit 11 Entertainment				
Getting started Talk about movies and TV shows you enjoyed when you were a child				
11A Ask and answer about entertainment experiences	Present perfect	Irregular past participles	Sentence stress; Sound and spelling: /ɜr/	
11B Talk about events you've been to	Present perfect or simple past	Music	Syllables	
11C Ask for and express opinions about things you've seen			Main stress and intonation	Asking for and expressing opinions
11D Write a review				
Review and extension More practice		WORDPOWER Multi-word verbs		
Unit 12 Travel				
Getting started Talk about photographs				
12A Talk about vacation plans	*be going to*	Geography	Syllables and word stress; Sentence stress	
12B Give advice about traveling	*should / shouldn't*	Travel collocations	*should / shouldn't*	
12C Use language for travel and tourism			Intonation to show surprise; Consonant clusters	Checking in at a hotel; Asking for tourist information
12D Write an email with travel advice				
Review and extension More practice		WORDPOWER *take*		
Phonemic symbols and Irregular verbs p. 129	**Communication Plus** p. 130	**Grammar Focus** p. 138		**Vocabulary Focus** p. 162

Listening	Reading	Speaking	Writing
A conversation about traveling	Three stories about vacations	A trip around your country	Notes about a trip around your country
A conversation about transportation in Moscow	A webpage about city transportation around the world; Four reviews of transportation systems	Subways you know; Disagreeing about transportation; Transportation you use	Notes about transportation
Air travel		Saying excuse me and I'm sorry; Showing interest	Unit Progress Test
A conversation about choosing a homestay family	Two online profiles; An email from Alejandro	Homestay families; English-speaking countries you'd like to visit	An email about yourself; Linking ideas with after, when, and while
A podcast about training for a marathon	An article about Paralympian Jonnie Peacock	Famous sporting events and people; Running and exercise; Present and past abilities	
Two monologues about exercise	An article about High Intensity Interval Training	Getting in shape; The things people have to do; Yoga; Parts of the body	Sentences and notes about what people have to do
At the gym		Health and how you feel; Expressing sympathy	Unit Progress Test
A conversation about a free-time activity	An email about a company blog; A blog article about a free-time activity	Free-time activities in your country; Your free-time activities	An article; Linking ideas with however; Adverbs of manner
Four phone conversations about meeting		Meeting friends in town; Saying where you are and what you're doing	Sentences about what you are doing
Two phone conversations about what people are wearing	Two blogs about living abroad; Text messages about what people are doing	Shopping; Festivals in your country; Clothes	Notes about what someone you know is wearing
Shopping for clothes		Choosing clothes; Paying for clothes; Saying something nice	Unit Progress Test
Four monologues about giving presents	Two thank-you emails	The presents you like to get; Giving presents and thanking people for them	A thank-you email; Writing formal and informal emails
A conversation about telephones	An online discussion about headphones and earbuds	Headphones and earbuds; Telephones; Comparing two similar things	Notes about two similar things
A radio show about languages	A blog about languages	Languages; Blogs and language websites; High numbers	
Asking for help		Asking for help; Checking instructions	Unit Progress Test
Three monologues about text messages	Four text messages; Six posts on an online discussion board	Sending messages; Social media posts	A post expressing an opinion; Linking ideas with also, too, and as well
A conversation about a magazine quiz	Three fact files about actresses; A magazine quiz about actresses; An article about actresses	Popular movies, TV shows, and books	Questions about movies, TV shows, and books
A conversation about music in Buenos Aires	An article about Buenos Aires	Buenos Aires; Kinds of music; Entertainment events in your town or city	Notes about entertainment events in your town or city
A night out		Going out in the evening; Asking for and expressing opinions; Responding to an opinion	Unit Progress Test
A conversation about a movie	Three movie reviews	Movies	A movie review; Structuring a review
Two conversations about vacations	A webpage about vacations	Natural places; Important things when on vacation; Vacation plans	
Two monologues about things people like when traveling	An article about living in a different country	Living in a different country; Traveling and vacations; Giving advice about traveling	
A prize vacation		Checking in at a hotel; Asking for tourist information; Showing surprise	Unit Progress Test
A conversation about a planned vacation	An email with travel advice; An email asking for travel advice	Planning vacations; Vancouver	An email with travel advice; Paragraph writing

3B | IMAGINE YOU DON'T HAVE THE INTERNET

At the end of this lesson, students will be able to:

- read and understand a text about using the Internet
- use a lexical set of technology words correctly
- understand conversations in which people talk about the technology they have and how they use it
- use the affirmative, negative, and question forms of *do, go,* and *have*
- talk about and give simple descriptions of their own and other people's possessions

1 READING

a Individually, students think about how they use the Internet and check the things in the list.

b 💬🔊 Students compare their ideas in small groups. Invite groups to share their answers as a class, and ask them if there's anything they think is missing from the list in 1a.

c Tell students they should read only the first part of the text *This month on TechBlog*. They then work individually, answering the questions. Check answers as a class.

> **Answers**
> 1 b
> 2 They are offline / without the Internet.

d Tell students to read the second part of the text *The Interview* and answer the questions. Pre-teach the words in the Vocabulary Support box. Students compare their answers in pairs. Check answers as a class.

> **Answers**
> 1 b, d
> 2 c, e, f

📖 VOCABULARY SUPPORT

upload (v.) (B1) – copy or move programs or information to a larger computer system or to the Internet

go online (v. + adv.) (A2) – access the Internet

chess (A2) – a popular game played on a square board

e 💬🔊 Put students into small groups to talk about the questions together; if possible, mix older and younger students together. Monitor, but don't interrupt fluency.

2 VOCABULARY Technology

⟳ LOA TIP ELICITING

- Consider eliciting some of the vocabulary in 2a by bringing in as many of the objects shown in the pictures as possible to show to the class. Ask students to close their books, explain *technology* (*electronic objects for science or personal use*), and elicit the words for each object. Drill each word for correct pronunciation.

a Individually, students match the words with the pictures. Check answers as a class.

> **Answers**
> | | |
> |---|---|
> | 1 smartwatch | 6 computer |
> | 2 printer | 7 headphones |
> | 3 laptop | 8 tablet |
> | 4 smartphone | 9 keyboard |
> | 5 camera | 10 speaker |

b ▶ 03.08 **Pronunciation** Play the recording for students to underline the stressed syllable. Check answers by writing the words on the board and asking individual students to come up and underline the stressed syllables on the board (see the underlining in the answers to 2a).

c Elicit possible answers to the first sentence from the class. Check that students understand that more than one answer may be possible for each sentence. Students decide what they think the people are talking about. Check answers as a class.

> **Suggested answers**
> 1 smartwatch, computer, laptop, smartphone, tablet
> 2 computer, laptop, smartphone, tablet
> 3 headphones
> 4 printer
> 5 smartwatch, laptop, smartphone, tablet

2 SAYING HELLO

a ▶ `00.02` Point to yourself and say your name, then point to two or three more students at random and elicit their names. Next, point to the man in the blue shirt in picture b and say *Tony*. Then, point to the woman and elicit *Joanna*. Finally, point to the man in the suit jacket and elicit *Pedro*. Say *Conversation 1* and hold up one finger. Individually, students put the sentences in the correct order. Play the recording for students to listen and check. Check answers as a class.

Answers
1 Hello. I'm Tony, and this is my wife, Joanna.
2 Hello. Nice to meet you. I'm Pedro.
3 Hello, Pedro. Nice to meet you.

b 💬 If you have real beginners, they may need some extra support to complete 2b and 2c. If so, consider writing model conversations on the board to guide students. As they are practicing, you can remove random words from the board so that ultimately they are relying on their memories.

Model the conversation by addressing a student: *Hello. I'm (your name)*. Elicit the response: *Hello. I'm (student's name)*. Do the same with another student and respond with: *Hello. Nice to meet you. I'm (your name)*. Drill the phrase *Nice to meet you*. Repeat these conversations with one or two more students until the class seems confident. If space allows, then gesture for students to stand up and mill around and say hello to their classmates. If there isn't enough space, have students work in pairs.

c 💬 Demonstrate the activity with three students. Say: *Hello. I'm (your name), and this is (Student A's name)*. Elicit a response from one of the other students: *Hello. Nice to meet you. I'm (Student B's name), and this is (Student C's name)*. In groups, students practice saying their names and introducing their partners. Monitor and praise students with a smile or a nod when they use the language for saying hello correctly.

d ▶ `00.03` Point to picture e and say *Conversation 2* and hold up two fingers. In pairs, students complete the conversation. Play the recording for students to listen and check. Drill the conversation.

Answers
1 How
2 fine
3 thanks

e 💬 If space allows, gesture for students to stand up and have conversations in small groups. If there isn't enough space, have students work sitting down in groups of three or four. Monitor, but don't interrupt fluency unless students make mistakes with the phrases for saying hello.

3 NUMBERS

a ▶ `00.04` Students may need some extra work on numbers before they continue. Be prepared to teach/review numbers 1–100. If you model the teen numbers in order, be careful that you don't inadvertently move the stress to the first syllable, i.e., *thirteen, fourteen, fifteen*, etc. NOT *thir*teen, *four*teen, *fif*teen, etc. Point to picture c and say *Conversation 3* and hold up three fingers. Say: *Numbers*. Point to the bill and play the recording for students to complete it. Students compare their answers in pairs. Then, check answers as a class. When checking answers, write the numbers on the board to make sure students have understood them.

Answers (For audioscript, see Conversation 3 p. 2)
COFFEE (2)	$6
ICE CREAM (2)	$7
TOTAL	$13

They pay $15.

b ▶ `00.07` Play the recording for students to listen and circle the numbers. They then check in pairs. Check answers as a class.

Answers
30
15
60
70
12

⟳ LOA TIP DRILLING

• Check that students can hear the difference between the pairs of numbers (*thirteen/thirty*, *fourteen/forty*, etc.) by beating the rhythm with your hand and showing where the stress falls.

---

c In pairs, students look at the options and choose the correct answers. After checking answers as a class, write some more numbers in numerals on the board and elicit from the class how to say and write them.

Answers
25 = twenty-five
61 = sixty-one
110 = a hundred and ten

d Students read the first sequence and continue it as a class. They then work in pairs, continuing the sequences.

Answers
5, 6, 7
40, 50, 60
45, 55, 65
37, 39, 41
200, 250, 300

💡 FAST FINISHERS

Ask fast finishers to invent new sequences like those in 3d to test their partner.

---

4 THE ALPHABET

a ▶ 00.08 Books closed. Say: *I'm (your name)*. Write your name on the board slowly, spelling the letters out as you go. Spell it again clearly, pointing to the letters. Then say: *The alphabet*. Students open their books. Play the recording or model the alphabet yourself for students to listen and repeat.

b **Pronunciation** Read the questions with the students. Model clearly the long "ee" sound, the word *see*, and the letter *B*. Elicit another letter with the same sound by modeling *A* and shaking your head. Model *C*, nod your head, and indicate students should write it. Individually, students complete the three groups. When checking answers, write the groups of letters on the board and drill them.

Answers
1 C, D, E, G, P, T, V, Z   2 A, J, K   3 L, M, N, S, X

c 💬🔊 Demonstrate the activity by pointing at two or three letters and eliciting them from the class. In pairs, students test each other on the letters. Monitor and correct students' pronunciation as appropriate.

> 💡 **EXTRA ACTIVITY**
>
> In pairs, students practice spelling their own names. They tell their partner their name: *I'm (student's name)*. Then, they spell it out, pointing to the letters in 4a. Monitor and correct students' pronunciation as appropriate.

d The question *How do you spell "…"?* isn't formally practiced until 7c on Student's Book (SB) p. 8. In 4d and 4e, don't distract students by using this question form, but elicit spelling "silently" by showing an open palm, pointing at letters, or standing with your pen positioned to write on the board as students call out the letters to you. Point to the red blot and elicit the word *red*. Write it on the board slowly, spelling the letters out as you go. Then say: *Colors*. Give students one minute to look at the colors and write down the ones they think they know. In pairs, students then practice saying and spelling the words. When checking answers, elicit the spelling from the class and write the colors on the board.

Answers
(from left to right) top: red, gray, blue, green, black
bottom: pink, brown, orange, yellow, white

e 💬🔊 Demonstrate the activity by saying two words to the class, e.g., *answer* and *number*, and eliciting the spelling. Students then write down another two words. Monitor and check their spelling or allow them to check the words in their dictionaries. In pairs, students practice spelling their partner's words.

f ▶ 00.05 Point to picture d and say *Conversation 4* and hold up four fingers. Point to the man in picture d and elicit *Mike*. Show students Mike's details in the Student's Book, pointing to the first line and saying *name* and the second and third lines and saying *address*. Play the recording for students to complete the name and address. Check answers as a class.

Answers
Mike <u>Kato</u>
<u>16</u> Lake Street
<u>Hudson</u>

g 💬🔊 Elicit the question *How do you spell your first name?* by writing *M-I-K-E* on the board and writing a question mark above it. In pairs, students say their names and addresses and ask each other to spell them. Students can, if they prefer, invent an address. Monitor, but don't interrupt fluency unless students make mistakes with the alphabet.

5 POSSESSIVE ADJECTIVES

a ▶ 00.06 Tell students to close their books. Write on the board: *I'm Tony, and this is … wife, Joanna*. Point to the blank. Elicit the missing word (*my*), and write it in the sentence. Leave the sentence on the board. Students open their books. Point to picture a, say *Conversation 5* and hold up five fingers. Play the recording for students to read and listen and underline the correct answers. Check answers as a class.

Answers
A … This is <u>my</u> wife and <u>her</u> brother.
B Oh, yes. Is that <u>your</u> apartment?
A Yes, that's <u>our</u> apartment in San Francisco …

b In the sentence on the board *I'm Tony, and this is my wife, Joanna*, circle the words *I* and *my*. Draw a line to link the two words and repeat them clearly for students. Point to the chart and read through the example sentences with *I/my* and *you/your*. Individually, students complete the chart. Check answers as a class.

Answers

He lives here.	This is <u>his</u> apartment.
She lives here.	This is <u>her</u> apartment.
We live here.	This is <u>our</u> apartment.
They live here.	This is <u>their</u> apartment.

c Individually, students complete the sentences. They then check in pairs. Check answers as a class.

Answers
1 His   2 their   3 your   4 our   5 her

> 🔄 **LOA TIP** REVIEW AND REFLECT
>
> • Draw a thumbs-up symbol in a box on the left of the board and a thumbs-down symbol in a box on the right of the board. Then stand in the middle, point to the thumbs up, and nod and look confident. Point to the thumbs down and shake your head and look worried. Ask students: *Possessive adjectives?* Elicit an indication of their confidence level.

> 💡 **EXTRA ACTIVITY**
>
> Students are usually very interested to learn something about their new teacher. Show students some photos of your family and/or friends and tell them something about the people, recycling simple language from the Welcome! unit and possessive adjectives, e.g., *This is my wife. Her name's Sarah. Mark is an old friend and that's his daughter*, etc.
>
> If students have pictures of family and/or friends on their cell phones, allow them to show each other some photos of their family and/or friends and make simple sentences.

6 CLASSROOM OBJECTS

a Books closed. Pre-teach some of the vocabulary by pointing to the classroom objects that you have in your classroom. Don't allow students to write anything down. Repeat the words several times and then "test" individual students by saying their name and pointing to an object. When you're confident that students can remember most of the vocabulary, elicit *dictionary* from a student and ask: *How do you spell that?* Students then open their books, look at the spelling of the vocabulary, and match objects 1–10 with a–j in the picture. Check answers as a class.

Answers

1 g 2 h 3 a 4 c 5 f 6 d 7 j 8 b 9 e 10 i

b ▶ 00.09 **Pronunciation** Play the recording and highlight the pronunciation for students. Individually or in pairs, students practice saying the words.

c Draw a large question mark on the board. Read the words in 6a quickly, placing extra emphasis on the article *a*. When you reach *an answer*, place extra emphasis on the article *an* and then point to the question mark on the board. Repeat if necessary, and then read the question in the Student's Book and elicit the answer as a class.

Answer

a before *a, e, i, o, u*

d Individually, students write *a* or *an* next to the words. They then check in pairs. Check answers as a class.

Answers

1 a book
2 an apple
3 a camera
4 a glass
5 an egg
6 a baby
7 a box
8 an ice cream cone

💡 FAST FINISHERS

Ask fast finishers to write a list of any "international English" words that they know, e.g., *orchestra, pizza, taxi*, and decide if they use *a* or *an*.

e Demonstrate the activity by thinking of one of the words yourself and eliciting questions from the class. Students then work in small groups and ask questions to guess each other's words. Monitor and help with vocabulary if necessary.

f Books closed. Pick up a pen, show the class, and say: *One pen.* Pick up another pen, and say: *Two …* to elicit the plural, *pens.* Point to three desks and say: *Three …* to elicit *desks.* Students open their books and complete the rules. Check answers as a class. Elicit an indication of their confidence level for the indefinite article and regular plural forms.

Answers

Most words add *-s* in the plural.
Change a final *-y* to *-i* and add *-es*.
If a word ends in *-s, -x, -sh,* or *-ch*, we add *-es*.

7 CLASSROOM INSTRUCTIONS

a ▶ 00.10 Play the recording, pausing after each item for students to follow the instructions. Elicit the actions for instructions 1 and 2. Repeat the recording, again pausing after each item, for students to identify which verbs they hear.

Answers

1 open, turn to, read (The first word of the text on SB p. 83 is *so.*)
2 turn to, look at (The place in the picture on SB p. 51 is Mexico City.)
3 close, look at
4 write
5 work, ask

Audioscript

1 Open your books and turn to page 83. Read the first word of the text. What is it?
2 Turn to page 51 and look at the picture. What place is it?
3 Close your books and look at the board.
4 Write a question on a piece of paper.
5 Work in pairs. Ask your question to your partner.

b ▶ 00.11 Individually, students underline the correct question words. Play the recording for students to listen and check. Check answers as a class.

Answers

1 What's   3 How   5 When's
2 Where's   4 Who's

🔄 LOA TIP CONCEPT CHECKING

Check that students understand the meaning of each question: for Question 1, point to the picture of the apple in 6d, ask the question, and elicit the answer: *It's an apple.* For Question 2, ask the question and elicit the answer: *Japan.* For Question 3, point to the word *dictionary* in 6a and elicit the pronunciation. For Question 4, ask the question and elicit the name of the president in the country where you are teaching or another country that has a president. For Question 5, ask the question and elicit the day(s) of your English classes with the students.

c Students read the questions and match them with the answers. Check answers as a class. Drill the questions, substituting other words for *amigo, night,* and *backpack*.

Answers

1 c 2 d 3 a 4 b

d Give students a few minutes to prepare their questions. Monitor and help as necessary. Students then work in small groups, asking and answering each other's questions.

💡 EXTRA ACTIVITY

Students prepare an end-of-section test for a partner. They write ten questions about the content of the unit using the question words in 7b and 7c, e.g., *How do you spell "whiteboard"?* or *How do you say "gelato" in English?* Monitor and help as necessary. Point out errors for students to self-correct.

In pairs, students ask and answer each other's questions. They then give their partner a score out of ten. Monitor the tests and give feedback to the class.

⟫ Photocopiable activities: Pronunciation Welcome!

UNIT 1
PEOPLE

🔄 UNIT OBJECTIVES

At the end of this unit, students will be able to:

- understand information, texts, and conversations about people and places, countries and nationalities, and people's personalities
- ask for and give information about themselves and other people, including their nationality and personality
- use simple phrases to check understanding
- introduce themselves in an online profile with correct capital letters and punctuation

UNIT CONTENTS

G GRAMMAR
- *be*: affirmative and negative
- *be*: questions and short answers

V VOCABULARY
- Countries: *Australia, Brazil, France, Japan, Mexico, Spain*, etc.
- Nationalities: *Australian, Brazilian, French, Japanese, Mexican, Spanish*, etc.
- Adjectives: *cool, fantastic, friendly, great, kind, nice, pleasant, popular, quiet, warm, well known, amazing, awful, modern, old, poor, rich, terrible, wonderful*
- Wordpower: *from* to talk about times, a starting place, our country or city, how far away something is

P PRONUNCIATION
- Word stress in nationalities
- Sound and spelling: /k/
- Rising and falling intonation
- Consonant clusters

C COMMUNICATION SKILLS
- Talking about where you are from
- Using adjectives for description
- Asking for and giving information
- Checking understanding using *So that's ...* and *Excuse me?*
- Discussing social networking and online profiles
- Writing an online profile about yourself

GETTING STARTED

💡 OPTIONAL LEAD-IN

Books closed. Review the alphabet by writing it on the board one letter at a time, saying each letter clearly, and asking the class to repeat it after you. When you have the complete alphabet on the board, point to letters at random to elicit them from the class. Repeat any letters that are problematic.

Say the word *alphabet* and then gesture for students to write it down as you spell it out: *A-L-P-H-A-B-E-T*. Check spelling by writing the word on the board. Repeat with *question, pink, textbook, address*, and *camera,* or choose words covered in the Welcome! unit containing letters which your students find difficult. Finish by asking students to spell the word *people*. Check meaning by gesturing to several students and saying *people*.

a 💬🗩 Give students one minute to think about their answers to the questions, and check that students understand the vocabulary in Questions 2 and 3. Discuss the answers as a class.

> **Suggested answers**
> 1 Brazil, Germany, Italy, Spain, the U.S.
> 2 for a sports game
> 3 Suggested answers: excited, good, happy

💡 EXTRA ACTIVITY

Write the country names from the picture on the board. Tell students to put the names of the countries in alphabetical order. They then compare their answers with a partner. Check answers as a class. (See the suggested answers above for the correct alphabetical order.)

b 💬🗩 Read the question and the ideas with the students, and check that they understand the vocabulary. Ask them when they usually meet people from other countries and ask students to share any other ideas they have. Help with vocabulary and pronunciation, but don't interrupt fluency.

💡 EXTRA ACTIVITY

Write *a music concert* on the board, point to yourself, and say: *I feel excited*. Write *watch sports* on the board, point to yourself, and say: *I feel bored*. Students then work in pairs and use the adjectives in Exercise a to say how they feel about the activities in Exercise b. Monitor and help as necessary.

Exercises **a** and **b** can be prepared as homework before this lesson to give students time to look up unfamiliar vocabulary. Ask students to look at the picture and to prepare their answers to the questions as homework to talk about in the next class.

1A | I'M FROM FRANCE

At the end of this lesson, students will be able to:

- understand a conversation about people's countries and nationalities
- use a lexical set of countries and nationalities correctly
- use simple present affirmative and negative forms of *be*
- ask for and give simple personal information about other people

💡 OPTIONAL LEAD-IN

Books closed. Draw a world map on the board and elicit the name in English of the country where you are teaching by pointing to it and writing the first letter on the board. When you have elicited the name of the country, ask: *How do you spell that?* Elicit the spelling from the class, writing it on the board as the class calls out the letters to you.

If you're from a different country, point to it and say the name of the country in English. Elicit the question *How do you spell that?* from the class before spelling the country for them. With multi-nationality classes, you could also ask some students to point to their country and see if they know how to say it in English. Don't worry if students don't know the names of the countries or how to spell them correctly at this point.

Leave the map on the board for 1a and 1b.

1 LISTENING AND READING

a 💬🗨 Give students one minute to think about their answers to the questions before talking about the pictures as a class. Don't check answers at this point.

b ▶ 01.01 Play the recording for students to listen and check. Check answers as a class. Play the recording again, or model the countries yourself for students to listen and repeat.

Answers
1 soccer
2 1 a 2 e 3 c 4 d 5 f 6 b

💡 EXTRA ACTIVITY

Quickly review the question *Where's (city)?* from the Welcome! unit by asking students about a city in the country where you are teaching. Then ask them about six other cities, one from each country in 1a, e.g., *Where's Sydney?* (Australia), *Where's Guadalajara?* (Mexico). If you used the optional lead-in, use the drawing of the world map on the board again and ask students to locate the cities using the question *Where's (city)?*

c ▶ 01.02 Ask students: *What's the World Cup?* Elicit possible answers, e.g., *It's a soccer championship for the world.* Remember that students will have very limited language at this point, so praise students who are able to express the basic idea, however simply. You may wish to pre-teach the word *team* (a group of people who play a sport or game together). Students listen to the conversation for general meaning and check the things André and Valentina talk about. Check answers as a class.

Answers
1 soccer ✓
2 countries ✓
4 a city ✓

d ▶ 01.02 Students listen to the recording again for specific words and complete the conversation. They compare in pairs. Check answers as a class. When checking answers, ask students: *How do you spell (word)?* Write the correct answers on the board.

Answers
1 name
2 from
3 where
4 France
5 great

e Play the recording again, or allow students to read the conversation at their own pace, and decide if the sentences are true or false. Check answers as a class.

Answers
1 F André and Valentina meet at the World Cup.
2 T
3 T
4 F Valentina says the French team's really good.

💡 FAST FINISHERS

Ask fast finishers to look at the pictures and identify all the colors, using the vocabulary from the Welcome! unit.

f Individually, students underline the two nationalities in the conversation. Check answers as a class.

Answers
Colombian, French

2 VOCABULARY Countries and nationalities

a ▶ 01.03 Read André's sentence with the class. Read the countries and nationalities in the box, and elicit another example of a country/nationality pair. Students work in pairs, matching the words. Play the recording for students to listen and check. Check answers as a class.

Answers and audioscript
She's from Colombia. She's Colombian.
They're from Brazil. They're Brazilian.
They're from Spain. They're Spanish.
They're from Germany. They're German.
They're from Japan. They're Japanese.

b ▶ 01.03 **Pronunciation** By counting on your fingers and breaking the words into chunks, show students how *Brazil* has two syllables, but *Brazilian* has four. Point out the dividing line between syllables in the Student's Book. Students read the other words in the box and count how many syllables there are in each. Play the recording again for students to underline the stressed syllable in each word. Check answers as a class.

Answers
Colombia, Brazilian, Spanish, Japan, Colombian, Germany, Japanese, German, Brazil, Spain

c ▶ 01.03 Play the recording again for students to listen and repeat.

> ### 🗣 LOA TIP DRILLING
>
> - Check that students are aware that the stress shifts from the second syllable in *Ja | pan* to the third syllable in *Ja | pa | nese*.
> - Highlight the changing vowel sound in *Spain* /speɪn/ and *Spanish* /ˈspænɪʃ/.

d Complete the first sentence as a class and elicit another example using picture a. Students work individually, writing sentences about the people in the pictures. They then check in pairs. Check answers as a class.

> **Answers**
> 1 Colombia
> 2 a Brazilian, Brazil   d Japanese, Japan
>   b French, France   e Spanish, Spain
>   c Australian, Australia   f Mexican, Mexico

e 💬 Individually, students complete the question. Before they work in pairs, quickly check that they have completed the question correctly (*Where*). Monitor and give students other nationalities if they are from countries other than those in 2a. If your students are from various different countries, ask each student: *Where are you from?*

f ≫ ▶ 01.04–01.05 Students complete the exercises in Vocabulary Focus 1A on SB p. 162. Play the recordings as necessary, monitor Exercises b and h, and check other answers as a class. Tell students to go back to SB p. 11.

> **Answers (Vocabulary Focus 1A SB p. 162)**
> **a** 1 the U.S.   6 Poland   11 Colombia   16 Ireland
>   2 Mexico   7 Saudi Arabia   12 South Africa   17 Italy
>   3 Turkey   8 Argentina   13 Canada   18 Pakistan
>   4 the U.K. / Britain 9 Australia   14 New Zealand   19 Russia
>   5 China   10 Iran   15 Nigeria   20 Ecuador
> **c** 1 a 2 c 3 d 4 e 5 b 6 f
> **d** 1 China – in Asia   3 Russia – speak Russian
>   2 Brazil – in South America   4 Spain – in Europe
> **e** 1 A 2 C 3 B 4 B 5 D 6 F
> **f** British, Chinese, Turkish, Mexican, Japanese, Brazilian, Canadian, Pakistani
> **g** 1 Chinese 2 different (Mexican, Japanese)

---

3 GRAMMAR *be*: affirmative and negative

a ▶ 01.06 Play the next part of the conversation for students to answer the question. Check the answer as a class.

> **Answer**
> b the town where André is from

> **Audioscript**
>
> **VALENTINA** So where are you from? Paris?
> **ANDRÉ** No, I'm not from Paris. I'm from a town called Rouen.
> **V** Hmm … Where's that?
> **A** Oh, it's a town near Paris. It's not very big.
> **V** Oh, right.
> **A** So are you here with friends?
> **V** Yes, we're a big group. We're all from Cartagena.
> **A** But they're not here.
> **V** No, they're all in the hotel. They say they're tired!
> **A** Oh, right. … Well, look, it's only 8:00, the game isn't on yet. So how about a coffee?
> **V** Hmm, yeah OK. Good idea! …

b ▶ 01.06 Students underline the correct answers. Play the recording again for students to listen and check. Check answers as a class.

> **Answers**
> 1 's not
> 2 are
> 3 aren't
> 4 It's

c Read the sentences with the students, and give them one minute to think about how to complete the rule before they work in pairs. Check the answer as a class.

> **Answer**
> 1 not

> ### 🌎 CAREFUL!
>
> There are several common student mistakes with *be* affirmative and negative. Common errors include: They miss *be* altogether, particularly before adjectives, e.g., ~~Brazil very big~~ (Correct form = *Brazil **is** very big*) and also in the second clause of a sentence, e.g., ~~This is a small town and the people very friendly~~ (Correct form = *This is a small town and the people **are** very friendly*). They confuse the forms *am/are/is*, e.g., ~~Here is the answers …~~ (Correct form = *Here **are** the answers to the homework*). They confuse colors because students often try to include the word *color* and may leave out *be*, e.g., ~~It a blue color~~ (Correct form = *It's blue*). Students may also have problems with word order, e.g., ~~They all are from Germany~~ (Correct form = *They **are** all from Germany*). They confuse capitals and apostrophes in the contracted forms, e.g., ~~Hes Spanish and i'm Brazilian~~ (Correct form = ***He's** Spanish and **I'm** Brazilian*). They may also use *have* instead of *be*, e.g., ~~She has 20 …~~ (Correct form = *She **is** 20 years old*).

d Individually, students complete the chart. They then check in pairs. Check answers as a class. Show students three fingers: point to the first finger and say *I*; point to the second and say *am*; and point to the third and say *not*. Then, close up the space between the first and second fingers to show how *I* and *am* are contracted as *I'm*. Repeat the process with *She's not*: close up the first and second fingers again to show how *she* and *is* are contracted as *she's*. Say *She is not*, point to your three fingers, and gesture to indicate for the class to show you which fingers should be closed up to represent the contraction *She's not* (i.e., first and second fingers). Repeat with *They are not*. Use this same strategy to show the alternative contraction that joins the form of *be* with *not*: *isn't* and *aren't*. Explain there are two possible answers, but the first contractions (*He's, She's, They're*) are more common in U.S. English.

> **Answers**
>
> | Affirmative (+) | Negative (−) |
> | --- | --- |
> | I'm from Cartagena.
He's a really good player.
They say they're tired. | I'm not French.
She's not from Medellín. / She isn't from Medellín.
They're not at the game. / They aren't at the game. |

e ⟫ ▶ 01.07 Students read the information in the Grammar Focus 1A on SB p. 138. Draw their attention to the different options for contractions that are possible. Play the recording where indicated, and ask students to listen and repeat. Students then complete the exercises. Check answers as a class, making sure students are using contractions correctly. Tell students to go back to SB p. 11.

Answers (Grammar Focus 1A SB p. 139)

a 2 is 3 are 4 are 5 am / 'm 6 is / 's 7 is 8 are

b 2 It's a beautiful city. It's not a beautiful city. / It isn't a beautiful city.
   3 We're from Los Angeles. We're not from Los Angeles. / We aren't from Los Angeles.
   4 They're at a party. They're not at a party. / They aren't at a party.
   5 I'm tired. I'm not tired.
   6 You're right. You're not right. / You aren't right.

c 3 'm 4 's not / isn't 5 's 6 aren't 7 is 8 's 9 aren't 10 're

d 2 He's not / He isn't a doctor. He's a student.
   3 They're not / They aren't my brothers. They're my friends.
   4 We're not / We aren't from London. We're from Toronto.
   5 I'm not a good cook. I'm a very bad cook.

f Complete the first sentence as an example with the class. Students work individually, adding the correct form of *be* to the sentences. Point out errors for students to self-correct. Check answers as a class.

Answers

1 My brother <u>is</u> in college in Madrid.
2 My mother and father <u>aren't</u> here.
3 Cartagena <u>is</u> very hot in August.
4 My friends <u>are</u> really interesting and fun.

💡 **EXTRA ACTIVITY**

Demonstrate 3g and 3h before students start to write their own sentences, two affirmative and two negative. Write *True or false?* on the board and then tell students four sentences about yourself using the verb *be*, e.g., *My mother and father are from Italy. I'm from Toronto.*, etc. Two of these should be true and two false. Students listen and try to identify the false sentences. Check answers as a class and correct the false sentences, e.g., *I'm not from Toronto. I'm from Ottawa.*, etc.

---

g Individually, students write four sentences about themselves. Monitor and help with vocabulary and give students ideas if necessary.

h 💬 In pairs, students decide if their partner's sentences are true or false. To make this a class activity, have each student then read one or two of their sentences for the class to guess if they're true or false.

---

4 SPEAKING

a ⟫ Divide the class into pairs and assign A and B roles. Student As read about Roberto on SB p. 130, and Student Bs read about Lora on SB p. 133. Monitor for any problems, and clarify these before students start on the pairwork stage. Put students into A/B pairs for them to ask and answer the questions about Roberto and Lora. As you monitor, don't interrupt fluency, but note any mistakes with *be*. After the activity, write these on the board, and ask students to correct them. Tell students to go back to SB p. 11.

b 💬 Put students into small groups to tell each other their names, countries, nationalities, and hometowns.

💡 **FAST FINISHERS**

Ask fast finishers to show each other pictures of their friends and families on their cell phones. They tell the group their names, countries, nationalities, and hometowns using the third person. Alternatively, ask fast finishers to continue talking about the other people in their group and practice giving information about each other using the third person.

⊕ **ADDITIONAL MATERIAL**

Workbook 1A

Photocopiable activities: Grammar 1A, Vocabulary 1A, Pronunciation 1A

1B | SHE'S A WONDERFUL PERSON

At the end of this lesson, students will be able to:

- read and understand short texts about pictures
- use a lexical set of personality adjectives correctly
- understand a conversation about people's nationalities and personalities
- use the simple present question form of *be*
- talk about people they know from other countries

♀ OPTIONAL LEAD-IN

Books closed. Draw the following puzzle on the board:

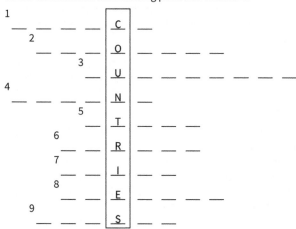

Point to the first line of the puzzle and say: *1 She's Mexican. She's from … .* Elicit *Mexico* as an example. Ask students to spell out the answer and fill it in. Students then work individually as you read clues 2–9 to the class:

2 *He's Colombian. He's from Bogotá in … .* (Colombia);
3 *They're not British. They're Australian. They're from … .* (Australia);
4 *He's Polish. He's from … .* (Poland);
5 *They're Italian. They're from Rome in … .* (Italy);
6 *She's not French. She's Turkish. She's from … .* (Turkey);
7 *They're Chinese. They're from … .* (China);
8 *She's Irish. She's from Dublin in … .* (Ireland);
9 *He's not Pakistani. He's Russian. He's from … .* (Russia).

Students check in pairs. Then, check answers as a class. When checking answers, ask students to spell out the countries to you as you write them in the puzzle.

1 READING

a 💬🗩 Discuss the question as a class and write students' ideas on the board.

b Students read the texts quickly and match them with the pictures. Check answers as a class and find out if students' guesses in 1a were correct. You may wish to help students with words in the Vocabulary Support box.

> **Answers**
> Suzi c (She's in Rio.)
> James d (He's in San Francisco.)
> Alex a
> Saddah b

📖 VOCABULARY SUPPORT

coworker (A2) – a person you work with at your job

cousin (A2) – the son/daughter of your father's/mother's brother/sister

c Read the first sentence with the class, and elicit who students think says it. Read the sentence aloud to justify the answer: *We're teachers and we work together in a school.* Individually, students decide who said the other sentences. They then check in pairs. When checking answers, elicit which words or sentences in the texts helped students decide.

> **Suggested answers**
> 1 Saddah   3 James
> 2 Alex   4 Suzi

d 💬🗩 In pairs, students talk about who they would like to meet and why. Ask students to share their answers to find out who the most popular person to meet is.

2 VOCABULARY Adjectives

a Point to picture c and read the sentence with the class. Read the adjectives again and elicit that the sentence is about Claudia.

> **Answer**
> Claudia

b Students work individually to find the other adjectives. You can tell them that there are two or three adjectives in each text. Check that students have found the correct words before they start to put them into the correct blanks. Students check in pairs. Then, check answers as a class.

> **Answers**
> 1 wonderful, great, fantastic
> 2 kind, nice
> 3 well known
> 4 quiet
> 5 popular

c **Pronunciation** Model the pronunciation of the three words from the text and highlight the /k/ sounds for students. Look at one or two words together as a class before students work individually, underlining the /k/ sounds and identifying the two words that don't have /k/. When checking answers, model and drill all the words for students to listen and repeat.

> **Answers**
> cold, car, kitchen, like, coffee, quick, back, key, come, make, school, cat
> *Cheap* and *know* don't have /k/.

♀ FAST FINISHERS

Ask fast finishers to look at the countries in Vocabulary Focus 1A on SB p. 162 and identify the seven countries that have the /k/ sound (Canada, Colombia, Mexico, Pakistan, South Africa, Turkey, the U.K.).

d 💬 Read the examples with the class. Students work in pairs or small groups, talking about people they know. If they wish, they can show pictures of the people they are talking about on their cell phones if they have them. Monitor, but don't interrupt fluency unless students make mistakes with the adjectives.

e ≫ ▶ 01.08–01.09 Students complete the exercises in Vocabulary Focus 1B on SB p. 163. Play the recordings as necessary and monitor students as they speak. Check answers as a class, making sure students are pronouncing the words correctly. Tell students to go back to SB p. 13.

> **Answers (Vocabulary Focus 1B SB p. 163)**
> **a** 1 not very good 2 very good 3 very good 4 not very good
> **b** old – modern; poor – rich

> 💡 **EXTRA ACTIVITY**
>
> Ask students to give an example for each adjective, e.g., *a rich celebrity, an awful national dish*. Remember that they still have limited vocabulary, so praise them for making the correct connections between the meaning of the adjectives and other words.

3 LISTENING

a ▶ 01.10 Point to the man in the first picture and say: *This is Roman.* Then ask: *What's his nationality?* Play the first part of the recording for students to listen and complete the nationality on the profile. Check the answer as a class. Then repeat the process with Diego and Mia and Laura. Make sure students understand that they should give the nationality, not the country, in each case. You may wish to pre-teach the word *married* (when you have a husband/wife).

> **Answers**
> 1 Polish 2 Mexican 3 Spanish

> **Audioscript**
>
> **1**
> A This is my good friend Roman. He's really friendly.
> B Is he from Poland?
> A Yes, he is.
>
> **2**
> A These are my friends Mia and Diego. They're really great.
> B Are they married?
> A Yes, they are.
> B Are they Brazilian?
> A No, they're not. They're from Mexico.
>
> **3**
> A This is my friend Laura. She's really cool.
> B Is she Italian?
> A No, she's not. She's from Spain.

b ▶ 01.10 Play the recording again without stopping for students to listen for the specific adjectives and complete the profiles. They compare in pairs. Then, check answers as a class. When checking answers, ask students: *How do you spell (word)?* Write the correct answers on the board.

> **Answers**
> 4 friendly 5 great 6 cool

4 GRAMMAR
be: questions and short answers

a ▶ 01.11 Look at picture c and text 1 on SB p. 12 again. Books closed. Write: *Claudia / Spanish (+)* on the board and elicit the affirmative sentence: *Claudia is Spanish.* Then write: *Claudia / French (–)* on the board and elicit the negative sentence: *Claudia's not French.* Finally, write *Claudia / Spanish (?)* on the board and see if students can form the question *Is Claudia Spanish?* Students open their books. Then, read the questions in 4a with the class. Individually, students complete the short answers. Play the recording for students to listen and check. Check answers as a class.

> **Answers**
> 1 's not 2 is 3 are 4 're not

b Individually, students complete the chart. Remind them that there are two possible alternatives for the negative form of *he/she* and *they*. They then check in pairs. Check answers by copying the chart onto the board and asking individual students to come up and complete the blanks.

> **Answers**
>
> | Questions (?) | Short answers | |
> |---|---|---|
> | <u>Are</u> you Australian? | Yes, I am. | No, I'm not. |
> | <u>Are</u> you Brazilian? | Yes, we are. | No, we're not./we aren't. |
> | <u>Is</u> he/she Turkish? | Yes, he/she <u>is</u>. | No, he/she <u>'s not</u>./<u>isn't</u>. |
> | <u>Are</u> they Ecuadorian? | Yes, they <u>are</u>. | No, they <u>'re not</u>./aren't. |

> 🔄 **LOA TIP** CONCEPT CHECKING
>
> - Write example questions on the board to check that students are assimilating correct word order. Point to each question one by one and ask students: *Is this correct?* Ask them to correct the questions as necessary, e.g., *She is Italian?* (No), *He French is?* (No), *From the U.S. is he?* (No), *Are they Pakistani?* (Yes), *They're Canadian?* (No).
> - Check that students understand that they also need to think about the verb forms. Write example questions with correct word order, but with incorrect verb forms and ask students to correct them, e.g., *Is they from Japan?* (Are they from Japan?), *Am Laura Spanish?* (Is Laura Spanish?), *Be you Chinese?* (Are you Chinese?).

> ◉ **CAREFUL!**
>
> The most common student mistake with *be* questions and short answers is for students to use *it* instead of *that* in Yes/No questions that ask if something is OK, e.g., ~~Is it OK?~~ (Correct form = Is **that** OK?), or ~~Is it good for you?~~ (Correct form = Is **that** good for you?). Students may also have problems with the inversion required to form questions, possibly because there is no change in the word order for questions in their own language, e.g., ~~Claudia is Spanish?~~ (Correct form = Is **Claudia** Spanish?).

c ≫ ▶ `01.12` Students read the information in Grammar Focus 1B on SB p. 138. Play the recording where indicated, and ask students to listen and repeat. Students then complete the exercises. Check answers as a class, making sure students are using correct word order and contractions where possible. Tell students to go back to SB p. 13.

> **Answers (Grammar Focus 1B SB p. 139)**
> **a** 2 Where are you from?   6 Are you friends?
>   3 Are you American?   7 Is it very cold?
>   4 Is she popular?   8 Is he from Chile?
>   5 What are your names?
> **b** 2 f   3 b   4 g   5 c   6 a   7 e
> **c** 1 are; 'm   2 's; 's; 's; 's   3 are; 're; 're
>   4 's; is; Are; 're not / aren't; 're; 're; are

💡 **FAST FINISHERS**

Ask fast finishers to write simple conversations of their own, using the conversations in Grammar Focus Exercise c as a model.

d ▶ `01.13` Individually, students complete the conversations. They then check in pairs. Play the recording for students to listen and check. Check answers as a class. Then, elicit an indication of their confidence level for *be*: affirmative, negative, questions, and short answers.

> **Answers**
> 2 's   6 're
> 3 Is   7 Are
> 4 is   8 're
> 5 are   9 're

💡 **EXTRA ACTIVITY**

Drill the questions *Is he from London?* and *Are they married?* and then tell students about some of your friends, using the conversations in 4d as a model. If possible, show students pictures of the people as you're talking about them. Elicit questions about your friends from individual students, e.g.:

Teacher   *My friend Fiona's Australian. She's very friendly.*

Student   *Is she from Sydney?*

Teacher   *No, she's not. She's from Melbourne.*

5 SPEAKING

a Give students a few minutes to prepare and write notes about the people they know. Monitor and help as necessary.

b 💬🗨 Students work in small groups, telling each other about the people they know and asking and answering each other's questions. Monitor and listen for correct usage of the target language from this lesson. You may ask each student to tell the class about one of the people they know and, if possible, show a picture.

⊕ **ADDITIONAL MATERIAL**

Workbook 1B

Photocopiable activities: Grammar 1B, Vocabulary 1B, Pronunciation 1B

1C | EVERYDAY ENGLISH
What's your last name?

At the end of this lesson, students will be able to:

- understand an informal conversation about registering for an exercise class
- use appropriate phrases for asking for and giving information
- use appropriate phrases for checking understanding
- identify how many sounds groups of letters have and pronounce them correctly
- maintain a conversation in which they register for a course

💡 **OPTIONAL LEAD-IN**

Write the adjectives from Lesson 1B on the board in random order: *amazing, awful, cool, fantastic, friendly, great, kind, modern, nice, old, rich, poor, popular, quiet, terrible, warm, well known, wonderful.* Say a variety of people/places/things which your students will know about and elicit adjectives to describe them, e.g., *Justin Bieber, New York, the weather in England.* As this is very subjective, students will likely disagree on which adjectives are appropriate, but accept all suggestions and clarify meaning as you go along.

1 LISTENING

a ▶ `01.14` Play Part 1 of the audio recording for students to choose the correct answers. Check answers as a class.

> **Answers**
> 1 a   2 b   3 b

> **Audioscript (Part 1)**
> **JENNY** Taxi!
> **RICHARD** Hello. The Market Street Hotel, please.
> **TAXI DRIVER** OK! Welcome to San Francisco.
> **J** Thank you! It's so beautiful tonight! Look – the ocean! Can you take us down to the water?
> **TD** Sure.
> **R** Jenny, it's late. It's after 9 o'clock.
> **J** But I want to see the city! Look at that bridge!
> **R** But I want to sleep. Can we go to the hotel, please? We can see the city tomorrow.

b ▶ `01.15` Play Part 2 of the audio recording for students to listen to the conversation for general meaning and answer the question. Check the answer as a class.

> **Answer**
> b take a yoga class

c ▶ **01.15** Students listen again for specific details. Play Part 2 of the audio recording again for students to decide if the sentences are true or false and correct the false sentences.

> **Answers**
> 1 T
> 2 F (Jenny wants to go to the yoga class. Richard wants to sleep.)
> 3 F (The fitness center is on the second floor.)

♀ EXTRA ACTIVITY

Ask students the following questions about Part 2 of the audio: *1 How do you spell Richard's last name? 2 What room is he in?* Play Part 2 of the audio recording again, repeating the relevant sections as necessary. Check answers as a class (*1 T-A-Y-L-O-R 2 418*).

2 USEFUL LANGUAGE
Asking for and giving information

a Individually, students decide who they think says each sentence. They then compare their ideas in pairs. Don't check answers at this point.

b ▶ **01.15** Students match the pairs of sentences. Play the recording for students to listen and check. Check answers as a class. Drill the key phrases from the conversation for correct intonation.

> **Answers**
> 1 (G) d (R)
> 2 (G) g (R)
> 3 (R) f (G)
> 4 (G) b (R)
> 5 (R) c (G)
> 6 (G) e (R)
> 7 (R) a (G)

c Students underline the correct answers. Check answers as a class and point out that we use *in* with a place and *at* with a time.

> **Answers**
> 1 Room 6
> 2 eight o'clock

d ▶ **01.16** Individually, students complete the conversation. They then check in pairs. Play the recording for students to listen and check. Check answers as a class.

> **Answers**
> 1 help
> 2 like
> 3 where's / where is
> 4 What's
> 5 spell

e 💬 ▣ Practice the conversation in 2d all together, with you taking the role of the receptionist and the class the role of the person who wants information. When students are confident in the role of the person who wants information, change roles so that they also practice the role of receptionist. In pairs, students practice the conversation, using their own last names. Monitor and correct students' pronunciation as appropriate.

♀ FAST FINISHERS

Ask fast finishers to change the additional information, e.g., *an (art) class, it's on (Friday) at (six) o'clock, in Room (3),* and practice the conversation again.

3 LISTENING

a ▶ **01.17** Students listen to Part 3 for specific details. Play the audio recording for students to decide if the sentences are true or false. Check answers as a class.

> **Answers**
> 1 F (It's 7:40.)
> 2 F (Richard is tired.)
> 3 T
> 4 F (Richard wants to drink coffee now.)

b 💬 ▣ Discuss the question as a class. Encourage students to justify their ideas as much as possible, e.g., *before work – It is quiet before work,* or *never – I'm lazy!*

4 CONVERSATION SKILLS
Checking understanding

a In pairs, students look at the mini-conversations and try to complete them. Check answers as a class.

> **Answers**
> 1 Excuse me?
> 2 So that's

b Give students a moment to think about the meaning of each expression individually before discussing them as a class.

> **Answers**
> 1 So that's
> 2 Excuse me?

c ▶ 01.18 **Pronunciation** Play the recording or model the sentences yourself and highlight the intonation for students. Drill the sentences, making sure students are using a rising intonation.

> **Answer**
> The intonation goes up.

d 💬 Read the dialogue map with students before they start. Remind students to make sure the intonation goes up on the expressions for checking understanding. In pairs, students practice conversations using their last names.

5 PRONUNCIATION Consonant clusters

a ▶ 01.19 Play the recording or model the example yourself and highlight the consonant clusters for students.

> 👁 **CAREFUL!**
>
> Many students have problems with the complex consonant clusters found in English because they are very different from the sound combinations that exist in their own language. These clusters can have up to four consonant sounds grouped together, but to start off simply, the examples in this section all contain just one or two sounds. When drilling, it may help students if you break consonant clusters down into their individual parts before putting them together for students, e.g., /k/ ❯ /l/ ❯ /kl/ and /θ/ ❯ /r/ ❯ /θr/. You may also wish to point out that in English, the number of letters in a written word frequently doesn't match the number of sounds.

b ▶ 01.20 Individually, students listen to the words and count how many consonant sounds the letters in **bold** have. They check in pairs. Then, check answers as a class. Model the pronunciation for students to listen and repeat.

> **Answers**
> **thr**ee – thr = two sounds: /θr/
> **six** – x = two sounds: /ks/
> ei**ght**y – ght = one sound: /t/

c ▶ 01.21 Play the recording or model the times yourself for students to listen and repeat. Test students by writing further times on the board in numerals and eliciting the times from the class.

6 SPEAKING

a ⫸ Divide the class into pairs and assign A and B roles. Student As read the first card on SB p. 131 and Student Bs read the first card on SB p. 133. Students then role-play the conversation. Monitor, but don't interrupt fluency unless students make mistakes with the content of this lesson. Students then read the second card and role-play the second situation.

> ↻ **LOA TIP** MONITORING
>
> - Listen to see if students are using the expressions for checking understanding at appropriate points. Praise students with a smile or a nod when they use this language correctly.
> - Monitor and identify students who use the language for asking for and giving information well. Ask these pairs to perform their conversations for the class.

> ⊕ **ADDITIONAL MATERIAL**
>
> Workbook 1C
> Unit Progress Test

At the end of this lesson, students will be able to:

• understand a conversation in which people introduce themselves
• understand written personal profiles
• use capital letters and punctuation correctly
• write a short personal profile introducing themselves

💡 OPTIONAL LEAD-IN

Write *social media site* on the board. Ask students: *What's a social media site?* Elicit possible answers, e.g., *a website where people or friends share information and photos on the Internet.* In monolingual classes, you may wish to ask students: *What's a "social media site" in (students' L1)?*

Draw a line running out from the words *social media site* on the board and start writing the name of a social media site which will be familiar to your students, e.g., *Instagram*, *Twitter*. Elicit the name of the site and then continue to draw lines from the words and elicit other social media sites your students know. You may also give students information from the Culture Notes below.

🌎 CULTURE NOTES

Social media sites change dramatically in popularity and can go in and out of fashion at great speed. At time of publication, some of the most important social networks around the world include the following:

Facebook (the first social network to have over a billion users around the world), Instagram (a picture-based social network, designed for use on smartphones and other mobile devices), LinkedIn (a business networking tool), and Twitter (a social network where users write short, public messages, called tweets, of up to 140 characters).

1 SPEAKING AND LISTENING

a 💬 Read the questions with the students, and then give them one minute to think about their answers. Discuss the questions as a class and find out which social media sites are most popular with your students.

b Check that students know the difference between *Lives in* (the place where they live now) and *From* (the place where they were born or grew up) in Kate's and Carla's profiles. Tell students to complete the chart, using the information in the two profiles. Check answers by copying the chart onto the board and asking students to complete the missing information. After students complete each item in the chart, point to it and ask the class: *Is it correct?* Elicit the general opinion before confirming if it's the correct answer or not.

Answers

She's …	20 years old	from Chicago	Mexican	a teacher	a student
Kate	DK	DK	DK	✓	✗
Carla	✓	✗	✓	✗	✓

c ▶ 01.22 Play the recording for students to listen for general meaning and answer the questions. Check answers as a class.

Answers
1 the first day
2 Chicago

Audioscript

KATE Welcome to the class, very nice to see you all. I'm Kate, as you know, and this is Mike. We're your two teachers, and we're both from the U.S. So, first, can we all say our names and where we're from? OK? Carla, you start …

CARLA Yes, of course. Hello, I'm Carla, and I'm from Mexico. I'm a student in Guadalajara. It's my first time in Chicago, so it's great to be here.

MASATO OK. Well, I'm Masato, and I live in Kyoto, Japan. I work in a restaurant in Kyoto, so English is really important to me.

CARMEN Yes, I'm Carmen. I'm from Barcelona, Spain. I'm also a student. I study computer science. It's not my first time in the U.S. I know Chicago pretty well, but it's nice to be here again.

ORHAN I'm Orhan and I'm from Turkey. I live in Chicago now with my family. I work for a bank here.

MARISA I'm Marisa and I'm a student in Recife, Brazil. It's my first time in Chicago, too, but my brother is here, so I can stay with him and his family.

K OK, great, thank you. Well, to start off then, I think I'll just explain what the class is all about…

💡 EXTRA ACTIVITY

Before students listen again, give them one minute to work in pairs and see what, if anything, they remember from the first listening. Ask them to look at the picture in the Student's Book, or project the picture on the board and ask students to close their books. Students say what they remember about the people, e.g., *Kate and Mike – teachers, from Chicago*; *Carmen – Spanish, from Barcelona*. Students share ideas as a class. Don't check answers at this point. This extra "scaffolding" will help students complete the task in 1d better.

d ▶ 01.22 Students listen to the recording again for specific details and complete the chart. Make sure students understand that they should give the country, not the nationality, in each case. They compare in pairs. Then, check answers as a class.

Answers

Name	Country	One other thing we know
Kate and Mike	U.S.	They're <u>teachers</u>.
Carla	Mexico	She's a <u>student (in Guadalajara)</u>.
Masato	<u>Japan</u>	English is <u>important</u> for his work.
Carmen	<u>Spain</u>	She's a computer science <u>student</u>.
Orhan	<u>Turkey</u>	His <u>family</u> is in Chicago.
Marisa	<u>Brazil</u>	Her <u>brother</u> is in Chicago.

e 💬 Put students into small groups, nominating the strongest student in each group, Student A, to be the "teacher." Students then work together, introducing themselves to their group. Monitor, but don't interrupt fluency.

- Elicit some example sentences from the class before students work in groups in 1e. Say *I'm ...* and then point to a person in the picture to elicit the person's name, e.g., *Marisa*. Then say: *I'm from ...* to elicit *I'm from Recife / Brazil / Recife in Brazil*. Continue with *I'm a ...* to elicit *student*.

- Keep in mind that although the language in the recording is A2 level, it does include items that have not yet been studied in this course. How much of this language you choose to use at this point will depend on the confidence level of your students.

♀ EXTRA ACTIVITY

Do the task in 1e "for real," i.e., with you introducing yourself to the class as if it were the first day of class and then asking each student to say who they are along with one more thing about themselves. Explain the task clearly first and give students one minute to prepare what they are going to say. Monitor and help with vocabulary and give students ideas if necessary. Then work as a class, with you welcoming the students and then inviting them to introduce themselves one after another. Choose students at random rather than working your way around the classroom systematically, as this will prevent students feeling stressed as they see their turn approaching.

2 READING

a Write *New information?* on the board and point to the text about Kate. Start reading and pause at her last name, and then point to the question on the board and ask: *Is it new information?* (No). Continue reading and pause after *Royal Oak*. Again, point to the question on the board and ask: *Is it new information?* (Yes). Indicate students should underline this. Individually, students continue reading the two texts and underline the new information. Check answers as a class.

> **Answers**
> Kate – It's a small city near Detroit, Michigan; I'm married and I have two young children, a boy and a girl; I like languages, music, and movies.
> Carla – I study marketing; I like running, swimming, and yoga.

3 WRITING SKILLS
Capital letters and punctuation

a Write *capital letters* on the board, then erase it and write *CAPITAL LETTERS*. Ask students: *What are capital letters?* and elicit possible answers, e.g., *big letters*. Complete the first one or two items in the list as examples before students work individually, putting a checkmark by the words that have capital letters. Check answers as a class.

> **Answers**
> 1 ✓
> 2 ✓
> 3 ✓
> 4 ✓
> 6 ✓
> 8 ✓
> 9 ✓

♀ FAST FINISHERS

Ask fast finishers to look back through the Welcome! unit and Unit 1 and find more examples of all the areas in 3a, e.g., *1 Pedro – SB p. 6; 5 soccer, 6 Cartagena – SB p. 10.*

b Students write the full forms of the words. Check answers by asking individual students to come up and write them on the board.

> **Answers**
> 1 it is
> 2 she is
> 3 you are
> 4 is not
> 5 are not

c Circle the words *it is* on the board from the previous exercise. Next to it, write *it's* and circle the apostrophe. Students then add apostrophes to the words in the book. Check answers as a class.

> **Answers**
> 1 I'm   4 he's
> 2 aren't   5 we're
> 3 isn't   6 they're

d Discuss the questions as a class and ask students to find examples of both commas and periods in Kate's and Carla's online profiles.

> **Answers**
> a periods
> b commas

e Students read the sentences and rewrite them with capital letters and the correct punctuation. They compare their answers in pairs. Check answers as a class by asking individual students to come up and write the sentences on the board.

> **Answers**
> 1 I'm from Shanghai. It's a big city in China.
> 2 I like basketball, old cars, and jazz.
> 3 I'm a French teacher in Australia.
> 4 This isn't my first time in Miami.
> 5 Are all the teachers American?

4 WRITING

a Individually, students write their profiles. Remind students to be careful with the use of capital letters and punctuation. Monitor and help with vocabulary and give students ideas if necessary. If you're short on time, this exercise can be completed for homework. Students could then bring their profiles to the next class.

b In pairs, students switch profiles and check their partner's work. They then give each other feedback. If they made any mistakes with capital letters and/or punctuation, they prepare a second draft of their profile and correct their mistakes. Finally, elicit an indication of students' confidence level for using capital letters and punctuation correctly.

⊕ ADDITIONAL MATERIAL

Workbook 1D

UNIT 1
Review and extension

1 VOCABULARY

a Individually, students complete the sentences. Check answers and spelling as a class by asking students to write the correct answers on the board.

Answers
1 Brazilian	3 German	5 French
2 Ecuadorian	4 Australian	6 Japanese

b Students complete the text, working individually. They check in pairs. Check answers as a class.

Answers
1 fantastic	3 kind	5 great	7 friendly
2 warm	4 nice	6 quiet	

> ♀ **FAST FINISHERS**
>
> Ask fast finishers to write sentences or a complete paragraph about their families, using the text in 1b as a model.

2 GRAMMAR

a Students complete the text with the correct form of the verb *be*. They check in pairs. Check answers as a class.

Answers
1 'm 2 'm 3 'm 4 'm 5 's 6 's 7 's 8 're 9 are 10 're

b Complete the first question as an example with the class. Individually, students write the questions. Monitor and help as necessary. Point out errors for students to self-correct.

Answers
1 Are you (French/Portuguese/Spanish, etc.)?
2 Is she kind?
3 Are they from (France/Portugal/Spain, etc.)?
4 What's your name?
5 Where are you from?

c Students write the questions and short answers. Remind them that there are two possible negative answers in some cases. Check answers as a class and drill the questions and short answers.

Answers
1 Are you Ecuadorian? Yes, I am.
2 Is she your sister? No, she isn't./she's not.
3 Are they friendly? Yes, they are.
4 Are you both from the U.S.? No, we aren't. / 're not.
5 Is he well known? No, he isn't./'s not.

d Check that students understand that contractions count as one word. Individually, students complete the conversation. Check answers as a class.

Answers
1 your	3 I'm	5 isn't/'s not	7 She's
2 Are	4 she	6 where's	

e 💬🗩 In pairs, students practice the conversation, using their own personal information. As you monitor, don't interrupt fluency, but note mistakes with the verb *be*. After the activity, write them on the board, and ask students to correct them.

3 WORDPOWER *from*

a Tell students to close their books. Write the four sentences from 3a on the board, leaving a blank in place of *from*. Point to the four blanks, and ask students: *What's this word?* Elicit *from*, and write it in a circle above the sentences. Students open their books, look at the sentences with *from*, and match them with the pictures. Check answers as a class.

Answers
1 c 2 a 3 d 4 b

b Students read the rules and match them with the sentences with *from* in 3a. They then check in pairs. Check answers as a class.

Answers
a 3 b 1 c 2 d 4

c Students read the sentences and match them with the rules in 3b. Check answers as a class.

Answers
1 a 2 d 3 b 4 c

d Write *I'm the U.S.* on the board and ask students: *Is this correct?* (No). Elicit the correct answer (*I'm from the U.S.*). Students then work individually, adding *from* to the sentences. Check answers by asking individual students to come up and write the sentences on the board.

Answers
1 This postcard is <u>from</u> New Zealand.
2 Breakfast is <u>from</u> seven o'clock to ten o'clock every morning.
3 The bank's only 200 meters <u>from</u> here.

e Write *the plane / this is / from Miami* on the board and use arrows to show how the phrases need to be put in order to make a sentence (*This is the plane from Miami.*). Students order the phrases to make sentences. Check answers as a class.

Answers
1 I'm from Denmark.
2 The supermarket's open from 7:30 a.m. to 9:30 p.m.
3 My place is two kilometers from school.

f As an example, make the sentences in 3e true for yourself, e.g., *I'm from the U.S.* Students then change the sentences to make them true for themselves. Monitor and point out errors for students to self-correct.

> ♀ **EXTRA ACTIVITY**
>
> Tell students four sentences about yourself, each including an example of *from*, e.g., *I'm from New York.*; *My place is five kilometers from the school.*; *The stores are only 100 meters from my house.*; *My day at school is from nine o'clock to seven thirty.* Make some true and some false, and ask students to identify which are true and which are false.

≫ Photocopiable activities: Wordpower 1

> 🔄 **LOA** REVIEW YOUR PROGRESS
>
> Students look back through the unit, think about what they studied, and decide how well they did. Students work on weak areas by using the appropriate sections of the Workbook and the Photocopiable activities.

WORK AND STUDY

UNIT 2

↻ UNIT OBJECTIVES

At the end of this unit, students will be able to:

- **understand information, texts, and conversations about work, jobs, and studying**
- **ask for and give information about themselves and other people, including their jobs and study habits**
- **tell the time**
- **use simple phrases to react to news**
- **identify and correct spelling mistakes in their written work**
- **complete a form explaining why English is important for them and why they want to improve their English**

UNIT CONTENTS

G GRAMMAR

- Simple present: affirmative and negative
- Simple present: questions and short answers

V VOCABULARY

- Jobs: *actor, businessman, businesswoman, chef, dentist, engineer, farmer, janitor, manager, mechanic, nurse, photographer, pilot, police officer, receptionist, salesperson, server, taxi driver, tour guide*
- Studying: *break, exam, get good/bad grades, pass/fail an exam, pass/fail a test, schedule, semester, study, take notes*
- Time: *o'clock, five after, ten after, (a) quarter after, thirty, (a) quarter to,* etc.
- Wordpower: *work* as a verb with *in* + place, *for* + company, *as* + job; *work* as a noun: *be at work, be out of work, go to work, leave work, start work,* etc.

P PRONUNCIATION

- Word stress in jobs
- Third person *-s*
- Simple present questions: *Do you*
- Sound and spelling: *ou*

C COMMUNICATION SKILLS

- Talking about jobs
- Talking about study habits
- Asking for things and replying
- Reacting to news using *That's too bad* and *No problem*
- Writing a competition entry about learning English

GETTING STARTED

♀ OPTIONAL LEAD-IN

Books closed. Write *jobs* on the board. Elicit the names of jobs students know and write them on the board, e.g., *banker, doctor, teacher.* If necessary, ask students: *How do you spell that?* In monolingual classes, you may ask: *What's "(doctor)" in (students' L1)?* Students then listen to you give four simple clues using *be,* e.g., *This person is very smart. / He or she knows about medicine. / You go to this person when you are sick.* Students then try to identify the job (*a doctor*). Unless students thought of the word *scientist* in the initial brainstorm, delete all the jobs from the board before reading out the following four clues: *This person works outside or in a laboratory. / This person is usually good with numbers. / This person is very smart.* Elicit the answer from the class or ask students to open their books and look at the photo. Write *scientist* on the board.

a 💬🔲 Give students one minute to think about their answers to the questions before talking about the picture as a class.

b 💬🔲 Read the ideas with the students and check that they understand *machines.* Discuss which kinds of work they think are interesting and ask students to share any other ideas they have.

♀ EXTRA ACTIVITY

If your students work, ask them to write down one good thing and one bad thing about their job, e.g., *It's an easy job, but it's very boring.* Ask students to say their sentences to the class, and ask the rest of the class: *Is it the same for you?* Don't let students tell each other exactly what their jobs are at this point, and tell them that they'll find out this information at the end of Lesson 2A. Then ask students to write down one good thing and one bad thing about being a student and to share their sentences with the class.

Exercises **a** and **b** can be prepared as homework before this lesson to give students time to look up unfamiliar vocabulary. Ask students to look at the picture and to prepare their answers to the questions as homework to talk about in the next class.

2A | SHE LOVES HER JOB

At the end of this lesson, students will be able to:
- read and understand a text about a dangerous job
- use a lexical set of jobs correctly
- use the affirmative and negative forms of the simple present
- talk about their jobs or the jobs of people they know

💡 OPTIONAL LEAD-IN

Books closed. Ask students: *What's a "gator girl"?* Tell them: *It's a job!* Write it on the board. Under *gator*, write *alligator* and help students to locate *gator* in the word by covering up *alli* with your hand. Help them understand that *gator* is a shortened version of the word "alligator." In a monolingual class, you could ask: *What's "alligator" in (students' L1)?* Alternatively, to help students connect the pictures with the job title and understand the job, point at the pictures and say: *This is an alligator. This is a girl.*

1 READING

a 💬 Individually, students look at the picture and answer the questions. Ask some students to tell the class their ideas, but don't check answers at this point.

b Students read the text quickly and check their answers to 1a. Check answers as a class. You may wish to help students with words in the Vocabulary Support box.

Answers
1 a in a park
2 b she works here
3 Students' own answers

📖 VOCABULARY SUPPORT

wild (B2) – an animal that lives away from people in natural conditions

smart (B1) – intelligent

c Read the sentences with students. Then, tell students to read the text again in detail and choose the correct answers. Check answers as a class.

Answers
1 don't like
2 likes
3 don't like
4 is
5 two jobs

d Make sure students understand that the information could be anywhere in the text, not necessarily in the section about Gabby. They check in pairs. Check answers as a class.

Possible answers
She works in a beautiful park; she loves her job; she teaches visitors about alligators; she also catches wild alligators.

💡 FAST FINISHERS

Ask fast finishers to look at the text again, find words that are new for them, and write them down in their notebooks, either with a definition, an example, or a translation.

e 💬 Students talk about the questions in pairs, small groups, or as a class. Encourage students to justify their ideas as much as possible, e.g., *I think Gabby's job is awful. It's very dangerous!*

2 VOCABULARY Jobs

a Ask students to cover the words and see how many of the jobs in the pictures they already know. Individually, students then match the words with the pictures. Monitor for any problems and clarify these as you check answers as a class.

Answers
1 i	4 f	7 g
2 d	5 e	8 h
3 c	6 b	9 a

💡 FAST FINISHERS

Ask fast finishers to write down all the other jobs they can think of. After they complete Vocabulary Focus 2A on p. 163, they can see how many jobs they had already thought of.

b ▶ 02.01 **Pronunciation** Look at the example with the class, and make sure students understand how the underlining relates to word stress by over-stressing the underlined syllable, i.e., *poLICE officer*. Play the recording for students to underline the stressed syllable. Check answers as a class.

Answers
engi<u>neer</u>
pho<u>tog</u>rapher
<u>den</u>tist

c 💬 Read the sentences with the students and then give them one minute to think about their answers. Check that students understand that there are no correct answers in this case. They then compare their ideas in pairs. Invite pairs to share their answers with the class.

Answers
Students' own answers

d ≫ ▶ 02.02 Students complete the exercises in Vocabulary Focus 2A on SB p. 163. Play the recording for students to check their answers to Exercise a, monitor Exercise c, and check other answers as a class. Tell students to go back to SB p. 21.

Answers (Vocabulary Focus 2A SB p. 163)
a
1 farmer	6 actor
2 chef	7 server
3 businessman / businesswoman	8 mechanic
4 receptionist	9 tour guide
5 manager	

b
a nurse	e chef	i receptionist
b tour guide	f dentist	j farmer
c actor	g mechanic	
d taxi driver	h pilot	

3 GRAMMAR
Simple present: affirmative and negative

a ▶02.03 Write the following three jumbled sentences about the text on SB p. 20 on the board and ask students to put them in order: *1 is / in Florida / Everglades Holiday Park* (Everglades Holiday Park is in Florida.) *2 animal park / It's / an* (It's an animal park.) *3 birds and alligators / It / has* (It has birds and alligators.) Say: *Sentence 3 is different.* Ask: *Why?* Elicit that it doesn't use the verb *be*. Students then look at the chart and complete it with the simple present verbs. Play the recording for students to listen and check. Check answers as a class.

Answers

	I / we / you / they	he / she / it
+	Tourists <u>come</u> to look at the alligators. Her parents <u>think</u> she's crazy.	She <u>works</u> at Everglades Holiday Park. She <u>catches</u> wild alligators.
–	They <u>don't go</u> too close to them. Alligators <u>don't attack</u> people.	Gabby <u>doesn't</u> always <u>work</u> at the park.

b Elicit the first two or three examples with the class. Students then underline the simple present verbs and classify them as affirmative or negative. Check answers by drawing two columns on the board and asking individual students to come up and write their examples on the board.

Answers

Affirmative forms: is, 's, has, visit, come, think, lives, works, loves, teaches, tells, swim, give, get, think, enjoys, thinks, has

Negative forms: don't (really) like, don't go, don't attack, don't like, doesn't (always) work, don't understand

---

◉ CAREFUL!

When using the simple present, students often make mistakes with the negative forms, either using *haven't* instead of *don't have* before a main verb, e.g., ~~I haven't a dangerous job~~ (Correct form = *I don't have a dangerous job*), or *didn't* instead of *don't*. This second type of error may sometimes cause misunderstandings, e.g., ~~I didn't like alligators.~~ (Correct form = *I don't like alligators. Simple present = it's not a usual action*).

Another problem area is subject/verb agreement. Students may either omit the *-s* on the third person singular, e.g., ~~Lisa work in a ...~~ (Correct form = *Lisa works in a hospital*), or use it where they shouldn't, e.g., ~~Our English classes finishes in June~~ (Correct form = *Our English classes finish in June*).

---

c ≫ ▶02.04 Students read the information in Grammar Focus 2A SB p. 140. Play the recording where indicated, and ask students to listen and repeat. Students then complete the exercises. Check answers as a class, making sure students are spelling the *-s* forms correctly and using *don't/doesn't* to form the negatives correctly. After students complete the Grammar Focus activities, ask them: *Is the simple present easy? Is it difficult?* Elicit an indication of their confidence level. Tell students to go back to SB p. 21.

Answers (Grammar Focus 2A SB p. 141)

a 2 finishes 4 buys 6 misses 8 teaches 10 watches
  3 relaxes 5 wants 7 says 9 worries
b 1 start   3 goes; leaves 5 get; makes 7 study; enjoy
  2 finishes; does 4 watches; tries 6 has; loves
c 2 don't drive 4 doesn't have 6 doesn't go
  3 don't cook 5 don't worry 7 don't do
d 2 ~~don't~~ doesn't 4 ~~haves~~ has   6 ~~I am love~~ I love
  3 ~~gos~~ goes 5 ~~no like~~ don't like

d Write the sentences on the board and ask the class to tell you which words to underline.

Answers
1 loves
2 catches

e ▶02.05 **Pronunciation** Play the recording for students to identify which verb has an extra syllable. Check answers as a class. If necessary, by counting on your fingers, show students how *love/loves* both have one syllable, how *catch* has one syllable, but the third person singular form *catches* has two.

Answer
Catches has an extra syllable.

f Give students one minute to read the rules and choose the correct answers. Check answers as a class.

Answers
1 add
2 don't add

g ▶02.06 You may wish to ask students to apply the rule from 3f to the verbs before they listen. Play the recording for students to check the verbs that have an extra syllable. Check answers as a class. Drill each pair of words, e.g., *work* (one syllable) − *works* (one syllable); *finish* (two syllables) − *finishes* (three syllables), to help students get a feel for when we add an extra syllable and when we don't.

Answers
✓ finishes ✓ uses ✓ catches ✓ teaches ✓ watches

h ≫ Divide the class into pairs and assign A and B roles. Student As read the sentences about a salesperson on p. 130, and Student Bs read the sentences about a nurse on SB p. 133. They complete the sentences. Monitor for any problems, and clarify these before the pairwork stage. Put students into A/B pairs for them to read aloud their sentences to each other and guess the jobs. Tell students to go back to SB p. 21.

◁ LOA TIP MONITORING

- Monitor the two stages of the pairwork activity closely. In the first step, check carefully that students are writing the verb forms with *-s* correctly, and point out any errors in spelling for students to self-correct.

- During the speaking stage, listen carefully to check that students are pronouncing the verb forms correctly. When students make a mistake with the pronunciation, try to catch their eye discreetly so that they can correct their mistake.

- If students continue to pronounce the verb forms incorrectly, you may wish to check this again or ask them to do the activity in Workbook 2A.

4 SPEAKING

a To help students, you may give them some example sentences about your own job, e.g., *I work in a really great place.* Make sure students understand that if they choose to write about someone they know, they will need to use the *-s* form of the verb. Monitor and help with vocabulary, and suggest ideas if necessary.

b 💬📱 Put students into pairs to tell their partner their sentences and try to guess the jobs.

c Students work in new pairs, or small groups, and tell each other what their partner told them. Point out that in this stage of the activity, all students will need to use the *-s* form of the verb. As you monitor, don't interrupt fluency, but note any mistakes with the pronunciation of the *-s* forms of the verbs. After the activity, write any verbs that caused pronunciation problems on the board and drill them.

2B | DO YOU WORRY ABOUT EXAMS?

At the end of this lesson, students will be able to:

- read and understand a text about exam stress
- use vocabulary for talking about studying correctly
- understand an interview about study routines
- tell the time using *o'clock, (a) quarter after, thirty*, etc.
- use the question form of the simple present
- ask and answer questions about studying

1 READING

a 💬📱 Give students one minute to think about their answers to the questions before talking about exams and tests as a class. You may wish to pre-teach the word *worry* (v.) (to think a lot about bad things).

b Students read the comments quickly and match them with the pictures. You may wish to pre-teach the words in the Vocabulary Support box. Check answers as a class.

Answers
1 c
2 b
3 a

c 💬📱 Tell students to read the comments again in detail. Students answer the questions in pairs. Then, check their ideas as a class. Check that students understand that there are no correct answers in this case.

2 VOCABULARY Studying

a Individually, students read the sentences and match them with the pictures. They then check in pairs. Check answers as a class. Check pronunciation by pointing to each word and asking students: *How do you say this word?* Elicit the correct pronunciation. Ask the class *Is that correct?* before modeling the pronunciation yourself if necessary.

Answers
1 j	5 g
2 h	6 d
3 e	7 i
4 f	

b Complete the first item as an example with the class. Students work individually, matching the words to make phrases. Check answers as a class.

Answers
1 pass/fail/take an exam
2 get good/bad grades
3 take notes
4 pass/fail/take a test

c 💬 Before students start asking and answering the questions in 2a, drill them for correct pronunciation. Monitor, but don't interrupt fluency unless students make mistakes with the vocabulary for studying.

3 LISTENING

a ▶ 02.07 Play the recording for students to listen for general meaning, and check the things Jack and Tania talk about. Check answers as a class.

Answers
1 ✓
2 ✓
4 ✓

Audioscript

JACK Umm, excuse me. Hi. Look, can I ask you a few questions about your study routine?
TANIA What?
J Your study routine.
T Umm … OK … but I have to …
J Great! So, first question, are you a full-time student or a part-time student?
T Part-time. I have a job – I'm a nurse and I have a family. I'm really busy.
J OK … and how many hours a week do you study?
T Well, at the university … about five hours.
J And at home?
T I don't know – maybe about ten hours.
J Do you study in the morning or afternoon?
T I usually study early in the morning or late at night.
J When do you start studying each day?
T Usually at eight thirty or nine o'clock.
J Do you finish studying very late?
T Well, it changes every day.
J Well, last night, for example.
T Hmm … last night … at a quarter after eleven.
J Wow, that's pretty late! And where do you study?
T Everywhere! On the bus, at work, at lunch time, in the kitchen, in the bedroom – everywhere!
J And in your free time?
T Free time?!
J What do you do in your free time?
T I don't have any free time!

b ▶ 02.07 Pre-teach the words *full-time* and *part-time* in the Vocabulary Support box. Students listen to the recording again for specific details and complete the information. They compare in pairs. Check answers as a class.

Answers
• part-time
• 15 hours a week
• early in the morning or late at night
• everywhere – on the bus, at work, at lunchtime, in the kitchen, in the bedroom

4 VOCABULARY Time

a Draw a question mark on the board and point to your watch to elicit the question: *What's the time?* or *What time is it?* Tell students what the time is using the simpler form they used in Lesson 1C, e.g., *It's ten twenty.*, *It's three twenty-five.*, etc. Look at the first clock in the Student's Book and say the time using this same system, i.e., *It's eleven fifteen.* Then, read the examples with the class for students to match them with what Tania said.

Answers
1 b
2 a

b Individually, students complete the sentences. Check answers as a class.

Answers
1 o'clock
2 thirty
3 after
4 to

c ⏵ `02.08` Students complete the exercises in Vocabulary Focus 2B on SB p. 164. Play the recording for students to check their answers to Exercise a and monitor Exercise b. Tell students to go back to SB p. 23.

Answers (Vocabulary Focus 2B SB p. 164)
a 1 c 2 e 3 g 4 d 5 h 6 a 7 f 8 i 9 b

5 GRAMMAR Simple present: questions

a ⏵ `02.09` Write the following three jumbled questions about Tania and Jack on the board, and ask students to put them in order: *1 Tania / busy / is ?* (1 Is Tania busy?) *2 a nurse / is / Jack ?* (2 Is Jack a nurse?) *3 students / they / are ?* (3 Are they students?). Ask students the questions and elicit the answers. (1 *Yes, she is.* 2 *No, he's not. He's a student.* 3 *Yes, they are.*) Point to the questions on the board and say *Questions with "be."* Then, point students to the Student's Book and say: *Simple present questions.* Students then look at the questions and decide which one is correct. Play the recording for students to listen and check. Check the answer as a class.

Answer
Question 2 is correct.

b Read the two questions as a class and elicit the word.

Answer
Do

c ⏵ `02.10` Tell students to listen to the next part of Jack and Tania's conversation for specific details about Ellie (Tania's daughter) and to complete the information. They compare in pairs. Check answers as a class. You may then wish to teach the word *library* (a place with lots of books that you can use to read or study).

Answers
- about 40 hours a week
- at about nine o'clock
- mostly at the university library and sometimes at home

Audioscript

JACK Are you the only student at home?

TANIA No, my daughter Ellie is a student, too.

J Can I ask about her ...?

T All right, but look, I really have to ...

J Thank you so much. So, Ellie is it?

T Yes.

J How many hours a week does she study?

T She's a full-time student, so she studies about 40 hours a week.

J What time does she start each day?

T I'm not sure. At about nine o'clock.

J Where does she study?

T Mostly at the university library and sometimes at home.

J Does she study more before an exam?

T Yes, I think so. Look, I really have no idea. I'm in a hurry ... I have to go. Goodbye!

J Please just one more question. Maybe not.

d Read the question as a class and refer students back to the questions in 5b. Elicit the difference.

Answer
Jack's question uses *Does,* not *Do.* It's a third person singular question form.

⏷ **LOA TIP** CONCEPT CHECKING

- Check that students understand the connection between the use of the auxiliary verb in simple present negative sentences and questions by writing *You study early in the morning.* After the sentence, write the plus sign (+) on the board. Directly underneath the (+), write (−) and elicit a negative sentence, e.g., *You don't study in the afternoon.* Under the (+) and the (−), write a question mark (?) and elicit a question, e.g., *Do you study early in the morning?* Circle the verb *study* in each sentence, and the auxiliaries *don't* and *do.*
- Repeat the process with a third person singular form, e.g., *Ellie studies full-time.* (+); *Ellie doesn't study part-time.* (−); *Does Ellie study full-time?* (?). Circle the *-s* ending of the verb in the affirmative sentence, and show students how this transfers to the auxiliary verb in the negative and in the question.

⊙ **CAREFUL!**

Students may have problems with the word order in simple present questions, particularly with the position of the auxiliary verb in relation to the subject and the main verb, e.g., ~~You do study at school~~ (Correct form = **Do you study** at school?), or they may omit the auxiliary verb completely, e.g., ~~Where you live?~~ (Correct form = Where **do** you live?).

Another common error is to use a period at the end of a question instead of a question mark or to omit the punctuation altogether, e.g., ~~What do you study~~ (Correct form = What do you study?). As students work through the Grammar Focus, make sure they are using correct word order and punctuation.

e ⏵ `02.11` Students read the information in Grammar Focus 2B on SB p. 140. Play the recording where indicated, and ask students to listen and repeat. Students then complete the exercises. Check answers as a class, making sure students are using *does/doesn't* for third person singular forms correctly. Tell students to go back to SB p. 23.

Answers (Grammar Focus 2B SB p. 141)
a 2 Do you go 5 What do they wear
  3 Does he want 6 What time do they have lunch
  4 Where do you play
b 2 Does 3 does 4 Do 5 don't 6 do 7 Does 8 doesn't
c 2 does she study 5 does the bus go
  3 does the store open 6 do you go to the gym
  4 do you want 7 do they work

f ⏵ `02.12` Students order the phrases to make questions. Play the recording for students to listen and check. Check answers as a class.

Answers
1 How many hours a week do you study?
2 Do you study grammar or vocabulary?
3 When do you study?
4 Where do you study?

g ⏵ `02.12` Pronunciation Play the recording again and highlight the pronunciation of *Do you* for students. Check the answer as a class.

Answer
No, you can't.

Ask students questions about specific times, and ask them to write down short answers in numerals in their notebooks, e.g., *1 What time does your English class start (on Tuesdays)? 2 What time do you go to bed on Mondays? 3 What time do you have dinner? 4 What time does your English class end today? 5 What's your favorite TV show? What time does it start?* In pairs, students compare the times they wrote down and try to make sentences using the information, e.g., *My English class starts at 10:00 on Tuesdays; I go to bed at 10:30 on Mondays.* Ask some students to tell the class their sentences.

Ask students in pairs or small groups to reconstruct the questions you originally asked them. Write the questions on the board for students to check their own answers, paying particular attention to the use of *Does* in the third-person question forms.

6 SPEAKING

a Give students one minute to write another question about study. Point out errors for students to self-correct.

b 💬 Students work in small groups, asking and answering the questions they wrote in 6a. Monitor, but don't interrupt fluency unless students make mistakes with the simple present forms.

Ask fast finishers to write sentences to summarize their discussion, e.g., *Sonia studies English because she loves it!*

c 💬 Discuss the question as a class. Praise students who are able to express their ideas, even if their English isn't perfect, and avoid correcting errors in front of the whole class.

⊕ **ADDITIONAL MATERIAL**

Workbook 2B

Photocopiable activities: Grammar 2B, Vocabulary 2B

2C | EVERYDAY ENGLISH
I'd like a latte

At the end of this lesson, students will be able to:

• understand informal conversations in which people make requests and respond
• use appropriate phrases for asking for things and replying
• use appropriate phrases for reacting to news
• relate the letters *ou* to the sounds /oʊ/ and /aʊ/
• maintain informal conversations in which they make requests and respond

💡 **OPTIONAL LEAD-IN**

Books closed. Ask students: *When you have trouble in your class(es), where do you go for help?* Depending on class size, you may put students into pairs to discuss their answers. Then, ask students to share their answers with the class. Ideas may include the Internet, friends or family, classmates, their teacher, etc. Give students suggestions if they have trouble answering the question. Then ask: *Do you help family or friends with their classes?* Students discuss their answers in pairs or with the class.

1 LISTENING

a 💬 Look at the three pictures on SB p. 24 with the class and read the question. Elicit students' ideas, but don't check the answer at this point.

b ▶ 02.13 Play Part 1 of the audio recording for students to check their answer to 1a. Check the answer as a class.

Answer
3 in a coffee shop

Audioscript (Part 1)

MARTINA Hey, Tomás. Thanks for meeting me here. I have to ask you something.

TOMÁS Anything for my sister.

SERVER Hi. Can I help you?

T I'd like a small coffee and … Martina, what do you want?

M Um, I don't know. I guess I'll have a large latte.

T Can we have a coffee and a latte, please?

S So, a small coffee and a large latte. Anything else?

T Yes. Could I have a croissant too, please?

S That's $7.25.

T Here you go.

S Thanks.

M So, tomorrow I have this –

T Actually, could I have a blueberry muffin instead?

S Of course. It's the same price.

M Tomás! I need your help – now!

T OK. What's up?

c 💬 In pairs, students read the sentences and see if they remember the answers from Part 1. Don't check answers at this point.

d ▶02.13 Students listen again for specific details. Play Part 1 of the audio recording again for students to check their answers to 1c.

Answers
1 small coffee, large latte, one muffin
2 $7.25
3 help

e ▶02.14 Play Part 2 of the audio recording for students to find out what Martina needs help with. Check the answer as a class.

Answer
b study for a test

Audioscript (Part 2)

TOMÁS What's going on, Martina?
MARTINA I need your help to get ready for a big math test and—
T Oh, sure! No problem.
M Could I come to your place tonight?
T Sorry, I have to work tonight.
M Oh, that's too bad.
T Do you want to come over on Friday for dinner?

M That sounds great but …
T Terrific. Friday night it is.
M BUT … my test is tomorrow.
T Oh! How about after we finish our coffee?
M Yes! Perfect. I have all my books here.
T Oh! Well, I think I'd like some more coffee, then.
M And I think I'll have a muffin now, too.

---

f ▶02.14 Students listen again for specific details. Play Part 2 of the audio recording again for students to decide if the sentences are true or false and correct the false sentences.

Answers
1 T
2 F (Tomás isn't free tonight. / Tomás has to work tonight.)
3 F (Martina is free on Friday.)
4 F (Martina's test is tomorrow.)

💡 **EXTRA ACTIVITY**

Write the following four jumbled sentences on the board (two from Part 1 and two from Part 2) and ask students to put them in order:

1 *ask / have / I / something / you / to* (I have to ask you something.)
2 *Can / have / coffee / and a / we / latte / a / please ?* (Can we have a coffee and a latte, please?)
3 *big math test / need / your / I / help / to get ready / a / for* (I need your help to get ready for a big math test.)
4 *tonight / work / sorry / have / I / to* (Sorry, I have to work tonight.)

Check answers by playing both parts of the audio recording again and pausing when the characters say the sentences for students to check their answers.

---

g 💬📋 In pairs, students discuss where they usually meet friends and family. Ask any students who think of different places to share their ideas with the class.

💡 **FAST FINISHERS**

Ask fast finishers to talk about what they usually do when they meet their friends, e.g., *play video games, chat, play sports,* etc.

---

2 USEFUL LANGUAGE
Asking for things and replying

a Individually, students decide who says each sentence. They then compare their ideas in pairs. Don't check answers at this point.

b ▶02.13–02.14 Check answers by playing both parts of the audio recording again and pausing each time Tomás and Martina ask for something. Elicit from the class which reply (a–d) they expect to hear before continuing to play the recording to find out if they were correct.

Answers
1 T   2 M   3 T   4 M
a 1   b 4   c 3   d 2

c 💬📋 Demonstrate the activity by asking one student: *Hello. Can I have a coffee, please?* and eliciting an appropriate response, e.g., *Sure. Small or large?* Encourage students to play around with the phrases and use their own ideas. Monitor and praise students with a smile or a nod when they use the language from this section correctly.

d ▶02.15 Point to each of the three photos on SB p. 25 one by one and ask: *Where is this?* Elicit *a a café, b a hospital, c an office.* Play the recording for students to listen and match the conversations with the pictures. Check answers as a class.

Answers
1 b   2 a   3 c

Audioscript

CONVERSATION 1
A Nurse!
B Yes?
A Could I have some water, please?
B Sure, no problem. Here you are.
A Thank you.

CONVERSATION 2
A Yes?
B I'd like a chicken sandwich, please.
A Sorry, we don't have chicken. We have cheese or roast beef.
B Oh, OK. Hmm … a cheese sandwich, then.

CONVERSATION 3
A Can I call you this afternoon? I'm very busy right now.
B Sure, no problem. Call me at about two?
A Yes, that's fine. Talk to you later.
B OK, bye.

---

e ▶02.15 Individually, students complete the sentences from the conversations. Play the recording again for students to listen and check. Check answers as a class.

Answers
1 Could I have   2 I'd like   3 Can I call

f Brainstorm phrases for each of the situations as a class and write these on the board for students to refer to in the next exercise, e.g., 1 *Pablo, can I have some water, please? – Sure, no problem.* 2 *Could I have a small espresso, please? – Of course.*

g 💬📋 In pairs, students role-play the four situations. Monitor and check that students are using appropriate ways to ask for things and to respond.

3 CONVERSATION SKILLS
Reacting to news

a ▶02.16 In pairs, students look at the mini-conversations and try to complete them. Play the recording for students to listen and check. Check answers as a class.

> **Answers**
> 1 problem
> 2 bad

b Read the mini-conversations as a class and check what the phrases mean.

> **Answers**
> 1 No problem.
> 2 That's too bad.

c Individually, students match the four phrases to the phrases in 3b with a similar meaning. Check answers as a class.

> **Answers**
> a 1
> b 2
> c 1
> d 2

4 PRONUNCIATION
Sound and spelling: *ou*

a ▶02.17 Play the recording and highlight the two possible sounds for the letters *ou* for students. Check the answer as a class.

> **Answer**
> Yes, they do.

b ▶02.18 Students classify the words into two groups. Play the recording for students to listen and check. Check answers as a class. Then ask students to repeat the words after the recording and practice the pronunciation.

> **Answers**
> four 1   your 1   about 2   sound 2

5 SPEAKING

a ≫ Divide the class into pairs and assign A and B roles. Student As read the first card on SB p. 130, and Student Bs read the first card on SB p. 133. Students then role-play the conversation. Monitor, but don't interrupt fluency unless students make mistakes with the content of this lesson. Students then read the second card and role-play the second situation.

SKILLS FOR WRITING

I need English for my job

At the end of this lesson, students will be able to:

- understand a conversation in which students talk about where they're from and why they're learning English
- understand personal information on a written form
- identify and correct spelling mistakes
- complete a form with their own personal information

💡 OPTIONAL LEAD-IN

Books closed. Tell students you have a list of common reasons for learning English (the reasons in 1a on SB p. 26). Give them a few minutes in pairs to try to guess the reasons on the list. Ask students to share their answers with the class, writing their ideas on the board. When a pair gives a reason that is in 1a, say: *Good job! That one is on the list.* If students have the same basic idea as one on the list, but express it in different words, congratulate them too, e.g., *to go to college in the U.S.* (= *to study something in English*). Write all their ideas on the board. Then, ask them to open their books and look at the ideas in 1a.

1 SPEAKING AND LISTENING

a 💬📋 Discuss the question as a class and find out why each of your students wants to study English. If you didn't use the optional lead-in, be prepared to help with vocabulary where necessary.

b ▶️ 02.19 Point to each of the three photos on SB p. 26 one by one and say: *This is Daniela / Said / Sakura.* Play the recording for students to listen for general meaning and underline the correct answers. Check answers as a class.

> **Answers**
> 1 Mexico City; job   2 Riyadh; job   3 Osaka; studies

Audioscript

DANIELA My name is Daniela, and I'm a police officer in Mexico City – but just traffic police. I need to speak English because sometimes tourists ask me questions in English. For example, they ask me for directions or some tourist information. I like studying at this college. The schedule works well – we have a two-hour break in the middle of the day. I want to improve my listening. I find listening pretty hard, and it's difficult to listen to something and take notes at the same time. So I need to do some extra listening practice.

SAID Hi. My name is Said, and I'm a dentist in Riyadh, Saudi Arabia. Sometimes English-speaking people come to my work, so I need to speak good English. This college is very good – the classes are very interesting and we do lots of different things in class. I want to stay here for a semester – until December. Listening and speaking are OK for me, but I need to work hard at reading and writing. I'd like to read books in English – maybe even some books about my work.

SAKURA Hello, my name's Sakura, and I'm a photographer for a newspaper in Osaka, Japan. In the future, I'd like to study at a university in the U.S., so I need better English to do that. Our teacher, Kate, is great. She's very friendly and she helps us a lot in class. Only one thing worries me a little: the grades I get on tests. I think my progress is OK, and I can speak better, but I'm not very good at tests and exams. But maybe I need to study grammar a bit more, too!

c ▶️ 02.19 Students listen to the recording again for specific details and complete the chart. They compare in pairs. Check answers as a class.

> **Answers**
>
> | | Likes at the college | Needs to improve |
> |---------|----------------------|---------------------|
> | Daniela | the schedule | listening |
> | Said | the classes | reading and writing |
> | Sakura | the teacher | grammar |

d 💬📋 Put students into small groups to talk about the questions together. Monitor, but don't interrupt fluency.

💡 FAST FINISHERS

Ask fast finishers to also talk about what they think is difficult to improve in English and why, e.g., *It's difficult to improve pronunciation because it's really irregular!*

e ▶️ 02.20 Play the recording for students to find out what you can win in the competition. Check the answer as a class.

> **Answer**
> an extra month of English lessons for free

Audioscript

KATE Hi, everyone. Before we begin the lesson, I just want to tell you about this competition we're having here at school. It's really good because you can win an extra month of English classes for free. That's right – an extra month for nothing. So all you need is … Well, you need to be a student at this school – and you all are – and you need to complete this entry form by hand – you know, you can't use a computer. But you also need to make sure that what you write on the entry form is correct – no mistakes! So if you want to enter, you can get an entry form from me or you can also get them from the receptionist. It's a really good competition – one more month of classes. So, are there any questions?

f ▶️ 02.20 Before students listen again, give them one minute to work in pairs and see what, if anything, they remember from the first listening. Play the recording again for students to answer the questions. Check answers as a class.

> **Answers**
> 1 No, they can't.
> 2 No, it isn't.
> 3 from Kate or from the receptionist

2 READING

a Individually, students read the information about Daniela and complete the form, using their own ideas for Daniela's last name and phone number. Check answers by copying Part 1 of the form onto the board and asking students to complete the information.

> **Answers**
> First name: Daniela
> Last name: Students' own answers
> Gender: female
> Nationality: Mexican
> Cell phone (U.S.): Students' own answers
> Email address: danielar@supermail.com
> Your class now: P1
> Class start date: July 6

b In pairs, students discuss what words complete Part 2 of the form. Don't check answers at this point.

c ▶ **02.21** Play the recording for students to listen to Daniela and check their answers. Check spelling by writing the words on the board.

> **Answers**
> 1 police officer
> 2 tourists
> 3 job
> 4 listening

3 WRITING SKILLS Spelling

a Write *Englesh speling* on the board. Students should realize that it is spelled incorrectly, so erase it and ask them *How do you spell it?* and write the correct spelling on the board. Tell students to cover SB p. 26 and look at the first copy of Daniela's entry form on SB p. 27. Look at the example together, and explain that there are eight more spelling problems. Ask students: *How many spelling problems are there in total?* Elicit the answer *nine* (the example plus eight more problems). Individually, students find and correct the spelling mistakes. Check answers as a class.

> **Answers**
> ~~offiser~~ officer
> ~~toorists~~ tourists
> ~~informashion~~ information
> ~~dificult~~ difficult
> ~~anser~~ answer
> ~~becos~~ because
> ~~listning~~ listening
> ~~scool~~ school

> ### ☉ FAST FINISHERS
> Ask fast finishers to make a list of words they know they often have problems spelling. They write the incorrect form of each word, strike it through, and put an X after it, and then write the correct spelling next to it with a checkmark after it, e.g., ~~riting~~ *X* writing ✓.

b As a class, discuss when it is important to use correct spelling.

> **Answers**
> 2 ✓
> 3 ✓

c Individually, students find and correct the spelling mistake in each sentence. Check answers by writing the sentences on the board and asking students to tell you where the mistake is. Strike the incorrect word through, and ask them to spell the correct word to you all together as you write it on the board.

> **Answers**
> 1 ~~see~~ sea
> 2 ~~right~~ write
> 3 ~~no~~ know
> 4 ~~here~~ hear
> 5 ~~bye~~ buy

d Discuss as a class how the incorrect and correct words in 3c are the same. Then, elicit an indication of students' confidence level for English spelling.

> **Answer**
> They're pronounced the same.

> ### 📖 LANGUAGE NOTES
> Homophones (words which have different spellings and meanings, but are pronounced the same) may not exist in your students' own languages, so the idea may seem very strange to them. Many problems with English spelling stem from homophones, like those in 3c. Some native speakers have real problems with even basic differences, such as *your* and *you're*; *there*, *they're*, and *their*. These problems have become even more noticeable in recent years with the advance of social media, where, oftentimes, people are not as careful with their grammar and spelling.

> ### ☉ EXTRA ACTIVITY
> Give students a spelling test with ten items from the class so far, e.g., *1 gray, 2 awful, 3 Australian, 4 amazing, 5 secretary, 6 Germany, 7 businesswoman, 8 interesting, 9 photographer, 10 schedule.* Ideally, personalize the test for your group by choosing words which you know your students often have problems spelling. Check answers by getting students to write the words on the board, spelling them aloud as they go. Students award themselves one point for each word they spell correctly.

4 WRITING

a Individually, students complete the form with their information. If you're short on time, this exercise and 4b can be completed for homework. Students could then bring their forms to the next class.

b Students write their answers to the two questions for the competition. Remind them to use their ideas from the discussion in 1d. If you used the Fast Finishers activity after 1d, make sure you have corrected any errors you heard students make in their speaking before they start writing in order for them not to repeat them in written form here.

> ### ↻ LOA TIP ELICITING
> • Before students start writing, consider eliciting orally another example about yourself. Use the texts about Daniela in 2a as a guide. Students close their books. Point to yourself and say: *I work as …* (elicit: an English teacher) *in …* (elicit: the city). *I love my job, but not the …* (elicit suggestions). Continue eliciting ideas for what you might say about yourself in answer to the first question.
>
> • After building up a paragraph about why the students' language is important to you, repeat the process with a second paragraph about what you want to improve in the students' language. This will also be valuable as it will help students understand that the problems they may be experiencing in learning English are relatively common and apply to people learning other languages, too.

c In pairs, students switch their forms and see if their ideas are the same. They can also check their partner's work for spelling mistakes. If students have made any spelling mistakes, or if their partner can offer any other ideas for improving their answers, they prepare a second draft of their answers before giving it to you for correction.

> ### ⊕ ADDITIONAL MATERIAL
> Workbook 2D

UNIT 2
Review and extension

1 GRAMMAR

a Individually, students complete the text. Check answers as a class by asking individual students to write the correct answers on the board.

Answers
1 work
2 start
3 don't start
4 doesn't have
5 works
6 doesn't like
7 work

b Students write possible questions for the answers. Monitor for any problems and clarify these before students start on the pairwork stage in 1c.

Possible answers
1 What do you do?
2 Do you work in an office?
3 Do you like your job?
4 When do you start work?
5 Does your husband work?
6 Where does he work?
7 Does he like his job?

c 💬 In pairs, students ask and answer the questions, making any changes necessary, e.g., *husband − wife, he − she.*

2 VOCABULARY

a Students put the letters in order. Check answers by writing the words on the board one letter at a time, saying each letter clearly and asking the class to repeat it after you.

Answers
1 nurse
2 dentist
3 pilot
4 engineer
5 janitor
6 photographer

b Students write the times in words. Check answers as a class.

Answers
1 eleven thirty
2 (a) quarter to one *or* twelve forty-five
3 six o'clock
4 (a) quarter after eight *or* eight fifteen
5 twenty to three *or* two forty
6 twenty after five *or* five twenty

c Individually, students match the parts of the sentences. Check answers as a class.

Answers
1 c   2 e   3 a   4 b   5 d

> 💡 **FAST FINISHERS**
>
> Ask fast finishers to write sentences using some of the other words from the Vocabulary: Studying section on SB p. 22, e.g., *schedule, study, pass a test.*

3 WORDPOWER *work*

a Tell students to close their books. Write the bold phrases from the three sentences in 3a on the board, i.e., *work in, work for,* and *work as.* Point to yourself and say: *I work in (a (language) school/university),* then: *I work for (name of your school/university),* and finally: *I work as a teacher.* Students open their books, look at the sentences, and match them with the pictures. Check answers as a class.

Answers
1 c   2 a   3 b

b Match the meanings with the marked phrases in 3a as a class.

Answers
1 work as   2 work in   3 work for

> 💡 **EXTRA ACTIVITY**
>
> If your students work, ask them to write sentences about themselves using the phrases in 3a. Ask each student one by one to tell the class their three sentences, and check they're using the words *in, for,* and *as* correctly.

c Give students one minute to think about the sentences individually before discussing them as a class.

Answer
It's a noun in all five sentences.

d Elicit the *work* phrases that match the meanings from the class. Check that students understand that these are normally used with the verb *be.*

Answers
a (be) out of work
b (be) at work

e Individually, students put the words in parentheses in the correct place in the sentences. They then check in pairs. Check answers as a class.

Answers
1 He works <u>as</u> a nurse at night.
2 We all <u>start</u> work at 6:00 p.m.
3 She'd like a job because now she's <u>out</u> of work.
4 She's a photographer and works <u>for</u> *The Times*.
5 When I'm <u>at</u> work, I have no free time.
6 We both work <u>in</u> a large office downtown.

f Give students one or two examples for someone you know using *work* as a verb and as a noun, e.g., *My best friend works as a doctor in a big hospital. She starts work at seven o'clock in the morning.* Monitor and listen for correct use of *work* as a verb and a noun. Point out errors for students to self-correct. If you wish, ask each student to tell the class about the person they wrote about.

⋙ Photocopiable activities: Wordpower 2

> 🔄 **LOA REVIEW YOUR PROGRESS**
>
> Students look back through the unit, think about what they've studied, and decide how well they did. Students work on weak areas by using the appropriate sections of the Workbook and the Photocopiable activities.

UNIT **3**
DAILY LIFE

⟳ UNIT OBJECTIVES

At the end of this unit, students will be able to:

- understand information, texts, and conversations and exchange information about daily life and routines and the role of the Internet and technology in people's lives
- talk about and give simple descriptions of their own and other people's possessions
- understand conversations in which people make plans and make plans themselves
- use simple phrases to hesitate while thinking about what they want to say
- write an informal invitation to an event and an appropriate reply

UNIT CONTENTS

G GRAMMAR
- Position of adverbs of frequency: *always, usually, often, sometimes, never*
- *do, go, have*

V VOCABULARY
- Time expressions: *every week/month/year, once a week/ month/year, twice a week/month/year, three times a week/ month/year*, etc.
- Common verbs: *buy, cost, decide, find, help, meet, prefer, sell, stay, try*
- Technology: *camera, computer, headphones, keyboard, laptop, printer, smartphone, smartwatch, speaker, tablet*
- Wordpower: Prepositions of time: *at* + times/*night, in* + months / parts of day / seasons, *on* + days / *the weekend*

P PRONUNCIATION
- Sentence stress on important words
- Sound and spelling: /ʌ/, /oʊ/, and /u/
- Word stress in technology words
- Main stress in sentences and intonation
- Pronunciation of *Hmm* when hesitating

C COMMUNICATION SKILLS
- Talking about your daily routine and the routines of people you know well
- Talking about the Internet and technology in your life
- Talking about your own and other people's possessions
- Making plans and responding appropriately
- Using appropriate phrases while thinking about what you want to say
- Writing an informal invitation to an event and writing a reply to an invitation you receive

GETTING STARTED

♀ OPTIONAL LEAD-IN

Divide the class into small groups. Ask half of the groups to brainstorm *jobs* and the other half to brainstorm *countries*. After two minutes, put students into pairs, one with a list of jobs and the other, a list of countries. Students take turns thinking of jobs/countries that aren't on their partner's list. When they say a new job/country, their partner asks them: *How do you spell that?* Students can check their partner's spelling in the Student's Book or a dictionary. Students win one point for every job/country not on their partner's list and an extra point for spelling it correctly. The student with the most points wins.

a Give students one minute to think about their answers before talking about the picture as a class. If you didn't use the optional lead-in, you could elicit a lot of possible countries and jobs for Questions 1 and 4 to give students some extra practice. You may also give students information from Culture Notes below.

🌐 CULTURE NOTES

The photo shows a subway train with a man dressed in a traditional Chinese opera costume. Chinese opera is one of the oldest dramatic art forms in the world. The costumes can be very expensive. For this reason, they are usually passed down from teacher to student.

b Read the questions and the ideas with the students and check that they understand the vocabulary. In pairs, they ask and answer the questions. Ask students to share their answers with the class, and then ask additional questions using the simple present, e.g., *Juan — you buy a newspaper. What newspaper do you buy?*; *Max — you listen to music on the bus. What kind of music?*

♀ EXTRA ACTIVITY

In pairs or small groups, students brainstorm other things they do every day. A1-level items which students will probably know include: *brush your teeth, drink coffee/tea, take a bath/shower, have breakfast/lunch/dinner, get up, go to work/school/college, watch TV*. Ask students to share their ideas with the class, and collate them on the board.

Exercises **a** and **b** can be prepared as homework before this lesson to give students time to look up unfamiliar vocabulary. Ask students to look at the picture and to prepare their answers to the questions as homework to talk about in the next class.

3A | SHE OFTEN TAKES AN ENGLISH CLASS

At the end of this lesson, students will be able to:

- read and understand a text about the daily life and routine of a woman in Norway
- use adverbs of frequency correctly with *be* and other common verbs
- understand a conversation in which people give information about the routines of themselves and others
- use time expressions to talk about how often things happen
- talk about what they do with people they know well and how often

◈ OPTIONAL LEAD-IN

Write ten common "daily routine" items on the board, e.g., *cook, get up, go home, go to bed, go to work/college, have breakfast, have dinner, have lunch, watch TV, work/study*. If you used the extra activity at the end of the Getting Started section, recycle some of the vocabulary students thought of then. In pairs, students decide what the usual "daily routine order" is for people in their country and if there is anything important missing from the list on the board. Add to the list if necessary, and then ask pairs to decide at what time people in their country do these things, e.g., *People have lunch at around two o'clock.* Have pairs share their answers with the class and check that students are saying the times correctly. Notice if students are using adverbs of frequency. Don't correct any mistakes with these, but see if students are having problems positioning them in the sentences.

1 READING

a 💬 Give students one minute to look at the pictures and think about their answers. Don't check answers at this point.

b Students read the text quickly and answer the questions. Check answers as a class.

> **Answers**
> 1 Answers will depend on work routines in different companies. Nora's work day is nine hours, but she gets breaks during the day, which probably help make her work life easy.
> 2 She has an English or knitting class during work time. The company has pets she can play with on her break.

c Tell students to read the text again in detail. Individually, students decide if the sentences are true or false. When checking answers, ask students to correct the false sentences.

> **Answers**
> 1 F (She has her breakfast at home.)
> 2 T
> 3 T
> 4 F (She takes an English class or a knitting class.)
> 5 T
> 6 F (She often has dinner at the company restaurant and goes home at 7:30 p.m.)

◈ FAST FINISHERS

Ask fast finishers to use the information in the text and write more true sentences about Nora's daily routine.

d 💬 In pairs, students talk about the good things in Nora's work life. Students share their answers with the class.

2 GRAMMAR
Position of adverbs of frequency

a Books closed. Write *She … arrives at work at about 8:15 a.m.* on the board. Point to the blank and ask students if they can remember what the word was (*usually*). Underneath, write: *Nora … leaves the office before 5:30 p.m.* and elicit the missing word (*never*). Individually, students look at the text in the book and underline more adverbs of frequency. Check answers as a class.

> **Answers**
> At about 10:15 or 10:30, Nora <u>usually</u> takes a break.
> She <u>often</u> takes an English class, but she <u>sometimes</u> takes a knitting class.
> … Nora <u>always</u> takes another break at about 3:00 p.m.
> … she <u>often</u> takes one of the dogs for a walk.
> Nora <u>never</u> leaves the office before 5:30 p.m.
> She <u>often</u> has dinner with her coworkers …

b Point to the two sentences on the board and show students that *never* is on the far left of the timeline. Elicit the correct position of *always* on the far right before students work individually, and put the other adverbs of frequency in the correct place. Check answers by drawing the timeline on the board and asking individual students to come up and write in the adverbs of frequency.

> **Answers**
> never sometimes often usually always
> 0% ├─────┼─────┼─────┼─────┤ 100%

◉ CAREFUL!

The most common student mistakes with adverbs of frequency involve word order. Students may place the adverbs before the subject, e.g., ~~Always I get up …~~ (Correct form = *I **always** get up at 7 a.m.*) or after verbs other than *be*, e.g., ~~I have usually coffee …~~ (Correct form = *I **usually have** coffee at breakfast*). They may also place the adverbs before the verb *be* instead of after it, e.g., ~~I often am tired …~~ (Correct form = *I **am often** tired after work*).

At this level, other errors are usually connected with spelling, e.g., ~~She's allways … / She's alway …~~ (Correct form = *She's **always** busy*); ~~He usualy has …~~ (Correct form = *He **usually** takes a nap after lunch*); ~~They sometime eat …~~ (Correct form = *They **sometimes** eat together*).

c ≫ ▶ 03.01 Students read the information in Grammar Focus 3A on SB p. 142. Play the recording where indicated, and ask students to listen and repeat. Students then complete the exercises on SB p. 143. Check answers as a class, making sure students position the adverbs of frequency correctly and use an affirmative verb with *never*. Tell students to go back to SB p. 30.

Answers (Grammar Focus 3A SB p. 143)

a 1 I <u>always</u> go and see them.
   2 I'm <u>sometimes</u> late for work, but my boss <u>never</u> gets angry.
   3 He <u>usually</u> comes here for a coffee at 10 o'clock – he's <u>never</u> late.
   4 We <u>often</u> have lunch together and talk. It's <u>always</u> good to see him.
   5 They're <u>never</u> away on vacation – they're <u>always</u> at home.
b 2 My parents sometimes eat in a restaurant.
   3 I often play tennis.
   4 Natasha's never late for work.
   5 We always watch TV in the evening.
c 2 Do you usually walk to work?
   3 Why are you always tired?
   4 Where do you usually go on weekends?
   5 How often do they play soccer?
   6 Is he often late for work?
   7 Why do you never write to me?

⟳ LOA TIP ELICITING

- After looking at the rules in Grammar Focus 3A on SB p. 142, write example affirmative and negative sentences and questions on the board to check that students are assimilating correct word order. Point to each sentence one by one, and ask students: *Is this correct?* Ask them to correct them as necessary, e.g., *I get up usually at seven o'clock.* (I <u>usually</u> get up …); *She often doesn't get up late.* (She doesn't <u>often</u> get up …); *Do sometimes you watch TV in the evening?* (Do you <u>sometimes</u> watch TV …?).

- Also check that students understand that although *never* is negative in meaning, it is used with an affirmative verb. Write three sentences with *never* on the board, and ask students: *Which is correct?*, e.g., *1 He doesn't never eat with his family. 2 He never eats with his family. 3 He doesn't eat never with his family.* (Sentence 2 is correct.)

d 💬 Students work in pairs or small groups, talking about the things they do. Monitor, but don't interrupt fluency unless students make mistakes with the position of the adverbs of frequency.

♀ EXTRA ACTIVITY

Play a guessing game with students. Tell students five sentences about something you do, and ask them to guess what it is, e.g., *1 I often do this in the morning and in the evening. 2 I sometimes do this at noon or after lunch. 3 I usually do this in the bathroom. 4 I never do this in class. 5 I always do this before I go to the dentist.* (The answer is *brush my teeth.*) Students then think of an activity themselves and write five clues using adverbs of frequency. In pairs or small groups, they then tell each other their sentences and try to guess the activity.

---

3 LISTENING

a 💬 Discuss the questions as a class.

b ▶03.02 Play the recording for students to listen for general meaning and answer the questions. You may wish to pre-teach the phrase *in a hurry* (doing things more quickly than usual). Check answers as a class.

Answers
1 They talk about their free time.
2 Martin wants the family to have dinner together once a week.

Audioscript

MARTIN Hey Katherine, I have an idea.
KATHERINE Oh yeah, what's that?
M I'd like us to have a family dinner together once a week.
K Oh really? … Why?
M Well, our lives are so busy and we're always in a hurry. You, me, and the kids, we never have dinner together these days. Spending some time together – just one night – it feels like a nice idea.
K OK, why not? When do you want to do it?
M When are you free?
K Most nights, but I go to my Spanish class once a week. It's on Wednesdays, so that's no good.
M OK, so not Wednesday. What about Liz and Pete?
K Well, Liz goes to volleyball practice.
M Of course. How often does she go?
K Twice a week – on Mondays and Thursdays.
M And Pete goes to band practice a lot.
K Yes, three times a week – on Mondays, Thursdays, and Fridays.
M OK. So that means … Tuesday! Yes, Tuesday night we can all have dinner together. Everyone's free then.
K Ah. No, they're not.
M What do you mean?
K I work late every Tuesday.
M Oh. But you said, "Most nights are free."
K Yeah, *most* nights – not *all* nights. You know I work late on Tuesdays. I don't need to tell you that!
M Sorry. Well, this is impossible!

c ▶03.02 Students listen to the recording again for specific details and complete the schedule. They compare in pairs. Check answers as a class.

Answers
Katherine – Tuesday: work late; Wednesday: Spanish class
Liz – Monday and Thursday: volleyball practice
Pete – Monday, Thursday, and Friday: band practice

d 💬 Students work in pairs or small groups, answering the questions. Share answers to Question 1 as a class.

♀ EXTRA ACTIVITY

Give students time for a "long turn" (a chance for the students to prepare what they're going to say on a topic and then talk to the whole class) at this point. This allows students to practice speaking under a little more pressure than normal and have the teacher's total attention for a few moments, both of which can be very beneficial. Ask students to think about their families' routines in more detail and to write notes, but not write complete sentences. Give students an example about yourself before they start, e.g., *In my family, we are always in a hurry! On Monday, my son goes to soccer practice, and my daughter …* Monitor and help as necessary as students write notes. Then, tell students not to look at their notes and to work with a partner, taking turns practicing what they are going to say. Discreetly point out errors for students to self-correct. Finally, ask students to speak to the class one by one about their families' routines. Remind students not to look at their notes while they're speaking, and choose students at random. After each long turn, allow two or three students to ask the speaker questions based on the speaker's talk.

4 VOCABULARY Time expressions

a ▶ 03.03 Read the sentences with the students. Ask: *Who gives this information in the recording?* (Katherine). Individually, students complete the sentences with the words in the box. Play the recording for students to listen and check. Check answers as a class.

> **Answers**
> 1 once
> 2 twice
> 3 a
> 4 every

b Elicit the rule as a class.

> **Answer**
> at the end of a sentence

📖 LANGUAGE NOTES

Time expressions like these can also be placed at the beginning of sentences when the speaker wishes to put more emphasis on the expression, e.g., *Once a week, we have a vocabulary test.* This difference is too subtle for students at A2 level, so, as with adverbs of frequency, students are taught only a limited part of a more complex rule at this point.

c ▶ 03.04 **Pronunciation** Play the recording. Highlight the stressed words for students by beating the rhythm with your hand to show where the stresses fall.

d Answer the question as a class. Drill the sentences in 4c.

> **Answer**
> a Important words like time expressions and verbs

e ▶ 03.05 Check that students understand that the lines of the conversation are in the correct order, but the words within each line are jumbled. Individually, students put the words in the correct order. Play the recording for students to listen and check.

> **Answers and audioscript**
> A How often do you and your family do things together?
> B About once a week.
> A What do you do?
> B We usually go on a picnic or to a restaurant.
> A Do you do that on weekends?
> B Yes, every Sunday, but we sometimes go to the movies.
> A Do you do anything else?
> B Well, about twice a year we go away for a weekend.
> A It sounds like you have a nice time with your family.

f ⟫ ▶ 03.06–03.07 Students complete the exercises in Vocabulary Focus 3A on SB p. 165. Play the recording for students to check their answers to Exercise a, and complete Exercise b as a class. Monitor Exercise c. Tell students to go back to SB p. 31.

> **Answers (Vocabulary Focus 3A SB p. 165)**
> **a** 1 b 2 f 3 e 4 g 5 a 6 d 7 c
> **b** 1 stay 2 long
> **c** Students' own answers

💡 FAST FINISHERS

Ask fast finishers to continue asking and answering questions with their partners after they have completed Exercise c, inventing their own questions using simple present verbs.

5 SPEAKING

a Give students a few minutes to prepare and write notes about the people they know well. Monitor and help as necessary.

b 💬 Students work in pairs or small groups, telling each other about the people they know well and asking and answering each other's questions. As you monitor, don't interrupt fluency, but note any mistakes with the position of adverbs of frequency and time expressions. After the activity, write them on the board and ask students to correct them.

⊕ ADDITIONAL MATERIALS

Workbook 3A

Photocopiable activities: Grammar 3A, Vocabulary 3A, Pronunciation 3A

3B IMAGINE YOU DON'T HAVE THE INTERNET

At the end of this lesson, students will be able to:

- read and understand a text about using the Internet
- use a lexical set of technology words correctly
- understand conversations in which people talk about the technology they have and how they use it
- use the affirmative, negative, and question forms of *do*, *go*, and *have*
- talk about and give simple descriptions of their own and other people's possessions

♀ OPTIONAL LEAD-IN

Before students arrive, write the incomplete text below on the board. If possible, show students a picture of yourself or other people in the 1990s to give context to the activity. Organize students into pairs. If you have a class with a variety of ages, try to mix older and younger students together as it will give them more to talk about. Students look at the sentences and choose a word to complete each blank. Check that students understand that they need to use the simple present form of the verb.

It's the 1990s! We:

1 usually … to the library to find information.

2 often … our friends at a café to talk.

3 sometimes … letters to family and friends.

4 often … games like Monopoly and Scrabble at home.

5 always … music from stores.

Check answers (*1 go 2 meet 3 write 4 play 5 buy*).
Then ask: *Life is very different today. Why?* Elicit the answer *because we have the Internet.* Students might be surprised to know that the Internet only became available to the general public in the early 1990s, but most people didn't use it in their daily life.

♀ FAST FINISHERS

Ask fast finishers to also talk about how much time they spend on the things in 1a every week and which websites they use to do each of the things.

2 VOCABULARY Technology

⟳ LOA TIP ELICITING

- Consider eliciting some of the vocabulary in 2a by bringing in as many of the objects shown in the pictures as possible to show to the class. Ask students to close their books, explain *technology* (*electronic objects for science or personal use*), and elicit the words for each object. Drill each word for correct pronunciation.

1 READING

a Individually, students think about how they use the Internet and check the things in the list.

b 💬 Students compare their ideas in small groups. Invite groups to share their answers as a class, and ask them if there's anything they think is missing from the list in 1a.

c Tell students they should read only the first part of the text *This month on TechBlog*. They then work individually, answering the questions. Check answers as a class.

> **Answers**
> 1 b
> 2 They are offline / without the Internet.

d Tell students to read the second part of the text *The Interview* and answer the questions. Pre-teach the words in the Vocabulary Support box. Students compare their answers in pairs. Check answers as a class.

> **Answers**
> 1 b, d
> 2 c, e, f

📖 VOCABULARY SUPPORT

upload (v.) (B1) – copy or move programs or information to a larger computer system or to the Internet

go online (v. + adv.) (A2) – access the Internet

chess (A2) – a popular game played on a square board

e 💬 Put students into small groups to talk about the questions together; if possible, mix older and younger students together. Monitor, but don't interrupt fluency.

a Individually, students match the words with the pictures. Check answers as a class.

> **Answers**
> 1 smartwatch   6 computer
> 2 printer   7 headphones
> 3 laptop   8 tablet
> 4 smartphone   9 keyboard
> 5 camera   10 speaker

b ▶ 03.08 **Pronunciation** Play the recording for students to underline the stressed syllable. Check answers by writing the words on the board and asking individual students to come up and underline the stressed syllables on the board (see the underlining in the answers to 2a).

c Elicit possible answers to the first sentence from the class. Check that students understand that more than one answer may be possible for each sentence. Students decide what they think the people are talking about. Check answers as a class.

> **Suggested answers**
> 1 smartwatch, computer, laptop, smartphone, tablet
> 2 computer, laptop, smartphone, tablet
> 3 headphones
> 4 printer
> 5 smartwatch, laptop, smartphone, tablet

♀ EXTRA ACTIVITY

Students write their own sentences about the technology items in 2a, using the sentences in 2c as a model. Monitor and help with vocabulary as necessary. In pairs or small groups, students read each other their sentences and try to guess what they are about.

③ LISTENING

a ▶ **03.09** Play the recording for students to listen to the answers and check the topics that are mentioned. Check answers as a class.

> **Answers**
> groceries, music, TV, movies, clothes

Audioscript

Conversation 1

MATT Do you often go to the movies, Don?

DON No, I don't go to the movies very often. I usually watch movies online. Or sometimes I download a movie onto my tablet. How about you?

MATT No, I don't go to the movies, either. I watch movies on TV, though. And I watch a lot of TV series, too.

Conversation 2

BELLA Oh no!

JOHN What is it, Bella?

B I want to listen to music on my way home, but I don't have my headphones.

J Here, do you want to use mine? I have my headphones right here.

B Thank you! Ooh, these are nice …

Conversation 3

SANDY Do you do all your shopping online, Peter?

PETER No, I don't do much shopping online. I buy some things online, like clothes sometimes, and books. But there's a great shopping mall near our house, and I go there to buy most things. My sister does all her grocery shopping online, though.

S How does she do that?

P Oh, she just sits in the kitchen with her smartphone and buys her groceries. She never goes to the grocery store.

b ▶ **03.09** Play the recording again for students to listen for specific details and complete the chart.

> **Answers**
>
> | | Gadgets | How do they use them? |
> |---|---|---|
> | Conversation 1 | 1 tablet
2 TV | to watch movies and TV series |
> | Conversation 2 | headphones | to listen to music |
> | Conversation 3 | smartphone | to buy groceries |

> 📖 **VOCABULARY SUPPORT**
>
> *gadget* (C1) – a small piece of technology that does a specific job

c ▶ **03.09** Students listen again and check their answers to Exercise b (given above). Check answers as a class.

④ GRAMMAR *do, go, have*

a Write *I … to the library* and *He … to the library* on the board. Underneath, write *go* and *goes*. Point to each sentence and elicit from students which verb form goes with each sentence. (*I go to the library. He goes to the library.*) Then, write the incomplete sentences *I … go online* and *He … go online*. Underneath, write the negative forms *don't go* and *doesn't go*. Ask students which negative form goes with each sentence. (*I don't go online. He doesn't go online.*) Tell them they now need to complete similar sentences about the reading on p. 32 and the listening on p. 33 they just finished.

> **Answers**
>
> | | | |
> |---|---|---|
> | 1 don't | 3 go | 5 goes |
> | 2 does | 4 don't | 6 doesn't |

b Students complete the chart, working individually. They then check in pairs. Check answers as a class.

> **Answers**
>
> | | I / We / You / They | He / She / It |
> |---|---|---|
> | *do* | do | does |
> | *go* | go | goes |
> | *have* | have | has |

c Draw students' attention to the spelling changes in the chart for *he*, *she*, and *it*: *do* ➔ *does*; *go* ➔ *goes*; *have* ➔ *has*. Read the questions aloud and elicit the answers from the class as a whole. If necessary, copy the chart onto the board to help students.

> **Answer**
> 1 They add -*es*.   2 It changes to *has*.

d ⟫ ▶ **03.10** Students read the information in Grammar Focus 3B on SB p. 142. Play the recording where indicated, and ask students to listen and repeat. Students then complete the exercises on SB p. 143. Check answers as a class, making sure students understand the mistakes in Ex a, the question and short answer form in Ex b, and the correct forms in Ex c. Tell students to go back to SB p. 33.

> **Answers (Grammar Focus 3B SB p. 143)**
>
> **a**
> 2 ~~has~~ have   4 ~~gos~~ goes   6 ~~don't~~ doesn't
> 3 ~~does~~ do   5 Does John **do**
>
> **b**
> 3 Does your mom have a digital camera? No, she doesn't.
> 4 Do your grandparents do yoga? No, they don't.
> 5 Do you go to the library every day? Yes, I do.
> 6 Does your sister do her shopping online? Yes, she does.
>
> **c**
> | | | | | |
> |---|---|---|---|---|
> | 3 has | 6 does, do | 9 Do | 12 has | 15 have |
> | 4 do, go | 7 does | 10 have | 13 Do, do | |
> | 5 go | 8 goes | 11 don't have | 14 do | |

e ▶ **03.11** **Pronunciation** Students listen and match the sound to the words. Check answers as a class.

> **Answers**
> a 3   b 1   c 2   d 2   e 1   f 2

f Organize students in pairs so they can take turns practicing saying the sentences in 4b.

g ▶ **03.12** Students read the phrases in the box. Play the recording and ask students to listen and repeat. Students then complete the exercise. Check answers as a class.

> **Answers**
> have a laptop, have a camera, have an e-book, have a car
> go to college, go to the movies, go shopping
> do yoga, do (your) homework

h Individually, students write sentences that are true for them. Monitor and point out errors for students to self-correct.

> 💡 **FAST FINISHERS**
>
> Ask fast finishers to write more sentences using the words and phrases in the box, but about their friends and families. Remind them to use the third-person forms correctly.

i Students write three questions with *go, have, do,* and the words and phrases in 4g. Monitor and point out any errors for students to self-correct before students start on the pairwork stage in the next section.

5 SPEAKING

a Students put the words in the correct order to make questions. Check answers by asking individual students to come up and write them on the board.

> **Answers**
> 1 What do you buy?
> 2 How often do you use it?
> 3 When do you do it?
> 4 Where do you go?

b 💬 Demonstrate the activity by asking one student: *Do you have a laptop?* and then asking one or two follow-up questions from 5a, e.g., *How often do you use it? Do you like it?* Students work in pairs, asking and answering their questions from 4i and asking additional questions from 5a. Monitor and listen for correct use of *do* and correct word order.

> 💡 **EXTRA ACTIVITY**
> Invite students to ask questions using the phrases in Exercise 4g. Answer clearly with *Yes, I do* or *No, I don't* to reinforce short answers. Encourage them to ask you other questions using the verbs and other words they know. At A2 level, students may know *dog/cat*, family members, *purse/wallet (have)*, *restaurant, snack bar (go)*.

> ⊕ **ADDITIONAL MATERIALS**
> Workbook 3B
> Photocopiable activities: Grammar 3B, Vocabulary 3B

3C EVERYDAY ENGLISH

How about next Wednesday?

At the end of this lesson, students will be able to:

- understand informal conversations in which people make plans
- use appropriate phrases for making plans and responding appropriately
- identify the main stress in sentences
- use appropriate phrases to hesitate while thinking about what they want to say
- maintain informal conversations in which they make plans

> 💡 **OPTIONAL LEAD-IN**
> Point to the first picture on SB p. 34, or project it on the board. Ask: *What is the woman doing?* and elicit *making a cooking show*. Ask students if they know how to cook and what kind of food they cook. Ask students if they think cooking shows help people learn to cook.

1 LISTENING

a 💬 Read the questions with the students and give them one minute to think about their answers before they work in pairs. Monitor and allow time for pairs to share their answers with the class.

b ▶03.13 Play Part 1 of the audio recording for students to answer the question. Check the answer as a class.

> **Answer**
> Yes, they do.

c ▶03.13 Students listen again for specific details. Play Part 1 of the audio recording again for students to decide if the sentences are true or false. When checking answers, ask students to correct the false sentences.

> **Answers**
> 1 F (It's called *Top Cook*.)
> 2 F (She always watches it.)
> 3 T

d ▶03.14 Play Part 2 of the audio recording for students to find out what they plan to do. Check the answer as a class.

> **Answer**
> They plan to go to a new restaurant for dinner.

Audioscript (Part 1)

PRIYA Hey, Jessica.
JESSICA Hi, Priya. What's up?
P It smells amazing in here. What are you cooking?
J It's chicken with tomatoes and rice.
P Wow! I live next door to a real chef!
J It's a recipe from my favorite TV show – the one about cooking.

P *Top Cook?* I always watch that one, too.
J It's on in five minutes ... want to stay and watch with me?
P Thank you! This is great. Cooking, food, restaurants. I love all that.
J So do I!

Audioscript (Part 2)

JESSICA I'm so sorry – everything is burned.
PRIYA No problem – I'm sorry your place is so smoky.
J Looks like I'm not such a great chef after all.
P Why don't we go out for dinner? I know this new restaurant near the river.
J That sounds great, but I think I'm done with food for tonight.

P How about next Wednesday?
J Hmm, maybe. Let me see. I'm sorry, I can't. I need to work late next Wednesday.
P Are you free next Friday?
J Hmm, possibly. Friday's fine. 7:30?
P That works for me! Hey look – your favorite show is on again.
J Great. I need all the help I can get.

e ▶ **03.14** Students watch or listen again for specific details. Play Part 2 of the audio recording again for students to answer the questions. Check answers as a class.

> **Answers**
> 1 The food is burned.
> 2 She thinks it's a great idea.
> 3 She works late on Wednesday.
> 4 They decide to go out on Friday.

> 💡 **EXTRA ACTIVITY**
>
> Ask students to answer questions 1–4 as a class. Play both parts of the audio recording again.
> 1 *What does Jessica try to make?* (chicken with tomatoes and rice)
> 2 *What does Priya love?* (cooking, food, restaurants)
> 3 *What is Jessica's place like?* (It is smoky.)
> 4 *Where is the new restaurant?* (near the river)

2 USEFUL LANGUAGE Making plans

a Individually, students match the beginnings with the endings of the sentences. They then check in pairs. Check answers as a class.

> **Answers**
> 1 c 2 e 3 b 4 a 5 f 6 d

b Students classify the questions and sentences in 2a. Check answers as a class.

> **Answers**
> Make suggestions – *Why don't we try it?; How about next Wednesday?; Are you free next Friday?*
> Say yes to suggestions – *That'd be great.; That works for me.; I'd love to.*

c Read Jessica's sentence to the class. Ask students which phrase means *no* (*I'm sorry, I can't.*). Tell students that in English, it's considered rude to say just *no* or *I can't*, so people usually use a phrase like *I'm sorry, I can't*, which includes an apology, and then also give an excuse (*I need to …*).

> **Answer**
> I'm sorry, I can't. I need to work late next Wednesday.

d ▶ **03.15** Tell students to work individually and order the sentences to make a conversation. Play the recording for students to listen and check. Check answers as a class.

> **Answers and audioscript**
> A Why don't we go to the movies?
> B The movies? I'd love to.
> A How about this Saturday?
> B I'm sorry, I can't. I'm busy this weekend.
> A Are you free on Monday?
> B Yes, Monday's fine. That works for me.

e 💬 In pairs, students practice the conversation and then make similar conversations using their own ideas. Monitor and correct the phrases for making plans as appropriate.

> 💡 **FAST FINISHERS**
>
> Ask fast finishers to close their books and practice the conversation and make similar conversations without looking at 2d to help them.

3 PRONUNCIATION Main stress

a ▶ **03.16** Play the recording and highlight the main stress for students.

b Individually, students choose the correct answer. Check the answer as a class.

> **Answer**
> a short and loud

c ▶ **03.17** Play the recording for students to underline the main stress. Check answers by writing the sentences on the board and asking individual students to come up and underline the main stress in each sentence.

> **Answers**
> 1 We'd <u>love</u> to.   3 That's a <u>great</u> idea.
> 2 That'd be <u>good</u>.   4 That'd be <u>fantastic</u>.

d 💬 Drill the sentences in 3c. Students then work in pairs, practicing saying the examples. Monitor and correct students' pronunciation as appropriate.

4 CONVERSATION SKILLS
Thinking about what you want to say

a Ask students to read the conversation and think about why Jessica uses the underlined phrases. Check the answer as a class.

> **Answer**
> b give her time to think

b ▶ **03.18** **Pronunciation** Play the recording for students to listen and notice the pronunciation of *Hmm* for hesitation. Ask students: *What do you say in your language when you don't know what to say?*

> 🔄 **LOA TIP ELICITING**
>
> • Drill Jessica's responses in the conversation in 4a before continuing. Drill her first response, building it up word by word until the class can say it together with correct pronunciation. Then ask Priya's first question: *How about next Wednesday?* Elicit the response from the class all together. Repeat with Jessica's second response, and then put the whole conversation together with you taking the part of Priya and the class taking the part of Jessica.
>
> • Pay particular attention to the intonation of the phrases for hesitation. Exaggerate the "musicality" as you drill them, and show students the up-and-down movements using hand gestures to give them a visual reference.

c 💬 Read the questions with the students. Remind students to use the underlined phrases in 4a and give themselves time to think before they reply. Monitor and correct students' pronunciation if they make mistakes with the phrases for hesitation.

> 💡 **FAST FINISHERS**
>
> Ask fast finishers to extend their conversations. If their partner says *no*, offer an alternative, just as Priya does in the conversation in 4a.

5 SPEAKING

a–b ≫ Divide the class into pairs and assign A and B roles. Student As read the first card on SB p. 35, and Student Bs read the first card on SB p. 132. Students then role-play the conversation. Monitor, but don't interrupt fluency unless students make mistakes with the content of this lesson. Students then read the second card and role-play the second situation. Tell Student Bs to go back to 5c on SB p. 35.

c 💬🗨 Students work in new pairs, or small groups, and tell each other about the plans they made in the two role plays.

💡 EXTRA ACTIVITY

Students work in small groups to plan a class party. They should use phrases from the Useful Language section to make suggestions and say *yes* and *no* and phrases from the Conversation Skills section to give themselves time to think. Write the following ideas on the board to help students keep the conversation going: *When? (in the evening? / on the weekend? / a different time?) Where? (at school? / in the park? / a different place?) Fun? (games? / music? / more ideas?) Food? (party food? / drinks? / other things?)* Monitor and praise students who are able to express their ideas, even if their English isn't perfect.

⊕ ADDITIONAL MATERIALS

Workbook 3C

Photocopiable activities: Pronunciation 3C

Unit Progress Test

3D SKILLS FOR WRITING
Can you join us?

At the end of this lesson, students will be able to:

- understand a person talking about his family and how they stay in contact
- understand emails inviting people to a family party
- use expressions for inviting and replying correctly
- write an invitation to an event and a reply to an invitation they receive

💡 OPTIONAL LEAD-IN

Ask students how many letters there are in the English alphabet and elicit them from the class. If necessary, students refer back to SB p. 7. Put students into small groups, and tell them they have three minutes to try to think of one country for each of the 26 letters. They aren't allowed to look at their books or their notes. When the three minutes are up, groups share their answers with class. Ask students to spell the countries they've seen in the class so far, but don't test them on any other countries they have thought of (the countries in parentheses). *Possible answers:* **A**rgentina, **B**ritain, **C**anada, **D**enmark, (**E**gypt), **F**rance, **G**ermany, (**H**ungary), **I**ran, **J**apan, (**K**enya), (**L**ibya), **M**exico, **N**igeria, (**O**man), **P**akistan, (**Q**atar), **R**ussia, **S**pain, **T**urkey, the **U**SA, (**V**ietnam), (**W**ales), (**X** – there isn't a country beginning with X), (**Y**emen), (**Z**ambia).

1 SPEAKING AND LISTENING

a 💬🗨 Read the questions with the students, and then give them one minute to think about their answers. Discuss the questions as a class, and find out who has family or friends in the most unusual places.

b ▶03.19 Play the recording for students to listen for general meaning and put the countries in order. Check answers as a class.

Answers

1 Ecuador	4 North Carolina
2 California	5 Puerto Rico
3 Canada	6 Italy

Audioscript

FELIPE I have a large family and we all live in many different places. I come from Cuenca, Ecuador, but I live in California now with my parents. I have a brother, Jorge, and sister, Viviana, in Canada. Some of our family is still in Ecuador, but I also have an uncle in North Carolina – he lives in Charlotte with his family – and another uncle in Puerto Rico. And I also have family in Italy. I don't know them very well. We all stay in contact by Skype and email, but we don't often see each other, unfortunately. But we always get together every five years, and we spend a long weekend together. It's always in Ecuador because my grandmother is there and she's very old. She's over 80 and she can't travel. We stay with family, and we have a big party. It's a great family occasion, but we also invite friends, so there are usually about 50 people there. It's a very nice way to keep in contact, and we always have a lot to talk about!

c ▶03.19 Students listen to the recording again for specific details and correct the mistakes in the summary text. They compare in pairs. Check answers as a class.

Answers

2 He has <u>a brother and a sister</u>.
3 … every <u>five</u> years …
4 … in <u>Ecuador</u>.
5 They stay <u>with family</u> and …
6 … have a big <u>party</u>.
7 This <u>isn't</u> only for people in the family …
8 … they <u>also</u> invite friends.

2 READING

a Individually, students read the emails quickly and decide why Felipe emails his friends. Check the answer as a class.

Answer
to invite them to the family party

b Tell students to read the emails again in detail and complete the information about the family party. They then check in pairs. Check answers as a class.

Answers
Place: Cuenca (in Ecuador)
Date: Friday, September 14 to Sunday, September 16
How many days: three days
Where to stay: Elena with Carolina, Carlos with Sergio (Carolina and Sergio are Felipe's friends from school.)

3 WRITING SKILLS Inviting and replying

a Look at the email to Elena with the class and check that students understand that they need to use the numbers 1–6 to complete this exercise. Elicit the answer to b as a class. Students then work individually, identifying the sentences. Check answers as a class.

Answers
b 1
c 6
d 2
e 5
f 3

b Make sure students are clear about the task before they start. Check answers as a class.

Answers

Email to Carlos	Email to Elena
1 How are you?	How are things?
2 same	same
3 same	same
4 Would you like to come?	Can you join us?
5 Sergio / he / his	Carolina / she / her
6 Please let me know if you would like to join us.	Please let me know if you can come.

c Individually, students read the questions and decide which ones are used to invite people. When checking answers, make sure students understand that Questions 2, 4, and 5 aren't possible because they're grammatically incorrect.

Answers
1 ✓
3 ✓
6 ✓
7 ✓

d Students order the words to make sentences and questions. Check answers as a class by asking individual students to write the correct answers on the board.

Answers
1 How are things?
2 It would be great to see you.
3 Hope you can make it.
4 I'd love to see you.
5 How are you?
6 I hope you can come.

e Students read the sentences and questions in 3d again and decide which mean the same. Check answers as a class.

Answers
1 and 5; 2 and 4; 3 and 6

f Students read the emails from Carlos and Elena for general meaning to find out if they can come. Check the answer as a class.

Answer
Elena can't come, but Carlos can.

g Individually, students look at the emails in 3f again and find sentences that match the meanings. They then check in pairs. Check answers as a class.

Answers
1 I'd love to come.
2 I'm afraid I can't.
3 Hope you all have a great time.

4 WRITING AND SPEAKING

a Students work individually to plan a party or other event. Monitor and help with vocabulary and give students ideas if necessary.

b 💬🗣 Tell students that this activity is about communication – it's not about perfect English. In small groups, students talk about their plans and see if their classmates have any additional ideas for the event.

- Although students won't be using the phrases for inviting and replying in this discussion stage, they'll be using other vocabulary and grammar structures that they'll probably need to use in their written invitation. Monitor and try to preempt any problems students may have, such as using words that they're incorrectly transferring from their L1 or making common mistakes, like confusing *fun* and *funny*.

- Note problems individual students have so that you can correct those on a one-to-one basis before students work on their written invitations in 4c.

c Individually, students write an invitation to their event to another student. You could tell them who to write to so that everyone gets an invitation. If you're short on time, this exercise can be completed for homework. Students could then bring their invitations to the next class.

d Students exchange invitations and check their partner has included the information in 4a.

e Students write a reply to the invitation they received, explaining why they can or can't go. Remind students that if they can't go, they shouldn't just say *no*, but should use one of the phrases in Lessons 3C or 3D and give an excuse. Students give their reply back to the student who invited them. Invite students to share their answers with the class and find out how many accept the invitation and how many of them say *no*.

EXTRA ACTIVITY

Write a short checklist on the board to help students when they check their invitations and replies in pairs: <u>Spelling</u>: check difficult words in the Student's Book, in a dictionary, or on your phone. <u>be</u>: negatives use *'m not / 're not / 's not*; questions use *Am/Are/Is* + subject. <u>Simple present</u>: negatives use *don't/ doesn't*; questions use *Do/Does* + subject + verb. <u>Word order</u>: check adverbs of frequency / time expressions are in the right position. <u>Phrases</u>: include phrases for making plans / inviting and replying. If students have made mistakes in any of these areas, they prepare a second draft of their invitation and/or reply before you collect pairs of invitations and replies to give feedback on them both.

ADDITIONAL MATERIALS

Workbook 3D

UNIT 3
Review and extension

1 GRAMMAR

a Students work individually, inserting the adverb of frequency in the correct place in each sentence. Check answers as a class.

Answers
1 He <u>often</u> gets up at about 10 or 11.
2 He <u>never</u> goes to bed before 2:00 a.m.
3 He <u>sometimes</u> studies all night.
4 He <u>usually</u> has black coffee and toast for breakfast.
5 He is <u>often</u> away for a week or more.
6 His windows are <u>always</u> closed, even in summer.

b Individually, students complete the text. They then check in pairs. Check answers as a class.

Answers
1 have	10 doesn't have
2 have	11 does
3 has	12 goes
4 goes	13 does
5 does	14 goes
6 have	15 has
7 don't have	16 goes
8 don't do	17 has
9 go	

2 VOCABULARY

a Students rewrite the sentences with time expressions in the correct position. Check answers as a class.

Answers
2 three times a year
3 twice a year
4 three times a week
5 every morning and evening / twice a day
6 four times a week

b Individually, students look at the pictures and write the names of the objects. Check answers and spelling as a class.

Answers
1 printer	6 camera
2 computer	7 smartphone
3 tablet	8 smartwatch
4 speaker	9 keyboard
5 headphones	10 laptop

3 WORDPOWER Prepositions of time

a Tell students to close their books. Write the following three blanked sentences on the board: *I work ... the morning., I start work ... 9 a.m., I never work ... Sunday.* Point to the three blanks and ask students about each missing word in turn. Write *in, at, on* on the board in each sentence. Students open their books, look at the sentences, and match them with the pictures. Check answers as a class.

Answers
1 c 2 b 3 a 4 e 5 d

b Individually, students answer the questions and find examples in 3a. Check answers as a class.

Answers
1 a at b on c in d in, at e in
2 a 3 (6 a.m., 1 p.m.)
  b 4 (weekdays, Sunday)
  c 5 (January)
  d 3 (the morning, the evening, night)
  e 1 (the summer)

c Students work individually, adding prepositions of time to the sentences. When checking answers, make sure students understand that this exercise is testing both the prepositions and their position. If students have used the wrong preposition, but put it in the correct position, then their answer can be considered partially correct.

Answers
1 I always get up <u>at</u> 6:30 <u>in</u> the morning <u>on</u> weekdays.
2 It's usually cold here <u>in</u> the winter, and it often snows <u>in</u> January.
3 Are you free <u>on</u> the weekend? I have tickets for a concert <u>on</u> Saturday. It starts <u>at</u> 7:30 p.m.

d As an example, make a sentence using *get up* which is true for yourself, e.g., *I get up at 7 a.m.* Students then write sentences that are true for themselves. Monitor and point out errors for students to self-correct.

Answers
Students' own answers

e Give students one or two example questions, using the things in 3d, e.g., *What time do you usually get up on weekends? What about on weekdays?*, etc. In pairs, students ask and answer questions. Monitor and listen for correct question formation and for correct use of the prepositions of time. Praise students with a smile or a nod when they use the language from this section correctly.

> **EXTRA ACTIVITY**
>
> Write jumbled questions a–d on the board. Ask students to put them in order and decide which things in 3d they are connected to: *a prefer / you / do / which ?* (Which do you prefer? 6); *b go / usually / where / you / do ?* (Where do you usually go? 4); *c what / have / you / do / usually ?* (What do you usually have? 3); *d things / kind / of / you / do / what / buy ?* (What kind of things do you buy? 5). Check answers as a class. Students can then use the questions to extend their conversations in 3d.

>> Photocopiable activities: Wordpower 3

> **LOA TIP ELICITING**
>
> Students look back through the unit, think about what they've studied, and decide how well they did. Students work on weak areas by using the appropriate sections of the Workbook and the Photocopiable activities.

UNIT 4

FOOD

UNIT CONTENTS

G GRAMMAR

- Count and noncount nouns
- *a/an*, *some*, *any*
- Quantifiers: *much*, *many*, *a lot (of)*

V VOCABULARY

- Food: *beans, burger, carrots, cereal, chicken, chips, cookie, garlic, grapes, jam, lamb, lemons, melon, mushrooms, onions, pears, salad, soda, steak, yogurt*
- Cooking verbs: *bake, boil, fry, grill, roast*
- Cooking adjectives: *baked, boiled, fried, grilled, roasted*
- Containers: *bag, bar, bottle, can, jar, package*
- Sequencing words: *first, then, next, after that, finally*
- Wordpower: *like* to talk about wants (*I'd like …*), make invitations (*Would you like … ?*), express general likes (*I like …*), ask "How is it?" (*What's it like … ?*), say "the same as" (*He's like me*), give examples (*… fruit, like apples*) and say "in that way" (*… live like that*).

P PRONUNCIATION

- Sound and spelling: *ea* (/i/, /eə/, and /eɪ/)
- Sound and spelling: /k/
- Stress in phrases with containers
- Word groups, e.g., *For my appetizer*, || *I'd like raw fish.*

C COMMUNICATION SKILLS

- Talking about shopping for food, eating habits, markets, and food likes and dislikes
- Discussing healthy and unhealthy food and describing ways of cooking
- Arriving at a restaurant and ordering a meal
- Changing what you say
- Asking and answering questions about cooking
- Writing a blog post

GETTING STARTED

⚑ OPTIONAL LEAD-IN

Books closed. Draw three digital clocks on the board, one with 7:30, one with 1:15, and one with 7:00, or other appropriate times for mealtimes. Write the words *breakfast*, *lunch*, and *dinner* on the board, but not connected in any way to the times. Say: *I usually have this at seven thirty in the morning.* Elicit *breakfast*. Draw a line from the 7:30 clock to *breakfast*. Repeat the process with *lunch* and *dinner*. Then, ask some students: *What time do you usually have breakfast/lunch/dinner?* Elicit the times.

a 💬🗣 If you didn't use the optional lead-in, check that students understand *breakfast*, *lunch*, and *dinner*. Give students one minute to think about their answers to the questions before talking about the picture as a class.

b 💬🗣 Read the questions with the students before they ask and answer them. Ask students to share vocabulary for what they usually have for breakfast, lunch, and dinner, and what they talk about when they eat as a family. Help with vocabulary and pronunciation, but don't interrupt fluency. Monitor to see what food vocabulary students already know.

⚑ EXTRA ACTIVITY

Review and consolidate A1-level food vocabulary by writing jumbled words on the board, e.g., *toatpo* (potato), *hicwands* (sandwich), etc. Use either A1-level items that students will probably know (*bread, cake, cheese, coffee, cookie, egg, fish, meat, milk, orange juice, tea, tomato, vegetables*), or consolidate the spelling of items you heard students use in Exercise b, or use a combination of both. Be careful, however, not to pre-empt the lexical set of food vocabulary in Lesson 4A.

Exercises **a** and **b** can be prepared as homework before this lesson to give students time to look up unfamiliar vocabulary. Ask students to look at the picture and to prepare their answers to the questions as homework to talk about in the next class.

4A TRY SOME INTERESTING FOOD

At the end of this lesson, students will be able to:

- read and understand a text about places to buy food
- identify count and noncount nouns
- use a lexical set of foods correctly
- understand a conversation about planning what to cook
- use *a/an*, *some*, and *any* correctly
- ask for food they need to cook dinner

⚲ OPTIONAL LEAD-IN

Write on the board: *Where do you buy food?* and under it write the following prompts: *in small stores? at a grocery store? online? at a market?* Check that students understand *market*. Tell the class where you usually buy food, e.g., *I usually buy food online.* Ask each student to tell the class where they buy food. Tell students to listen to what their classmates say, and elicit from the class where most people usually go grocery shopping.

1 READING

a 💬 Give students one minute to think about their answers to the questions before talking about the pictures as a class. Encourage students to justify their ideas as much as possible.

b Students read the texts quickly and match them with the pictures. Check answers as a class. You may also give students information from Culture Notes below.

> **Answers**
> 1 b
> 2 c
> 3 a

🌍 CULTURE NOTES

Union Square Greenmarket started in 1976 and has become more and more successful over the years. The market takes place year round. At peak times of the year, over 100 farmers may be selling their products in the heart of Manhattan, giving New Yorkers the opportunity to buy fresh, locally produced ingredients.

The Municipal Market opened in the center of São Paulo in 1933 in a historic building that is known for its eclectic style and stained glass windows. It is filled with market stalls selling a huge variety of foods, including most of the exotic fruit that is native to Brazil.

Nishiki Market is the largest traditional food market in Kyoto. It is styled as a traditional *shotengai* (shopping street) so visitors can get an idea of what this would have looked like. As well as market stalls selling the main ingredients of traditional Kyoto cuisine, there are some restaurants and food stands with takeout food.

c Read the first sentence with the class, and elicit where students think Joshua is. Read aloud the end of the final sentence of text 3 to justify the answer: *At Nishiki Market, you can try local foods such as tofu, pickled vegetables, grilled fish, and sweets.* Individually, students decide where Madison and Sarah are. They then check in pairs. When checking answers, elicit which words or sentences in the texts helped students decide. You may wish to help students with words in the Vocabulary Support box.

> **Answers**
> Joshua is at the Nishiki Market in Kyoto.
> Madison is at the Municipal Market of São Paulo in São Paulo.
> Sarah is at the Union Square Greenmarket in New York.

📖 VOCABULARY SUPPORT

amazing (A2) – very good

customer (A2) – a person who buys something in a store or market

dish (A2) – food that is prepared and cooked for people to eat

historic (B1) – interesting because it is old

d 💬 Students talk about the questions in pairs, small groups, or as a class. Students share their answers as a class.

2 GRAMMAR Count and noncount nouns

a Write the four nouns on the board, and ask students which two words have plural endings. Circle the *-s* of *vegetables*, then cover the *-s* with your hand and say *one vegetable.* Next, uncover the *-s* and say *two vegetables.* Point to *tomatoes*, and hold your pen up to the board for students to tell you to circle the *-es*. Again, cover the plural ending and say *one tomato.* Then, uncover it and say *two tomatoes.*

> **Answer**
> *Vegetables* and *tomatoes* have plural endings.

b Elicit the rule as a class.

> **Answer**
> never

📖 LANGUAGE NOTES

Note that in 2c, the words *cheese, chocolate,* and *fish* are treated as noncount. They can, however, be count in certain circumstances, e.g., *Go to the store and buy me a good cheese.* (= a complete cheese, not only a part), *Do you want a chocolate?* (= referring to a chocolate from a box of chocolates), *I have a pet fish named Nemo!* (= referring to the living creature).

Unless students ask about this, don't mention it at this point, but be prepared to explain if necessary. After students have studied *some/any* later in this lesson and the containers in Lesson 4B, you may like to give further explanation.

c Individually, students complete the chart. Check answers by copying the chart onto the board and asking students to add the words.

> **Answers**
> Count nouns: potatoes, carrots, mushrooms, spices, sandwiches, pastries, sweets
> Noncount nouns: pasta, meat, bread, chocolate, tofu, fish

⚲ FAST FINISHERS

Ask fast finishers to add the food words that they thought of in Exercise b of the Getting Started section to the chart.

3 VOCABULARY Food

a Ask students to cover the words and see how many words for the food in the pictures they already know. Individually, students then match the words with the pictures. Monitor for any problems, and clarify these as you check answers as a class.

Answers			
1 chicken	4 lamb	7 carrots	9 lemons
2 pears	5 mushrooms	8 grapes	10 onions
3 steak	6 beans		

b Complete the first item as an example with the class. Students work individually, identifying the different word in the other groups. They then check in pairs. Check answers as a class.

Answers
1 carrot – It's not fruit. It's a vegetable.
2 lamb – It's not a vegetable. It's meat.
3 grape – It's not meat. It's fruit.

♀ EXTRA ACTIVITY

Students classify the vocabulary from 3a as count or noncount and add it to the chart in 2c. Check answers as a class. If you drew the chart on the board in 2c, check answers by asking students to add the words to the chart (Count nouns – *beans, lemons, mushrooms, onions, pears, carrots, grapes*; Noncount nouns* – *chicken, steak, lamb*).

*See Language Notes on the previous page. Both *chicken* and *lamb*, like *fish*, can be count when referring to the living creature. Note that we also use *a chicken* when buying the complete animal in a meat market, and *a steak* when buying or ordering an individual steak.

c ▶04.01 **Pronunciation** Answer the first question as a class. Individually, students then match the pairs of words. Play the recording for students to listen and check.

Answers
1 All the words have *ea* in them.
2 green – bean; hair – pear; make – steak

d ▶04.02 Read the examples, and check that students understand that the three phonemic symbols at the top of the chart are the same as the ones in 3c. Students add the words to the sound groups. Play the recording for students to listen and check. Drill each word.

Answers and audioscript

Sound 1 /eɪ/	Sound 2 /i/	Sound 3 /eə/
steak	bean	pear
eight	eat	where
rain	these	wear
day	green	fair

e 💬 In pairs, students talk about the food they like and don't like. Monitor, but don't interrupt fluency unless students add -s to noncount nouns.

f ≫ ▶04.03–04.05 Students complete the exercises in Vocabulary Focus 4A on SB p. 166. Play the recording for students to check their answers to Exercise a and complete the Pronunciation activities. Monitor Exercises d and f, and check other answers as a class. Tell students to go back to SB p. 41.

Answers (Vocabulary Focus 4A SB p. 166)

a 1 e 2 d 3 c 4 b 5 j 6 f 7 g 8 i 9 h 10 a
c 1 b 2 a 3 a 4 a
e 1 chicken; steak; lamb
2 salad; onions; carrots; beans; mushrooms
3 cereal; yogurt; jam 4 pears; grapes; melon 5 chips; soda

4 LISTENING

a 💬 Discuss the questions as a class. Find out how many students like cooking.

b ▶04.06 Play the recording for students to listen for specific details and answer the questions. They compare in pairs. Check answers as a class.

Answers	
1 No, she doesn't.	3 at the farmers' market
2 Milly	4 Tom

Audioscript

TOM We have almost nothing to eat for dinner.
MILLY OK. We can order some pizza then.
T Not again.
M Well, it's the weekend – I don't really want to cook.
T All right, fine. I can cook.
M OK. If you want to.
T But you can come to the store with me.
M Like I said – it's the weekend. I don't cook and I don't go to the supermarket.
T We can take a nice walk to the farmers' market then. It's open today.
M OK, fine. What do we need?
T Well, we have some potatoes, so we can have roasted potatoes, maybe. But we don't have any meat.
M Do you want to make that chicken and mushroom dish – you know, the one you like to make?
T Yeah – good idea. Do we have any mushrooms?
M No, I don't think so.
T OK, we can get some. And I need an onion and a chicken, of course.
M So, let's put that on the shopping list – a chicken, some mushrooms, and an onion. Is that all?
T Yeah, I think so.
M Oh, and Tom … I don't have any money at the moment, so … .
T All right, Milly. I can pay.

c ▶04.06 Students listen to the recording again and check the food that Tom and Milly need. Check answers as a class. If students checked *potatoes*, clarify that Tom says that they have potatoes, so they don't need to buy more.

Answers
✓ chicken ✓ an onion ✓ mushrooms

5 GRAMMAR *a / an, some, any*

a ▶04.07 Pick up two pens and say to the class: *I have two pens.* Then, add another two pens, and elicit from the class how many pens you have: *I have four pens.* Finally, add several other pens so that students can't see the exact number and say: *I have [silence] pens.* Elicit/Teach the word *some*. Look at the first sentence in the Student's Book, and complete it as a class. Individually, students complete the other sentences. Check answers as a class.

Answers			
1 some	2 any	3 an	4 any

b Show the students all the pens again, and say: *I have.* Ask: *Affirmative or negative?* (affirmative), *count or noncount?* (count), *singular or plural?* (plural). Then look at sentence 1 in 5a, and ask the same questions. Show students how to complete the first space in the chart with *some.* Students complete the chart. Check answers by copying the chart onto the board and asking individual students to come up and complete it.

Answers

	Count	Noncount
+	a potato some potatoes	some fruit
– / ?	an onion any onions	any cheese

> ### ↻ LOA TIP ELICITING
>
> - Check that students fully understand when we use *a/an, some,* and *any* by asking them further questions, e.g., *What word do we use with a noncount noun in a question?* ("any"); *What word do we use with a singular count noun in an affirmative sentence?* ("a"), etc.
>
> - Write sentences 1–3 on the board:
>   *1 We need to buy ... vegetables from the market.*
>   *2 I'm hungry. Do you have ... food?*
>   *3 I don't want ... burger, thank you.*
>   Point to sentence 1, and ask students: *What's the noun?* (vegetables); *Is it count or noncount?* (count); *Is it singular or plural?* (plural); *Is the sentence affirmative or negative, or is it a question?* (affirmative). Once students have answered all four questions correctly, ask them what word goes in the blank. Repeat with sentences 2 and 3 (Answers *1 some, 2 any, 3 a*).

> ### ◉ CAREFUL!
>
> The most common student mistake with count and noncount nouns is adding a final *-s* to noncount words like *fruit, furniture, hair, homework,* and *money.*
>
> Students may also have problems with the indefinite article and include it where it isn't needed, e.g., *I travel to school by a bus (Correct form = I travel to school **by bus**),* or not include it where it is needed, e.g., *This smartphone has very good camera ... (Correct form = This smartphone has **a** very good camera).* They may also confuse *the* and *a,* e.g., *There's the big market ... (Correct form = There's **a** big market in my town).*
>
> When using the determiners *some* and *any,* students may leave them out, e.g., *I want new shoes (Correct form = I want **some** new shoes)* or *Do you have money? (Correct form = Do you have **any** money?).* In some cases, students may use *a* instead of *some,* e.g., *I need a bread ... (Correct form = I need **some** bread to make a sandwich).*

c ⏩ ▶ 04.08 Students read the information in Grammar Focus 4A on SB p. 144. Play the recording where indicated, and ask students to listen and repeat. Students then complete the exercises. Check answers as a class, making sure students are clear on the differences between count and noncount nouns. Tell students to go back to SB p. 41.

Answers (Grammar Focus 4A SB p. 145)

a 2 C   3 N   4 N   5 N   6 N   7 C   8 N   9 C   10 N
b 2 a   4 any   6 a   8 some   10 any
  3 some   5 an   7 any   9 any
c 2 ~~furnitures~~ any furniture   5 ~~a~~ some cheese   7 long ~~hairs~~ hair
  3 any ~~moneys~~ money   6 ~~some~~ any meat   8 ~~any~~ an apple
  4 ~~a~~ an onion

> ### ♀ FAST FINISHERS
>
> Ask fast finishers to rewrite the conversation in Grammar Focus Exercise b using vegetables instead of fruit.

d ▶ 04.09 Individually, students complete the conversation. They then check in pairs. Play the recording for students to listen and check.

Answers
1 a
2 an
3 some
4 any
5 any
6 some

6 SPEAKING

a ⏩ Divide the class into pairs and assign A and B roles. Student As read the instructions and look at the picture on SB p. 130, and Student Bs read the instructions and look at the words on SB p. 133. Students then role-play the conversation. Monitor, but don't interrupt fluency unless students make mistakes with the content of this lesson. Students then role-play the second conversation.

> ### ♀ EXTRA ACTIVITY
>
> Play a "listing game" (see p. 153) with students. Mime having a bag of groceries and say: *These are my groceries. I have two melons.* Pass the "bag of groceries" to a student who has to repeat your sentence and add an item, e.g., *These are my groceries. I have two melons and some chicken.* They pass it on to the next student, who repeats the sentence and adds an item, and so on until the list is too long to remember. Students can then play in small groups. Monitor and check students are using *a/an* and *some* correctly.

> ### ⊕ ADDITIONAL MATERIALS
>
> Workbook 4A
>
> Photocopiable activities: Grammar 4A, Vocabulary 4A, Pronunciation 4A

4B | HOW MUCH CHOCOLATE DO YOU NEED?

At the end of this lesson, students will be able to:
- read and understand short friendly emails
- use a lexical set of verbs and adjectives about cooking correctly
- understand a conversation about recipes
- use the quantifiers *much*, *many*, and *a lot (of)* correctly
- ask and answer questions about the food they eat

♀ OPTIONAL LEAD-IN

Write *My favorite meal is …* on the board. Tell the students what your favorite three-course meal is using vocabulary from the previous lesson, e.g., *My favorite meal is soup – either French onion soup or mushroom soup – then meat (I love lamb!) with some vegetables – carrots, beans, and potatoes. To finish, I love ice cream – banana and chocolate ice cream. Delicious!* Students then think about their own favorite meal and share it with a small group or the class.

1 READING

a 💬🔊 Give students a few minutes to think about their answers to the questions and read the text about Aarón Sánchez before they discuss the questions in small groups. Ask students to share their ideas. You may give students information from Culture Notes below.

🌍 CULTURE NOTES

Aarón Sánchez (b. 1976) is one of the most famous celebrity chefs in the U.S. He began cooking when he was a child by helping his mom prepare traditional Mexican dishes for her restaurant. When his family moved to New York, he started working in the family's restaurant as a professional chef. After helping other people open different restaurants, he opened his own called *Johnny Sánchez* in 2014. Sánchez's food is referred to as Pan-Latin because it combines flavors and ingredients from Central and South America, reflecting his heritage. Sánchez has appeared on many TV shows, such as *Masterchef*, *Chopped*, and *Chopped Junior*.

b Tell students they should only read the first email. They then work individually, answering the questions. Check answers as a class.

Answers
1 Josh lives in New Orleans.
2 He wants to go to *Johnny Sánchez*.
3 It looks fun and his friend Pete says the food is good.

c Tell students to read the second email for general meaning and find out if Josh's dad wants to go to *Johnny Sánchez*. Check the answer as a class.

Answer
No, he doesn't.

d Students read Josh's dad's email again in detail. Individually, students underline the correct answers. Encourage students to guess the meaning of any new words from the context. Check answers as a class.

Answers
1 different
2 normal
3 expensive for Josh

♀ EXTRA ACTIVITY

Ask students to read both emails again and also look at the information about Aarón Sánchez in 1a. Ask students to decide if the following sentences are true or false.

1 *Aarón Sánchez is famous because he has written two cookbooks.* (F – He is famous because he makes creative dishes.)
2 *Josh's dad wants to take Josh for dinner.* (F – Josh wants to take his dad for dinner.)
3 *Josh loves the grilled fish at Johnny Sánchez.* (F – Josh's friend's mother loves the grilled fish at *Johnny Sánchez*.)
4 *Josh's dad likes his wife's cooking.* (T)
5 *Josh's dad wants him to cook roasted chicken and boiled potatoes.* (F – He wants to go to a normal restaurant or have a can of soup at Josh's place.)

e 💬🔊 Discuss the questions as a class. Encourage students to justify their answers as much as possible.

2 VOCABULARY Cooking

a Individually, students read the cooking instructions and match them with the pictures. Check answers as a class. Drill each word.

Answers
1 c
2 e
3 a
4 d
5 b

b ▶04.10 Individually, students complete the chart. Play the recording for students to listen and check. Check answers as a class.

Answers

Verb	Adjective
boil	boiled
fry	fried
grill	grilled
bake	baked
roast	roasted

c Look at the example together and check that students understand that the base verb is *boil*, so *-ed* has been added to form the adjective. Students complete the examples, working individually. They then check in pairs. Check answers as a class.

Answers
- add *-ed*   grilled, roasted
- add *-d*   baked
- changes *-y* to *-ied*   fried

📖 **LANGUAGE NOTES**

Students may confuse the words *roast* and *bake* or be unsure about the distinction, as they are both used for cooking in the oven. To help them understand, explain that *roast* is generally used for things that are cooked with oil, e.g., beef, chicken, potatoes, etc., while *bake* is used for things that are made with flour, e.g., cookies, bread, and cakes.

d 💬 Put students into pairs or small groups to talk about the questions. Pre-teach the words *healthy* (good for your body) and *unhealthy* (bad for your body). Monitor, but don't interrupt fluency unless students make mistakes with the vocabulary for cooking.

e ⟫ ▶04.11 Students complete the exercises in Vocabulary Focus 4B on SB p. 166. Play the recording as necessary and monitor students as they speak. Check answers as a class, making sure students pronounce and stress the phrases correctly. Tell students to go back to SB p. 43.

Answers (Vocabulary Focus 4B SB p. 166)
a 1 d 2 a 3 e 4 b 5 c 6 f
b 1 the nouns
c 2 a jar of jam   5 a can of tuna
    3 a package of spaghetti 6 a bag of apples
    4 a bar of chocolate

💡 **FAST FINISHERS**

Ask fast finishers to think of other things that can collocate with the containers, e.g., *a bottle of soda*, *a package of cereal*, etc.

3 LISTENING

a ▶04.12 Pre-teach the word *recipe* (written information about how to make a dish). Students listen to the conversation for general meaning, and check the two recipes Olivia and Harry talk about. Check answers as a class.

Answers
✓ Superb mashed potatoes
✓ Chocolate coffee sauce

Audioscript

OLIVIA I want to try this recipe from my favorite cooking blog.
HARRY Which one?
O Superb mashed potatoes.
H Mashed potatoes? That's kind of boring.
O But it says "superb" – you know, really great.
H What's so special about it?
O Well, it says to use 250 grams of butter.
H 250 grams? That's a lot of butter.
O I know! That's why I want to try it. And then you boil the potatoes and add garlic and herbs. I'm going to make it today. Anyway, look at the blog. Which recipe do you want to try?

H Something sweet. Let's see … oh yes, this one, chocolate coffee sauce. Sounds really good! I can put it on ice cream.
O What's in it?
H Well, some coffee beans, of course.
O How many do you need?
H It says you need 50.
O Whoa! That's a lot! And how much chocolate?
H Only a little – 50 grams. But I need dark chocolate, not milk chocolate.
O How many grams of butter?
H Let's see … *only* 200 grams! And 200 grams of sugar, too … and that's all. It looks really easy to make. I just boil everything together. Now, no more talking. I'm hungry! Let's get cooking.

b ▶04.12 Play the recording again for students to underline the specific food words. They compare in pairs. Then check answers as a class.

Answers
1 potatoes, butter
2 boil
3 sugar, coffee beans, dark chocolate
4 boil

c 💬 Discuss the question as a class. If students are interested in learning more about Aarón Sánchez's recipes, more information and pictures are readily available by searching the Internet.

💡 **EXTRA ACTIVITY**

Give the class some additional listening practice through a "live listening." Tell the group about a typical dish from your country, e.g., roasted chicken, and explain how to make it using the food vocabulary from Lesson 4A and the cooking verbs and adjectives from this lesson, e.g., *This is my recipe for roasted chicken with onions, lemon, and garlic. Fry the onions and the garlic in a little oil. Put two lemons inside the chicken with the onion and garlic, and roast it in the oven for around two hours.* Students write down the ingredients and the main steps of the recipe. They then check in pairs, and ask you to clarify any steps they are not sure of, e.g., *Where do you put the lemons?*

4 GRAMMAR
Quantifiers: *much, many, a lot (of)*

a ▶04.13 Look at the first sentence in the Student's Book and complete it as a class. Individually, students complete the other sentences. Check answers as a class.

Answers
1 a lot
2 much; a little
3 many

b Read the first mini-conversation as a class, and make sure students understand that it's possible to use all four phrases. Ask them: *Is butter a count or a noncount noun?* (noncount). Repeat the process with the second mini-conversation: *Are beans count or noncount?* (count). Repeat with the final sentence: *Are potatoes count or noncount?* (count). Ask: *What about chocolate?* (noncount). Check students understand that *a lot (of)* can be used with both count and noncount nouns. Also point out that *of* is only used when followed by a noun.

> **Answers**
> 1 noncount nouns
> 2 count nouns
> 3 both

⊙ CAREFUL!

At this level, students will probably use *How much* correctly, but may still make mistakes with *How many*, sometimes using it in place of *How much*, e.g., ~~How many cheese do~~ … (Correct form = ***How much*** *cheese do we need?*). Another common error is using *much/many* in contexts where *a lot of* would sound more natural, e.g., ~~There are many people~~ … (Correct form = *There are **a lot of** people at the restaurant*) or ~~We always have much fun~~ … (Correct form = *We always have **a lot of** fun in class*). Students also often use *much* instead of *many*, e.g., ~~Aarón doesn't have much restaurants~~ (Correct form = *Aarón doesn't have **many** restaurants*), and may occasionally use *many* instead of *much*. They also sometimes spell *a lot* as one word or include *of* when *a lot* appears at the end of a sentence, e.g., ~~I like this dish alot / a lot of~~ (Correct form = *I like this dish **a lot***).

c ≫ ▶04.14–04.15 Students read the information in Grammar Focus 4B on SB p. 144. Play the recording where indicated, and ask students to listen and repeat. Students then complete the exercises. Check answers as a class, making sure students are clear about which quantifiers are used with count nouns and which are used with noncount nouns. For Exercise a, tell students that they should choose from the quantifiers in the chart on p. 144. Tell students to go back to SB p. 43.

> **Answers (Grammar Focus 4B SB p. 145)**
> **a** 2 little   3 a lot of   4 few   5 much   6 a lot of
> **b** 2 much   4 many   6 many   8 much
>   3 much   5 much   7 much
> **c** 1 much   3 many   5 much   7 much
>   2 much   4 a little   6 a lot of   8 a few

♀ FAST FINISHERS

Ask fast finishers to look at the picture of the market stall on SB p. 130 and write sentences about it using the quantifiers.

d ▶04.16 Individually, students complete the conversation and put it in order. Play the recording for students to listen and check. Check answers as a class.

> **Answers**
> 1 lot
> 2 much
> 3 many
> 4 much

> **Answers and audioscript**
> **A** How much fruit do you eat a day?
> **B** A lot – about five or six pieces.
> **A** And what about drinks? How many glasses of water do you have a day?
> **B** About two.
> **A** Really? That's not much water.

↻ LOA TIP ELICITING

- Draw a smiley face ☺ on the left of the board, a neutral face ☺ in the center of the board, and a sad face ☹ on the right of the board.
- Point to the smiley face and give a thumbs up, the neutral face and give a "so-so" shaky-hand gesture, and the sad face and give a thumbs down. Ask students: *Count and noncount nouns?* Elicit an indication of their confidence level. Repeat with *Some and any?* and *Much, many, and a lot of?*

e 💬🗨 Discuss the question as a class. Encourage students to justify their answers as much as possible.

5 SPEAKING

a Students work individually, writing questions to ask their partner about the food they eat. Monitor and point out errors for students to self-correct.

b 💬🗨 Put students into pairs to ask and answer their questions. Tell them to take notes on their partner's answers.

c 💬🗨 Students read the information on SB p. 131 and then look at their notes from 5b. Ask volunteers to share their answers to find out who eats in a healthy way.

⊕ ADDITIONAL MATERIALS

Workbook 4B

Photocopiable activities: Grammar 4B, Vocabulary 4B

4C EVERYDAY ENGLISH

Do we need a reservation?

💡 OPTIONAL LEAD-IN

Ask a student to write *American* on the board. To confirm the student has spelled it correctly, point to the board and ask the rest of the class: *Is that correct?* Repeat the process with: *British, Chinese, French, Greek, Indian, Italian, Japanese, Mexican, South African.* Ask students: *What kind of restaurants are popular in your country?* Elicit their ideas. Finally, ask students: *What kind of restaurants do you think are popular in the U.S.?* (Food from many different countries is popular in the U.S., but Chinese, Italian, and Mexican restaurants are especially popular.)

1 LISTENING

a 💬 Pre-teach the phrase *eat out* (have a meal in a restaurant, not at home). Give students one minute to think about their answers to the questions before talking about restaurants and eating out as a class.

b 💬 Ask students to look at the picture in pairs. They decide why the restaurant is empty. Elicit students' ideas, but don't check the answer at this point.

c ▶️04.17 Play Part 1 of the audio recording for students to check their answer to 1b. Check the answer as a class.

> **Answer**
> 3 It's very early.

Audioscript (Part 1)

EMILY Is this the right restaurant, Tim?

TIM Yes. This is it, Emily.

E Are you sure? It's empty.

T Maybe it isn't open yet.

S Hello. Good evening.

E Hello. Are you open?

T Yes, of course. Do you have a reservation?

E No, we don't. Do we *need a* reservation?

S Um, not really. It's pretty early ...

T OK, then, we'd like a table for two.

S OK. How about this table here?

E Um ... Can we have a table by the window?

S Sure. The two tables over there are free.

T What do you think? The one on the left?

E That's fine with me. Although, what about the one on the right? It has a better view ...

T OK, if you like that one ...

E Maybe not. The one on the left is fine. It's farther from the door ...

S Tell you what ... go ahead and choose any table you want while I get your menus.

d ▶️04.17 Students listen again for specific details. Play Part 1 of the audio recording again for students to decide if the sentences are true or false and correct the false sentences. Check answers as a class.

> **Answers**
> 1 F (They don't have a reservation.)
> 2 F (They want a table by the window.)
> 3 T

2 USEFUL LANGUAGE
Arriving at a restaurant

a Check that students understand that the lines of the conversation aren't in the correct order, but that they don't have to put them in order yet. They read for general meaning to identify which speaker is the server. Check the answer as a class.

> **Answer**
> The server is A.

b ▶️04.18 Students read the sentences again in detail. Individually, students put them in order to make a conversation. Play the recording for students to listen and check. Check answers as a class.

> **Answers and audioscript**
> A Good evening. Do you have a reservation?
> B No, we don't. We'd like a table for four.
> A No problem.
> B Can we have a table by the window?
> A Yes, of course. This way, please.

c 💬 Drill the conversation before students work in pairs. Monitor and correct students' pronunciation as appropriate.

d 💬 Read the sentences with the students and, if possible, organize them into pairs with a new partner to practice the conversation with the new information.

💡 FAST FINISHERS

Ask fast finishers to invent their own conversations with different information, e.g., *Can we have a table in the corner?* or *We have a reservation for three people at 8:30 p.m. I'm sorry we're late. The name's Wilson.*

3 LISTENING

a Look at the menu with the students. Ask: *What do you eat first? An appetizer or an entree?* (an appetizer) Check the meaning of *dip, mixed,* and *pie* if necessary. Then look at picture b, and read what the friends say. Individually, students predict what they choose for their main course. Don't check answers at this point.

b ▶️04.19 Play Part 2 of the audio recording for students to check their answers to 3a, and find out who can't decide what to have. They check in pairs. Check answers as a class.

> **Answers**
> 1 Tim – chicken soup and lamb; Emily – chicken wings and lamb
> 2 Emily can't decide what she wants to have.

SERVER Are you ready to order?

EMILY Oh, it's so hard to decide. OK, I think I'm ready.

S What would you like for your appetizer?

E I'll have the chicken wings to start. No, wait! I'll have the salad, please. Yes. That sounds good.

S And for your entrée?

E For my entrée … I'd like … the spaghetti. Yep. And I'll have garlic bread with that. That's it.

S Very good. And for your appetizer, sir?

TIM I'd like the chicken soup, please.

E Ooh, chicken soup - that sounds really good. Can I change my order?

S That's fine, ma'am. Chicken soup to start.

E I think so …

T And then for my entrée, I'll have the lamb.

S Would you like rice with that?

T Yes, please.

E Oh, lamb! That sounds nice. I'm sorry, can I change my order again?

S Of course.

E I'll have the same as Tim – lamb for my entrée.

S And chicken soup to start.

E Mmmm. You know what? I'm sorry. Let's go with chicken wings, my first idea. I'm sorry.

S So, that's the chicken wings appetizer?

E Yes.

S And what would you like to drink with that?

E To drink? Oh, wow …

S Would you like a moment to think about that?

T Why don't you come back in about 20 minutes?

> ♀ **EXTRA ACTIVITY**
>
> Play both parts of the audio recording again, and ask students to answer questions 1 and 2: *1 What time of day is it?* (evening) *2 What do the friends choose for their appetizers?* (Tim – chicken soup; Emily – chicken wings).

c 💬 Discuss the questions as a class. Encourage students to justify their answers as much as possible.

4 USEFUL LANGUAGE
Ordering a meal in a restaurant

a Individually, students complete the conversations. They then check in pairs. Check answers as a class.

> **Answers**
> 1 have   2 I'd   3 like   4 then   5 with

> ♀ **FAST FINISHERS**
>
> Ask fast finishers to invent more short conversations by changing words and phrases in the conversations in 4a.

b Refer students to the conversations in 4a and, as a class, elicit which two phrases we use to order food.

> **Answers**
> 2 ✓ I'd like
> 4 ✓ I'll have

c ▶ 04.20 Individually, students put the words in the correct order. Play the recording for students to listen and check. Check answers as a class. Drill the sentences.

> **Answers**
> 1 I'd like salad for my appetizer.
> 2 I'll have spaghetti for my entrée.
> 3 I'd like chicken curry with rice.

5 PRONUNCIATION Word groups

a ▶ 04.21 Play the first sentence, and highlight the break between the word groups for students. Then, play the rest of the recording for students to listen and mark where the new word groups start. They check in pairs. Check answers as a class. You may wish to teach the word *raw* (not cooked).

> **Answers**
> 2 And I'll have steak tacos || for my entrée.
> 3 I'd like cucumber salad || for my appetizer.

b ▶ 04.21 Point out the underlined words in the sentences in 5a. Play the recording again. Highlight the main stresses for students by beating the rhythm with your hand to show where the stresses fall.

c ▶ 04.22 Play the recording for students to listen and mark where the new word groups start. Check answers by copying the text onto the board and asking students to mark the word groups. Drill the text before students work in pairs in 5d.

> **Answers**
> For my appetizer, || I'll have tomato soup. || And then I'd like a cheeseburger || for my entrée. || And I'll have some fries || with my burger.

d 💬 In pairs, students practice saying the text in 5c. Monitor and help as necessary.

6 CONVERSATION SKILLS
Changing what you say

a Ask students to read the sentences from the conversation, and underline the phrases Emily uses to change what she wants to say. Check answers as a class.

> **Answers**
> 1 Maybe not.
> 2 No, wait.

b ▶ 04.23 Individually, students complete the sentences. Play the recording for students to listen and check. Check answers as a class.

> **Answers**
> 1 not
> 2 wait

7 SPEAKING

a 💬 Put students into small groups, and tell them to decide together on one more appetizer and one more entrée for the menu. Students may well add the word *steak* to the menu. If so, be prepared to feed in the question *How would you like your steak?* and the answers *rare*, *medium*, and *well done*.

- Drill some of the key phrases students will need to complete the task in 7b before they start. Try focusing on the main stress in each phrase first before adding the other words, e.g., *table* – *Can we have a* – *Can we have a table* – *window* – *by the* – *by the window* / *Can we have a table by the window?*

- Once students are confident with the phrases, ask them to repeat them back to you. Then, give them a new word so that they have to repeat each phrase immediately with a slight change, e.g., Students: *Can we have a table by the window?* Teacher: *door.* Students: *Can we have a table by the door?* Other phrases that work well with this type of substitution drill include: *I'd like the fried fish, please.* (Teacher: *chicken salad*), *And I'll have the vegetable pie for my main course.* (Teacher: *spaghetti with tomato sauce*), *Would you like rice with that?* (Teacher: *potatoes*).

b 💬🗨 Read the instructions with the students. Remind students to use the phrases in 6a when they change what they say. Monitor, but don't interrupt fluency unless students make mistakes with the content of this lesson.

⊕ ADDITIONAL MATERIALS

Workbook 4C

Photocopiable activities: Pronunciation 4C

Unit Progress Test

4D SKILLS FOR WRITING

Next, decide on your menu

At the end of this lesson, students will be able to:

- understand people talking about cooking
- understand information on a blog about learning how to cook
- make the order of items in a written text clear
- write a blog post about something they know how to do and explain how to do it better

💡 OPTIONAL LEAD-IN

Ask students to look at pictures a–d. Write on the board: *cheese, chicken, chocolate, fish, ice cream, lemon, pasta, pie, sauce, tomatoes, vegetables.* Organize students into pairs or small groups to decide what the ingredients of each of the four dishes are. Invite pairs or small groups to share their ideas with the class before students talk about the questions in 1a *(dish a: chocolate, ice cream, pie; dish b: cheese, pasta, sauce, tomatoes; dish c: water, chicken, vegetables; dish d: fish, lemon, tomatoes).*

1 SPEAKING AND LISTENING

a 💬🗨 Read the questions with students, then put them into pairs or small groups to ask and answer the questions together. Monitor and allow time for all students to share their ideas.

b ▶ 04.24 Play the recording for students to listen for general meaning and underline the correct answers. Students check in pairs. Check answers as a class. If you wish, elicit the names of the four dishes and write them on the board (dish a: *pear cake with chocolate sauce*; dish b: *spaghetti with tomato and mushroom sauce*; dish c: *vegetable soup*; dish d: *grilled fish with lemon sauce*).

Answers

Name	Talks about		
Jake	himself	a bad cook	picture b
Rosa	her husband	a good cook	picture c
Johanna	herself	a good cook	picture d
Marco	his mother	a good cook	picture a

Audioscript

JAKE I'm really bad at cooking. I eat a lot of fast food and frozen meals. I'm OK at making pasta – usually spaghetti with sauce. The one sauce I make is tomato and mushroom. It's not very fancy, but I like it! So, I eat a lot of pasta because it's easy to make.

ROSA My husband's a great cook, and he does all the cooking at home. He can look in our fridge and find some vegetables and cheese and then make a dish from it that's wonderful to eat, like a vegetable soup. I don't know how he does it. But I'm lucky to have a husband like that!

JOHANNA My friends say I'm a good cook. I'm not sure about that, but I definitely enjoy cooking. I think it's fun to try new dishes, and I certainly like eating the things I make! Tonight, I want to try a new fish dish. First, you grill the fish, then you make a lemon sauce. I think it'll go well with a bean salad I like to make.

MARCO My mother is a fantastic cook. But isn't everyone's mother a fantastic cook?! I eat everything she makes, and I always want more. I really, really like the cakes and cookies she makes. My favorite is her pear cake – I love eating it warm with chocolate sauce.

c ▶ 04.24 Students listen to the recording again for specific details and answer the questions. They then compare in pairs. Check answers as a class.

Answers
1 Marco
2 Jake
3 Rosa
4 Johanna

d Individually, students think of someone they know who's a good cook and take notes. Monitor and help with vocabulary if necessary.

> ↻ **LOA TIP** ELICITING
>
> • Students close their books. In order to elicit similar questions to those in the speech balloons in 1e and other questions which students might find useful in 1e, write sentences on the board about a person you know who's a good cook, e.g., *My brother is a good cook. He makes great fish tacos. He's a good cook because he always finds new and unusual recipes. He watches Aarón Sánchez on TV every week.*
>
> • Point to the sentences on the board, and elicit possible questions from the class, e.g., *Who do you know who's a good cook? What does he/she make? Why is he/she a good cook? Does he/she watch cooking shows?* Write these questions on the board. Students then open their books and refer to the questions on the board during 1e.

e 💬🗩 In pairs, students ask and answer questions about a good cook they know. Monitor, but don't interrupt fluency. Ask some students to tell the class about the person their partner talked about, and make sure they are using the third person *-s* form correctly.

> ♀ **FAST FINISHERS**
>
> Ask fast finishers to write sentences about the people their partners told them about, e.g., *Ahmed's sister is a great cook. She makes fantastic cakes and cookies.*

2 READING

a Point to the picture on SB p. 46 and say: *This is Jake.* Tell students they should only read the text *Jake Cooks!* They then work individually, answering the question. Check the answer as a class.

Answer
b people who want to learn how to cook

b Tell students to read the second part of the text, *My food − shared!*, and answer the question. Check the answer as a class. Ask students: *What kind of text is this?* (a blog). Then ask: *Do you write a blog?* to find out if anyone in the class has their own blog.

Answer
b planning a dinner

c Students read *My food − shared!* again in detail. Individually, students decide if the sentences are true or false. When checking answers, ask students to correct the false sentences.

Answers
1 T
2 T
3 F (It's too hard to try new dishes.)
4 F (Call or text to invite your friends and agree on a night that's good for everyone.)
5 T

> ♀ **EXTRA ACTIVITY**
>
> Ask students to read both texts again and answer Questions 1−5:
> 1 *Is Jake a good cook?* (No, he's not.)
> 2 *Who sometimes helps Jake?* (his family and friends)
> 3 *How many people does Jake usually invite?* (four)
> 4 *Does Jake always call his friends to invite them to dinner?* (No, he calls or texts them.)
> 5 *Why does Jake prefer Saturday or Sunday for cooking dinner?* (He has all day to prepare.)

d 💬🗩 Discuss the questions as a class. Encourage students to justify their answers as much as possible.

3 WRITING SKILLS
Making the order clear

a Books closed. Write on the board: *… , think about how many people you want to invite.* and *… , call or text to invite your friends.* Point to the blank in the first sentence, and ask: *Do you remember this word?* Write *First* on the board in the sentence. Repeat the process with the second sentence, and write *Next* on the board in the sentence. Ask students: *What kind of words are these?* Elicit *words to make the order clear.* If you wish, introduce the term *sequencing words.*

Answers
After that; Finally

b Answer the questions as a class. Check that students understand that *after that, next,* and *then* mean the same in this context.

Answers
We can replace *next* and *after that* with *then*.
We use a comma after these phrases.

> 📖 **LANGUAGE NOTES**
>
> There are many ways to indicate sequence in a written text (e.g., the simple past and the past perfect; connectors like *when/ while*), but at this level, students need some words to use as "flags" in their writing. For this reason, basic sequencing words are presented in the simplest possible way. *First* is used for the first item; *after that, next,* and *then* are presented as synonyms for the next items; and *finally* is used for the last item. Most of the verbs in the model texts are imperatives, which also helps to keep the text as grammatically simple as possible and will allow students to focus their attention on the sequencing words.

c Individually, students read the sentences and put them in the correct order. Students then check in pairs. Check answers as a class.

> **Answers**
> 2 Leave the beans ...
> 3 Put lemon and oil ...
> 4 Add salt and pepper ...

d Read the example sentence with the students. Check that they understand that more than one answer may be possible for each sentence. Students then add the words to the sentences in 3c. Check answers as a class and clarify that in sentences 2–4, the sequencing words can be used in any order.

> **Answers**
> 1 First, cook the beans in hot water with a little salt.
> 2 After that / Next / Then, leave the beans until they are warm.
> 3 After that / Next / Then, put lemon and oil on the warm beans – not too much.
> 4 After that / Next / Then, add salt and pepper and mix everything together.
> 5 Finally, place the bean salad in a nice bowl and serve your guests.

♀ FAST FINISHERS

Ask fast finishers to write simple instructions for another recipe using the five sequencing words.

---

4 WRITING

a Read the questions with the class. Students work individually to plan their blogs. Monitor and help with vocabulary, and give students ideas if necessary.

b Students write their blogs, working individually. Remind students to use sequencing words to make the order clear. If you're short on time, this exercise can be completed for homework. Students could then bring their blogs to the next class.

c In pairs, students switch blogs and check their partner's work. Tell them to check that their partners have used the sequencing words correctly. They then give each other feedback. If they made any mistakes with the sequencing words or in other areas, they prepare a second draft of their blogs before giving them to you for correction.

⊕ ADDITIONAL MATERIALS

Workbook 4D

UNIT 4
Review and extension

1 GRAMMAR

a Individually, students read the text and correct the words that are wrong. Check answers and spelling as a class by asking students to write the correct answers on the board.

Answers

1 ✓	6 ~~butters~~ butter
2 vegetable<u>s</u>	7 ✓
3 ~~fruits~~ fruit	8 egg<u>s</u>
4 potato<u>es</u>	9 ~~fishes~~ fish
5 ✓	10 ✓

b Students underline the correct words to complete the questions. Check answers as a class and drill the questions.

Answers

1 any	4 some
2 much	5 any
3 many	6 much

c Check that students understand that only one of the three options is possible. They then choose the correct answers, working individually. Check answers as a class.

Answers

1 c   2 b   3 b   4 a

2 VOCABULARY

a Students match the words with the categories, and then add one more word to each group. They compare in pairs. Check answers and students' suggested words as a class.

Answers

1 chicken, lamb
2 potato, carrot
3 pear, grape
4 cheese, yogurt
5 grilled, boiled

b Individually, students read the list and decide if the items are normal or unusual (or impossible). Check answers by drawing a checkmark and a cross on the board and asking individual students to come up and write the word on the board under the correct heading.

Answers

3 ✓	7 ✓
4 ✗	8 ✓
5 ✓	9 ✓
6 ✗	

> ♥ **FAST FINISHERS**
>
> Ask fast finishers to write down all the other normal combinations they can think of with *baked*, *boiled*, *fried*, *grilled*, and *roasted*.

3 WORDPOWER *like*

a Books closed. Ask more confident students the following questions: *Do you like cooking?*; *I have a tablet in my bag. Would you like to see it?*; *Do you have a favorite café? What's it like?* Don't worry if they have problems answering, but notice if students can understand the questions. Then, write the three questions with *like* on the board, leaving a blank in place of *like*. Point to the blanks, and ask: *What's this word?* Elicit *like* and write it in a circle above the questions. Students open their books and match the conversation with the picture. Check the answer as a class.

Answer

Conversation 2

b Students read the questions and match them with the questions in 3a. Check answers as a class.

Answers

1 What vegetables would you like?   3 What kind of fruit do you like?
2 Would you like to join us?

c Students read the sentences and match them with the questions in 3b. Check answers as a class.

Answers

a 3   b 2   c 1

d Individually, students match the words in bold with the meanings. Check answers as a class.

Answers

1 c   2 d   3 b   4 a

e As an example, elicit a question with *like* for the first situation from the class. Students work individually for the other situations. Monitor and point out errors for students to self-correct. They then compare ideas in pairs. Elicit possible questions and write them on the board.

Suggested answers

1 Would you like to come to the movies on Friday?
2 I'd like some apples, please.
3 Would you like cream and sugar?
4 What would you like for lunch/dinner?
5 What's New York like?

f  Put students into pairs to ask and answer the questions from 3e. As you monitor, don't interrupt fluency, but note mistakes with *like* and the auxiliaries *would* and *do*. After the activity, write these on the board and ask students to correct them.

> ♥ **EXTRA ACTIVITY**
>
> Ask students questions with *like* and talk about them as a class, e.g., *Would you like to try Japanese/Russian/Mexican food? Why/ Why not?*; *What food from your country do you like? What food from your country don't you like? Why?*; *Are you like your parents? Are your children like you? In what ways?*; *What's it like to study in this class?*

>> Photocopiable activities: Wordpower 4

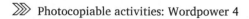

> **LOA TIP** ELICITING
>
> Students look back through the unit, think about what they've studied, and decide how well they did. Students work on weak areas by using the appropriate sections of the Workbook and the Photocopiable activities.

UNIT OBJECTIVES

At the end of this unit, students will be able to:

- understand information, texts, and conversations about towns and cities, homes and furniture, and neighborhoods
- ask for and give information about places in a town or city
- describe their home and talk about their furniture
- understand conversations in which people give directions and ask for and give directions themselves
- use simple phrases to check what other people say
- write a description of their neighborhood

UNIT CONTENTS

G GRAMMAR
- *there is / there are*
- Possessive pronouns and possessive *'s*

V VOCABULARY
- Places in a city: *apartment, bridge, building, café, church, concert hall, downtown, fitness center, hotel, park, police station, post office, restaurant, river, square, stadium, street, subway station, theater*
- Furniture: *armchair, bookcase, couch, curtains, dresser, lamp, mirror, nightstand, sink, stove, wardrobe, washing machine*
- Linking ideas with *and, but,* and *so*
- Wordpower: Prepositions of place: *across from, at the end of, behind, between, in, in front of, next to, on, on the corner of*

P PRONUNCIATION
- Words that end in /s/ and /z/
- Sound and spelling: /b/ and /p/
- Sound and spelling: vowels before *r*
- Sentence stress

C COMMUNICATION SKILLS
- Talking about where you live and the things you like in your town or city
- Asking and answering questions about what there is in a town or city
- Describing the furniture in the different rooms in your home
- Using appropriate phrases to check what other people say
- Asking for and giving directions
- Asking and answering questions about your neighborhood
- Writing a description of your neighborhood

GETTING STARTED

♀ OPTIONAL LEAD-IN

Books closed. Write these questions on the board: *What's your home like? Is it big or small? Who do you live with? Where's your home? Do you like it? Why / Why not? Would you like to live somewhere else? Where?* Put students into pairs or small groups to discuss the questions. Monitor and praise students who are able to express their ideas, even if their English isn't perfect.

Students may show each other pictures of their homes on their cell phones if they have them. Ask students to open their books and look at the picture. Ask: *Would you like to live here?* Elicit a short reaction from the class.

a ⌨ Give students one minute to read the ideas and decide which they think are true before talking about the picture as a class.

🌐 CULTURE NOTES

This picture shows an abandoned cabin in Colorado in the U.S.

b ⌨ Read the questions and the ideas with the students, and check that they understand the vocabulary. Organize students into pairs to discuss reasons why this is a good or bad place for a home. Ask students for their ideas about what a "good home" is and to share any other ideas they have. Help with vocabulary and pronunciation, but don't interrupt fluency.

♀ EXTRA ACTIVITY

Ask students to discuss the good and bad aspects of some specific homes in the area where you're teaching. Give them three contrasting real locations, giving the names of a place or street if possible, e.g., a big house in a small town up in the mountains, a small apartment in the town/city near your school, a beach house on the coast. Organize students into pairs or small groups to discuss their ideas. Ask all students to share their ideas.

Exercises **a** and **b** can be prepared as homework before this lesson to give students time to look up unfamiliar vocabulary. Ask students to look at the picture and to prepare their answers to the questions as homework to talk about in the next class.

5A | THERE AREN'T ANY PARKS OR SQUARES

At the end of this lesson, students will be able to:
- read and understand a text about a town
- use a lexical set of places in a city correctly
- use affirmative, negative, question, and short answer forms of *there is / there are*
- ask for and give information about places in a town or city

 OPTIONAL LEAD-IN

Give students the chance to learn something more about you. Organize students into pairs or small groups to brainstorm things they would like to ask you about where you come from, e.g., *Where do you come from? Is it a good place for a home? Why / Why not? Does your town/city have a lot of cafés / a fitness center / a theater? What are the bad things about where you live?*, etc. Monitor, and point out errors for students to self-correct.

Students take turns asking you their questions. Encourage them to ask additional questions if they wish.

1 READING

a Discuss the question as a class, and write students' ideas on the board. If you used the optional lead-in, you might like to ask students which picture they think is most like the place where you come from. Don't check answers at this point.

📖 **VOCABULARY SUPPORT**

unusual (A2) – different in a way that is surprising or interesting

roof (A2) – the covering over the top of a building

tunnel (B1) – a long passage under or through the ground

b Students read the text quickly and check their answers to 1a. Check the answer as a class. If you wish, give students information from Culture Notes below.

Answer
Everything is in one building; you get there through a tunnel.

🌍 **CULTURE NOTES**

Whittier is a very remote town; it can only be reached by ocean or by a one-lane tunnel that is closed at night and in which traffic can run in only one direction. Around 80% of the town's residents live in one building, and the building houses services such as a grocery store and even a bed and breakfast. All tenants also have access to small storage areas under the main building to store the things they can't fit in their apartments.

c Tell students to read the text again in detail. Individually, students answer the questions. Encourage students to guess the meaning of any new words from the context. Check answers as a class.

Answers
1 No
2 No
3 Yes
4 Yes
5 No
6 No

 EXTRA ACTIVITY

Ask students to read the text again and answer Questions 1–5: *1 Do people live in other places in the town?* (Yes, they do.) *2 Do people work in the main building* (Yes, they do.) *3 How long is the tunnel to Whittier?* (3 km) *4 How often do cars pass through the tunnel?* (once every hour) *5 What happens if you want to leave Whittier at 11 p.m.?* (You can't leave. You have to wait until the next morning.)

d In pairs, students talk about if they would like to visit or live in Whittier. Ask all students to share their ideas. Encourage students to justify their answers as much as possible.

2 VOCABULARY Places in a city

a Elicit the first two or three examples with the class. Students then underline the places in the text and identify the ones they can see in the pictures. Check answers as a class. Drill each word.

Answers
Buildings or in buildings:
building, store, church, police station, hospital, apartment, office, college, university, school, café
Outside:
street, park, square (*also* street café)

b ≫ 🔊 05.01–05.02 Students complete the exercises in Vocabulary Focus 5A on SB p. 164. Play the recording for students to check their answers to Exercise a and complete the Pronunciation activity. Monitor Exercise d, and check other answers as a class. Tell students to go back to SB p. 51.

Answers (Vocabulary Focus 5A SB p. 164)
a 1 concert hall   3 post office   5 police station
  2 stadium   4 fitness center   6 theater
b a stadium   d bridge   g square
  b park   e theater   h concert hall
  c post office   f police station   i fitness center
c The /p/ sounds in *park* and *post office* are produced with extra air.

c Students work in small groups, brainstorming more places in a city. Check answers by drawing three columns on the board and asking individual students to come up and write their words on the board. Drill each word.

Answers
Students' own answers

d In pairs, students tell each other about three places they like in their town or city. Monitor, but don't interrupt fluency unless students make mistakes with the vocabulary for places in a city. Ask some students to tell the class about the places they chose.

💡 **FAST FINISHERS**

Ask fast finishers to talk about places that they don't like in their towns or cities and to justify their answers as much as possible.

3 GRAMMAR *there is / there are*

a Books closed. Write on the board: *Affirmative or negative? Singular or plural?* Read the complete first sentence to the class (*There aren't any parks or squares.*) and point to the two questions on the board to elicit that it's negative and plural. Students open their books. Individually, they complete the sentences in the book. Check answers as a class.

Answers

1 There aren't	2 There's	3 There isn't	4 There are

b Point to the first column in the chart and say *affirmative,* then point to the second column and elicit *negative.* Point to the first row and say *singular,* then point to the second row and elicit *plural.* Students complete the chart. They then compare answers in pairs. Check answers as a class.

Answers

+	–
There*'s* a police station.	There *isn't* a normal road.
There *are* a few stores.	There *aren't* any street cafés.

c Students match the questions with the answers. They compare in pairs. Check answers as a class.

Answers

1 b	2 c	3 d	4 a

d Individually, students complete the chart. They compare answers in pairs. Check answers as a class. Ask students: *When do we use "there is"?* (affirmative, singular) and *When do we use "there are"?* (affirmative, plural) Repeat with the negative forms. Then ask: *How is the word order of questions with "there is" and "there are" different from the word order of affirmative or negative sentences with "there is" and "there are"?* (We put "is" or "are" first.)

Answers

Yes/No questions	Short answers	
Is there a good hotel in the town?	Yes, there *is.*	No, there *isn't.*
Are there any good restaurants?	Yes, *there are.*	No, *there aren't.*

👁 CAREFUL!

There are several common student mistakes with *there is / there are.* As students work through the Grammar Focus, make sure they understand that the verb and the noun must always agree, e.g., ~~There isn't many buildings~~ (Correct form = There **aren't** many buildings). Mistakes with agreement are particularly common before noncount nouns like *information,* e.g., ~~There are more informations ...~~ (Correct form = There **'s** more information ...) and with lists. Point out that we use a singular verb before a list if the first item is singular, e.g., ~~There are a river, a town square ...~~ (Correct form = There **is** a river, a town square, and a lot of cafés).

e ▷ **05.03** Students read the information in Grammar Focus 5A on SB p. 146. Play the recording where indicated, and ask students to listen and repeat. Students then complete the exercises. Check answers as a class, making sure students are using contractions where appropriate, ordering the words correctly, and distinguishing between singular and plural. Tell students to go back to SB p. 51.

Answers (Grammar Focus 5A SB p. 147)

a
2 There are six cafés.	6 There aren't many schools.
3 There isn't a stadium.	7 There's a river.
4 There are a lot of stores.	8 There are two bridges.
5 There are four parks.	

b 2 How many cafés are there in the town? There are six (cafés).
3 Is there a stadium in the town? No, there isn't.
4 Are there any stores in the town? Yes, there are a lot (of stores).
5 How many parks are there in the town? There are four (parks).
6 Is there a school in the town? Yes, there is (but there aren't many).
7 Is there a river in the town? Yes, there is.
8 How many bridges are there in the town? There are two (bridges).

c Students' own answers

💡 FAST FINISHERS

Ask fast finishers to write additional sentences about other things in their towns using *there is/isn't/are/aren't.*

f ▷ **05.04** **Pronunciation** Play the recording for students to answer the questions. Check that students hear the /s/ sound at the end of words like *markets* and the /z/ sound at the end of words like *there's.*

Answers

1 markets, parks, restaurants, maps   2 buildings, trains, cafés, there's

g ⟫ Divide the class into pairs, and assign A and B roles. Student As read the instructions and look at the picture on SB p. 131 and Student Bs read the instructions and look at the picture on SB p. 132. Students then ask and answer questions to find the six differences. Tell students to go back to SB p. 51.

4 SPEAKING

a ▷ **05.05** Point to the picture, and ask students: *Is Mexico City a good place to visit? Why / Why not?* Individually, students complete the conversation. Play the recording for students to listen and check. Check answers as a class.

Answers

1 There are	4 there are	7 Is there
2 there are	5 Are there	8 there isn't
3 Are there	6 there are	9 there are

🔄 LOA TIP DRILLING

- Practice the conversation in 4a as a split-class choral drill. Divide the class in half down the middle, and tell the group on your left that they are "Tom" and the group on your right that they are "Gabriela." Drill Tom's first question with the group on the left and Gabriela's response with the group on the right. Then, put the two pieces together with the groups asking and answering the first question all together. Repeat the process until students can perform the whole conversation without you having to model the lines for them.

- Pay particular attention to the pronunciation of *there is / there are* and the vocabulary for places in a city.

b 💬 Organize students into pairs, and then put pairs together to make groups of four. Assign Pair A and Pair B roles. Ask each group to choose a town or city and to follow the instructions. Monitor and help as necessary.

c 💬 In their groups of four, students role-play the conversation. Monitor, but don't interrupt fluency unless students make mistakes with the content of this lesson. Students may switch roles and repeat the activity with a different town or city.

💡 **EXTRA ACTIVITY**

To consolidate work on places in a city and *there is / there are*, ask students to produce a written conversation between two people about a famous tourist city in their country using the conversation in 4a as a model. They can use their ideas from 4b and 4c or choose a different town or city.

If you and your students have the technology available, students could work in pairs and record their conversations. Then, instead of giving you a written script, they can give you an audio recording to correct.

⊕ **ADDITIONAL MATERIAL**

Workbook 5A

Photocopiable activities: Grammar 5A, Vocabulary 5A, Pronunciation 5A

5B | WHOSE COUCH IS THAT?

At the end of this lesson, students will be able to:

- use a lexical set of furniture correctly
- understand a conversation in which people talk about the furniture in their home
- use possessive pronouns and possessive 's
- describe their home and talk about their furniture

💡 **OPTIONAL LEAD-IN**

Books closed. Draw a simple floor plan of your home on the board or of a fictional house/apartment if you prefer. Draw a bed in the bedroom(s), a television in the living room, a shower in the bathroom, and a stove in the kitchen, leaving room to draw other items of furniture in each room as taught in 1c below. Point to the different rooms on the floor plan, and ask students: *What room is this?* Elicit and label the rooms. If you wish, tell students a little more about your home as you elicit the name of each room, e.g., *I cook our meals here. It's really nice because there's a park outside and I can hear the birds.*

1 VOCABULARY Furniture

a 💬 Students discuss the questions in pairs or small groups. Invite students to share their ideas with the class.

b Students read the advertisement quickly and find out who the store is for. You may wish to pre-teach the words in the Vocabulary Support box. Check the answer as a class and ask students: *Do you know any stores like this?*

> **Answer**
> b people who don't want to spend too much money on furniture

📖 **VOCABULARY SUPPORT**

classic (B2) – something that people like and that doesn't change over time

crazy (A2) – different, strange, or unusual; in this context, in a positive way

quality (B1) – the way something is made; it can be good or bad

c Individually, students match the words with the pictures. Check answers as a class. Drill each word. If you used the optional lead-in, you could now go back and add the furniture in your home to the floor plan on the board with labels. Use *there is / there are* and tell students what you're drawing as you go along, e.g., *In the living room, there's a couch here, and there are two armchairs there. In the kitchen, there's a sink here*, etc.

> **Answers**
> a armchair
> b stove
> c nightstand
> d curtains
> e bookcase
> f mirror
> g washing machine
> h wardrobe
> i sink
> j lamp
> k couch
> l dresser

💡 **FAST FINISHERS**

Ask fast finishers to brainstorm other things that you typically find in a house, e.g., *bathtub, carpet, dishwasher*, etc.

d ▶ 05.06 **Pronunciation** Play the recording for students to listen and decide which letters in bold have the same sounds. Check answers as a class.

> **Answers**
> 1, 3, and 6 have the same sound.
> 2, 4, and 5 have the same sound.

e Answer the questions as a class. Drill the words in 1d and *floor, nurse, verb,* and *store.*

> **Answers**
> floor – wardrobe, door, your
> nurse – furniture, curtains, her
> verb – furniture, curtains, her
> store – wardrobe, door, your

f Give students a few minutes to prepare and write notes about the furniture in the room they're in now. Monitor and help as necessary.

g 💬 In pairs, students compare their lists. Monitor and check they're using *there is / there are* and the vocabulary from this lesson correctly.

2 LISTENING

a 💬 Discuss the questions as a class. Encourage students to justify their ideas as much as possible, e.g., *My favorite room is my living room because there's a comfortable couch and I have a big TV there.*

b ▶ 05.07 Play the recording for students to listen for general meaning and identify which rooms Jim shows Eva. Check answers as a class.

> **Answers**
> b the living room   d the bedroom

Audioscript

JIM So, what do you think of this room?

EVA Mmm … Nice and big. I love that armchair.

J Yes, it's … interesting.

E Is it yours?

J No, it's David's. He's my roommate.

E I love it. That mirror over there. Is that Mom and Dad's?

J Well, yes, but really it's mine now.

E Well, no it isn't. It comes from my old room. It's really mine.

J Are you sure? I don't remember it in your room. Well, it's Mom and Dad's, not ours.

E But it comes from my old room at their place.

J Yes, well, anyway – let's take a look at another room. … So, this is my favorite room, of course.

E Beautiful – it's nice and light and clean.

J And it's a good size.

E Whose dresser is that? Is it Mom and Dad's?

J Yeah, it's theirs. It's from home. They said I can use it.

E But that's from their bedroom.

J They got a new one.

E So it's all our parents' furniture in here?

J Well … I guess … some of it. The bed's mine.

E Are you sure?

c ▶ 05.07 Students listen to the recording again for specific details and write down the furniture they talk about in each room. Students compare in pairs. Check answers as a class.

> **Answers**
> Room 1: armchair, mirror
> Room 2: dresser, bed

d Elicit the answer to the question from the entire class.

> **Answer**
> She thinks most of it isn't Jim's.

3 GRAMMAR
Possessive pronouns and possessive *'s*

a ▶ 05.08 Books closed. Show the students your book, and say: *This is my book.* Borrow a pen from a student, point to him/her, and say to the class: *This is his/her pen.* Finally, point to a backpack and ask the student nearest to it: *Is this your backpack?* Write the three sentences on the board, and circle the possessive adjectives. Ask students: *What are the other possessive adjectives?* Elicit *its, our, their.* Students open their books. Explain that this section is about other ways to talk about possession. Students then look at the conversation and complete it with words from the box. Play the recording for students to listen and check. Check answers as a class.

> **Answers**
> 1 yours
> 2 David's
> 3 Mom and Dad's
> 4 mine

b Individually, students decide which sentences are correct. Check answers as a class.

> **Answers**
> 3 ✓ It's Jim's apartment.
> 6 ✓ It's my parents' apartment.

c Students look at the question and the example answers. Then, answer the questions as a class.

> **Answers**
> 1 No, we don't.
> 2 b is better.

d Elicit the first answer from the class. Students then complete the sentences with the words in the box. Check answers as a class. Ask students: *Which possessive adjective in sentences 1–5 ("my," "your," etc.) is the same as the possessive pronoun in the answers?* (his).

Answers
1 mine
2 yours
3 hers
4 theirs
5 his

⊙ CAREFUL!

Emphasize for students the importance of using possessive adjectives (especially *my, your*) and possessive pronouns (especially *mine, yours*) correctly, e.g., ~~This is mine house.~~ (Correct form = This is **my** house.); ~~Is this yours bedroom?~~ (Correct form = Is this **your** bedroom?); ~~It's my!~~ (Correct form = Don't take that book. It's **mine**!).

Highlight that the possessive *'s* can cause problems even for native speakers when writing. Make sure students avoid using the possessive *'s* where it shouldn't be used, e.g., ~~I always go to the fitness' center ...~~ (Correct form = I always go to the **fitness** center on Saturdays). Make sure they don't use it instead of plurals, e.g., ~~There are a lot of café's and restaurant's ...~~ (Correct form = There are a lot of **cafés** and **restaurants** here).

e ≫ ▶05.09–05.11 Students read the information in Grammar Focus 5B on SB p. 146. Play the recording where indicated, and ask students to listen and repeat. Students then complete the exercises. Check answers as a class, making sure students put apostrophes in the correct position and distinguish between possessive adjectives and possessive pronouns. After students complete the Grammar Focus activities, ask them: *Is talking about possession easy or difficult?* Elicit an indication of their confidence level. Tell students to go back to SB p. 53.

Answers (Grammar Focus 5B SB p. 147)
a 2 hers   3 theirs   4 his   5 ours   6 yours
b 2 It's   4 parents'   6 Whose   8 your
    3 Our   5 mine   7 Anita's
c What's (C – is) your brother's name (P); he's in my class (C – is); you're Paul's sister (P); That's right. (C – is);
My name's Nadia. (C – is); What's your name? (C – is); I'm Alexis. (C - am); It's nice (C – is)

⊙ FAST FINISHERS

Ask fast finishers to look around the classroom at other objects and write sentences about them similar to the sentences in Exercise a, e.g., *It's that man's bag., They're her boots.,* etc.

f ▶05.12 Individually, students complete the text about Antonio's apartment with the words in the box. Play the recording for students to listen and check. Check answers as a class.

Answers
1 mine   5 mine
2 parents'   6 mother's
3 sister's   7 yours
4 hers   8 mine

⊙ EXTRA ACTIVITY

Play a memory game (see p. 153) with students. Ask each student to choose one personal object from their bag that they don't mind sharing with the class and lending you for a few minutes. They then take turns giving you their objects. Say clearly what each person is giving you, e.g., *This is Sara's pencil, This is Pablo's notebook,* and show it to the class before putting each object out of sight, either in a bag or a box, or simply behind your desk. Don't allow students to take notes at this point.

When you have collected one object from each student, organize students into pairs and give them three minutes to write down the objects you have, e.g., *Sara's pencil, Pablo's notebook.* Get answers by asking students: *What objects do I have?* or *What objects are in the bag/box?* Elicit answers with *You have ...* or *There's ....* As you take each object out and return it to its owner, confirm whose it is by asking: *Is this yours?* If there are any objects students are unsure about, ask the class questions like *Is it his or is it hers?* or *Whose is this?* Pairs win one point for every object they remembered correctly. The pair with the most points wins.

4 SPEAKING

a Give students a few minutes to write their sentences, using Antonio's words in 3f to help them. Point out errors for students to self-correct.

b 💬 Students work in pairs, reading their sentences to each other and trying to remember the information. Don't allow students to take notes.

c 💬 Students try to remember what their partner said about their home. Monitor, but don't interrupt fluency unless students make mistakes with possessive adjectives, possessive pronouns, or *'s.*

⊕ ADDITIONAL MATERIAL

Workbook 5B

Photocopiable activities: Grammar 5B, Vocabulary 5B

5C EVERYDAY ENGLISH

Is there a theater near here?

At the end of this lesson, students will be able to:
- understand conversations in which people talk about where things are and give directions
- use appropriate phrases to check what other people say
- use appropriate phrases to ask for and give directions
- identify the stressed words when we give directions
- maintain a conversation in which they ask for and give a friend directions

♀ OPTIONAL LEAD-IN

Show students a tourist map of the town (or project a map app onto the board). Invite them to point to different places and make sentences using *This is / That is,* etc. and the places, e.g., *This is the fitness center.*

1 LISTENING

a 💬📱 Read the questions and look at pictures a and b with the class. Elicit ideas from students and write them on the board.

b ▶05.13 Play Part 1 of the audio recording for students to check their answers to 1a. Check answers as a class.

> **Answers**
> 1 a a theater
> 2 They don't know how to get to the theater.

> **Audioscript (Part 1)**
> **LANDON** Come on, Jess. The show's about to start. We can't be late.
> **JESS** Do you know where you're going, Landon? Want to look at my phone?
> **L** No, thanks. I have a great sense of direction. It's this way.
> **J** Are you sure?
> **L** I think so.
> **J** OK, but this street sign says we're on Bedford Street, and my phone says we want Park Road.
> **L** Why? The theater is on South Street.
> **J** Are you positive it's on South Street?
> **L** Yes.
> **J** OK, and South Street is off Park Road.
> **L** Can I look at your phone?
> **J** What about your great sense of direction?

c ▶05.13 Students listen again for specific details. Play Part 1 of the audio recording again for students to choose the correct answers. Check answers as a class.

> **Answers**
> 1 b Park Road
> 2 a off Park Road
> 3 b late

2 CONVERSATION SKILLS

Checking what other people say

a ▶05.14 Individually, students read the sentences and answer the questions. They check in pairs. Check answers as a class. Drill the questions as they appear in the Student's Book, and then drill them again reversing *sure* and *positive.*

> **Answers**
> 1 Yes, they are.
> 2 b She wants to check something with Landon.

3 LISTENING

a 💬📱 Individually, students read the ideas and choose what they usually do when they are lost. Don't check answers at this point.

b ▶05.15 Play Part 2 of the audio recording for students to check their answer to 3a. Check the answer as a class.

> **Answer**
> Students' own answers (Jess and Landon ask someone for help to find the theater.)

> **Audioscript (Part 2)**
> **JESS** My phone shows there's a theater on the corner of Park Road and South Street.
> **LANDON** But we're on Henrietta Street.
> **J** Let's ask this guy. Excuse me, sir. Is there a theater near here?
> **MAN** A theater? Yes. There's a theater just down the block. It's just about 50 meters or so.
> **L** Thanks very much. Let's go.

c ▶05.15 Students listen again for specific details. Play Part 2 of the audio recording again for students to decide if the sentences are true or false. When checking answers, ask students to correct the false sentence.

> **Answers**
> 1 T
> 2 F (The man on the street says there's a theater about 50 meters away.)

d 💬📱 In pairs, students look at picture c and guess what the problem is. Elicit ideas from students and check that they understand that Landon and Jess still can't find the theater.

e ▶05.16 Play Part 3 of the audio recording for students to answer the questions. Check answers as a class.

> **Answers**
> 1 No, they don't.
> 2 Yes, she does.

> **Audioscript (Part 3)**
> **JESS** Are you positive this is the right theater?
> **LANDON** I think so... but I'm not sure. The directions said South Street.
> **J** This is Henrietta Street, not South Street.
> **L** Excuse me, ma'am. Can you tell us how to get to South Street?
> **W** Sure. Go that way, then turn right at the corner.
> **L** Onto King Street?
> **W** That's right. Then go about 100 meters on King Street until you come to Park Road.
> **L** OK.
> **W** Turn right onto Park Road, go straight ahead about a block, and South Street is on your left.
> **J** Great, thanks.
> **L** That's exactly where our car is parked. Told you I have a great sense of direction.

f ▶05.16 Students listen again for specific details. Play Part 3 of the audio recording again for students to follow the woman's directions and write *South Street* on the map. Check the answer as a class.

Answer

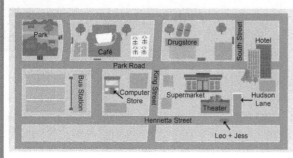

4 USEFUL LANGUAGE
Asking for and giving directions

a Individually, students complete the questions with the words in the box. They then compare in pairs. Check answers as a class.

Answers

1 there	3 How
2 tell	4 Where

b Students change the words in bold. Check that they understand that the meaning may change when they change the words in bold for words in the box that fit the sentences. Check answers as a class. Ask students: *Which sentence has the same meaning when you change the word?* (sentence 1).

Answers

1 Go straight <u>on</u> this road.
2 The bank is on your <u>left</u>.
3 Go straight until you come to <u>a supermarket</u>.

c Complete the exercise as a class. Ask students: *When do we use "at"?* (with a specific place) and *When do we use "onto"?* (with the name of a road or street).

Answers

1 b   2 a

d ▶05.17 Individually, students complete the conversation. They then check in pairs. Play the recording for students to listen and check. Check answers as a class.

Answers

1 can	5 go
2 get	6 come
3 go	7 turn
4 turn	8 go

e 💬 In pairs, students practice the conversation, taking turns being A and B. Monitor and correct students' pronunciation as appropriate.

💡 FAST FINISHERS

Ask fast finishers to change the place, the street names, and the distance in the conversation and practice it again.

5 PRONUNCIATION   Sentence stress

a ▶05.18 Play the recording and highlight the stressed words for students.

b Answer the question as a class.

Answer
2 the words for direction and place

💡 EXTRA ACTIVITY

Give students some additional practice in identifying stressed words in directions. Write sentences 1–5 on the board (without the underlining) and ask students to decide which words are stressed: *1 Go <u>right</u> at the <u>subway</u> <u>station</u>. 2 Then, <u>turn</u> <u>left</u> onto <u>Park</u> <u>Road</u>. 3 Go <u>straight</u> until you come to the <u>supermarket</u>. 4 <u>Downtown</u> is about a <u>hundred</u> <u>meters</u> away. 5 Go <u>down</u> <u>South</u> <u>Street</u> and the <u>café</u> is on your <u>right</u>.*

Check answers by asking individual students to come up and underline the stressed words on the board.

c 💬 In pairs, students ask for and give directions using the conversation in 4d as a model, the phrases from 4, and the map in 3f.

🔄 LOA TIP CONCEPT CHECKING

- Monitor 5c and note any mistakes students make with the phrases for asking for and giving directions. Also note any pronunciation problems students are having. After the activity, write the mistakes on the board for students to correct, and provide additional help with difficult pronunciation. Remind students that they should avoid repeating the same mistakes in the next exercise.

- In 6a, monitor, but don't interrupt fluency. However, if students repeat mistakes that you drew their attention to after 5c, try to catch their eyes discreetly so that they can correct their mistakes.

6 SPEAKING

a ≫ Divide the class into pairs, and assign A and B roles. Student As read the first card on SB p. 131 and Student Bs read the first card on SB p. 132. Students then role-play the conversation. Students then read the second card and role-play the second situation.

💡 FAST FINISHERS

Ask fast finishers to use the map on SB p. 55, invent additional situations like those on the cards, and practice them together.

⊕ ADDITIONAL MATERIAL

Workbook 5C

Photocopiable activities: Pronunciation 5C

Unit Progress Test

5D

SKILLS FOR WRITING It isn't very exciting, but it's a nice place to live

At the end of this lesson, students will be able to:

- understand people talking about what makes a good neighborhood
- understand a website in which people describe their neighborhood
- link their ideas with *and*, *but*, and *so*
- write a description of their neighborhood

💡 OPTIONAL LEAD-IN

Books closed. Write *In this neighborhood …* on the board, and explain that *neighborhood* means the area of a town or city where people live or work. Draw two columns underneath headed *there is / are* and *there isn't / aren't*. Put students into pairs or small groups to think of as many complete sentences beginning with *there is / are* or *there isn't / aren't* as possible, e.g., *There's a very big fitness center.*, *There aren't any cafés or restaurants.*, etc. Monitor and point out any errors in spelling for students to self-correct. Check that students are only giving facts in their sentences and aren't giving opinions about what makes a good or bad neighborhood. Ask students to share their ideas with the class and collate them on the board.

1 SPEAKING AND LISTENING

a Individually, students check four things they think make a good neighborhood.

b 💬🗨 In pairs or small groups, students compare their ideas in 1a. If you used the optional lead-in, students could also discuss if they think any of the things on the board are essential to a good neighborhood. Ask students to share their answers, plus any others they have for what makes a good neighborhood.

c ▶ 05.19 Play the recording for students to listen for general meaning and answer the questions. Check answers as a class.

Answers
1 a Sara b Lexie c Jacob
2 Students' own answers

Audioscript

LEXIE For me, it's very important for a neighborhood to have lots of restaurants. I like an exciting neighborhood. I like going out and meeting my friends a lot. I like a neighborhood with lots of people in it. My neighborhood is pretty exciting. There's also a museum near my house, so I'm really lucky.

JACOB I think a good neighborhood is a quiet one. So, for example, no clubs or restaurants – nothing like that – only houses. My neighborhood isn't like that – there are lots of stores and restaurants. And there's a movie theater close to my house – I really don't like that.

SARA I think a good neighborhood is a new one – new houses and stores. I also like a neighborhood that is close to a shopping mall. It's good to have lots of new stores near you – it's interesting. In my neighborhood, there aren't any stores – there's only a park. It's a little boring.

d ▶ 05.19 Students listen to the recording again for specific details and write the places in the box next to the people. They compare in pairs. Check answers as a class.

Answers
1 Lexie –restaurants, museum
2 Jacob – clubs, restaurants, houses, stores, movie theater
3 Sara – houses, stores, shopping mall, park

Lexie likes her neighborhood. Jacob and Sara don't like their neighborhoods.

e 💬🗨 In pairs, students ask and answer questions about their neighborhoods. Monitor, but don't interrupt fluency.

💡 FAST FINISHERS

Ask fast finishers to talk about the best neighborhoods in their town/city and discuss anything that those neighborhoods have that their own doesn't.

2 READING

a Tell students they should read only *Around the World Online*. They then work individually, answering the questions. Check answers as a class.

Answers
1 You can read about different neighborhoods from around the world.
2 It wants you to write about your neighborhood.

b Tell students to read *In My Neighborhood* on SB p. 57. Check the answer as a class.

Answer
No, they don't.

c Individually, students decide if the sentences are about Hannah or Marianna. They compare in pairs. Check answers as a class. When checking answers, elicit which words or sentences in the texts helped students decide.

Answers
1 Hannah   3 Hannah   5 Marianna
2 Marianna   4 Hannah

💡 EXTRA ACTIVITY

Ask students to read the complete text again and decide if sentences 1–5 are true or false:

1 *The places on the website are all popular with tourists.* (F – They are places tourists never go.)
2 *It's very difficult for Marianna to get downtown.* (F – It's easy because there's a subway station near her house.)
3 *Marianna is happy in her neighborhood.* (T)
4 *Hannah often goes downtown.* (F – She doesn't go downtown very often.)
5 *Hannah lives in a modern part of the city.* (F – There are some beautiful old buildings there.)

3 WRITING SKILLS
Linking ideas with *and*, *but*, and *so*

a Books closed. Write sentences 1–3 on the board, and give students one minute to decide which word in each sentence connects two ideas. Check answers as a class. Ask students: *What kind of words are these?* Elicit *words to connect ideas.* Introduce the term *linking words*.

Answers

1 and   2 but   3 so

b Complete the rules as a class. Show students how *and* adds an extra idea by pointing to the first part of the first sentence on the board and saying *one idea* and then pointing to the second part and saying *an extra idea.* Repeat the process with *but* (first part: *one idea*; second part: *a different idea*) and *so* (first part: *one idea*; second part: *the result of the idea*).

Answers

1 *and*   2 *but*   3 *so*

📖 VOCABULARY SUPPORT

Linking words don't generally cause students any serious problems. However, some students might not be clear about the difference between *so* and *because*.

So is used to introduce a result, whereas *because* is used to introduce a cause. Most sentences with *so* can be rewritten with *because* and vice versa, e.g., *There aren't any restaurants or bars in the area, so it's nice and quiet. / It's nice and quiet because there aren't any restaurants or bars in the area.*

c Students read *In My Neighborhood* again and underline examples of *and*, *but*, and *so*. They then compare answers in pairs. Check answers by eliciting the number of examples of each word in the text (*and* 4, *but* 3, *so* 5).

Answers

… downtown, <u>but</u> everything I need …
… in my neighborhood, <u>so</u> I don't go …
… the art museum, <u>and</u> there are some …
… old buildings here, <u>so</u> it's an interesting part …
… restaurants in my neighborhood, <u>and</u> my apartment's …
… their food, <u>and</u> it's cheap, <u>so</u> I eat …
… from downtown, <u>but</u> there's a …
… near my house, <u>so</u> it's easy …
… in the area, <u>so</u> it's nice …
… isn't very exciting, <u>but</u> it's a nice …

💡 EXTRA ACTIVITY

Write incomplete sentences 1–6 on the board, and ask students to complete them with *and, but,* and *so*: *1 There's a café … a restaurant on our street.* (and) *2 It's very expensive here, … a lot of houses are empty.* (so) *3 There's a river in my town, … there is only one bridge.* (but) *4 My office is close to my apartment, … I can walk to work.* (so) *5 There are two movie theaters here, … there isn't a concert hall.* (but) *6 We have everything here – a post office, a supermarket, … a fitness center.* (and).

d Students work individually, putting the linking words in the correct place in each sentence. They then check in pairs. Check answers as a class.

Answers

1 … downtown, <u>and</u> there are a lot …
2 … near the university, <u>so</u> there are a lot …
3 … during the day, <u>but</u> it's nice and quiet …
4 … near a park, <u>and</u> there's a small river …
5 … very friendly, <u>so</u> it's a nice place to live, <u>but</u> sometimes it's …
6 … in my neighborhood, <u>but</u> I don't like coffee, <u>so</u> I never …

💡 FAST FINISHERS

Ask fast finishers to look for sentences that contain the linking words in the conversation in 4a on SB p. 51.

4 WRITING

a Students work individually to plan their descriptions. Monitor and help with vocabulary and give students ideas if necessary.

🔄 LOA TIP ELICITING

- If students need more support or ideas, collate words and phrases for the four categories in 4a on the board after students have had a few minutes to start taking notes. They will then be able to borrow ideas from each other and use a wider range of vocabulary in their writing. As you monitor 4a, notice if students think of interesting words or phrases. Then, during a class brainstorming stage, say things like: *Jo has a very good word meaning "very big" – can you guess what it is?* Elicit ideas from the class before asking the student to share the word he/she originally thought of.

- Take some of the ideas from the brainstorming stage, and ask students to connect them with *and, but,* and *so*. For example, point to *downtown* and *expensive* on the board and ask students to connect them, e.g., *Tina lives downtown, so it's expensive.*

b Students write about their neighborhoods, working individually. Remind students to use *and, but,* and *so* to link their ideas. If you're short on time, this exercise can be completed for homework. Students could then bring their descriptions to the next class.

c In pairs, students switch descriptions and check their partner's work. Tell them to check that their partner has used linking words correctly. They then give each other feedback. If they've made any mistakes with the linking words, or mistakes in other areas, they prepare a second draft of their description before giving it to you for correction.

d After correcting students' work, ask them to make a final version to share with other students. Display the descriptions around the classroom for other students to read and decide which neighborhood is the most different from their own. Alternatively, if you and your students have the technology available, set up a class blog where students can post their written work and comment on each other's texts.

⊕ ADDITIONAL MATERIAL

Workbook 5D

UNIT 5
Review and extension

1 GRAMMAR

a Individually, students complete the conversation. Check answers as a class, and check that students are using contractions where appropriate. Drill the conversation.

Answers

1 There's	5 is there
2 Is there	6 there's
3 there isn't	7 are there
4 there's	8 There are

b Highlight the example, and complete the second item with the class. Check that students understand that they can use possessive pronouns or possessive *'s*. Monitor and help as necessary. Point out errors for students to self-correct. Check answers as a class.

Answers

2 mine 3 ours 4 hers 5 his 6 his 7 mine 8 yours

2 VOCABULARY

a Students underline the correct words in each sentence. Check answers as a class.

Answers

1 apartment	4 park
2 hotel	5 bridge
3 restaurants; square	6 station

b Students complete the sentences, working individually. Check answers and spelling as a class by asking students to write the correct answers on the board.

Answers

1 mirror	5 washing machine
2 sink	6 stove
3 dresser	7 nightstand
4 couch	

> **♀ FAST FINISHERS**
>
> Ask fast finishers to write similar sentences about things you find in a room with the other vocabulary from Lesson 5B, e.g., *armchair, bookcase, curtains,* and *lamp.*

3 WORDPOWER Prepositions of place

a Tell students to close their books. Ask a student to come to the front of the class and help you. Stand immediately behind your student, and ask the class: *Where am I?* Elicit: *You're behind (student's name).* Then, to elicit *in front of,* change places with the student, and ask: *Now where am I?* To elicit *behind* again, stay in the same position, and ask: *Where's (student's name)?* To elicit *next to,* stand alongside the student, and ask: *Where am I now?* Thank the student, and ask him/her to sit down. Say *behind, in front of,* and *next to,* and ask: *What kind of words are these?* Elicit *prepositions of place.* Students then look at the map in their book and find the cafés. Check answers as a class.

Answers

1 d 2 f 3 a 4 e 5 b 6 c

b Highlight the underlined examples in 3a. Then, to elicit *behind,* point behind you, and ask: *What was this preposition?* Repeat the process with *in front of* and *next to.* Students underline the other prepositions of place in 3a. Check answers as a class.

Answers

2 <u>On the corner of</u> Newton Street and Green Street.
3 ... just <u>in front of</u> the train station.
4 ... <u>on</u> Green Street, <u>between</u> the market and the library.
5 <u>At the end of</u> Newton Street, <u>across from</u> the station.
6 It's <u>on</u> a small street <u>behind</u> Rex Theaters.

c Individually, students add one word to each sentence to make them correct. They then check in pairs. Check answers as a class.

Answers

1 ... next <u>to</u> the supermarket.
2 ... ATM <u>at</u> the end of ...
3 ... in front <u>of</u> the bank ...
4 ... bookstore <u>on</u> the corner of ...

> **⊙ CAREFUL!**
>
> Students often confuse the prepositions of place *in* and *on* with the prepositions of movement *into* and *onto*. Check that students understand that when we use a preposition with a verb indicating movement, we usually use a preposition of movement, e.g., *Turn right <u>onto</u> King Street.* However, when the verb doesn't indicate movement, we usually use a preposition of place, e.g., *The café is <u>on</u> Park Road.* In 3d, students are not being asked to describe movement, only position, and should therefore only be using prepositions of place.

d 💬 Describe one of the places yourself as an example before students work in pairs to describe and guess a place. Monitor and listen for correct use of the prepositions of place. Point out errors for students to self-correct.

> **♀ EXTRA ACTIVITY**
>
> Ask students to work in pairs and assign A and B roles. Student A is a tourist downtown. Student B lives in the city and knows it well. Ask them to decide exactly where the conversation takes place before they start. Student A stops Student B and asks for directions to a common tourist destination, e.g., a museum. Student B then gives directions. Students then change roles and role-play a second conversation.

≫ Photocopiable activities: Wordpower 5

> **◐ LOA REVIEW YOUR PROGRESS**
>
> Students look back through the unit, think about what they've studied, and decide how well they did. Students work on weak areas by using the appropriate sections of the Workbook and the Photocopiable activities.

⟲ UNIT OBJECTIVES

At the end of this unit, students will be able to:

- understand information, texts, and conversations and exchange information about family, family relationships, life events, and childhood hobbies
- talk about their family tree
- leave a voicemail message
- make a phone call and use appropriate phrases to ask for someone and ask someone to wait
- write the life story of someone in their family

UNIT CONTENTS

G GRAMMAR
- Simple past: *be*
- Simple past: affirmative

V VOCABULARY
- Family: *aunt, brother, cousin, grandchildren, granddaughter, grandfather, grandmother, grandparents, grandson, parents, sister, uncle*
- Years and dates
- Simple past irregular verbs: *ate, became, bought, brought, came, cost, cut, did, found, gave, got, lost, made, read, sold, spent, thought, told, went, won*
- Linking ideas in the past: *in, when, later*
- Wordpower: *go – go by (bus/train), go home, go out, go shopping, go to (a party / the movies)*

P PRONUNCIATION
- /ʌ/ in family words: **cou**sin, grandm**o**ther, grands**o**n, **u**ncle
- *was* and *were* in sentences, questions, and short answers
- Simple past *-ed* endings
- Sound and spelling: *a* (/æ/, /ɔ/, /ɪ/, /eɪ/)

C COMMUNICATION SKILLS
- Talking about families and asking and answering questions about a family tree
- Talking about your hobbies when you were young
- Leaving a voicemail message and making a phone call
- Using appropriate phrases when asking someone to wait
- Writing the life story of someone in your family

GETTING STARTED

♀ OPTIONAL LEAD-IN

Use a "live listening" to review the basic family words that students will need in Getting Started, i.e., *grandfather, grandmother, grandparents, mother, father, parents, brother, sister, son, daughter,* and *children*. Be careful not to include other family words as these will be introduced in Lesson 6A. Tell students about your immediate family, e.g., *My family all lives in the same neighborhood in Chicago. My mother is a dentist and my father is a photographer, and they live in a small house downtown. I have one brother and one sister. My sister lives in an apartment near my parents, and my brother lives with Mom and Dad. They don't have any children, but I do. I have two sons and a daughter.* Students listen and note any information about you that they didn't know before. They then open their books and compare your family with the family in the picture.

a 💬🎙 Give students one minute to think about their answers to the questions before talking about the picture as a class.

b 💬🎙 Read the questions and check that students understand that they should talk about a family they know well, but not their own family. In pairs, they ask and answer the questions. Ask students to share their ideas. You may also tell the class about a family you know.

♀ EXTRA ACTIVITY

Put students into pairs or small groups to prepare a description of a famous family. Check that each pair/group writes about a different family, and monitor and help with vocabulary if necessary. Finally, ask pairs/groups to read their descriptions to the class, but to say *beep* instead of the people's names. Their classmates listen and identify the missing names of the famous people.

Exercises **a** and **b** can be prepared as homework before this lesson to give students time to look up unfamiliar vocabulary. Ask students to look at the picture and to prepare their answers to the questions as homework to talk about in the next class.

6A | SHE WAS A DOCTOR

At the end of this lesson, students will be able to:
- use a lexical set of family words correctly
- understand a conversation in which people talk about family and life events
- use the affirmative and negative simple past forms of *be*
- talk about years and dates correctly
- ask and answer questions about their family tree

💡 OPTIONAL LEAD-IN

Review possessive *'s* by writing *your father's mother* on the board. If students are still encountering problems with the possessive *'s*, write *the mother of your father* in parentheses after it. Ask: *Who is your father's mother?* Elicit *your grandmother*. Dictate phrases 1–6 and ask students to write them down, paying attention to the possessive *'s*. Point out that they don't need to write the answers, only the phrase itself: *1 your mother's sister 2 your daughter's son 3 your sister's mother and father 4 your parents' parents 5 your father's brother 6 your mother's brother's son*. Check the phrases by writing them on the board. Don't elicit the answers to phrases 1–6 until 1b below (*1 aunt 2 grandson 3 parents 4 grandparents 5 uncle 6 cousin*).

1 VOCABULARY Family

a 💬 Give students a few minutes to prepare and write notes about their parents, brothers, and sisters. Put students into pairs or small groups to talk about the people in their families.

b ▶ 06.01 If you used the optional lead-in, ask students to match the definitions on the board with the family words before you start this exercise. Point to the illustration, and ask students: *What's this in English?* Elicit/Teach *family tree*. Ask *Where's Greg?* for students to find him on the family tree. You may also wish to pre-teach the phrase *be born* (come out of a mother's body and start to live). Play the recording for students to listen for general meaning and check the people Greg talks about. Check answers as a class.

> **Answers**
> Greg mentions all of the people except *granddaughter* and *grandson*.

Audioscript

FRIEND What's this, Greg?

GREG Oh, it's my family tree. You can download a special program to make it.

F That's really good. So are these your grandparents?

G Yes. Sally, she's my grandmother, and that's my grandfather, Nathan. They're my mother's parents. They have two children – a son and a daughter. Michael's their son, he's my uncle, and they have a daughter, Mary – that's my mother.

F And so Alejandro's your father?

G Yeah. They have three children – there's me, there's my brother, Rick, and my sister, Lily – that's her there.

F Alejandro's a Spanish name, right?

G Yeah, it is. His parents, Pablo and Lucia, are from Honduras, but he was born here in New York. And his brother Fernando was born here, too – so Fernando's my other uncle.

F Right. So, he's married, too.

G Yes, you can see here – he's married to my aunt Alice. And they have two children, Hugo and Olivia. They're my cousins.

F So your grandparents from Honduras have five grandchildren?

G Yes, they're very happy about it!

c Individually, students choose words from 1b to complete the family tree. They compare in pairs. Don't check answers at this point.

d ▶ 06.01 Students listen to the recording again for specific details. They check their answers to 1c and identify which people in the family were born in Honduras. Check answers as a class.

> **Answers**
> **1c** Pablo: grandfather; Lucia: grandmother; Nathan: grandfather; Sally: grandmother; Alice: aunt; Fernando: uncle; Michael: uncle; Hugo: cousin; Olivia: cousin; Lily: sister; Rick: brother
> **1d** Fernando and Alejandro's parents were born in Honduras.

e ▶ 06.02 **Pronunciation** Play the recording for students to check the family words that have the same sound as *but* /ʌ/. Check answers as a class and drill each word.

> **Answers**
> ✓ cousin, ✓ uncle, ✓ grandmother, ✓ grandson

f Look at the example as a class and check that students understand that Greg, Lily, and Rick could all say the sentence. Individually, students identify who can say the other sentences. They then check in pairs. Check answers as a class.

> **Answers**
> 2 Greg, Lily, Rick
> 3 Pablo, Lucia, Nathan, Sally
> 4 Hugo, Olivia
> 5 Sally, Nathan

💡 EXTRA ACTIVITY

Tell the class about your extended family, using the vocabulary from this section. If you used the optional lead-in on the Getting Started page, elicit information about your immediate family that students already know. Draw that part of your family tree on the board and write each person's name. Then, continue talking about your extended family. If you didn't use the optional lead-in, start by describing your immediate family before talking about your more extended family. Name the people and talk about their relationships to you and/or to other people in your family, e.g., *My mom's name's Jennifer, and she's Barbara and Frank's daughter, so they are my grandparents.* Complete your family tree on the board, write the names of the people, and elicit their relationships to you and/or to other people from the class as you go along.

g 💬 Individually, students draw their family trees. Monitor and help with any other vocabulary students might need to talk about their families, e.g., *stepmother/ father/brother/sister, half brother/sister, only child*, etc.

Then, put students into pairs to show each other their family trees and talk about their families. Monitor and point out errors for students to self-correct.

2 LISTENING

a ▶**06.03** Look at the timeline with students and show them how it runs from left to right. Students listen to the recording again for specific details and complete the timeline. Check answers as a class.

Answers
1943 2 (grandfather was born)
1945 6 (grandmother was born)
1964 5 (went to college)
1968 1 (got married)
1969 4 (photographer took the picture)
2010 3 (grandmother retired from her job)

> 📖 **VOCABULARY SUPPORT**
>
> *alive* (B1) – something that is living and not dead
>
> *romantic* (B1) – relating to love or a close loving relationship

Audioscript

FRIEND So, your grandparents are all still alive?

GREG Yes, they are.

F Your grandmother, Sally – she looks nice and friendly.

G She's great, yes, but she's very old now, of course. Look – here's a photo of her with my grandfather. I think this is from about 1969, yeah, you can see that she was a very beautiful woman.

F Oh, yes. She really was. So, when was she born?

G Um, she was born in 1945, I think, I'm not sure. But I know her birthday's July 16th. And my grandfather was born two years before her.

F Mmm... interesting.

G Yes, my grandmother's a really interesting woman. She was a doctor at the university hospital in Chicago for about 40 years, I think, until she was 65. So, until 2010.

F Until 2010? Wow, that's a long time. What about your grandfather? Was he a doctor, too?

G Yes, he was. And they were high school classmates.

F Really? Were they in the same class?

G No, they weren't. They weren't even friends in high school. But then when they were college students, they met again and of course then things were very different ....

F Ah, right.

G Yes, in fact they got married in 1968. They were still students.

F Oh, so in this photo she was ... 24 and just married?

G Yes, that's right.

F Ah, that's so romantic.

3 GRAMMAR Simple past: *be*

a Books closed. Write on the board: *Greg's grandfather ... born in 1943 and his grandmother ... born in 1945.* Point to the blanks, and ask students: *What's this word?* Elicit *was* and say: *This is called the simple past. What's the verb?* Elicit *be.* Students then open their books and underline the correct word in each sentence. Check answers as a class.

Answers
1 are 2 isn't 3 was 4 were 5 weren't

b Complete the rules as a class. Then, ask students to circle all the examples of *n't* in 3a and tell them that the position of the apostrophe is important.

Answers
1 b the past
2 b *n't*

c Individually, students complete the chart. Check answers by copying the chart onto the board and asking individual students to come up and complete the sentences.

Answers

(+)	(–)
I was sick. She <u>was</u> a doctor.	I wasn't sick. He <u>wasn't</u> a teacher. He was a doctor.
We were classmates. They <u>were</u> friends in college.	No, we <u>weren't</u> in the same class. They <u>weren't</u> married yet in 1960.

> 🗣 **LOA TIP** CONCEPT CHECKING
>
> • Write the pronouns *I, you, he, she, it, we,* and *they* on the board and ask students: *With the simple present of "be," which forms are the same?* (the *you, we,* and *they* forms – they are all *are*). Ask: *What are the "I" and the "he/she/it" forms?* (*am* and *is*). Remind students of the affirmative contracted forms by showing them two fingers representing *I* and *am* and closing them up to illustrate *I'm.* Repeat the process with the other simple present forms.
>
> • Repeat the process with the simple past by asking: *With the simple past of "be," which forms are the same?* (the *you, we,* and *they* forms – they are all *were*). Elicit that the *I* and the *he/she/it* forms are also the same: *was.* Ask students: *Do we contract the simple past affirmative of the verb "be"?* (no) *What about negatives?* (yes). Show students three fingers representing *I, was,* and *not* and close up the second and third fingers to illustrate *I wasn't.* Repeat the process with the other negative simple past forms.

d ▶**06.04** Play the recording for students to complete the conversation. Check answers as a class. Make sure students understand that the verb is repeated in the question and the answer, although affirmative turns to negative in a negative answer.

Answers
1 Was   4 weren't
2 was   5 was
3 Were   6 was

> ⊙ **CAREFUL!**
>
> Since *be* has more forms than other verbs and uses different grammar, students are likely to make mistakes. Highlight the following typical errors: tense – this type of error may be obvious, e.g., ~~I am ...~~ (Correct form = *I **was** there yesterday*), but may sometimes cause misunderstandings, e.g., ~~My grandmother is ...~~ (Correct form = *My grandmother **was** very friendly.* Simple past = the grandmother is no longer alive); word order in questions, e.g., ~~Your whole family was ...~~ (Correct form = ***Was your whole family** at the party?*); subject/verb agreement, e.g., ~~My parents wasn't ...~~ (Correct form = *My parents **weren't** at home last night*); auxiliary verbs – students may incorrectly use *didn't* to form negatives, e.g., ~~It didn't expensive~~ (Correct form = *It **wasn't** expensive*).

68

e ▶ 06.05 Students read the information in Grammar Focus 6A on SB p. 148. Play the recording where indicated, and ask students to listen and repeat. Students then complete the exercises. Check answers as a class. After students complete the Grammar Focus activities, ask them: *Is the simple past with "be" easy or difficult?* Elicit an indication of their confidence level. Tell students to go back to SB p. 61.

> **Answers (Grammar Focus 6A SB p. 149)**
> **a** 2 were   4 wasn't   6 were   8 were
>   3 Weren't   5 were   7 Was
> **b** 2 They weren't friends.
>   3 **A** Was your grandfather rich? **B** No, he wasn't.
>   4 We were in school together.
>   5 It was a beautiful day.
>   6 My teacher's name was Miss Smith.
>   7 She wasn't at home.
>   8 There were 20 people in my class.
>   9 I wasn't tired.
>   10 **A** Were you happy? **B** Yes, I was.
> **c** 2 Was the movie good?
>   3 Were there a lot of people at the party?
>   4 What was your grandmother's name?
>   5 Were you at school yesterday?
>   6 Was there a pool at your hotel?

> ♀ **FAST FINISHERS**
>
> Ask fast finishers to look at the questions in Grammar Focus 6A Exercise c on p. 149 and to write short answers to the questions.

f ▶ 06.06 **Pronunciation** Play the recording for students to underline *was/were* when they are stressed. Check answers as a class.

> **Answers**
> 4 Was she a doctor? Yes, she <u>was</u>.

g Complete the rules as a class. Drill the sentences in 3f.

> **Answers**
> aren't; are

h Individually, students complete the questions. Check answers as a class. Drill the questions before students ask and answer them in 3i.

> **Answers**
> 1 were   2 was   3 was   4 Was

i 💬 In pairs, students ask and answer the questions. Monitor and correct students' pronunciation as appropriate.

4 VOCABULARY Years and dates

a ▶ 06.07 Play the recording for students to listen and answer the questions about years and dates. Check answers as a class. Ask students: *What's the date today?* and elicit the date, including the year, in the correct format.

> **Answers**
> 1 b nineteen forty-five
> 2 c both a and b are correct
> 3 We add -*th* to 16.

b ▶ 06.08 Play the recording for students to listen and check the years they hear. Check answers as a class.

> **Answers**
> ✓ 2012   ✓ 1930   ✓ 1989   ✓ 2001

> ♀ **EXTRA ACTIVITY**
>
> Play bingo (see p. 152) with the class. Write 25 different years on the board in numerals. Ask students to draw a bingo grid with four columns and two rows. Tell them to complete it with eight years from the board. Read aloud the years on the board in random order, making a note of the ones you read aloud. The first student to complete his/her card calls out "Bingo!" After you have checked that his/her card is correct, that student is the winner.

c ▶ 06.09–06.10 Students complete the exercises in Vocabulary Focus 6A on SB p. 165. Play the recording for students to check their answers to Exercises a and b and to repeat the months in Exercise a. Monitor Exercise e and check other answers as a class. Tell students to go back to SB p. 61.

> **Answers (Vocabulary Focus 6A SB p. 165)**
> **a** January, February, March, April, May, June, July, August, September, October, November, December
> **b** 1 in   2 on   3 in
> **c** 2 February <u>twenty-first</u> (February 21)
>   3 <u>two thousand and</u> seven (2007)
>   4 July <u>seventh</u> (July 7)
>   5 <u>nineteen</u> ninety-eight (1998)
>   6 December <u>second</u> (December 2)

5 SPEAKING

a Students write more detailed notes about the people in their family trees from 1g. Give students any jobs that they don't know how to say in English.

b 💬 In pairs, students ask and answer questions about their family trees. Monitor and listen for correct use of family vocabulary, years, dates, and *be*.

> ♀ **FAST FINISHERS**
>
> Ask fast finishers to cover their family trees. They work in pairs and take turns trying to draw each other's family tree as their partner says each person's name and their relationship to other people in the family tree.

> ⊕ **ADDITIONAL MATERIAL**
>
> Workbook 6A
>
> Photocopiable activities: Grammar 6A, Vocabulary 6A, Pronunciation 6A

I PLAYED ANYTHING AND EVERYTHING

At the end of this lesson, students will be able to:

- read and understand a text about the life of Steve Jobs
- use the simple past affirmative form of regular verbs
- understand people talking about childhood hobbies
- use a lexical set of simple past irregular verbs correctly
- talk about a childhood hobby in some detail

♀ OPTIONAL LEAD-IN

Books closed. Put students into pairs. On the board, draw a simple complete outline of an apple with a short stem sticking out the top. Ask students: *What's the first thing you think of when you see this ... ?* Tell pairs to discuss their ideas. Don't ask them to share their ideas at this point. Write these years on the board: *1666, 1968, 2007.* Ask students: *How are these years connected with apples?* Students discuss the question in their pairs. Invite students to share their ideas with the class. (*1666 – an apple falls on Isaac Newton's head and he understands gravity; 1968 – The Beatles start Apple Records; 2007 – Apple Inc. sells the first iPhone.*) Find out how many students in the class first thought of the fruit when they saw the apple, and ask students if any of them thought of anything else, e.g., *Adam and Eve, Snow White, Johnny Appleseed,* etc.

📖 1 READING

a 💬 Look at the pictures, and discuss the answers to the questions as a class. You may give students information from Culture Notes below. Ask students: *Do you have any Apple products?*

🌍 CULTURE NOTES

Steve Jobs (1955–2011) is remembered as one of the great visionaries of the digital age. In fact, it was his friend Steve Wozniak who designed the first Apple computers, but it was Jobs who had an innate ability to know what people wanted to buy before they even knew it themselves, and he was one of the first people to see the enormous potential of home computing.

Jobs was fired from Apple in 1985 and used his fortune to take over Pixar Animation Studios, where he helped produce *Toy Story.* In his absence, Apple went from bad to worse, and in 1997 he returned to the company. In the following years, he is credited with creating some of the most innovative products in the history of personal computing, including the iMac, iPod, iPhone, and iPad. He was diagnosed with pancreatic cancer in 2003 and died in 2011. At the time of his death, his personal fortune was estimated at over $7 billion.

b 💬 Pre-teach the word *secret* (not known to many people, very private). In pairs, students talk about the ideas and choose one. Don't check the answer at this point.

c Pre-teach the phrase *be adopted* in the Vocabulary Support box (you may wish to wait until Exercise 1d to pre-teach the other words). Students read the text quickly and check their answer to 1b. Check the answer as a class.

Answer
2 He had a secret sister.

📖 VOCABULARY SUPPORT

be adopted (B2) – be legally taken as a child by people who are not your biological parents, but who make you part of their family

be worth (B1) – have a specific value in money

close (adj) (A2) – with a very good relationship and who know each other well

electronics (B2) – small pieces of technological equipment used inside things like computers, phones, etc.

d Students read the text again in detail. Individually, students put the events in the correct order. Encourage students to guess the meaning of any new words from the context. Check answers as a class.

Answers
1 d (Steve's birth parents couldn't keep him.)
2 f (Clara and Paul Jobs became Steve's parents.)
3 b (His sister Mona was born.)
4 a (Steve started a new hobby: electronics.)
5 c (Steve became friends with Steve Wozniak.)
6 h (Apple Computers began.)
7 g (The two Steves became very rich.)
8 e (Steve met his sister.)

♀ EXTRA ACTIVITY

Ask students to read the text again and decide if sentences 1–5 are true or false: *1 Most people don't know who Steve Jobs is.* (F – We all think we know Steve Jobs's story.) *2 Steve Jobs's real parents were born in 1955.* (F – Steve Jobs was born in 1955. His parents were college students at that time.) *3 There are lots of big technology companies near Mountain View in California.* (T) *4 In 1980, Apple Computers was worth $1.2 billion.* (T) *5 Steve's real mother, Mona, is now a famous writer.* (F – His sister, Mona, is now a famous writer.).

📝 2 GRAMMAR Simple past: affirmative

a Tell students to close their books. Write sentences 1–5 on the board (not the verbs in parentheses): *1 Steve's real parents ... not to keep their son.* (decided) *2 The Jobs family ... in California.* (lived) *3 The two Steves both ... electronics.* (loved) *4 In 1976, they ... Apple Computers.* (started) *5 They ... hard.* (worked). Ask students: *Are the sentences about the past, present, or future?* (past). Then ask: *Can you remember the verbs?* Put students into pairs or small groups to try and remember. Elicit the answers (in parentheses) from the class, making sure you pronounce the words correctly. Don't write the simple past forms on the board. Students open their books, look at the verbs, and find the simple past forms in the text. Check answers as a class.

Answers
1 worked   4 decided
2 started   5 loved
3 lived

b Ask students to look at the simple past forms of the verbs in 2a. Complete the rule as a class.

> **Answer**
> -ed or -d

c ▶️ 06.11 **Pronunciation** Play the recording for students to listen and identify which two verbs have an extra syllable in the past. Check answers as a class.

> **Answers**
> started; decided

d Say the two verbs from 2c that have an extra syllable, i.e., *start – started, decide – decided*, and complete the rule as a class.

> **Answer**
> /t/, /d/

e ▶️ 06.12 💬 Students work individually or in pairs and identify the simple past forms that have an extra syllable. Play the recording for students to listen and check. Check answers as a class. Drill the base and simple past forms of each verb.

> **Answers**
> hated; waited; wanted; needed

f Students look at the verbs and find the simple past forms in the text. Check answers as a class. Ask students: *Where can you find a list of irregular verbs in this book?* (on SB p. 129).

> **Answers**
> 1 had   2 found   3 made   4 became
> These verbs are irregular.

> 👁 **CAREFUL!**
>
> When using the simple past form of verbs other than *be*, students often use the base form where they should use the simple past, e.g., ~~Steve Jobs love …~~ (Correct form = *Steve Jobs* **loved** *his sister, Mona*) and may also use the simple past where they should use the present, e.g., ~~We can watched …~~ (Correct form = *We can* **watch** *the movie tomorrow*). They also often confuse specific verbs, particularly *had* and *got*, e.g., ~~I had …~~ (Correct form = *I* **got** *my first job in 2001*) and *did* and *had*, e.g., ~~I did …~~ (Correct form = *I* **had** *a great time*). Students may also make mistakes with word order in more complex sentences, e.g., ~~They started in 1976 Apple Computers~~ (Correct form = *They started* **Apple Computers in 1976**), or ~~To live with the Jobs family went Steve~~ (Correct form = **Steve went to live** *with the Jobs family*).

g ≫ ▶️ 06.13 Students read the information in Grammar Focus 6B on SB p. 148. Play the recording where indicated, and ask students to listen and repeat. Students then complete the exercises. Check answers as a class, making sure students refer to the Irregular Verbs list on SB p. 129 if necessary. Tell students to go back to SB p. 63.

> **Answers (Grammar Focus 6B SB p. 149)**
> **a** 1 R 3 I 5 R 7 R   9 R 11 I 13 R 15 I 17 R 19 R
>   2 I 4 I 6 R 8 I 10 I 12 R 14 R 16 I 18 I 20 I
> **b** 2 cooked   4 enjoyed   6 liked   8 played   10 worked
>   3 decided   5 finished   7 planned   9 tried
> **c** 2 became   4 told   6 wrote   8 went
>   3 found   5 won   7 bought   9 got
> **d** 2 ~~buyed~~ bought   4 ~~eated~~ ate   6 ~~dicide~~ decided
>   3 ~~liket~~ liked   5 ~~gotten~~ got

> 💡 **FAST FINISHERS**
>
> Ask fast finishers to test themselves on the irregular simple past verbs by covering the simple past columns in the verbs list on SB p. 129 and trying to remember the simple past forms and correct spelling.

3 LISTENING

a Individually, students check the hobbies they had as children. Ask them to share their answers with the whole class. Elicit other common hobbies and write them on the board. You may then wish to teach the word *childhood* (the part of your life when you're a child, not an adult).

b ▶️ 06.14 Play the recording for students to listen for general meaning and identify what Hannah's and Charlie's childhood hobbies were. Check answers as a class.

> **Answers**
> Hannah: sports
> Charlie: baking

> **Audioscript**
>
> **HANNAH** My childhood hobby was sports. I loved them. I played anything and everything: basketball, tennis, swimming, soccer. But I think my favorite was tennis – I played every summer. Every day of the week, I went to some kind of sports activity or game. My parents, poor things, spent all the time driving me to different activities and games and things like that. I never took a train or bus. I think it was really difficult for them! I don't play sports very much now – I don't have the time.
>
> **CHARLIE** My hobby when I was a child was kind of unusual, I think. I really loved sweet things – cakes, cookies – food like that. So, my hobby was baking. After school and on the weekends, I made cakes and cookies, and my friends came to my place and ate them. My parents bought all the things I needed. They told me it cost a lot, but they were always happy to eat the things I made. I still bake cookies and cakes now. My wife loves it because she never needs to bake anything.

c ▶️ 06.14 Students listen to the recording again and complete the notes. They compare in pairs. Check answers as a class.

> **Answers**
>
> | | Hannah | Charlie |
> |---|---|---|
> | hobby details | basketball, tennis, swimming, soccer | cakes, cookies |
> | parents' problem | They spent all their time driving her to activities and games. | It was expensive because they bought all the things he needed. |
> | now | She doesn't have time to play sports. | He still bakes and his wife loves it because she doesn't have to bake. |

4 VOCABULARY
Simple past irregular verbs

a Individually, students match the simple past forms in the box with the base forms. They check their answers by looking at the Irregular Verbs list on SB p. 129.

Answers
1 bought
2 ate
3 told
4 went
5 cost
6 spent
7 made
8 got
9 came

b ≫ ▶06.15–06.17 Students complete the exercises in Vocabulary Focus 6B on SB p. 165. Play the recording for students to check their answers to Exercises a and c and complete the Pronunciation activity. Monitor Exercise d. Tell students to go back to SB p. 63.

Answers (Vocabulary Focus 6B SB p. 165)

a
1 did	4 thought	7 lost	10 cut
2 read	5 brought	8 found	11 sold
3 gave	6 won	9 became	

b They sound different. The present *read* is pronounced /rid/. The past *read* is pronounced /red/.

c
| 1 won | 3 bought | 5 gave | 7 found out | 9 thought |
| 2 did | 4 sold | 6 read | 8 became | 10 cut |

♀ EXTRA ACTIVITY

Reinforce simple regular and irregular forms by playing a game of "tennis" (see p. 153). Demonstrate the activity by asking a stronger student to help you. Say the base form of a verb from this lesson, e.g., *spend,* and ask the student to respond with the simple past form, i.e., *spent.* The student continues with a different base form, and you respond with the simple past. For example: **A** *spend*; **B** *spent – become*; **A** *became – remember*; **B** *remembered*, etc. Check that students understand the game before playing in pairs. Tell them they should continue for as long as possible. If they make a mistake or pause for more than three seconds, they lose the game and start again.

c 💬📣 Put students into pairs or small groups to talk about the topics. Monitor, but don't interrupt fluency unless students make mistakes with the simple past forms.

5 SPEAKING

a ▶06.18 Individually, students complete the text. They then compare in pairs. Play the recording for students to listen and check. Check answers as a class.

Answers
1 liked
2 bought
3 started
4 had
5 listened
6 played

b Students write notes about hobbies they had when they were children.

↻ LOA TIP MONITORING

- Effective preparation in 5b is essential for effective task completion in 5c, so monitor the note-taking stage intensively. Make sure students aren't writing full sentences, and check that they know how to pronounce any difficult words. Students may also need specific words to talk about their hobbies, so be prepared to give them these and to model the correct pronunciation before the speaking stage.

- During the speaking stage, monitor for correct usage of any specific language you gave students during 5b. If students make mistakes with this, try to catch their eyes discreetly so that they can correct their mistakes. Also, note any mistakes with the simple past. After the activity, write these on the board and ask students to correct them.

c 💬📣 In pairs, students talk about their hobbies. Encourage them to ask each other questions to keep the conversation going.

♀ FAST FINISHERS

Ask fast finishers to talk about the hobbies of other people in their families, or any other people they know who have particularly unusual hobbies.

⊕ ADDITIONAL MATERIAL

Workbook 6B

Photocopiable activities: Grammar 6B, Vocabulary 6B, Pronunciation 6B

6C EVERYDAY ENGLISH

Can he call you back?

At the end of this lesson, students will be able to:

- understand voicemail messages and phone calls
- use appropriate phrases when leaving a voicemail message and asking for someone on the phone
- use appropriate phrases for asking someone to wait
- relate the letter *a* to the sounds /æ/, /ɔ/, /ɪ/, and /eɪ/
- make an informal phone call

💡 OPTIONAL LEAD-IN

When all students are in the classroom, glance quickly at your cell phone and say: *Oh sorry! I have a message.* Gesture for students to wait with an apologetic expression as you listen to the "message." As you listen, look bewildered, and then when you hang up say: *Sorry. It was my mom. I need to call her – one minute.*

Simulate making a phone call, gesture to students that they should listen, and pause at each "…" as if your mother was saying something to you, e.g., *Hi, Mom – it's me. … No, I'm at work. … Well, yes, but I'm a little busy right now. … OK, quickly. … What? … A penguin? … There's a penguin in your kitchen? … It's in the sink?* [roll your eyes as if your mother was talking nonsense] *… Well, I don't know how it got there. … No, Mom, I don't know what penguins eat! … Do you have any fish? … Look, I need to go. I have class now. … Talk to you later!*

Check that students understood the gist of the conversation by asking: *Who was the message from?* (your mother) and *What is the problem at home?* (There's a penguin in the sink in the kitchen!)

1 LISTENING

a 💬 Individually, students read the ideas and choose what they usually do when there's no answer. They then compare in pairs.

b ▶ 06.19 Play Part 1 of the audio recording for students to find out who Sofia calls. Check the answer as a class.

> **Answer**
> She calls her brother, Mateo.

Audioscript (Part 1)

MATEO "Hello…"	**M** "I can't answer your call right now. Please leave me a message."
SOFIA Mateo, it's Sofia. Where are you? You said—	
M "I can't answer your call right now. Please leave me a message."	**S** Mateo! It's Sofia. Your sister. You are in so much trouble! You promised to drive me to the airport this afternoon. Grandma arrives at 2:30. We need to pick her up and take her to Dad's house. We can't be late! Call me back – now.
S Come on, Mateo, answer your phone.	
M "Hello…"	
S Mateo? Is this you or your voicemail—	

c ▶ 06.19 Students listen again for specific details. Play Part 1 of the audio recording again for students to decide if the sentences are true or false. When checking answers, ask students to correct the false sentence.

> **Answers**
> 1 F (Mateo doesn't answer his phone.)
> 2 F (Sofia tells Mateo to call her back now.)

2 USEFUL LANGUAGE

Leaving a voicemail message

a Complete the first item as an example with the class. Individually, students read the sentences and decide who says them. Don't check answers at this point.

b ▶ 06.19 Play Part 1 of the audio recording again for students to check their answers to 2a. Check answers as a class.

> **Answers**
> 1 M   2 S   3 S   4 M   5 M

c ▶ 06.20 Individually, students complete the messages. Play the recording for students to listen and check. Check answers as a class.

> **Answers**
> 1 this
> 2 here
> 3 message
> 4 it's
> 5 back
> 6 call

📖 LANGUAGE NOTES

When identifying themselves on the phone, some students may say *I'm (name)* because saying *This is* or *It's* to introduce themselves may seem very unnatural. In English, until a caller has been clearly identified, we tend to speak in the third person on the phone, e.g., *Who's calling?* not *Who are you?* If students have problems understanding this, tell them that what we are really saying when we start a phone call is *This (voice that you can hear now) is Lisa('s voice)* or *It's Lisa('s voice that you can hear now)*.

🔄 LOA TIP DRILLING

- Drill the voicemail message and the caller's message before students work in pairs in 2d. Work on the messages in small chunks, e.g., *Hello, this is Alex. | Sorry, | I'm not here right now. | Please leave a message | and I'll call you later.* Repeat the chunks as many times as necessary, and make sure students can repeat each chunk correctly before putting them together.

- Pay particular attention to the intonation in the messages. To make them sound friendly, students should use a wide pitch range and be careful not to sound too flat. As you drill the messages, consider showing students the up-and-down movements, using hand gestures to give them a visual reference.

d 💬🎙 Tell students that they can now practice leaving a voicemail message. Check that students understand the dialogue map before they start. In pairs, students take turns giving their voicemail message and leaving a message for their partner. Monitor and praise students with a smile or a nod when they use the language from this section correctly.

> 💡 **EXTRA ACTIVITY**
>
> If you and your students have the technology available, ask them to make an audio recording of their voicemail messages to give to you to evaluate their pronunciation. Students could use their smartphones to do this, or any other recording device they have available, and then email you the recording.

3 LISTENING

a ▶️ 06.21 Read the events with the class. Students then work individually and put them in a logical order. Play Part 2 of the audio recording for students to listen and check. Check answers as a class.

> **Answers**
> 2 c (Chris answers the phone.)
> 3 e (Sofia tells Chris her message is important.)
> 4 a (Mateo beats his high score on a video game.)
> 5 d (Sofia talks to Mateo.)

> **Audioscript (Part 2)**
>
> **CHRIS** Hi, Sofia. This is Chris, Mateo's roommate.
> **SOFIA** Oh, hi Chris. Is Mateo there? Why did you answer his phone?
> **MATEO** Go! Go! Noooo!
> **C** He's here, but he's busy right now. He asked me to answer his phone because it rang so many times.
> **S** What's he doing? Please put him on the phone.
> **C** He can't talk now. Can he call you back?
> **S** Tell him it's important.
> **C** Um, OK. Mateo?
> **M** ARRRRGH! Oh oh oh oh oh oh…
> **S** What is going on?!
> **C** He just beat his high score on this video game. Here he is.
> **S** Are you kidding me?
> **M** Hey, Sof!
> **S** Mateo. I left you 14 messages.
> **M** You did? Oh, sorry, I was—
> **S** I know. Video game. High score. Congratulations.
> **M** Thanks!
> **S** Do you remember who promised to pick up Grandma at the airport this afternoon?
> **M** Dad.
> **S** That's—what?
> **M** Dad left a message. He got off work early and he's picking Grandma up at the airport.
> **S** Why didn't you tell me?
> **M** I was working on my—
> **S** High score. Right. OK, bye.
> **M** Bye, Sof.

b Individually, students answer the questions. If necessary, play Part 2 of the audio recording again. Check answers as a class.

> **Answers**
> 1 c 2 b 3 b 4 a

4 USEFUL LANGUAGE
Asking for someone on the phone

a ▶️ 06.21 Students look at Sofia's questions and Chris's answers and underline the correct words. Check answers by playing the beginning of Part 2 again and pausing each time Sofia and Chris say one of the sentences. Drill the questions and answers.

> **Answers**
> 1 there 2 here 3 back

b 💬🎙 Check that students understand the dialogue map before they start. Put them into pairs to practice making phone calls, each time asking for someone, and then asking him/her to call them back. Monitor and correct students' pronunciation as appropriate.

5 CONVERSATION SKILLS
Asking someone to wait

a Individually, students complete the conversation. They then check in pairs. Check answers as a class.

> **Answers**
> 1 wait
> 2 minute
> 3 Just
> 4 minute

b Answer the question as a class.

> **Answer**
> b "a short time"

c 💬🎙 If possible, put students into new pairs so they're not working with the same partner as in 4b. Students practice making phone calls again, but this time asking the person to wait a short time until the other person is available.

> 💡 **FAST FINISHERS**
>
> Ask fast finishers to invent different contexts for the call, e.g., *She went to get coffee*, *He's on the phone / his cell*, etc. Also, tell them to make polite conversation with the other caller while they wait, e.g., by talking about the weather.

6 PRONUNCIATION
Sound and spelling: *a*

a ▶️ 06.22 Play the recording and highlight the four possible sounds for the letter *a*.

> 📖 **LANGUAGE NOTES**
>
> This section introduces some of the most frequent sounds that correspond to the letter *a*: /æ/, /ɔ/, /ɪ/, and /eɪ/. Don't ask students to look for other examples of words with *a*, since they may well find words that contain the letter *a* but aren't pronounced with the four sounds being worked on.

b ▶️ 06.23 Students classify the words into four groups. Play the recording for students to listen and check. Check answers as a class. Ask students to repeat the words after the recording and practice the pronunciation.

> **Answers**
>
> | Sound 1 /æ/ | Sound 2 /ɔ/ | Sound 3 /ɪ/ | Sound 4 /eɪ/ |
> | --- | --- | --- | --- |
> | th**a**nks | c**a**ll | mess**a**ge | l**a**ter |
> | b**a**ck | t**a**lk | vill**a**ge | w**a**it |
> | bl**a**ck | t**a**ll | lugg**a**ge | voicem**a**il |
> | | sm**a**ll | | s**a**me |
> | | | | t**a**ble |

c 💬🗣 In pairs, students test each other on words that have the same sound. Monitor and correct students' pronunciation as appropriate.

7 SPEAKING

a ▶️06.24 Play the recording for students to listen and complete the phone conversation. Check answers as a class. Ask students: _Is this a formal or an informal conversation?_ (informal, especially the second part)

Answers

1 It's	3 message	5 call	7 It's
2 here	4 back	6 minute	8 called

b ≫ Divide the class into groups of three, and assign A, B, and C roles. Student As read the first card on SB p. 131, Student Bs read the first card on SB p. 132, and Student Cs read the first card on SB p. 130. Students then role-play the conversation. Monitor, but don't interrupt fluency unless students make mistakes with the content of this lesson. Students then read the second card and role-play the second situation, and then finally the third.

6D SKILLS FOR WRITING
Five months later, we got married

At the end of this lesson, students will be able to:

- understand someone talking about important events in their life
- understand a series of life events and put them in a logical order
- link ideas in the past using _in_, _when_, and _later_
- write the life story of a person in their family

1 LISTENING AND SPEAKING

a Individually, students write down two important years in their lives and take notes about what happened in each. Monitor and help with vocabulary, and give students ideas if necessary. Point out that, as students are going to tell a partner what happened in those years, they should choose something they are happy to share.

b 💬🗣 In pairs, students talk about their two important years. You may allow time for students to share their answers and ask students to tell the class about one of the important years in their lives.

c ▶️06.25 Point to the picture of Eva on SB p. 66 and say: _This is Eva. She's from Colombia._ Then, point to the list of events and years and tell students to match the phrases with the years in a logical order for Eva. Play the recording for students to listen for general meaning and check. Check answers as a class.

Answers

1992 d (was born)
2005 b (went to live in the U.S.)
2014 a (got a job as a teacher)
2017 e (met her husband)
2019 c (moved to Germany)

Audioscript

EVA OK, well, 1992 was a very important year for me. I was born that year! I was born in a small town in northern Colombia, near Cartagena. My whole family lived there – my parents, my grandparents, uncles, aunts, cousins, everyone. It's a very nice place, very hot, tropical. I really loved it. And then 2005 was a very important year. Everything changed. My parents moved to the U.S. My father got a job in Minnesota, so we went to live in the U.S. and I went to school there. I learned English pretty quickly. In 2014, I got my first job. I was an elementary school teacher. I taught young kids, six to ten years old. It was great. Then in 2017, I met Niko – he's my husband. He's German, but we met in the U.S., and then in 2019 I moved to Germany to be near him, and we got married. And then I found a job. I teach English to business people, so here I am today.

d ▶ 06.25 Students listen to the recording again for specific details and underline the correct answers. They compare in pairs. If necessary, play the recording again. Check answers as a class.

Answers
1 small
2 with her parents
3 young children
4 to be near Niko

e 💬 Students work individually and write two more important years. Put students into pairs, and tell them to try to guess what happened in the years their partner chose.

> **💡 FAST FINISHERS**
>
> Ask fast finishers to close their books. They write down everything they can remember about Eva from 1c and 1d before referring back to the Student's Book to check.

2 READING

a Point to the picture of George on SB p. 67, and explain that the timeline across the top of the page represents his life. Tell students to cover sentences a–f. In pairs, they look at the timeline, say the years, and talk about what they can see in the pictures. They then look at the sentences and put them in the correct order. Check answers as a class.

Answers
2 a
3 f
4 c
5 e
6 b

> **💡 FAST FINISHERS**
>
> Ask fast finishers to circle the verbs in sentences a–f, decide if they are regular or irregular, and then write the base form of each verb.

3 WRITING SKILLS
Linking ideas in the past

a Books closed. Write the first sentence on the board, leaving a blank in place of *and*. Point to the blank and ask students: *What's this word?* Elicit *and* and ask: *What other words can we use to link ideas?* Elicit *but* and *so* from the previous unit. Students then open their books and complete the second sentence. Check the answer as a class.

Answer
2 When

b Individually, students complete the three sentences. They then compare in pairs. Check answers and answer the final question as a class.

Answers
1 when
2 In
3 When
a *in*
b *when*

> **🔄 LOA TIP ELICITING**
>
> • Before students complete 3c, write possible endings to the seven sentences in random order on the board, but without including *in* or *when*, e.g., *1991, I was 19, I was a student*, etc. Include three distractors, which don't correspond to any of the sentences, to make a total of ten endings. Read the first sentence *I started school …* and point to the board. Elicit a sentence from the class using the ending and *in* or *when*.
>
> • As students complete each sentence orally, ask them to change the linking word so that they transform sentences with *in* to sentences with *when* and vice versa.

c As an example, complete the first sentence so that it's true for you. Students then work individually, completing the sentences. Monitor and check that students are completing the sentences with *in* or *when*, and point out errors for students to self-correct. Ask each student to tell the class one or two of their sentences.

Answers
Students' own answers

d Read sentence 1, and then elicit ideas from students to complete sentence 2 as a class.

Answer
2 later

e Write the sentences from 3d on the board, and circle the phrases *In 2010* and *A year later* to highlight how students should change the sentences. Students work individually, rewriting the underlined expressions with a time expression and *later*. Check answers as a class.

Answers
1 A year later / One year later
2 Five months later
3 Three years later

f Check that students understand that they should write two sentences, one with *in* and one with *later*. Monitor and point out errors for students to self-correct.

g 💬🔊 In pairs, students take turns reading aloud their sentences with *later*, stopping after *later* to see if their partner can guess how the sentence ends.

4 WRITING AND SPEAKING

a Students work individually to draw a timeline about someone in their family and add notes. Monitor and help with vocabulary, and give students ideas if necessary.

b Individually, students write the life story of their person using their notes. Check that students understand that they shouldn't include their relationship to the person or the person's name in the life story. Remind them to use linking words to connect their ideas. If you're short on time, this exercise can be completed for homework. Students could then bring their life stories to the next class.

c 💬🔊 In pairs, students switch their life stories and try to guess who the people are.

d Ask students to read each other's life stories again and check that their partner has used linking words correctly. They then give each other feedback. If they made any mistakes with the linking words or in any other areas, they prepare a second draft of the life story before giving it to you for correction.

UNIT 6
Review and extension

1 GRAMMAR

a Individually, students complete the conversation. Check answers as a class and check that students are using contractions where appropriate. Drill the conversation.

Answers
1 are	6 Was
2 'm	7 wasn't
3 Were	8 was
4 was	9 Is
5 wasn't	10 's

b Individually, students complete the text. They then check in pairs. Check answers as a class.

Answers
1 was	5 was
2 wanted	6 decided
3 loved	7 studied
4 had	8 found

c Complete the first blank as an example with the class. Check that students understand that they can use the simple present or the simple past, so they need to think carefully about the meaning. Check answers as a class.

Answers
1 stayed; cooked
2 went; had
3 plays; gets; got
4 spent; were; see

2 VOCABULARY

a Students complete the text with the correct family words. Check answers as a class, and then ask students to draw the family tree for the text to check that they have understood the meaning.

Answers
1 grandparents	4 aunt
2 grandmother	5 uncle
3 grandfather	6 cousins

b Read the example with the students. They then write the dates in words. Check answers by asking individual students to come up and write them on the board.

Answers
1 October nineteenth, twenty fourteen / two thousand and fourteen
2 June twelfth, nineteen eighty-five
3 September third, nineteen ninety
4 April twenty-second, two thousand and eight
5 August thirty-first, twenty twenty / two thousand and twenty
6 January ninth, two thousand and twelve / twenty twelve

> ♀ **FAST FINISHERS**
>
> Ask fast finishers to write down dates, first in numbers and then in words, when important things happened to them. Next to the dates, they write a short note of why they're important.

3 WORDPOWER go

a Books closed. In a column on the board, write: *home, by bus, shopping, swimming, out to a restaurant.* Ask students: *What word can I write before all of these?* Elicit *go*. Students open their books, look at the conversation, and answer the questions. Check answers as a class.

Answers
1 Viv
2 to go out to a restaurant

b Students match the phrases with *go* with the meanings. Students check in pairs. Check answers as a class.

Answers
a 2 go by	c 3 go shopping
b 1 go home	d 4 go out

c Individually, students match the verbs and the nouns to make more phrases with *go*. Check answers as a class and elicit alternative nouns for each phrase from the class, e.g., *go to a café / friend's house, go by car/taxi*, etc.

Answers
1 c 2 a 3 d 4 b

d Students read the sentences and, working individually, find and correct the mistakes. Check answers as a class.

Answers
1 They want to go to home now.
2 I need to go for shopping in town this afternoon.
3 I'd like to go to the movies this evening.
4 He usually goes to work by bus.

e As an additional example, change the example sentence so that it's true for you. Students then write sentences about their lives using the prompts. Monitor and point out errors for students to self-correct.

Answers
Students' own answers

f 💬 In pairs, students tell each other their sentences and decide how similar they are. Ask students to share their ideas with the class, and ask pairs to justify why they think they are similar or different, e.g., *Antoni goes home at 6:00 p.m. every day, but I go home two and a half hours later at 8:30 p.m.*

> ♀ **EXTRA ACTIVITY**
>
> Play a drawing game with students. Choose one of the phrases with *go* and start drawing a simple picture on the board. When students think they know what it is, they raise their hands. Continue the game either as a whole class, with the first student who guesses correctly being the next to draw on the board, or in pairs or small groups. The student who guesses the most phrases correctly wins.

≫ Photocopiable activities: Wordpower 6

> 🔄 **LOA TIP** REVIEW YOUR PROGRESS
>
> Students look back through the unit, think about what they studied, and decide how well they did. Students work on weak areas by using the appropriate sections of the Workbook and the Photocopiable activities.

UNIT 7
TRIPS

⟳ UNIT OBJECTIVES

At the end of this unit, students will be able to:

- understand information, texts, and conversations about travel and transportation
- exchange information and express opinions about travel and transportation
- get someone's attention, apologize, and show interest in the other participants in a conversation
- introduce themselves using personal emails

UNIT CONTENTS

G GRAMMAR

- Simple past: negative and questions
- *love / like / don't mind / hate* + verb + *-ing*

V VOCABULARY

- Transportation: *airplane (plane), bike, bus, cruise ship, ferry, helicopter, motorcycle, scooter, speedboat, train*
- Transportation collocations: *catch (the train), change (trains), get off (the train), get on (the train), miss (the train), take (the train)*
- Transportation adjectives: *cheap – expensive, clean – dirty, comfortable – uncomfortable, empty – crowded/full, fast – slow, safe – dangerous*
- Linking ideas with *after, when,* and *while*
- Wordpower: *get* meaning *arrive, become, bring, receive, take, travel on*

P PRONUNCIATION

- Simple past questions: *did you* /ˈdɪdʒə/
- Stress in adjectives
- Intonation for saying *excuse me*
- Emphasizing what we say

C COMMUNICATION SKILLS

- Talking about different trips
- Evaluating different forms of transportation
- Saying *excuse me* and *I'm sorry*
- Showing interest
- Discussing English-speaking countries you'd like to visit
- Writing an email about yourself

GETTING STARTED

♀ OPTIONAL LEAD-IN

Books closed. Write the following wordsnake on the board:

tbusrtaxiiboatpcars

Tell students to find four kinds of transportation in the wordsnake. Tell them that there are seven extra letters, which form a word connected with transportation. Students work individually, finding the kinds of transportation and the word connected with transportation. They compare in pairs. Check answers by asking individual students to circle the kinds of transportation in the wordsnake on the board and to open their books and look at the title of the unit. (Answers: *bus, taxi, boat, car. The other letters spell "trips."*)

a 💬📢 Give students one minute to think about their answers to the questions before talking about the picture as a class.

🌍 CULTURE NOTES

This picture shows three tourists riding their bikes through Alentejo. Alentejo is a region in south central and southern Portugal. Although it's not very popular among tourists, Alentejo is known for its beautiful scenery and Roman history.

b 💬📢 Read the questions with students and then put them into pairs to discuss their imaginary travel plans. Help with vocabulary and pronunciation, but don't interrupt fluency.

♀ EXTRA ACTIVITY

Individually, students draw the routes they want to take on the trips they discussed in Exercise b and then check in their pairs. Tell them to mark the places they would like to visit and the sights they would like to see. Make sure they know how to say the names of these places in English.

Divide up the pairs students worked in for Exercise b and put students into new small groups, if possible, so that each student in the group has a different country. Students take turns talking about their trip. Students in each group then decide which trip they think is best and why.

Exercises **a** and **b** can be prepared as homework before this lesson to give students time to look up unfamiliar vocabulary. Ask students to look at the picture and to prepare their answers to the questions as homework to talk about in the next class.

7A | THE BUS DIDN'T ARRIVE

At the end of this lesson, students will be able to:

- read and understand blog posts about travel
- use a lexical set of transportation words and transportation collocations correctly
- use the negative and question forms of the simple past
- understand a conversation about a long trip
- ask and answer questions about trips

💡 OPTIONAL LEAD-IN

Draw a rough world map on the board and elicit the names of the different parts of the world from Vocabulary Focus 1A by pointing to the different geographical areas and asking: *What part of the world is this?* (*Africa, Asia, Central and South America, Europe, North America, Oceania*)

Drill the pronunciation of each part of the world and ask students: *Where's the stress?* Underline the stressed syllable in each.

Tell students you're going to read out three famous tourist attractions for each part of the world. They listen and write down the part of the world. *1 the Leaning Tower of Pisa, the Eiffel Tower, Big Ben* (Europe) *2 Victoria Falls, the Pyramids, Serengeti National Park* (Africa) *3 Machu Picchu, Sugarloaf Mountain, Panama Canal* (Central and South America) *4 Uluru / Ayers Rock, Botany Bay National Park, Milford Sound* (Oceania) *5 the Golden Gate Bridge, the Rockies, Yellowstone National Park* (North America) *6 Mount Everest, the Taj Mahal, the Forbidden City* (Asia). Students compare in pairs. Check answers as a class.

1 READING

a 💬 If you used the optional lead-in, before students open their books, mark the three trip destinations on the map on the board and elicit the countries by asking students: *Where does this trip start/finish?* In pairs, students open their books, look at the trips, and discuss which one they would like to go on and why. Ask some students to tell the class their ideas and justify their decisions as much as possible.

b Students work individually, answering the questions. Check answers as a class. Ask students if they know about any of the three places mentioned in the blog posts. If you wish, give students information from Culture Notes below about Valdez Glacier.

Answers
a = Ethan
b = Kayla
c = Jessica

🌍 CULTURE NOTES

Valdez Glacier is located in Valdez, Alaska, the snowiest place in the United States. In the late 1800s, many people used the Valdez Glacier to enter Alaska and look for gold.

The best way to see the glacier is by kayak, but it can be very dangerous to get close to the glacier. As the ice melts, large portions of ice break off, which can change the water levels a lot in a very short time.

c Students read the blog quickly and match the sentences with the people. Check answers as a class and ask students: *Which words helped you find the answers?*

Answers
1 E   2 K   3 J   4 E   5 J   6 K

📖 VOCABULARY SUPPORT

selfie stick – a long tool you can attach to your cell phone and use for taking a selfie (a photograph of yourself)

kayak – a light, narrow canoe that is covered over the top

fly(-ies) – a small insect with two wings

mosquito – a small, flying insect that bites people and animals and sucks their blood

makeup – colored powder and liquid used on your face to change or improve its look

💡 FAST FINISHERS

Ask fast finishers to write more sentences that they think Jessica, Ethan, or Kayla might say about their trips.

💡 EXTRA ACTIVITY

Ask students to read all three texts again and answer questions 1–5:

1 *How long did it take Jessica to get from Cartagena to Playa Blanca on the speedboat?* (forty-five minutes)

2 *Who traveled in the water?* (Jessica and Ethan)

3 *Who made a new friend?* (Jessica)

4 *Who do you think traveled the farthest?* (probably Kayla)

5 *Whose trip do you think was most expensive?* (probably Ethan's)

d 💬 Tell students that in this activity, the emphasis is on communication and not on perfect English. In pairs, students talk about the questions.

🔄 LOA TIP MONITORING

- Asking students who perform well on a task to share what they said can provide a realistic and achievable model for students. If you use yourself as a model, this can sometimes set up an unrealistic expectation and a sense of "Of course I can't do it as well as the teacher."

- Monitor 1d intensively and identify students who give good, clear arguments for why they think Jessica's, Ethan's, or Kayla's trip was best. Allow time so students can share their ideas with the class. Ask the other students: *Who do you agree with most? Why?*

2 VOCABULARY Transportation

a Ask students to cover the words in the box and see how many of the kinds of transportation in the pictures they already know. Individually, students then match the words with the pictures. Monitor for any problems and clarify these as you check answers as a class. Check that students understand that *airplane* is the more formal word, but *plane* is more common in everyday English. Explain that *speedboat* and *cruise ship* are two forms of water transportation, but a *speedboat* is very fast and for a small number of people, while a *cruise ship* is a lot bigger, goes more slowly, and can hold many more people. Drill the vocabulary.

Answers

1 cruise ship	5 speedboat
2 train	6 ferry
3 bus	7 helicopter
4 airplane (plane)	8 scooter

b 💬 Read the questions with the students and check that they understand the task. Give them one minute to think about answers for the questions before they work in pairs. Monitor, but don't interrupt fluency. Check ideas with the class.

Suggested answers
- transportation people often use to go on vacation – airplane, bus, ferry, cruise ship, train
- transportation people normally use to get to work or school – scooter, train, bus
- unusual transportation for people to use in your country / transportation you normally use – Students' own answers

> 💡 **FAST FINISHERS**
> Ask fast finishers to brainstorm other kinds of transportation.

c ⟫ ▶ 07.01–07.03 Students complete the exercises in the Vocabulary Focus 7A on SB p. 167. Play the recordings as necessary and monitor students as they speak. Check other answers as a class. Tell students to go back to SB p. 71.

Answers (Vocabulary Focus 7A SB p. 167)
a 1 d 2 e 3 f 4 a 5 b 6 c
b 1 take 2 miss 3 get off 4 caught 5 took 6 on
c 1 bought, saw

3 GRAMMAR Simple past: negative

a Read the two sentences and complete them as a class.

Answers
1 didn't
2 buy

b Students check in pairs. Elicit the rule and concept-check the position of the auxiliary verb in relation to the base form by asking students: *Which comes first in negative sentences, "didn't" or the main verb?*

Answer
didn't

c Individually, students look at Jessica's and Kayla's blog posts again to find more examples of the simple past negative forms.

Answer
Jessica's blog post: *didn't arrive*
Kayla's blog post: *didn't use, didn't know, didn't wear*

4 LISTENING

a ▶ 07.04 Students listen to the conversation for general meaning and answer the questions. Check the answers as a class.

Answers
1 Kayla's story
2 Carly
3 food

Audioscript

SCOTT Which story did you like most?
CARLY Kayla's – it's very funny.
S It sure is.
C Lipstick on a scooter - you don't think of things like that.
S What about your vacations? Any stories to tell?
C Um … well … nothing like that – nothing funny.
S But?
C Well, when I went to Mexico with two of my best friends …
S Did you go last year?
C That's right.
S How did you travel there?
C By plane. We went to Mexico City.
S Right.
C …and we tried to order food from this place – it was a very simple restaurant.
S What did you choose?

C Well, that was the problem. We didn't speak Spanish and we didn't understand the words on the menu.
S Oh, dear. What did you do?
C Well, we started to use the dictionaries on our cell phones.
S A long, slow process.
C Sure was. But then this Mexican man saw us, and he offered to help. He told us what things were and then he ordered the food for us.
S Wow! What a nice guy!
C Exactly – we said "thank you" about a hundred times! And then he went away. But that's not all.
S Oh?
C Yeah, we went to pay for the meal and the man – he paid for our meals before he left!
S Unbelievable! That's incredible.
C Yeah – just so kind.

b ▶ 07.04 Students listen to the conversation again for specific details and underline the correct answers. Tell them that for some items, they may need to underline more than one word. Students compare in pairs. Check answers as a class.

Answers
1 Mexico City
2 two friends
3 menu
4 cell phone
5 food
6 paid then left

c 💬 Discuss the question briefly as a class. If possible, share a simple personal story of your own. In pairs, students answer the question.

5 GRAMMAR Simple past: questions

a ▶️07.05 Write the affirmative sentence: *Carly went to Mexico City.* (+) on the board. Then, write *Carly / go / Mexico City* (–) on the board and elicit the negative sentence: *Carly didn't go to Mexico City.* Finally, write *Carly / go / Mexico City* (?) on the board, and see if students can form the question: *Did Carly go to Mexico City?* Tell the class that now they are going to look at simple past questions. Individually, students complete the questions in the book. Play the recording for students to listen and check. Check answers as a class.

> **Answers**
> 1 Did   2 did   3 did

b Students check in pairs. Write the following jumbled question on the board: *you / visit / Mexico / did ?* Ask students: *What's the correct order?* (Did you visit Mexico?) and elicit the rule (*did* + subject + base form).

> **Answer**
> *did*

c ▶️07.05 **Pronunciation** Play the recording and ask students to listen to the pronunciation of *did you*. Elicit that you can't hear both words clearly and that *did you* is pronounced as one word /ˈdɪdʒə/. Play the recording again for students to listen and repeat. Then, drill the questions. Ask students to give themselves a grade for their pronunciation: *3 Good, people can understand me – no problem!, 2 OK, but I need to practice this more!, 1 This is very difficult for me!*

d ≫ ▶️07.06 Students read the information in Grammar Focus 7A on SB p. 150. Play the recording where indicated and ask students to listen and repeat. Students then complete the exercises. Check answers as a class, making sure students are using the auxiliary verb correctly. Tell students to go back to SB p. 71.

> **Answers (Grammar Focus 7A SB p. 151)**
> **a** 2 didn't take   4 didn't answer   6 didn't see
>   3 didn't want   5 didn't like   7 didn't get
> **b** 2 They didn't travel to Playa Blanca.
>   3 We didn't have a good time.
>   4 The tickets didn't cost a lot of money.
>   5 She didn't visit China.
>   6 They didn't stay in hotels.
>   7 The people didn't speak English, so I didn't understand them.
> **c** 2 Did, spend, didn't
>   3 Did, enjoy, didn't
>   4 Did, travel, did
> **d** 2 How much did the trip cost?
>   3 How many countries did you visit?
>   4 Where did you stay?
>   5 When did you arrive home?

e ▶️07.07 Tell students that this is a friendly, informal conversation. Individually, students complete the conversation. They then check in pairs. Play the recording for students to listen and check. Check answers as a class.

> **Answers**
> 1 was
> 2 was
> 3 did (you) visit
> 4 went
> 5 did (you) travel
> 6 took
> 7 rented
> 8 did (you) enjoy
> 9 loved

6 SPEAKING

a Tell students that now they can practice using all the language from the lesson with a partner. Read the instructions with the students and check that they understand the task. Give them one minute to write notes and help with vocabulary if necessary.

b 💬 In pairs, students ask and answer each other's questions about their trips. Tell them to use questions similar to those in 5e, such as: *How was your trip to __?; How did you travel around __?; What did you enjoy most?* Monitor, but don't interrupt fluency unless students make mistakes with the simple past.

c 💬 In groups, students share their partners' stories. Don't interrupt fluency unless students make mistakes with the simple past.

> ⊕ **ADDITIONAL MATERIAL**
>
> Workbook 7A
>
> Photocopiable activities: Grammar 7A, Vocabulary 7A, Pronunciation 7A

7B | I LIKE THE STATIONS

At the end of this lesson, students will be able to:

- read and understand a website with information and reviews
- use a lexical set of transportation adjectives correctly
- understand a conversation in which people talk about trips and give their opinions
- use *love / like / don't mind / hate* + verb + *-ing*
- talk about the types of transportation they use

♀ OPTIONAL LEAD-IN

Books closed. Tell students not to look at their books or their notes. Ask students: *What were the eight kinds of transportation we learned last lesson?* Elicit the eight words from Lesson 7A orally, but don't let students write anything down. Drill the kinds of transportation, but don't check the spelling.

Then, draw this puzzle on the board:

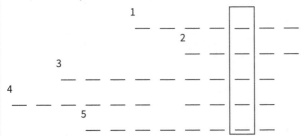

In pairs, students complete the puzzle with five kinds of transportation from Lesson 7A. Explain that the vertical box is another word for a kind of transportation. Check answers as a class by asking students to complete the puzzle on the board or spell the answers out to you. (Answers: *1 scooter 2 ferry 3 speedboat 4 cruise ship 5 airplane. The vertical word is "train."*)

1 READING

a 💬🗩 In pairs, students talk about the question. Brainstorm as a class cities that have subways and/or express buses.

b Students read the text quickly and match the cities with the pictures. Tell students they should only read the text "Fast City Transportation Around the World," not "From the locals." You may wish to pre-teach the words in the Vocabulary Support box. Check answers as a class.

Answers
a Bogotá
b Moscow
c London

📖 VOCABULARY SUPPORT

above ground – above the level of the streets and roads

bridge (A2) – a structure built over a river, road, or railway to allow people and vehicles to cross

deep (A2) – a long way down into the earth

palace (B1) – a large house that is the official home of a king, queen, or other important person

platform (A2) – a flat raised area or structure

statue (B1) – a model usually made of stone and often of a person

steps (B1) – the individual blocks which, when joined together, form "stairs"

system (B1) – a set of connected things that operate together

c Tell students to read the text again in detail. Individually, students answer the questions. Students compare in pairs. Check answers as a class and ask students to read the sections of the text which helped them answer the questions.

Answers
1 London
2 Bogotá
3 Bogotá
4 Moscow
5 Bogotá
6 Students' own answers

d Individually, students look at the text again and underline two things that surprise them. They then compare their ideas in pairs. Ask pairs to share their answers with the class to find out what surprised students most.

e Ask students: *What do you think people say about the subway and express buses in Bogotá/Moscow/London?* and elicit ideas, e.g., *It's new/expensive/slow.* If students have visited any of the cities, ask about their experiences. Tell students to read the opinions of people that use the different forms of transportation in "From the locals" and answer the questions. Check answers as a class.

Suggested answers
Sergei – Moscow: stations like palaces
Antonia – Bogotá: buses, roads are busy
Bill – London: expensive, underground
Joanna – London: trains are full, over 300 steps

f 💬🗩 In pairs, students answer the questions. Invite students to share their answers with the class.

♀ EXTRA ACTIVITY

Write sentences 1–5 on the board for students to decide if they are true or false. When checking answers, ask students to correct the false sentences.

1 *The London Underground isn't a popular way to travel.*
   (F – The trains are often full.)

2 *Traffic is a problem for the express bus system in Bogotá.*
   (F – Traffic isn't a problem – the buses have their own lanes.)

3 *The Moscow Metro is very dangerous at night.* (F – There are police at the stations, so it's very safe.)

4 *In Bogotá, you pay for the bus with a card.* (T)

5 *The London Underground is a very cheap way to travel.*
   (F – The London Underground is expensive.)

2 VOCABULARY Transportation adjectives

a Ask students to cover the texts and see if they know any of the words to complete the chart. Individually, students then look at the texts and find the opposite adjectives. Don't check answers at this point.

b ▶ **07.08** **Pronunciation** Play the recording for students to check their answers. Play the recording again for students to listen and repeat.

> **Answers**
> safe – dangerous
> empty – crowded / full
> comfortable – uncomfortable
> cheap – expensive
> clean – dirty

c Tell students to classify the adjectives in the chart as positive or negative. Complete the first two items (positive: *fast*; negative: *slow*) as an example. Individually, students decide if the other words are positive or negative. Check answers as a class by asking students to write the correct answers in two groups on the board.

> **Answers**
> Positive: fast, safe, empty, comfortable, cheap, clean
> Negative: slow, dangerous, crowded, uncomfortable, expensive, dirty

d ▶ **07.09** **Pronunciation** Play the recording for students to underline the stressed syllable in each word. Check answers as a class. Model the pronunciation for students to listen and repeat.

> **Answers**
> comfortable
> dangerous
> expensive

e 💬🔊 Divide the class into pairs and ask one pair to read the example. In a speech bubble on the board, write: *I don't agree.* Ask: *What other expressions do you know to say "I don't agree"?* Elicit ideas, e.g., *I disagree, I'm not sure*, and write them on the board. Students work in pairs, making sentences and responding, and taking turns being A and B. Monitor, but don't interrupt fluency unless students make mistakes with the transportation adjectives.

> ### 💡 EXTRA ACTIVITY
>
> Work as a class to build up a paragraph on the board for the website citytripper.com about the subway or bus system in the students' own area. Tell students to look for phrases and sentences in the texts on SB p. 72 that they can use and adapt for their own city. Tell students that when they do their written work, it is fine to use and adapt phrases from the model texts and elicit sentences from the class, e.g., *The Rome Metro is unusual because it's in a capital city, but it has only two underground lines. There are very old buildings above and below the ground everywhere in Rome, so it's very difficult to build metro lines downtown.*

3 GRAMMAR AND LISTENING
Love / like / don't mind / hate + verb + -ing

a 💬🔊 Tell the class how you usually travel when you go to meet a friend, e.g., *I always use public transportation because it's fast and cheap.* Discuss the question as a class. Encourage students to justify their decisions using transportation adjectives from the previous section.

b ▶ **07.10** Students listen to the conversation for general meaning and complete the chart. Check answers as a class. You may wish to pre-teach the word *traffic* (n.) (a lot of cars, buses, etc. on the road at the same time).

> **Answers**
>
> | | She came by … | The trip took … |
> | --- | --- | --- |
> | Svetlana | Metro | half an hour |
> | Alex | car | one hour |

> **Audioscript**
>
> **ALEX** Hi, Svetlana. Sorry I'm late. It was the traffic.
> **SVETLANA** Was it bad? I didn't notice the traffic.
> **A** Really? So how did you get here?
> **S** On the Metro, of course.
> **A** Really? Do you use the Metro?
> **S** Yes, I love going on the Metro; it's so quick. It only took half an hour. Don't you use the Metro?
> **A** No, I don't like using the Metro; it's so crowded. And it isn't always very clean in the trains. And the stations, they're terrible. So many people.
> **S** Oh, I love the stations. I think they're beautiful. So did you come by car?
> **A** Yes, of course, I go everywhere by car. I like driving in Moscow.
> **S** You like it? But it's always so slow. How long did it take you to get here?
> **A** About an hour, maybe. The traffic was bad.
> **S** But it's always bad. I hate sitting in traffic. It's so boring.
> **A** Oh, I don't mind it; it's not too bad. You can listen to the radio or an audiobook.
> **S** Well, you must have a very nice car.
> **A** Yes, it is a pretty nice car. It's very comfortable and big inside.
> **S** Ah.

c ▶ **07.10** Tell students that now they need to listen for Svetlana's and Alex's specific opinions on the different kinds of transportation. Play the recording again for students to complete the chart. Students compare in pairs. Check answers as a class.

> **Answers**
>
> | | Svetlana thinks | Alex thinks |
> | --- | --- | --- |
> | the Metro is … | quick | crowded, dirty |
> | the stations are … | beautiful | terrible |
> | driving is … | slow | not too bad |
> | Alex's / Her car is … | very nice | nice, comfortable, big |

d ▶)07.11 Tell students to close their books. Write on the board: *I ... going on the Metro.* Ask students: *Can you remember what Svetlana said?* (love) Then ask students: *What's the opposite of "love"?* (hate) Tell students that they are going to look at verbs of preference in detail. Students look at the sentences in their books and try to complete them. Play the recording for students to listen and check. Check answers as a class.

Answers
1 love
2 don't like
3 love
4 like
5 hate
6 don't mind

e Students then match the verbs in 3d with the meanings. Check answers as a class.

Answers
1 love
2 hate
3 don't mind

🔄 **LOA TIP** CONCEPT CHECKING

- Draw emoticons on the board and ask students to write the five answers to 3d next to them to check that they understand the meaning:

  ☺☺☺   (love)

  ☺   (like)

  ☺   (don't mind)

  ☹   (don't like)

  ☹☹☹   (hate)

- Ask students: *What kinds of word can come after "love," "like," "don't mind," and "hate"?* Students look at the examples in 3d and elicit the possibilities: *the "-ing" form or a noun/pronoun.*

⊙ **CAREFUL!**

When verbs of preference are followed by a verb, students are likely to use the wrong form for the second verb. They may use the base form of the verb, e.g., *I hate use ...* (Correct form = *I hate using* public transportation), or they may use the infinitive, e.g. *I love to go ...* (Correct form = *I love going* by car). Note that the infinitive form is in fact acceptable and used by native speakers in certain circumstances. However, at this level, students should always use the *-ing* form as the difference in meaning between the verb followed by the *-ing* form or by the infinitive is complicated.

Some students may add the *-ing* form to the verb of preference when it isn't followed by another verb, e.g., *I loving cars* (Correct form = *I love cars*).

Students may also start to overuse *like* and use it instead of *would like*, e.g., *I like traveling ...* (Correct form = *I would like to travel* to the Valdez Glacier).

---

f ≫ ▶)07.12 Students read the information in Grammar Focus 7B on SB p. 150. Play the recording where indicated and ask students to listen and repeat. Students then complete the exercises. Check answers as a class, making sure students are using *-ing* forms after the verbs where necessary and spelling them correctly. Tell students to go back to SB p. 73.

Answers (Grammar Focus 7B SB p. 151)
a 2 driving   5 flying   8 having   11 standing   14 trying
    3 walking   6 relaxing   9 speaking   12 staying   15 using
    4 getting   7 being   10 sitting   13 running   16 agreeing
b 1 He doesn't mind cooking. He doesn't mind getting pizza. He loves trying new food.
    2 Lisa likes eating in restaurants. She hates cooking. She doesn't like getting pizza. She loves trying new food.
c Students' own answers

---

4 SPEAKING

a Individually, students choose three kinds of transportation from the list.

b Read the instructions with the students and check that they understand the task. Give them one minute to write notes and help with vocabulary if necessary.

c 💬 In pairs, students tell each other their ideas and find out how similar they are. As you monitor, don't interrupt fluency, but note any problems with pronunciation and write down any mistakes with *love / like / don't mind / hate* + verb + *-ing*. After the activity, write these on the board and ask students to correct them.

💡 **FAST FINISHERS**

Ask fast finishers to work together in their pairs and complete the sentence: *I ..., but (my partner) ... .* in as many ways as possible using information they learned about their partner in 4c, e.g., *I don't like taking the plane, but Sophia loves it!*

⊕ **ADDITIONAL MATERIAL**

Workbook 7B

Photocopiable activities: Grammar 7B, Vocabulary 7B, Pronunciation 7B

At the end of this lesson, students will be able to:

- understand informal conversations in which people say *excuse me* and *I'm sorry* and talk about where they are traveling
- use appropriate phrases to say *excuse me* and *I'm sorry*
- emphasize what they say appropriately
- use appropriate phrases to show interest during a conversation
- maintain an informal conversation in which they apologize about something and show interest

OPTIONAL LEAD-IN

Books closed. Write *going away for the weekend* in the middle of the board. Ask students: *What does "going away" mean?* (go and stay in a place away from your home). Create a word map on the board by drawing a circle around *going away for the weekend* and adding three lines. At the end of the lines, write *places*, *activities*, and *people*. Elicit places to go, e.g., *the beach, a spa, a big city*; typical activities, e.g., *swimming in the ocean, visiting museums, sleeping late*; people to go with, e.g., *friends, family, partner*, and add them to the word map.

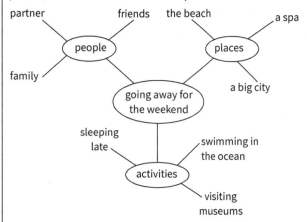

In pairs, students add more vocabulary to the word map. Invite pairs to share their answers with the class and add their ideas to the word map on the board. Leave the word map on the board for students to refer to in 1a.

1 LISTENING

a Discuss the questions as a class. If you used the optional lead-in, remind students that they can use the vocabulary on the board.

b Tell students to look at picture a and ask them what they can see. They then work in pairs, answering the questions. Ask some students to tell the class their ideas, but don't tell them if they are right or wrong.

c ▶07.13 Play Part 1 of the audio recording for students to listen and check their answers to 1b. Check answers as a class.

> **Answers**
> 1 They're in an airport.
> 2 They're boarding a flight.

Audioscript (Part 1)

ANNOUNCEMENT Attention passengers. Flight 135 to Dallas is now boarding.
ISSA (on the phone) I have to hang up now, Mom. I'll see you in few hours. Bye.
JAYDEN Hey, watch out! Your coffee! Oh, no!
I Oh! I'm so sorry.
J That's all right.
I I didn't see you there. My coffee – it's all over your shirt.
J Don't worry. It's just a little spot.
I Do you want my napkin?
J That's OK.

d ▶07.13 Play Part 1 of the audio recording again for students to listen and check their answers to 1d. Check answers as a class.

> **Answers**
> 1 She's traveling to Dallas.
> 2 She spills coffee on his shirt.
> 3 a He is calm.

e ▶07.14 Play Part 2 of the audio recording for students to listen and check their answers. Check answers as a class.

> **Answers**
> 1 Jayden
> 2 Issa
> 3 Jayden

Audioscript (Part 2)

ANNOUNCEMENT Welcome aboard Flight 135. Please take your seats.
JAYDEN Excuse me, please. Oh, hi!
ISSA We meet again!
J Excuse me, but I think you're sitting in my seat. I have a window seat.
I Oh. I'm very sorry. I just sat down. I didn't check. I'm really sorry. Just let me grab my water.
J It's no problem, really! I'll sit on the aisle.
I Thank you. That's very kind— Oh, no! I spilled on you again! I'm so sorry!
J It's just water this time – don't worry!

2 USEFUL LANGUAGE

Saying *excuse me* and *I'm sorry*

EXTRA ACTIVITY

Write *Excuse me, please.* and *I'm sorry!* in two speech bubbles on the board. Walk around the class and mime accidentally bumping into a student with your elbow. Look embarrassed, and then point to your mouth and to the two phrases on the board to elicit which you should use (*I'm sorry!*). Then, try to reach a part of the classroom that you can't get to because a student is in the way. Look frustrated, gesture for the student to move, and point to the phrases again to elicit which one you should use (*Excuse me, please.*). Tell students that now they're going to look at how to say *excuse me* and *I'm sorry*.

a Individually, students match the phrases with the meanings. Check answers as a class.

> **Answers**
> 1 b
> 2 a

b ▶07.15 **Pronunciation** Play the recording and highlight the intonation for students.

c Discuss the questions as a class and check that students are clear about the two different uses of *excuse me*. Drill the phrases, completing the first one appropriately, e.g., *Excuse me, but I don't understand.*

> **Answers**
> a Excuse me, but … b Excuse me, please.

d Elicit the rule as a class. Make sure students understand the position of *very, really,* and *so* in the expression by writing *I'm very/really/so sorry.* on the board with *very/really/so* underlined, circled, or in a different color.

> **Answer**
> You put *very*, *really*, and *so* before *sorry*.

e ▶️07.16 Students match the pairs of sentences. Play the recording for students to listen and check. Check answers as a class. Ask students to underline *very, really,* and *so* in the sentences to help them remember the position.

> **Answers**
> 1 e 2 c 3 b 4 a 5 d

f If you used the extra activity earlier, once again mime accidentally bumping into a student with your elbow. Say *I'm sorry!* and gesture to elicit a response from the student. Students then think about which replies are correct to use when someone apologizes. Check answers as a class.

> **Answers**
> 1 ✓ That's all right.   3 ✓ No problem.
> 2 ✓ That's OK.   5 ✓ Don't worry.

g ▶️07.17 Tell students to work individually and order the sentences to make two short, separate conversations. Play the recording for students to listen and check. Check answers as a class.

> **Answers and audioscript**
> **Conversation 1**
> b **A** Excuse me, but I think that's my coat.
> c **B** Is it? I'm so sorry. I took the wrong one.
> a **A** No problem. They all look the same.
>
> **Conversation 2**
> f **A** Excuse me, but I think this is my seat.
> e **B** Oh, I'm sorry. I thought this was number 35.
> d **A** Don't worry. The seat numbers are hard to read.

h 💬 In pairs, students practice the conversations. Monitor and correct students' pronunciation as appropriate. Then, elicit an indication of students' confidence level for saying *excuse me* and *I'm sorry*.

3 PRONUNCIATION
Emphasizing what we say

a ▶️07.18 Play the recording and highlight the stress for students.

b Individually, students choose the best answer. Check the answer as a class.

> **Answer**
> 2 We want to sound more sorry.

c 💬 Students work in pairs, practicing saying the sentences in 3a. Monitor and correct students' pronunciation as appropriate.

> 🔄 **LOA TIP** DRILLING
>
> - Before students work together in 3c, drill the sentences in 3a to check that they are emphasizing *very/really/so* and *sorry* and giving the other underlined words enough stress.
> - Model the very weak pronunciation of *I'm* /əm/ in isolation and make sure students don't start to overemphasize it once they start to practice at sentence level. This is particularly important for students whose L1 is a syllable-timed language (e.g., French, Chinese, Spanish), as they are more likely to try to give each syllable equal weight. In contrast, students whose L1 is a stress-timed language (e.g., Portuguese, Russian, Arabic) will probably have fewer problems with the pronunciation.

4 CONVERSATION SKILLS Showing interest

a ▶️07.19 Read the sentences as a class. Then, play Part 3 of the audio recording for students to decide if they are true or false. When checking answers, ask students to correct the false sentences.

> **Answers**
> 1 F (Issa is going to Dallas. Jayden is going to Fort Worth.)
> 2 F (Issa is visiting her mother.)
> 3 T

> **Audioscript (Part 3)**
> **ISSA** Are you visiting Dallas?
> **JAYDEN** No, Fort Worth. I went to college there.
> **I** Great! I love Fort Worth.
> **J** How about you?
> **I** I'm going to Dallas. My mom lives there. I go to see her every month.
> **J** Really? That's so nice. Oh, yikes!
> **I** Uh oh. I can't believe I did it again. And soda this time.
> **J** My shirt was already wet. No problem.
> **I** I'm really, really, really sorry this time. How can I make it up to you?
> **J** Have dinner with me in Dallas – or Fort Worth?
> **I** Really? Well, sure. OK.
> **J** But no more spills, please...
> **I** Maybe you should bring an extra shirt or two, just in case …

b ▶️07.19 In pairs, students look at the two extracts and try to remember which two words aren't correct. Check that all students have the correct answers by playing the audio recording again and asking students to shout *Stop!* when they hear the different words.

> **Answers**
> **ISSA** ~~Right.~~ Great!   **JAYDEN** ~~Oh.~~ Really?

c Discuss the question as a class. Remind students that an important part of communication is showing interest.

> **Answer**
> 2 to show they are interested

> 📖 **LANGUAGE NOTES**
>
> Some students may feel uncomfortable using what seems to them to be exaggerated intonation patterns for interjections such as *Great!* and *Really?*
>
> To help students understand the importance of showing interest, drill the conversations in 4b with flat, bored intonation and use *Oh* rather than *Great!* and *Really?* Ask students how they would feel if someone talked to them in that way. Then, drill the conversation again, this time with *Great!* and *Really?* and the intonation patterns in 2b. Ask students which conversation they would prefer to be part of.

5 SPEAKING

a 💬🔊 Tell students that they can now practice using all the language from the lesson with a partner. Check that students understand the dialogue map before they start. In pairs, students take turns being A and B. Monitor and correct students' pronunciation as appropriate, and listen for correct usage of the target language from this lesson.

b 💬🔊 In pairs, students practice new conversations using different reasons for being late. Remind students to be careful to use the correct intonation and to use the phrases for emphasizing and showing interest. Nominate a few pairs to perform their conversations for the class.

♥ FAST FINISHERS

Ask fast finishers to practice additional conversations based on their own ideas, e.g., *someone waiting at an airport to meet a friend*, *a coworker apologizing for arriving late to a meeting*.

⊕ ADDITIONAL MATERIAL

Workbook 7C

Unit Progress Test

7D | SKILLS FOR WRITING

It really is hard to choose

At the end of this lesson, students will be able to:

- understand a person discussing with a friend which homestay family he would prefer to stay with
- understand an email in which someone introduces himself/herself
- link ideas using *after*, *when*, and *while*
- write an email introducing themselves to a homestay family

♥ OPTIONAL LEAD-IN

Books closed. Write the following question on the board: *What makes a house a home?* Give students a few ideas, e.g., *a cat or a dog; a comfortable sofa and a big TV; a nice yard.* Students work in small groups to think of ideas. Ask groups to share their answers with the class and write their ideas on the board.

Ask students: *Do you stay in other people's houses? When? Why?* Elicit some answers, e.g., *at a friend's after a night out*, etc. Pre-teach *stay with a homestay family* (be with a family in their house while a person studies or works), and find out if any students are staying or have ever stayed with a homestay family. If they are/have, ask them to tell the class about their experiences.

Tell students that they can use the ideas and useful language from this activity to help them with their writing later in the lesson. Give them time to note any new words or expressions. Alternatively, if you have an interactive whiteboard, save the vocabulary brainstorm for students to refer back to later in the lesson.

1 SPEAKING AND LISTENING

a 💬🔊 Individually, students choose three ideas from the list. They then compare their ideas in pairs.

b 💬🔊 Students work in pairs, read the profiles, and answer the questions. Monitor, but don't interrupt fluency. Ask pairs to share their answers with the class and find out which family is more popular and why.

♥ EXTRA ACTIVITY

Students work individually using the profiles in 1b to create a homestay family profile for their own family. When students have completed their profiles, collect them. Divide the class into small groups and give each group an equal number of profiles. Students discuss which of the profiles would be the most attractive for a foreign student coming to their country to study. If students are not comfortable talking about their own family situation in class, tell them to invent the information in their profile.

c ▶07.20 Students listen to the conversation for general meaning and answer the question. Play the recording and check the answer as a class.

Answer
No, he doesn't.

Audioscript

ALEJANDRO So here are the photos and the profiles of the families I can choose from.

JUSTIN Hmm – interesting – two very different kinds of families.

A Yes, it's hard to decide.

J Well, both families look very friendly.

A Yes, they do.

J And the Conways look very kind.

A But maybe they're a little too quiet?

J Maybe. The Philips like doing active things – swimming, surfing – that kind of thing.

A Yes, but I don't like going to the beach much. I like playing football.

J You mean soccer. In New Zealand, they say soccer, not football. Like in the U.S.

A That's right.

J And, I have to say, in New Zealand soccer is not that popular. Everyone loves rugby – it's the national sport.

A But the Conways like watching any sport, so maybe I can watch soccer with them. That'd be nice.

J Yeah, that's true. But you like listening to pop music, don't you?

A Yes, I do.

J And the Philips like listening to pop music, too.

A I'm not sure about children, though.

J Children are fun.

A Yes, but they aren't quiet!

J No, not if you want to study.

A And I really want to study a lot.

J Then there's transportation. It's pretty expensive in Auckland.

A So I can save money if I stay at the Conways?

J Yeah, you probably can.

A It really is hard to choose.

J It sounds like it! But you are the only person who can decide!

d ▶️07.20 Students listen to the recording again for specific details and check the true phrases. They compare in pairs. Check answers as a class.

> **Answers**
> 2 ✓ likes watching sports
> 3 ✓ likes listening to pop music
> 6 ✓ wants to study a lot
> 7 ✓ likes playing soccer

e 💬 Students work in pairs, talking about which family is good for Alejandro and why. Monitor, but don't interrupt fluency. Ask some students to share their ideas with the class. Encourage students to justify their decisions as much as possible.

> 💡 **FAST FINISHERS**
>
> Ask fast finishers to list all the personal information they know about Alejandro, e.g., *Alejandro likes playing soccer / listening to music.* When they finish 2b, they check what extra information in the email isn't on their lists.

2 READING

a Tell students that Alejandro thinks it would be a good idea to send an email to the Conways. Students read the email quickly and check the main reason he writes to them. Check the answer.

> **Answer**
> 3 ✓ to tell them about himself

b Tell students to read the email again in detail. Individually, students number the information in the order they find it. Encourage students to guess the meaning of any new words from the context. Check answers as a class.

> **Answers**
> 1 his hometown   3 his hobbies
> 2 his family's jobs   4 his future plans

3 WRITING SKILLS
Linking ideas with *after*, *when*, and *while*

a Ask students to identify the word in each sentence that is different from Alejandro's email. They then check their own answers by looking back at the email. Check answers as a class.

> **Answers**
> 1 while
> 2 when
> 3 after
> 4 When

b Individually, students complete the rules. Check answers as a class.

> **Answers**
> 1 *while*
> 2 *after*
> 3 beginning

> 👁 **CAREFUL!**
>
> A common learner error is to use *will* after *after/when/while*. Although students have not yet studied the future form in this course, it is something they may have learned in the past and may transfer to this structure, e.g., ~~When I will be ...~~ (Correct form = *When I'm in Sydney, I want to ...*), ~~I want to be a teacher after I will finish ...~~ (Correct form = *I want to be a teacher after I finish college*). When students are writing their emails, monitor to make sure they don't make this mistake.

c Students read the sentences and underline the correct words. Students compare in pairs. Check answers as a class.

> **Answers**
> 1 After, When
> 2 when, while
> 3 after, when
> 4 After, When
> 5 when, while

4 SPEAKING AND WRITING

> 🗨 **LOA TIP** ELICITING
>
> • Elicit some English-speaking countries as a class, e.g., Australia, Canada, New Zealand, the U.K., the U.S., etc. by projecting the countries' flags one after the other onto the board.
>
> • Alternatively, draw a rough world map on the board. Point to the different countries and ask: *What country is this?* and *How do you spell that?*

a Use the LOA Tip to elicit some English-speaking countries as a class. Alternatively, ask students to work in pairs and brainstorm English-speaking countries. Ask pairs to share their answers with the class and collate students' ideas on the board. You may also give students information from Culture Notes on the next page.

> **Suggested answers**
> Australia, Canada, New Zealand, the U.K., the U.S.

b 💬 Give students one minute to think about which country they would like to visit and why. In pairs, students discuss the countries in 4a. Ask some students to share their ideas with the class. Encourage them to justify their decisions as much as possible.

c Students plan their emails, working individually. Tell them to use the ideas from the lesson and the linking words *after*, *when*, and *while*. Monitor and help with vocabulary and suggest more ideas if necessary. If you're short on time, 4c–d can be completed for homework. Students could then bring their emails to the next class.

d Read the checklist with students before they start writing their emails. Tell them to make sure they check each box in the checklist. Students write a first draft of their emails.

e 💬 Remind students of the importance of checking their work carefully before handing it in. In pairs, students switch emails and check that their partner has included all the ideas in 4d. They then give each other feedback. If they have missed any of the points, they prepare a second draft of their emails and make sure all areas are covered.

⊕ **ADDITIONAL MATERIAL**

Workbook 7D

UNIT 7
Review and extension

1 GRAMMAR

a Individually, students complete the text. They then check in pairs. Check answers and spelling as a class by asking individual students to write the correct answers on the board.

Answers

1 called	6 was
2 didn't come	7 landed
3 took	8 arrived
4 was	9 asked
5 waited	10 didn't have

b Students look at the example and then complete the questions. Check answers as a class and drill the questions.

Answers

2 How did you get there?	5 How long did you stay?
3 Did you have a good time?	6 Was it hot?
4 Where did you stay?	

c 💬 Give students one minute to choose a place they've visited and think about the answers to the questions in 1b. In pairs, students take turns asking and answering the questions.

d Students complete the sentences, working individually. Check answers as a class.

Answers

2 Clare/She hates listening to Mozart.
3 Clare/She doesn't mind taking the subway.
4 Clare/She doesn't like watching baseball.
5 Clare/She likes speaking French.

> ### ⚲ EXTRA ACTIVITY
>
> Give students a spelling test using regular and irregular simple past forms and -ing forms. Test students on words that you've noticed they often have problems with. Alternatively, give each student a small slip of paper and ask them to write down one simple past or -ing form that they find difficult to spell. Collect the papers and use these words for the test. Check answers by asking individual students to write the words on the board.

2 VOCABULARY

a Individually, students complete the words. They then compare in pairs. Check answers as a class.

Answers

2 train	5 ferry
3 ship	6 scooter
4 helicopter	

b Students correct the sentences. Check answers and spelling as a class by asking individual students to write the correct answers on the board.

Answers

2 dirty	5 dangerous
3 uncomfortable	6 expensive
4 fast	

3 WORDPOWER get

a Tell students to close their books. On the left of the board, in a vertical column, write *arrive, become, bring, receive, take,* and *travel on.* Draw an = sign in the middle of the board and ask students: *Which word can mean all of these?* Elicit *get.* Write *get* in a circle on the right of the board. Students open their books and match the questions and answers. Check answers as a class.

Answers

1 d   2 e   3 a   4 b   5 c

b Students read the verbs and match them with the answers with *get* in 3a. They then check in pairs. Check answers as a class.

Answers

1 d   2 c   3 e   4 a   5 b

c Individually, students read the story and think about what happened next. Ask some students to share their ideas with the class. They then identify the meanings of *get* in the story. Check answers as a class.

Answers

1 Students' own answers
2 a 2 receive   b 5 take or bring   c 3 travel on   d 4 arrive   e 1 become

d Tell students to classify the phrases in the box according to the meaning of *get.* Complete the first two items as an example. Ask: *What does "get" mean in "get angry"?* Elicit *become.* Then ask: *Which two phrases in the box can we use with "become"?* Elicit *sad* and *better.* Individually, students match the phrases with 1–5. Check answers as a class and elicit the meanings of *get.*

Answers

1 get sad, get better (= become)
2 get a phone call, get an email (= receive)
3 get a taxi, get the train (= travel on)
4 get to the airport, get to school (= arrive)
5 get a glass of water (= take or bring)

e Before students write sentences about their lives, give students one or two examples about yourself using *get* and the phrases in 3d, e.g., *I never get angry with my students!* and *I got an email from my cousin in New Zealand yesterday.* Monitor and help as necessary. Point out errors for students to self-correct.

Answers

Students' own answers

f 💬 In pairs, students tell each other their sentences and find out how similar they are.

> ### ⚲ FAST FINISHERS
>
> Using information they learned in 3f, ask fast finishers to complete the sentence: *We both …* in as many ways as possible, e.g., *We both get the train home in the evening.*

≫ Photocopiable activities: Wordpower 7

> ### ⟳ LOA TIP REVIEW YOUR PROGRESS
>
> Students look back through the unit, think about what they've studied, and decide how well they did. Students work on weak areas by using the appropriate sections of the Workbook and the Photocopiable activities.

HEALTHY AND IN SHAPE

🔄 UNIT OBJECTIVES

At the end of this unit, students will be able to:

- understand information, texts, and conversations and exchange information about sports, sports personalities, events, free-time activities, doing exercise, and getting in shape
- ask for and give information about abilities
- talk about what is necessary and what isn't necessary when doing sports and free-time activities
- understand conversations in which people talk about health and how they feel
- use appropriate phrases to express sympathy
- write an article about a free-time activity

UNIT CONTENTS

G GRAMMAR
- *can / can't, could / couldn't* for ability
- *have to / don't have to*

V VOCABULARY
- Sports and exercise: *dance, do yoga, play badminton, ride a bike, skate, ski*
- Sports and exercise collocations: *do exercises / martial arts; go fishing/running/sailing/snowboarding; play (American) football/golf/hockey/soccer/volleyball*
- Parts of the body: *arm, back, finger, foot, hand, head, leg, neck, stomach, toe*
- Appearance: *attractive, curly/dark/blonde/long/short/straight hair, in good shape, good-looking, out of shape, pretty, thin*
- Linking ideas with *however*
- Adverbs of manner
- Wordpower: *tell / say*

P PRONUNCIATION
- *can, can't, could,* and *couldn't*
- *have to*
- Stress in adjectives
- Connecting words

C COMMUNICATION SKILLS
- Talking about which free-time activities you could/couldn't do well as a child and which you can/can't do now
- Talking about what you have to do and have to have for different activities
- Talking about health and how you feel
- Expressing sympathy
- Writing an article about a free-time activity

GETTING STARTED

♀ OPTIONAL LEAD-IN

Write *Last week …* on the board and under it, write the following jumbled sentences and ask students to put them in order: *1 I / to the gym / five times / went; 2 every morning / walked /to work / I; 3 a lot of / and vegetables / I / salad, fruit, / ate; 4 two liters / I / every day / drank / of water* (1 I went to the gym five times. 2 I walked to work every morning. 3 I ate a lot of salad, fruit, and vegetables. 4 I drank two liters of water every day.)

Write *I'm … and … !* on the board and ask for suggestions to complete it. Tell students to look at the title of Unit 8. Elicit the sentence: *I'm <u>healthy</u> and <u>in shape</u>!*

a 💬📱 Give students one minute to think about their answers to the questions before talking about the picture as a class. You may give students information from Culture Notes below.

🌍 CULTURE NOTES

This picture shows the sport sepak takraw, or kick volleyball. The sport began in Malaysia approximately 500 years ago, but it's played throughout Asia in Cambodia, India, Indonesia, Singapore, Laos, Myanmar, Singapore, Thailand, and Vietnam. Scoring is similar to volleyball, but unlike volleyball, players may not use their hands. They can only use their feet, knees, chest, and head to touch the ball.

b Individually, students make a list of other sports and exercise the men in the picture would like. Help with vocabulary, as necessary.

Exercises **a** and **b** can be prepared as homework before this lesson to give students time to look up unfamiliar vocabulary. Ask students to look at the picture and to prepare their answers to the questions as homework to talk about in the next class.

c 💬📱 Put students into pairs to share their lists and see if they thought of the same things. Ask pairs to share their answers with the class and find out how many different ideas the class had in total.

♀ EXTRA ACTIVITY

Extend the discussion and get students to talk more about the sports and exercise they thought of in Exercise b. Write the following questions on the board and put students into small groups to discuss them: *Which sports and exercise from Exercise b do you like? How often do you do them? Who do you do them with? Are you good at them? Which do you like watching? Do you watch them on TV, at a stadium, or somewhere else? Which don't you like watching? Why?*

8A | THEY CAN DO THINGS MOST PEOPLE CAN'T

At the end of this lesson, students will be able to:

- read and understand a text about a sports personality
- use *can / can't, could / couldn't* correctly to talk about ability
- understand a podcast in which people talk about running marathons
- use a lexical set of sports and exercise words correctly
- ask for and give information about their abilities

💡 OPTIONAL LEAD-IN

Draw the Olympic rings on the board and ask students what they represent. Write sentences 1–5 under the rings and put students into pairs or small groups to try and complete them with a place or a person: *1 The first modern Olympic Games were in …* (Athens); *2 The person with the most Olympic medals is …* (Michael Phelps (at time of publication)); *3 The first Paralympic Games were in …* (Rome); *4 The Olympic torch always comes from …* (Olympia); *5 The first Olympic Games shown on television were in …* (Berlin). If students don't understand *medal* and/or *torch*, draw pictures on the board to clarify the meaning. Check answers as a class.

1 READING

a 💬🔊 Read the questions with the students and check that they understand that questions 3a–d refer to the picture of Jonnie Peacock (the man on SB p. 80). Put students into pairs to ask and answer the questions. Don't check answers at this point.

b Students read the text quickly and check their answers to 1a. Ask students what other things they wanted to know about Jonnie Peacock and see if the questions they wrote in 1a were answered in the text. If you wish, give students information from Culture Notes below.

Answers
3 a He runs / does track.   c He's at the Paralympic Games.
   b He's from Cambridge.   d Students' own questions

🌍 CULTURE NOTES

Jonnie Peacock (b. 1993) started competing in track and field competitions in 2009, but he didn't become a household name until the final of the 100 meters at the London 2012 Paralympic Games. At the age of 19, only 14 years after spending four days in a coma and losing his right leg, he set a new Paralympic record with his winning time of 10.90 seconds. He was the youngest athlete competing in the final, and his win was watched by over six million people. Peacock also won gold for the 100 meters at the IPC Athletics World Championships in Lyon, France, in 2013. He was awarded an MBE in 2013 for his services to track and field. Then, in 2016, he won a gold medal again at the 2016 Paralympic Games in Rio de Janeiro with an even faster time.

c Tell students to read the text again in detail. Individually, students answer the questions. Check answers as a class. You may wish to help students with words in the Vocabulary Support box.

Answers
1 He was like most boys. He loved to play sports.
2 He became very sick with meningitis. The doctors saved his life, but they couldn't save his right leg.
3 They were surprised because he could do so much only 18 months after he lost his leg.
4 Some of the Paralympic athletes can't walk, and some can't see at all or very well. But in their sports, they can do things that most people can't.
5 Jonnie is famous because he won gold in the 2012 and 2016 Paralympic Games. He also competed on a TV show called *Strictly Come Dancing*.

📖 VOCABULARY SUPPORT

artificial (B2) – something made by people, not a natural thing

athlete (B1) – a person who is good at physical activities like running, jumping, etc. and who is often in competitions

disabled (B1) – someone who has trouble doing things because of a physical or mental problem

meningitis – a very dangerous infection usually caused by bacteria, viruses, or fungi in the brain and spine

surprised (A2) – the feeling when something happens that you didn't expect

💡 EXTRA ACTIVITY

Ask students to read the text again and decide if sentences 1–5 are true or false: *1 Jonnie nearly died because his parents didn't take him to the hospital.* (F – His parents took him to the hospital and he nearly died there.) *2 Running was always Jonnie's favorite sport.* (F – Soccer was his favorite sport when he was a child.) *3 Jonnie's parents gave him his artificial leg.* (F – The doctors gave him his artificial leg.) *4 One of the first activities Jonnie did with his new artificial leg was dancing.* (T) *5 Jonnie started to practice a lot a year before the London 2012 Paralympic Games.* (F – He started to practice a lot two years before the London 2012 Paralympic Games.)

d Individually, students underline the parts of the text that surprise them. They then tell a partner.

e 💬🔊 Discuss the question as a class.

2 GRAMMAR
can / can't, could / couldn't for ability

a Books closed. On the board, write *I … speak English really well.* Point to yourself, show students a confident face, and then point to the blank. Elicit the missing word (*can*), and write it in the sentence. Then, write on the board *I … speak Chinese at all.* (Change *Chinese* to a language you can't speak, if necessary.) Again, point to yourself, but this time show students a frustrated face. Elicit the missing word (*can't*), and write it on the board. Ask students: *Do we use "can" to talk about something that's possible or something that's necessary?* Elicit *something that's possible.* Students open their books and complete the exercise. Check answers as a class.

Answers
1 couldn't
2 could
3 can't
4 can; can't
5 Can

b Give students one minute to read the rules and complete them. Check answers as a class.

> **Answers**
> present; past
> question

c Elicit the two correct answers as a class.

> **Answers**
> b and c

d ⏵ **08.01** **Pronunciation** Play the recording for students to listen and answer the question. Check the answer as a class. Drill the sentences, making sure students are not pronouncing /l/ in *could /couldn't.*

> **Answer**
> No, you can't.

⊙ CAREFUL!

There are several common student mistakes with *can / can't, could / couldn't* for ability. Highlight the following typical errors:

- using the present in place of the past and vice versa – this type of error may be obvious, e.g., *... and can't believe it.* (Correct form = *His parents were very surprised and* **couldn't** *believe it*).
- not using the base form of the verb after *can/can't/could/ couldn't*, e.g., *I couldn't to swim ...* (Correct form = *I* **couldn't** **swim** *when I was a child*), or using *-ing*, e.g., *Later, we can playing soccer ...* (Correct form = *Later, we* **can play** *soccer in the park*).

---

e ⏵⏵ ⏵ **08.02** Students read the information in Grammar Focus 8A on SB p. 152. Play the recording where indicated and ask students to listen and repeat. Students then complete the exercises. Check answers as a class, making sure students are not confusing past and present and are using the base form after *can / can't, could / couldn't.* Tell students to go to SB p. 81.

Answers (Grammar Focus 8A SB p. 153)

a 2 couldn't 4 can't 6 can
   3 can   5 couldn't 7 could

b 2 Rob couldn't cook a meal when he was a boy. He can cook a meal now.
   3 Rob could ride a bike when he was a boy. He can't ride a bike now.
   4 Rob couldn't run 25 km when he was a boy. He can run 25 km now.
   5 Rob couldn't speak Spanish when he was a boy. He can speak Spanish now.

c 2 She ~~cans~~ can speak ...
   3 ... ~~you can swim~~ can you swim?
   4 I could ~~ran~~ run ...
   5 I ~~didn't could~~ couldn't understand ...
   6 ~~Does he can~~ Can he cook?
   7 Yes, he ~~did~~ could.

♀ FAST FINISHERS

Ask fast finishers to write sentences like those in Grammar Focus, Exercise b about themselves, e.g., *I couldn't speak English when I was a girl. I can speak English now.*

94

---

3 LISTENING

a 💬🎙 Give students one minute to review items 1–4. Ask students how they would form the questions to ask their classmates about items 1–4. Write on the board the correct forms: *Do you go running? Have you ever run in a marathon or half-marathon? How often do you exercise?* Students get up and ask and answer each other's questions to find someone who 1) often goes running, 2) never goes running, 3) once ran in a marathon or half-marathon, and 4) exercises once a week or more. As you monitor, don't interrupt fluency. Once it appears that students have asked most or all of their classmates, ask them to share their findings in complete sentences.

b Give students one minute to read the question and form an opinion. Invite students to share their answers with the class, and encourage students to justify their answers as much as possible.

c ⏵ **08.03** Play the recording for students to listen for general meaning and answer the question. Check the answers as a class.

> **Answers**
> 1 running, exercise
> 2 running too much

Audioscript

HOST Hanna, welcome.
HANNA Thank you.
HO So, it's an interesting question. Running is very popular, lots of people train for marathons. But is it actually good for you?
HA Well, yes, running is good for you. It's good for your heart, it makes you feel good, it's fun ...
HO But it can be bad for you?
HA Sure. If you train over a long time, or if you do too much, it can be bad for your heart. That's quite clear.
HO OK, someone wants to train for a marathon. What do you tell them? How can they stay safe?
HA Well, first I'd say, don't do a marathon; start with a half-marathon!
HO OK, half-marathon.
HA And then – basically follow three rules.
HO OK.
HA Number one: don't do too much. Don't go from nothing to two hours' running. Start

with 20 minutes, then do a bit more, then a bit more.
HO So you build up slowly.
HA Exactly. Then number two: drink a lot of water, and I mean a lot. When you run, your body gets hot, so you need water. You see people in marathons sometimes - they seem just fine, then suddenly boom, they're down. They can't continue. Usually — I'd say, 70, 80 percent of the time — it's because they didn't drink enough water. Simple as that.
HO OK, so water. What's rule number three?
HA Listen to your body; that's really important. You feel tired ... stop. Your foot hurts ... stop. People often fight against it. They think, "Yeah, I can do this," but that's how you have problems. And also - enjoy it. It's for fun, it's not your work.
HO OK, so that's rule number four!
HA I guess so, yeah.

---

d ⏵ **08.03** Students listen to the recording again for specific details and answer the questions. They compare in pairs. Check answers as a class.

> **Answers**
> Rule No. 1: Don't <u>do too much.</u>
>   At the start, run <u>for 20 minutes.</u>
> Rule No. 2: <u>Drink</u> a lot of <u>water.</u>
>   When you run, you <u>need water.</u>
> Rule No. 3: Listen <u>to your body.</u>
>   If you feel tired, <u>stop.</u>
>   If your foot hurts, <u>stop.</u>
> Rule No. 4: <u>Enjoy it!</u>

e 💬🎙 Students work in small groups, discussing their ideas. Groups share their answers with the class.

4 VOCABULARY Sports and exercise

a Individually, students match the words with the pictures. Check answers as a class. Drill each word.

> **Answers**
> a play badminton   d skate
> b do yoga   e ride a bike
> c dance   f ski

b ⟫ ▶08.04–08.05 Students complete the exercises in Vocabulary Focus 8A on SB p. 167. Play the recording for students to complete the Pronunciation activities. Monitor Exercise f and check other answers as a class. Tell students to go back to SB p. 81.

> **Answers (Vocabulary Focus SB p. 167)**
> **a** 1 martial arts   5 (American) football   9 snowboarding
>   2 fishing   6 volleyball   10 soccer
>   3 golf   7 running   11 exercises
>   4 hockey   8 sailing
> **b**
>
> | go | play | do |
> | --- | --- | --- |
> | fishing
sailing
snowboarding | hockey
(American) football
volleyball
soccer | exercises |
>
> **c** 1 *play*   2 *go*   3 *do*
> **d** different
> **e** 1 football   2 football   3 judo   4 football   5 judo   6 judo
> **f** Students' own answers

> 💡 **FAST FINISHERS**
>
> Ask fast finishers to add more activities to the columns in Vocabulary Focus, Exercise b, e.g., *go climbing/surfing*, *play tennis/basketball*, *do aerobics*, etc.

c Individually, students read the sentences and put them in order. They then check in pairs. Check answers as a class. Ask students which of the sentences is true for them.

> **Answers**
> 1 c (I can play baseball really well.)
> 2 a (I can play baseball pretty well.)
> 3 b (I can't play baseball very well.)
> 4 d (I can't play baseball at all.)

d 💬 In pairs or small groups, students ask and answer questions about the activities. Monitor, but don't interrupt fluency unless students make mistakes with *can/can't*.

5 SPEAKING

a Give students a few minutes to prepare and write sentences for the four categories. Monitor and help as necessary.

> 💡 **EXTRA ACTIVITY**
>
> Before students work together in 5b, drill some example sentences and questions to check that students are stressing them correctly. Check that students understand that in affirmative sentences and questions, *can/can't/could/couldn't* isn't stressed, e.g., *I can <u>dance</u> the <u>samba</u>. Can you <u>dance</u> the <u>samba</u>?* However, in negative sentences, both *can't/couldn't* and the main verb are stressed, e.g., *I <u>can't</u> <u>dance</u> the <u>samba</u>.* The rhythm is very important as native speakers differentiate affirmative from negative primarily by the stress of the sentence, not by the /t/ on the end of *can't*, which, as in the example above (*I can't dance …*), is often omitted.
>
> Students may also benefit from hearing you clap out the rhythm for them so that they can then apply the rhythm to the sentence, e.g., *I can <u>dance</u> the <u>samba</u>* would be "clap clap CLAP clap CLAP clap."

b 💬 Students work in small groups, asking and answering each other's questions to find out if they can or could do the same things. As you monitor, don't interrupt fluency, but note any mistakes with the content of this lesson. After 5c, write the mistakes on the board and ask students to correct them.

c 💬 Read the examples with the class. Then, ask students to share the things they have in common.

> 🔄 **LOA TIP REVIEW AND REFLECT**
>
> • Draw a scale on the board from 1 to 5. Under 1, write: *This is difficult for me.* Under 5, write: *This is easy for me.*
>
> • Students put their hands behind their backs. Tell them that you will count down (3, 2, 1 …) and then you want them to show you between one and five fingers, depending on how confident they feel about the topics *can / can't* and then *could / couldn't*.

> ⊕ **ADDITIONAL MATERIAL**
>
> Workbook 8A
>
> Photocopiable activities: Grammar 8A, Vocabulary 8A, Pronunciation 8A

8B HOW EASY IS IT TO GET IN SHAPE?

At the end of this lesson, students will be able to:
- read and understand a text about a new type of exercise
- use *have to / don't have to* correctly to talk about rules and things they need and don't need to do
- understand people talking about doing exercise
- use a lexical set of parts of the body correctly
- talk about what they have to do and have to have for different activities

💡 OPTIONAL LEAD-IN

Before students arrive, write a mini-questionnaire on the board.

Are you healthy and in shape?
Can you …
– swim for 30 minutes?
– ride a bike 10 kilometers?
– run a half-marathon?
– do a lot of exercise and not feel tired?

Do you …
– eat healthy food?
– drink two liters of water every day?
– sleep eight hours every night?
– go to the gym every week?

As students arrive, put them into pairs or small groups to talk about the questions. Monitor and check that they are using the correct auxiliary verbs in the short answers. Invite students to share their answers with the class and find out if any students can answer yes to all the questions.

1 READING

a 💬 Pre-teach the phrase *get in shape* (to become healthy and strong after a lot of exercise). Give students one minute to think about their answers to the questions. They then talk about getting in shape and doing exercise in pairs or small groups. If you used the optional lead-in, students can also discuss which of the things in the mini-questionnaire they think are important for getting in shape.

b Tell students they should read only the first paragraph of the article ("Only Five Minutes of Exercise a Day …"). They then work individually, answering the questions in that paragraph.

c 💬 Elicit from the class what they think the new type of exercise is. They then read the rest of the text for general meaning to find out if they were correct. You may then wish to teach the word *intensity* (the level you do something, usually high, medium, or low).

> **Answer**
> The new type of exercise is High Intensity Interval Training (HIIT).

d Students read the text again in detail. Individually, they complete the fact sheet. Check answers as a class. You may wish to help students with words in the Vocabulary Support box.

> **Answers**
> warm up ➔ 20 to 30 seconds of intense exercise ➔ rest (repeat 2 times)
> How often? Time: a few minutes a day
> Good for: Getting in shape, preventing diabetes and heart disease

📖 VOCABULARY SUPPORT

diabetes – a problem where the body can't control the quantity of sugar in the blood correctly

heart disease – a serious problem with the heart, often caused by bad diet and/or insufficient exercise

muscle (B2) – the parts of your body that are connected to bones and make them move

scientist (B1) – a person that works in science

e 💬 Discuss the questions as a class and find out if any students have tried an exercise routine like HIIT.

2 GRAMMAR *have to / don't have to*

a Books closed. Write incomplete sentences 1–3 on the board and ask students to complete them orally as a class. Don't complete the sentences on the board yet. Drill the sentences. Students open their books and complete the sentences. Check answers by completing the sentences on the board.

> **Answers**
> 1 have to
> 2 don't have to
> 3 have to

b Individually, students choose the correct answers. They compare in pairs. Check answers as a class.

> **Answers**
> a need to
> b don't need to
> c need to

🔄 LOA TIP CONCEPT CHECKING

- Check that students have fully understood the meaning of *have to / don't have to*. Write sentences 1–3 and meanings a–c on the board. Ask students to match 1–3 with a–c: *1 You don't have to bring a dictionary to class. 2 You have to be quiet during the exam. 3 You have to spend more time studying. a This is a rule. b This is something that is necessary. c This is something that isn't necessary.* (Answers: 1 c, 2 a, 3 b)

- Focus students' attention on the negative (*You don't have to bring a dictionary to class.*) and ask: *Is it necessary to bring a dictionary to class?* (no), *Is there a problem if you bring a dictionary to class?* (no), *Can you do it if you want?* (yes).

c ▶ 08.06 **Pronunciation** Play the recording for students to answer the questions. Check answers as a class. Drill the sentences.

> **Answers**
> 1 /f/   2 unstressed

⊙ CAREFUL!

At this level, students will probably use *have to* correctly. However, when they are not working on it in controlled exercises, they may inadvertently substitute *must* in contexts where it isn't appropriate, e.g., ~~Why do I must practice?~~ (Correct form = *Why do I **have to** practice?*). The most common error with the negative is the formation. Students may make the negative with *nothing*, e.g., ~~You have to pay nothing!~~ (Correct form = *You **don't** have to pay **anything**!*) or may omit the auxiliary *don't*, e.g., ~~I have not to take the bus …~~ (Correct form = *I **don't have to** take the bus to work. I can walk.*).

d ≫ ▶ `08.07` Students read the information in Grammar Focus 8B on SB p. 152. Play the recording where indicated and ask students to listen and repeat. Students then complete the exercises. Check answers as a class, making sure students are forming the negative sentences with the auxiliary *don't* correctly. Tell students to go back to SB p. 83.

Answers (Grammar Focus 8B SB p. 153)

a 2 f 3 g 4 h 5 c 6 b 7 a 8 e
b 2 Do you have to buy; I do
   3 I don't have to pay
   4 I have to wear
   5 do we have to do
   6 I have to give; you don't
   7 does he have to be
   8 you have to walk
c Students' own answers

♀ FAST FINISHERS

Ask fast finishers to write sentences about things they *have to / don't have to* do in class, e.g., *We have to speak only in English.*, *We don't have to do homework every night.*, etc.

e Students work individually and write their sentences. Monitor and point out errors for students to self-correct.

f 💬🗨 Read the example with the students. Then, put them into pairs to tell each other about things they have to do and ask each other follow-up questions. Monitor and listen for correct use of *have to / don't have to* and check that students are forming the questions correctly.

♀ EXTRA ACTIVITY

Read out the following to students: *I'm a(n) …. I have to answer the phone, write emails, and take messages. I usually have to make people coffee, too! I don't have to work on weekends, but sometimes I have to work late in the evening.* Ask students to write down what job they think you're describing. When all students have decided, tell them to say the job at the same time to find out if they are correct. Count down *3, 2, 1 …* and elicit the answer from the class. (*receptionist*)

Individually, students then prepare their own clues for a job. Monitor and help as necessary. Then, put students into small groups to read their sentences and try to guess the jobs they are describing.

3 LISTENING

a 💬🗨 Tell students to look at pictures a and b. In pairs, students answer the questions. Check the answer to question 1 (yoga) as a class.

b ▶ `08.08` Play the recording for students to listen for general meaning and match the speakers and the pictures. Check answers as a class.

Answers

Stella – picture a; Mariana – picture b

Audioscript

STELLA Yoga is a great way to be in shape, strong, and healthy, and anyone can do it. My friends and I go to yoga classes every week. My favorite yoga position is very difficult, but it feels really good. You put your arms on the floor, then you put your legs in the air and try to touch your head with your toes. It's not easy, but I love it. But, please, don't try it at home! I needed years of practice to do that!

MARIANA I only started yoga three weeks ago. I'm very lazy, so I wanted to do some exercise that's easy. But, you know, it's not so simple! You need to think about how you move different parts of your body: your stomach, arms, and legs … And sometimes you don't move at all – you just stand in one place for two or three minutes. But my favorite part is the end of the class. We all lie on the floor and relax for five minutes. Can I tell you something? Last class, I was so tired that I fell sleep on the floor in the middle of the studio!

c ▶ `08.08` Students listen to the recording again for specific details and decide if the sentences are true or false. They then check in pairs. When checking answers, ask students to correct the false sentences and, if possible, to justify their answers.

Answers

1 T
2 F (Her favorite yoga exercise is very difficult to do.)
3 T
4 F (Mariana doesn't think beginner yoga is easy.)
5 T
6 F (The end of each yoga lesson is her favorite part of the class.)

4 VOCABULARY Parts of the body

a Books closed. Pre-teach the vocabulary and correct pronunciation by pointing to parts of your body and eliciting the word if students know it, or saying it yourself if they don't. Drill each word. Don't allow students to write anything down. As you introduce new items, keep going back to review items you've already taught by pointing at that part of your body again. Increase the pace as you go to increase the challenge for students. When you've taught all the words, students open their books and match the words in the box with the picture. Check answers as a class.

Answers

 1 head
 2 back
 3 neck
 4 stomach
 5 arm
 6 hand
 7 finger
 8 leg
 9 foot
10 toe

b 💬🗨 In pairs or small groups, students talk about the questions. Check answers as a class.

Suggested answers

1 arm, back, finger, foot, hand, leg, neck, toe
2 back, head, neck, stomach

c ▶ 08.09–08.10 Students complete the exercises in Vocabulary Focus 8B on SB p. 168. Play the recording for students to check their answers to Exercise c and complete the Pronunciation activity. Monitor Exercises e and h and check other answers as a class. Tell students to go back to SB p. 83.

> **Answers (Vocabulary Focus 8B SB p. 168)**
>
> **a** 1 f 2 h 3 d 4 a
> **b** short / long
> **c** b She has short curly dark hair.
>   c He has short curly blonde hair.
>   e He has long straight dark hair.
>   g She has long curly blonde hair.
> **d** and **e** Students' own answers
> **f** 1 e 2 a 3 d 4 f 5 b 6 c
> **g** prett | y a | ttrac | tive good-look | ing

> 💡 **FAST FINISHERS**
>
> Ask fast finishers to write sentences to describe people in their families using the vocabulary for appearance.

5 SPEAKING

a Give students a few minutes to choose one of the activities and write notes. Monitor and help as necessary.

b 💬🗨 Put students into pairs. Students then tell each other about what people have to do to get ready for the activity they have chosen and what they have to have. They try to guess each other's activity.

> ⊕ **ADDITIONAL MATERIAL**
>
> Workbook 8B
>
> Photocopiable activities: Grammar 8B, Vocabulary 8B

8C EVERYDAY ENGLISH
I'm a little tired

At the end of this lesson, students will be able to:

- understand informal conversations in which people talk about health and how they feel
- use appropriate phrases to talk about health and how they feel
- use appropriate phrases to express sympathy
- connect words ending in /t/ and /d/ to the next word in a sentence
- talk about health and how they feel

> 💡 **OPTIONAL LEAD-IN**
>
> Tell students you're going to give them four clues to guess a sport or free-time activity. Read the following clues: *1 You have to play this game on a team. 2 You can watch this game at a stadium. 3 You can't touch the ball with your hands. 4 You don't have to wear special clothes or shoes to play it.* (soccer) Repeat the process with: *1 You have to do this activity with a partner. 2 You can do it at a gym. 3 You can't wear shoes to do this activity. 4 You have to wear special white clothes.* (martial arts)
>
> Put students into pairs to choose another sport or free-time activity and write four clues. If students use *can/could* and *have to / don't have to*, check that they are using them correctly. However, don't insist that they use them in every sentence. Pairs then read their clues to the class for other students to guess.

1 LISTENING

a 💬🗨 In pairs, students look at the pictures and answer the questions. Elicit students' ideas, but don't check answers at this point.

b ▶ 08.11 Play Part 1 of the audio recording for students to check their answers in 1a and find out what Kate tells Alex to do. Check answers as a class.

> **Answers**
>
> 1 They are at a gym.   3 Yes, she's in good shape.
> 2 Alex feels a little tired/awful.   4 Kate tells Alex to sit down.

> **Audioscript (Part 1)**
>
> **KATE** This gym is great, right? How's your first workout?
> **ALEX** Terrific! I feel healthier already! How far do you run on this treadmill?
> **K** Five miles.
> **A** Great! Me too.
> **K** You don't have to, you know. You can stop anytime.
> **A** If you can run five miles, I can run five miles, too.
>
> **K** Just be sure to take it slow.
> **A** Uh, huh.
> **K** Hey, are you all right?
> **A** Um, I think so.
> **K** Are you sure? You don't look so good.
> **A** Yes, I'm a little tired. Actually, I feel awful …
> **K** Oh, no. Come and sit down. Just take a break. Drink some water.

c ▶ 08.12 Read the questions with the class. Play Part 2 of the audio recording for students to choose the correct answers. Check answers as a class.

> **Answers**
>
> 1 c
> 2 b

2 USEFUL LANGUAGE
Talking about health and how you feel

a Individually, students complete the mini-conversations.

b ▶ 08.11–08.12 Play Parts 1 and 2 of the audio recording again for students to check their answers in 2a. Check answers as a class.

> **Answers**
> 1 all right
> 2 look so good
> 3 'm a little tired
> 4 the matter
> 5 feel well

c Read the words in the box and check that students understand the meaning by asking them: *What's a toothache?* In monolingual classes, you could ask: *What's "toothache" in (students' L1)?* Individually, students decide which words in the box they can use instead of the words in bold in the sentences. They then check in pairs. Check answers as a class.

> **Answers**
> I'm sick/hungry.
> I have a stomachache / a cold / a toothache / a fever.
> My arm/foot hurts.

d 💬🗩 In pairs, students take turns inventing health problems and asking each other how they feel. Monitor and check that students are using *feel*, *have*, and *hurts* for the correct problems.

> 💡 **EXTRA ACTIVITY**
>
> Play a listing game (see p. 153) with students. Mime having a sudden pain from your tooth and say *I have …* to elicit *a toothache*. Then, mime a pain in your back and say *My back …* to elicit *hurts*. Point to your tooth and then at your back to elicit *I have a toothache and my back hurts*. Clutch your stomach and look sick to elicit *I'm sick*. Then, point to all three things to elicit *I have a toothache, my back hurts, and I'm sick*. Gesture for another student to continue and add another problem and elicit it from the class. They then nominate another student to continue and so on until the list is too long to remember. Students can then play in small groups.

3 CONVERSATION SKILLS
Expressing sympathy

a Suddenly hold your hand up to your head and groan loudly. Elicit an appropriate question from the class, e.g., *Are you all right?* or *What's the matter?* Say: *I'm not sure. I don't feel well. I have a headache and I'm sick.* Gesture to elicit a response and see if students can remember an appropriate phrase, e.g., *Oh no, I'm sorry to hear that,* or *That's too bad.* Students look at the extracts from the audio and complete what Kate says. Check answers as a class.

> **Answers**
> 1 no
> 2 sorry
> 3 bad

b Answer the question as a class.

> **Answer**
> 1 I feel sorry for you.

c 💬🗩 In pairs, students take turns saying the sentences and giving sympathy with appropriate phrases.

> 🔄 **LOA TIP** CONCEPT CHECKING
>
> • As students practice telling each other the problems, monitor and check that they are using correct sentence stress and falling intonation in the phrases for expressing sympathy. If necessary, clap out the rhythm of the sentences and phrases for them so that they can then apply the rhythm to the sentence, e.g., Oh <u>no</u>. would be "clap CLAP." You could also show students the downward movement at the end of the phrases using hand gestures to give them a visual reference.

4 PRONUNCIATION Connecting words

a ▶ 08.13 Play the recording for students to listen to sentences 1–4 and underline the correct words in the sentence. They then check in pairs. Check answers as a class.

> **Answers**
> connects; no

> 📖 **LANGUAGE NOTES**
>
> Connecting words can cause serious problems for students trying to understand English spoken by native speakers. The most common example of this is covered in 4a, when, in connected speech, a word which ends in /t/ and /d/ transfers this sound to the beginning of the following word, or even loses it completely. This type of exercise helps students understand that what they hear in spoken English may not correspond with breaks between words when the words are written down.

b 💬🗩 Students work in pairs, practicing saying the sentences and giving replies. Monitor and correct students' pronunciation as appropriate.

5 SPEAKING

a–b ≫ Divide the class into pairs and assign A and B roles. Student As read the first card on SB p. 85 and Student Bs read the first card on SB p. 134. Students then role-play the conversation. Monitor, but don't interrupt fluency unless students make mistakes with the content of this lesson. Students then read the second card and role-play the second situation.

♀ **FAST FINISHERS**

Ask fast finishers to close their books and invent similar conversations without looking at the phrases in 2a or 3a to help them.

⊕ **ADDITIONAL MATERIAL**

Workbook 8C

Photocopiable activities: Pronunciation 8C

Unit Progress Test

8D SKILLS FOR WRITING
However, I improved quickly

At the end of this lesson, students will be able to:

- understand an informal conversation in which people talk about a free-time activity
- ask and answer questions about something they do in their free time
- understand an article about a free-time activity
- link ideas with *however*
- use adverbs of manner correctly
- write an article about a free-time activity

♀ **OPTIONAL LEAD-IN**

Write the following free-time activities on the board: *using social media, exercising, eating at restaurants, online shopping, watching TV*. Tell students that these are five of the most popular free-time activities in the U.S. Put students into pairs or small groups and ask them to put them in order from 1 to 5 (with 1 being the favorite activity). Ask groups to share their answers with the class and tell students the correct order. (*1 watching TV, 2 using social media, 3 eating at restaurants, 4 online shopping, 5 exercising*) Ask students if they think the order would be similar or different in their country and ask them if they are surprised by any of the things that are or aren't on the list.

1 SPEAKING AND LISTENING

a 💬▶ Read the questions with the students and, if necessary, check the meaning of the six items in 1 by referring students to the pictures. Students then work in pairs or small groups, asking and answering the questions. If you used the optional lead-in, students can also discuss the five extra activities on the board. Invite students to share their answers with the class, and ask students what their favorite free-time activity is.

b Point to the picture of Gina and Andy next to the staff email and ask students: *Where do they work?* (in an office) and *What do you think they do?* (businessman/ businesswoman, manager, receptionist, etc.). Students then read the email and answer the questions. Check answers as a class.

Answers
1 b It's kind of boring.
2 a information about their free time

c ▶08.14 Play the recording for students to listen for general meaning and answer the questions. Check answers as a class. If your students work, ask them: *Would you write an article for your company blog? Why / Why not?*

Answers
1 riding a bike
2 No, he doesn't.

Audioscript

GINA Did you see the email about writing an article for the company blog?

ANDY Yes, I did.

G I guess it's true. We don't know each other very well. I mean, I have no idea if you have a hobby or not. You seem to be in good shape so … I don't know … maybe you play some kind of sport?

A Yeah, you're right. About a year ago, a friend of mine asked me to go on a bike ride with him. I laughed and said, "I can't do that – I don't have a bike." "No problem," he said. "I can lend you one." Well, I went and it was amazing. About two weeks later, I bought my own bike.

G That's great!

A Yeah, I ride my bike all the time – almost every day after work. I love it because it's a way of staying in shape and being outdoors at the same time. I could never go to a gym!

G No, I hate gyms, too.

A Riding a bike can be kind of dangerous in the city, and you always have to be careful in the traffic. A couple of months ago, a car sort of hit me.

G Oh no!

A I wasn't hurt badly – I just hurt my arm and my foot a little. But I try to get out of the city into the country. For example, last weekend I went for a two-day ride in the hills. There was almost no one on the road. It was amazing – I couldn't believe it.

G Well, there's something I didn't know about. You could write an article about that.

A Me? Write an article? No, I couldn't do that. I don't have time.

d ▶ 08.14 Students listen to the recording again for specific details and match the beginnings with the endings of the sentences. They then check in pairs. Check answers as a class.

Answers

1 f	4 d
2 a	5 c
3 b	6 e

> ♀ **EXTRA ACTIVITY**
>
> Ask students to listen again and decide if sentences 1–5 are true or false: *1 Andy and Gina are good friends.* (F – They don't know each other very well.) *2 Gina thinks Andy looks healthy.* (T) *3 Andy's friend lent him a bike the first time he went on a bike ride.* (T) *4 Gina and Andy both love the gym.* (F – They both hate gyms.) *5 Andy hurt his hand and his leg badly.* (F – Andy hurt his arm and his foot a little.)

e Students work individually. They think about an activity and answer the questions. Tell students to write notes, but not write complete sentences. Monitor and help as necessary.

> ⟳ **LOA TIP** ELICITING
>
> • When students have finished writing their notes in 1e, give them an opportunity to review question words and brainstorm useful questions before continuing. To elicit *what, where, when, who, which, whose,* etc., write a large *W* on the board and say: *Tell me question words!* Point out that some common questions start with *H* and elicit *how, how often, how much/many,* etc.
>
> • Ask students to look at their notes from 1e and try to predict questions that their partner could ask them, e.g., *Why did you start doing it?, How much does it cost to do it?,* etc. As students share their questions with the class, write them on the board for students to refer to in 1f. If students need more support, consider giving them prompts to help them formulate useful questions, e.g., *Why / start?, How much / cost / do?,* etc.

f 💬 Tell students that in this activity, the emphasis is on communication, not on perfect English. In pairs, students ask and answer questions about their activities.

> ♀ **FAST FINISHERS**
>
> Ask fast finishers to write a short paragraph to summarize the information their partner told them.

2 READING

a Point to the picture of Dylan and the article and say: *This is Dylan. He works for the same company as Andy and Gina. He wrote this article for the company blog. What's his favorite free-time activity?* Elicit *hiking.* Students then read the article quickly and check the things that are the same. Check answers as a class.

Answers

1 ✔ they do their free-time activities outdoors
3 ✔ they get in shape doing their free-time activities

b Tell students to read the article again in detail and decide if the sentences are true or false and correct the false sentences. They compare in pairs. Check answers as a class.

Answers

1 T
2 F (He didn't like the idea of hiking immediately because it didn't sound very interesting.)
3 T
4 T
5 F (It's easy to learn how to go hiking because you only have to know how to walk.)

3 WRITING SKILLS
Linking ideas with *however*; adverbs of manner

a Books closed. Write the example sentences on the board, leaving a blank in place of *However.* Point to the blank and ask students: *What's this word?* If students suggest *but,* point clearly at the period and tell them that we don't usually start a new sentence with *but.* Elicit *however.* Students then open their books and answer the question. Check the answer as a class.

Answer

Yes, it is.

b Students read Dylan's article again and underline three more examples of *however.* Check answers as a class.

Answers

However, I was really out of shape.
However, I decided it could be good exercise for me, so I went along.
However, I improved quickly …
However, you have to buy special boots …

We use a comma after *however.*

c Students work individually, linking the sentences with *however.* Monitor and check that students are writing them as two sentences and putting a comma after *however.* Check answers as a class.

Answers

1 c I can only do very simple exercises. However, I feel really in shape.
2 b I started doing yoga about six years ago. However, I can't do the difficult positions.
3 a I fell off my bike and hurt my leg. However, I didn't stop riding.

d Read the example sentence and answer the question as a class.

Answer

It tells us how he did it.

e Individually, students look at the article in 2a again and find the adverbs that go with the verbs. Check answers as a class.

Answers

1 walk <u>slowly</u>; walk pretty <u>fast</u>
2 improve <u>quickly</u>

f Read the rule with the class and elicit which adverb from the article is different.

Answer

Fast is different because it is irregular.

4 WRITING

a Students work individually to plan an article about a free-time activity. Suggest they write about the activity they talked about in 1f, but allow them to choose a different activity if they prefer. Monitor and help with vocabulary and suggest ideas if necessary.

b Remind students to use adverbs of manner when writing their articles. If you're short on time, this exercise can be completed for homework. Students could then bring their articles to the next class.

c In pairs, students switch articles and check their partner's work. They then give each other feedback.

⚲ EXTRA ACTIVITY

If you normally use a code or abbreviations when correcting students' written work, e.g., *GR* for a grammar mistake, *WW* for a wrong word, *SP* for spelling, remind students of the system in place and ask them, in pencil, to find mistakes in their partner's work. If you don't normally use a code or abbreviations, ask students to circle things in pencil which they think their partner should check. Monitor and help as necessary. If students have not included the items in 4c, or have made any other mistakes, they prepare a second draft of the article.

⊕ ADDITIONAL MATERIAL

Workbook 8D

UNIT 8
Review and extension

1 VOCABULARY

a Complete the first sentence as an example with the class. Students then complete the other sentences with the words in the box. Check answers as a class.

> **Answers**
> 1 baseball 2 ski 3 bike 4 badminton 5 dance 6 yoga

b Students look at pictures 1–3 and then complete the words for the body. Check answers and spelling by asking individual students to write the correct answers on the board.

> **Answers**
> 1 head, neck 2 arm, hand, finger 3 leg, foot, toe

2 GRAMMAR

a Individually, students complete the text. They then check in pairs. Check answers as a class.

> **Answers**
> 1 can   4 can't
> 2 can   5 can
> 3 could   6 couldn't

b Students complete the sentences with the correct form of *have to*. Check answers as a class.

> **Answers**
> 1 have to   4 have to
> 2 don't have to   5 has to
> 3 Do (I) have to

3 WORDPOWER *tell / say*

a Books closed. Dictate sentences 1–3, saying *beep* instead of *told* and *say*. Students listen and write down the sentences. They then check in pairs and try to decide together the word they think can complete each sentence. Check that they understand that they don't have to use the same word in all three sentences. Students open their books, look at the sentences, and check their answers. Finally, they match the sentences with the pictures. Check answers as a class.

> **Answers**
> 1 c 2 a 3 b

b Point to the bold words in 3a and elicit which word, *tell* or *say*, matches each group of phrases as a class.

> **Answers**
> 1 say 2 tell

⊙ CAREFUL!

Students often have problems with the constructions which follow *tell* and *say*. Most mistakes are usually connected with the indirect object and word order. Students may use *to* after *tell*, e.g., ~~I told to my little sister a story~~ (Correct form = I **told my little sister** a story), or they may not use *to* after *say*, e.g., ~~He said me hello quickly~~ (Correct form = He **said** hello **to me** quickly).

Other problems relate to the specific collocations, e.g., *tell a story / the truth, say hello/sorry,* etc. If students ask, tell them that they have to memorize these as there is no clear rule governing when to use *tell* and when to use *say*.

c Individually, students complete the sentences with *to* if possible. Check answers as a class and ask students: *Which verb do we use* to *with? Say or* tell*?* (say).

> **Answers**
> 1 –
> 2 to
> 3 –
> 4 to
> 5 –

d Students complete the sentences, working individually. They then check in pairs. Check answers as a class.

> **Answers**
> 1 story
> 2 me
> 3 truth
> 4 thanks
> 5 sorry
> 6 you

e As an example, complete one or two of the sentences so that they are true for you. Students then complete the sentences with their own ideas. Monitor and point out errors for students to self-correct.

f 💬 In pairs, students tell each other their sentences. Encourage students to ask follow-up questions if possible.

♀ EXTRA ACTIVITY

Write the following jumbled sentences on the board and ask students to put them in order:
1 never / she / to her brother / sorry / says;
2 tell / can / a really funny joke / me / you ?;
3 thank you / I / to them / for lunch / didn't say;
4 a really strange story / me / told / my friend / yesterday;
5 I / the truth / don't think / told / me / he
(Answers: 1 She never says sorry to her brother.
2 Can you tell me a really funny joke?
3 I didn't say thank you to them for lunch.
4 My friend told me a really strange story yesterday.
5 I don't think he told me the truth.)

≫ Photocopiable activities: Wordpower 8

↻ LOA REVIEW YOUR PROGRESS

Students look back through the unit, think about what they've studied, and decide how well they did. Students work on weak areas by using the appropriate sections of the Workbook and the Photocopiable activities.

UNIT 9

CLOTHES AND SHOPPING

At the end of this unit, students will be able to:

- understand information, texts, and conversations about shopping and shopping malls, what people shop for, and buying clothes and presents
- ask for and give information about where people are, what they are doing, and what clothes they are wearing
- shop and pay for clothes
- use appropriate phrases when choosing and paying for clothes and when saying something nice
- distinguish between formal and informal emails
- write formal and informal thank-you emails

UNIT CONTENTS

G GRAMMAR
- Present continuous
- Simple present or present continuous

V VOCABULARY
- Shopping: *bookstore, bus stop, coffee shop, parking lot, ATM, drugstore, clothing store, department store, entrance, fast food restaurant, information desk, stairs*
- Money and prices
- Clothes: *boots, dress, earrings, gloves, jeans, jewelry, necklace, pants, raincoat, ring, scarf, shirt, shoes, shorts, skirt, sneakers, socks, sweater, T-shirt, watch*
- Wordpower: *time*

P PRONUNCIATION
- Word stress in compound nouns
- Sentence stress with the present continuous
- Sound and spelling: *o* (/ɑ/, /u/, /ʌ/, and /oʊ/)
- Silent letters
- Connecting words

C COMMUNICATION SKILLS
- Asking and answering questions about what people are doing
- Talking about festivals in your country and which festival you would like to go to
- Describing what a person is wearing
- Choosing clothes in a store and paying for them
- Using appropriate phrases to say something nice
- Talking about who you give presents to and how you say thank you
- Writing formal and informal emails to say thank you for a present

GETTING STARTED

☿ OPTIONAL LEAD-IN

Books closed. Write these sentences on the board: *I love going shopping – it's my favorite thing to do. I hate buying clothes – I can never find what I want. I prefer shopping in small, local stores, not big stores downtown.* Put students into pairs or small groups to discuss the sentences and say if they agree or disagree and why. Monitor and praise students who are able to express their ideas, even if their English isn't perfect. Invite pairs or small groups to share their answers with the class. Encourage students to justify their ideas as much as possible. Ask students to open their books and look at the picture. Ask: *Did you like shopping when you were a child?* Elicit a short reaction from the class.

a 💬🗩 Give students one minute to think about their answers to the questions before talking about the picture as a class.

b 💬🗩 Read the question with students and then put them into pairs to discuss where the best places to shop are. Help with vocabulary and pronunciation, but don't interrupt fluency. Students share their ideas as a class.

☿ EXTRA ACTIVITY

Individually, students write down two sentences about their shopping habits, e.g., *I go to the mall every Saturday, but I never spend any money; I bought this watch for $10 near my house.* One sentence should be true and one false. Monitor and point out errors for students to self-correct. In pairs, they then read their sentences to each other and decide if they are true or false. Each student then chooses one of their sentences to read to the class for the other students to decide if it is true or false.

Exercises **a** and **b** can be prepared as homework before this lesson to give students time to look up unfamiliar vocabulary. Ask students to look at the picture and to prepare their answers to the questions as homework to talk about in the next class.

9A WE'RE NOT BUYING ANYTHING

At the end of this lesson, students will be able to:
- use a lexical set of shopping words correctly
- understand conversations in which people plan to meet at a shopping mall
- use the affirmative, negative, and question forms of the present continuous
- ask and answer questions about what people are doing

💡 OPTIONAL LEAD-IN

Books closed. Write the following questions on the board:

Where do you usually go to …

get a new book or magazine?

sit down and relax with coffee?

have a burger, chips, and soda?

choose some new clothes for a party?

look for the perfect present for someone?

buy something when you have a headache?

Give students one or two examples, e.g., *When I go downtown, I always go to my favorite bookstore, Barnes & Noble. They sell thousands of books; My favorite place to sit down and relax with a coffee is Hot Numbers on my street;* etc. to make it clear that you want them to discuss specific places in their area. Put students into pairs or small groups to talk about the questions. Invite pairs or small groups to share their answers with the class and find out which places are particularly popular.

1 VOCABULARY Shopping

a Individually, students look at pictures 1–6 and match them with the words in the box. They compare in pairs. Check answers as a class. If you used the optional lead-in, students can match the places they talked about with the words in the box, e.g., *Barnes & Noble is a bookstore., Hot Numbers is a coffee shop.,* etc.

Answers

1 a coffee shop	4 a clothing store
2 a bookstore	5 a drugstore
3 a fast food restaurant	6 a department store

b Point to the map of the shopping mall and ask students to match the words in the box with the letters on the map. Check answers as a class.

Answers

a bus stop	d information desk
b entrance	e ATM
c stairs	f parking lot

c ▶️ **09.01 Pronunciation** Play the recording for students to identify which word is stressed in each case. Check the answer as a class. Drill each word.

Answer
the first word

d Complete the first item as an example with the class. You may wish to pre-teach the word *aspirin* (medicine to stop a part of your body from hurting). Students work individually, deciding where the people can go in the shopping mall. They then check in pairs. Check answers as a class.

Answers

1 clothing store / department store	4 drugstore
	5 parking lot
2 department store	6 fast food restaurant / coffee shop
3 bookstore	7 ATM

💡 FAST FINISHERS

Ask fast finishers to write sentences about some of the places not included in 1d (*bus stop, entrance, information desk, stairs*).

e ≫ ▶️ **09.02** Students complete the exercises in Vocabulary Focus 9A on p. 169. Play the recording for students to check their answers to Exercise a and repeat the prices. Monitor Exercise b and drill the prices. Tell students to go back to SB p. 90.

Answers (Vocabulary Focus 9A SB p. 169)
a 1a 2b 3b 4b 5a 6b 7b 8a

💡 EXTRA ACTIVITY

Play Bingo (see p. 152) with the class. Write 25 different prices on the board in numerals. Also include some pairs of numbers that you know often cause students problems, e.g., *$19 and $90*, or *$76.99 and $67.99*, etc. Students draw a Bingo grid and complete it with eight prices from the board. Play the game as a class.

2 LISTENING

a 💬 Students discuss the question in pairs or small groups. Invite pairs or small groups to share their answers with the class.

b Look at the map of the shopping mall and elicit suggestions for a good place for a group of friends to meet.

Answer
Students' own answers

c ▶️ **09.03** Play the recording for students to listen and answer the questions. Check answers as a class.

Answers
Sam wants to meet Addie at the mall. They might have problems finding each other.

Audioscript

CONVERSATION 1
ADDIE Hello?
SAM Hey, Addie. It's Sam. Do you want to go and see a movie tonight with Amy and Diego?
A Yeah, great idea, I'd love to.
S Let's meet at the mall at around seven. OK?
A Where? The mall's really big!
S Oh, I don't know. I'll call you when we get there and we can find each other.
A OK …

105

d ▶09.04 Tell students that they are going to listen to two more phone conversations. Play the recording for students to listen and underline the correct answers. Check answers as a class, and ask students to show you where the four people are on the map of the mall.

> **Answers**
> 1 in the bookstore   3 in the department store
> 2 at the bus stop   4 at the ATM

Audioscript

CONVERSATION 2
SAM Hello?
ADDIE Sam! Hi! Where are you? Are you getting a coffee?
S No, I'm just buying that new book I told you about. What are you doing?
A I'm just getting off the bus. So where do you want to meet? It's almost seven.
S Let's meet at the entrance in five minutes.
A All right.
S And can you call Amy and Diego to tell them where to meet?
A Yeah, sure, no problem. Hurry up!

CONVERSATION 3
DIEGO Hello?
ADDIE Diego, it's Addie. Where are you?
D Oh! Hi, Addie. I'm just getting some cash. Amy's looking at furniture.
A Furniture? Are you buying furniture?
D No, we're not buying anything. She's just looking.
A OK, well, can you meet Sam and me at the entrance to the movie theater in five minutes?
D Yeah, sure. See you there!

e 💬 Point to the pictures of Sam and Addie on their phones. Put students into pairs to answer the questions.

f ▶09.05 Play the recording for students to listen and check. Check answers as a class.

> **Answers**
> 1 Sam is looking at his watch because the movie's about to start.
> 2 Addie feels worried because Sam might be late for the movie.

Audioscript

CONVERSATION 4
ADDIE Hi, Amy! Hi, Diego!
AMY Hi!
DIEGO Hi!
AD Great to see you!
D Good to see you, too! Where's Sam?
AD I don't know. He told me to meet him here. Let me just call him.
SAM Hello?

AD Sam, where are you waiting for us?
S I'm standing by the entrance – you aren't here!
AD Yes, we are! We're waiting for you. I just bought our tickets.
S What? … Oh, no! I'm at the main entrance, not the movie theater entrance.
AD What? Quick, run! The movie is about to start!

3 GRAMMAR Present continuous

a ▶09.06 Books closed. Write the following four jumbled sentences on the board. Tell students they are about the information in 2d and ask them to put them in order: *1 a book / Sam / buying / is* (Sam is buying a book.); *2 getting off / Addie / is / the bus* (Addie is getting off the bus.); *3 is / Amy / at furniture / looking* (Amy is looking at furniture.); *4 Diego / some cash / is / getting* (Diego is getting some cash.). Ask: *What's similar about all four sentences?* Elicit that they all have the verb *be* and the *-ing* form of the verb. Tell students that this is called the present continuous. Students then match the questions and answers in the book. Play the recording for students to listen and check. Check answers as a class.

> **Answers**
> 1 b   2 d   3 a   4 c

106

b Complete the rule as a class.

> **Answer**
> a now

c Individually, students complete the charts. Check answers by copying the charts onto the board and asking individual students to come up and complete the sentences.

> **Answers**
>
> | Affirmative (+) | | Negative (–) | |
> | --- | --- | --- | --- |
> | I'm
We're
He's/She's | <u>reading</u> a magazine.
<u>talking</u> on the phone. | I'm not
We're not / We aren't
He's not / He isn't
She's not / She isn't | <u>drinking</u> coffee.
<u>waiting</u> at the entrance. |
>
> | *Yes/No* questions (?) | |
> | --- | --- |
> | Are you
Is he/she | <u>parking</u> the car? |

d ▶09.07 **Pronunciation** Play the recording for students to listen and notice the stress.

> 👁 **CAREFUL!**
>
> One of the most common student mistakes with the present continuous is with the spelling of the *-ing* forms. The spelling rules for *-ing* forms are highlighted in Grammar Focus 7B on SB p. 150. Highlight the correct spelling and the top five errors at this level: *writing* (NOT ~~writting~~), *coming* (NOT ~~comeing~~ or ~~comming~~), *studying* (NOT ~~studing~~), and *swimming* (NOT ~~swiming~~).

e ≫ ▶09.08 Students read the information in Grammar Focus 9A on SB p. 154. Play the recording where indicated and ask students to listen and repeat. Students then complete the exercises. Check answers as a class, making sure students are spelling the *-ing* forms correctly. Tell students to go back to SB p. 91.

> **Answers (Grammar Focus 9A SB p. 155)**
> **a** 2 They're talking.
>   3 He's not riding a horse. / He isn't riding a horse.
>   4 I'm doing a grammar exercise.
>   5 She's not wearing shoes. / She isn't wearing shoes.
>   6 They're playing tennis.
> **b** 2 is (she) smiling; 's feeling
>   3 Are (you) sleeping; 'm not
>   4 are (they) standing; 're not standing / aren't standing
>   5 Is (your brother) playing; 's not / isn't; 's playing
> **c** 2 I'm shopping   5 I'm standing   8 we're not stopping/
>   3 We're looking   6 are you wearing   we aren't stopping
>   4 We're driving   7 I'm wearing

> 💡 **FAST FINISHERS**
>
> Ask fast finishers to choose other pictures of people in the Student's Book and write sentences like those in Exercise a about what they are doing.

f Give students a few minutes to prepare and write three sentences. Monitor and check that they are spelling the *-ing* forms correctly and point out errors for them to self-correct.

g 💬 Read the example with the students. Put students into pairs to tell their partner their sentences and try to guess where they are. Monitor, but don't interrupt fluency unless students make mistakes with the present continuous forms.

4 SPEAKING

a ⟫ Divide the class into pairs and assign A and B roles. Student As read the instructions and look at the picture on SB p. 134. Student Bs read the instructions and look at the picture on SB p.136. Students then ask and answer questions to find the five differences.

9B EVERYONE'S DANCING IN THE STREETS

At the end of this lesson, students will be able to:

- read and understand posts about people's shopping habits and local festivals
- talk about festivals in their country
- distinguish between the simple present for things we usually do and the present continuous for things happening at the time of speaking
- understand conversations in which people talk about what they are wearing
- describe what a person is wearing

⚐ OPTIONAL LEAD-IN

Tell students you're going to describe a picture from Units 1–8 in the Student's Book. Tell students to close their books and listen. Read the following sentence twice: *They're riding their bicycles.* Say: *OK. Open your books. Find the picture!* (SB p. 69) Repeat the process with: *She's talking on the phone, and he's playing a video game.* (top left and middle left, SB p. 64) *They're sitting at their desks in a big room. They're taking an exam.* (bottom left, SB p. 22) *He's looking at clothes in a clothing store. (middle left, p. 56) They're in a restaurant, and they're looking at the menu and talking.* (bottom, SB pp. 44–45) Put students into pairs and ask them to write two or three similar sentences about pictures in the Student's Book using the present continuous. Monitor and point out errors for students to self-correct. Put students into larger groups. Separate students from their original partners. Students read their sentences and find the pictures.

1 READING

a 💬 Give students one minute to think about their answers to the questions before talking as a class about when they go shopping.

b Point to the two posts and ask students: *What kind of website is this?* (It's a social media site.) You may want to pre-teach the word *mask* using the picture on SB p. 92. Students read the texts quickly and match the people with the things they write about. Check answers as a class.

Answers
a B   b D   c J   d J

c Tell students to read the texts again in detail. Individually, students decide if the sentences are true or false. When checking answers, ask students to correct the false sentences. If you wish, give students information from Culture Notes on the next page.

Answers
1 F (He speaks English at work because his coworkers all speak English.)
2 T
3 T
4 F (She loves Venice in the winter.)
5 T
6 F (It's Carnevale and the whole city is like one big party.)

d Individually, students read the messages and decide
which is José's and which is Diana's. Check answers as a
class. You may wish to teach the word *dragon* using the
picture on SB p. 92.

> **Answers**
> left message – José
> right message – Diana

e Students discuss the questions in pairs or small
groups. Invite pairs or small groups to share their
answers with the class.

2 GRAMMAR
Simple present or present continuous

a Books closed. Write prompts 1 and 2 on the board and ask
students to write the complete sentences that appear in
José's online post and message: *1 I / meet / friends / mall*
(I usually meet friends at a mall.), *2 We / watch / dragon*
(We're watching a big, beautiful dragon). Students check
answers by looking at the complete sentences in the book.
Students match the sentences with the correct meaning.
Then, ask students to look at José's online post and
message and find more examples of his normal routine,
e.g., *In my free time, I sometimes study Mandarin and relax.*,
and things happening now, e.g., *Everyone's wearing red.*

> **Answers**
> 1 a   2 b

b Complete the rule as a class.

> **Answers**
> simple present; present continuous

c Students read Diana's online post and message again
and underline more examples of the simple present and
present continuous.

> **Answers**
> I <u>love</u> it here in Venice!
> It<u>'s</u> so beautiful…
> … but on the weekends I <u>get</u> some free time.
> I usually <u>walk</u> around and <u>look</u> at the old buildings…
> I <u>go</u> to museums.
> There <u>are</u> so many interesting …
> It<u>'s</u> very different …
> This week it<u>'s</u> Carnevale and the whole city <u>is</u> like one big party.
> It<u>'s</u> tonight…
> Everyone<u>'s dancing</u> in the streets and <u>having</u> a great time.
> We<u>'re</u> all <u>wearing</u> amazing clothes – I<u>'m</u> even <u>wearing</u> a dress!

d Students read the information in Grammar Focus 9B
on SB p. 154. Students then complete the exercises. Check
answers as a class, making sure students understand why
the simple present or present continuous is correct in
each case. Tell students to go back to SB p. 93.

> **Answers (Grammar Focus 9B SB p. 155)**
> **a** 2 today   4 this morning   6 'm enjoying   8 often
>   3 never   5 's dancing   7 on weekends
> **b** 1 We're getting; I'm watching
>   2 He's singing; he sings; They often play
>   3 Are you playing; I'm not; I'm trying; are you doing
> **c** Students' own answers

e ▶ **09.09** Students work individually, completing the conversation. Play the recording for students to listen and check. Check answers as a class.

Answers
1 'm getting   2 don't go   3 are arriving

3 LISTENING AND VOCABULARY Clothes

a ▶ **09.10** Play the recording for students to listen for general meaning and answer the questions. Check answers as a class.

Answers
1 b   2 c

Audioscript

Conversation 1

JOSÉ Hello?

TINA Hi José, it's Tina.

J Oh, Tina – hi!

T I just read your message. Sounds like you're having fun.

J Yeah, it's great here – I love it.

T I can't believe you're wearing red.

J I know, I know.

T You hate red.

J Yes, but it's Chinese New Year – everyone's wearing red – I'm even wearing red socks and a red belt. And someone also gave me a red scarf.

T I hope you're not wearing red shoes.

J No, no – I'm wearing black boots.

Conversation 2

DIANA Hello?

PETE Hi, Diana. It's Pete.

D Oh hi, Pete! Thanks for calling!

P Thanks for the message and the picture.

D No problem. I'm having such a great time here.

P That doesn't look like you in the picture.

D Yeah, that's me.

P But you're wearing a dress. You never wear dresses! And gloves, too. You look so cool.

D Thanks. I wear dresses sometimes you know.

P Yeah, but I normally see you in sweaters and jeans. And you're wearing jewelry, too – those are pretty earrings.

D Well, this is special – it's *Carnevale*. I'm having so much fun.

b ▶ **09.10** Students listen to the recording again for specific details and check the clothes words they hear. They compare in pairs. Check answers as a class.

Answers
José: ✓ socks, ✓ scarf, ✓ shoes, ✓ boots
(They don't talk about pants or a shirt.)
Diana: ✓ gloves, ✓ dress, ✓ earrings, ✓ jeans, ✓ sweater
(They don't talk about a raincoat.)

💡 EXTRA ACTIVITY

Play the recording again and ask students to write down what José and Diana are wearing. Point out that they both use some clothes words, but say that they are not wearing these items. Check answers as a class and check that students understand the meaning of *belt* by showing them your belt if you're wearing one or drawing a picture on the board. (*José is wearing red socks, a red belt, a red scarf, and black boots. Diana is wearing a dress, gloves, and earrings.*)

c **Pronunciation** Model the four words and the four vowel sounds in the chart. Elicit from students which column *shoe* should go in.

Answer
Sound 2 /u/ – boot, shoe

📖 LANGUAGE NOTES

3c and 3d introduce some of the most frequent sounds which correspond to the letter *o*: /ɑ/, /u/, /ʌ/, and /oʊ/. Don't ask students to look for other examples of words with *o*, as they may well find words which contain the letter *o*, but are not pronounced with the four sounds being worked on.

d ▶ **09.11** Students match the words with the sounds. Play the recording for students to listen and check. Check answers as a class. Then, drill each word.

Answers and audioscript

Sound 1 /ɑ/	Sound 2 /u/	Sound 3 /ʌ/	Sound 4 /oʊ/
sock	boot	glove	coat
shop	shoe	come	know
box	group	mother	phone
	two		

e ▶▶ ▶ **09.12–09.14** Students complete the exercises in Vocabulary Focus 9B on SB p. 168. Play the recording for students to check their answers to Exercise a and complete the Pronunciation activities. Monitor Exercise d and correct students' pronunciation as appropriate. Tell students to go back to SB p. 93.

Answers (Vocabulary Focus 9B SB p. 168)

a 1 d (skirt)   3 a (T-shirt)   5 h (sneakers)   7 b (watch)
  2 g (necklace)   4 e (shorts)   6 c (jewelry)   8 f (ring)
b jewelry
c 1 vegetable   3 chocolate   5 comfortable
  2 interesting   4 camera

4 SPEAKING

a Individually, students think of someone that they saw before class and write notes about what that person is wearing. Monitor and help with any other vocabulary students might need to talk about the people, e.g., *high heels, leggings, suit, tie*, etc.

b 💬 In pairs, students talk about the people they chose. Monitor and listen for correct use of clothes vocabulary and the present continuous.

💡 FAST FINISHERS

Ask fast finishers to close their eyes and, from memory, describe what their partner is wearing in as much detail as possible.

⊕ ADDITIONAL MATERIAL

Workbook 9B

Photocopiable activities: Grammar 9B, Vocabulary 9B, Pronunciation 9B

9C EVERYDAY ENGLISH

It looks really good on you

At the end of this lesson, students will be able to:

- understand conversations in which people choose clothes in a store and pay for them
- use appropriate phrases for shopping in a clothing store
- use appropriate phrases to say something is nice
- connect words to the next word in the sentence by moving the final consonant sound
- ask for something in a clothing store, ask to try it on, and pay for it

♀ OPTIONAL LEAD-IN

Play "Guess who?" (see p. 153) with students. Tell them that you're thinking of a person in the class and that they have to guess who it is by asking questions about what they are wearing. They are allowed to ask you five *Yes/No* questions with the present continuous to find out who it is, e.g., *Is this person wearing jeans?* and *Is this person wearing earrings?* Make sure you reply only with *yes* or *no* (NOT ~~*Yes, he/she is*~~) in order not to give away if it is a man or a woman. Once you're sure students have understood what they have to do, they can continue playing the game in small groups. Monitor and check that students form the present continuous correctly and pronounce the clothes words from Lesson 9B correctly.

1 LISTENING

a 💬 Put students into pairs to ask and answer the questions. Invite pairs to share their answers with the class.

b ▶09.15 Tell students to look at the picture at the bottom of the page and ask them where James and Daniela are. Play Part 1 of the audio recording for students to answer the question. Check the answer as a class.

> **Answer**
> James

Audioscript (Part 1)

DANIELA Hi, James!

JAMES Hi, Daniela, are you free at lunchtime?

D Yes.

J Could you help me? I need help buying some clothes.

D Yeah, sure. But what about Camila? Can't she help?

J Well, I'm meeting her for dinner tonight. She always says I wear the same old clothes, so I want to get something new. I want to surprise her.

D OK, sure. I'd love to. I'm free at 12:30.

c ▶09.15 Students listen again for specific details. Play Part 1 of the audio recording again for students to identify the incorrect information in the text. When checking answers, ask students to correct the information.

> **Answers**
> ... ~~to go to a concert~~ <u>for dinner</u>
> ... she's free at ~~12:00~~ <u>12:30</u>.
> She ~~isn't~~ <u>is</u> happy ...

d ▶09.16 Play Part 2 of the audio recording for students to answer the questions. They then check in pairs. Check answers as a class.

> **Answers**
> 1 a shirt and pants
> 2 pants: 34; shirt: large
> 3 No, he probably doesn't enjoy shopping.

Audioscript (Part 2)

SALESPERSON Hi, there. Let me know if you need any help.

JAMES Thanks.

DANIELA So what are you looking for?

J I don't really know. A shirt and a pair of pants, I think. Just something casual.

D OK. What size are you?

J In pants? 34 in the waist.

D And probably a large for the shirt?

J Yeah, I guess so.

D What color would you like? Try this purple. And this yellow one. Ooh, this pink is nice!

J Really?! I thought maybe just something ... dark.

D Why don't you try them on?

J OK. Excuse me, where are the fitting rooms?

SP They're right over there.

e 💬 Students ask and answer the questions in pairs or small groups. Invite pairs or small groups to share their answers with the class.

2 USEFUL LANGUAGE Choosing clothes

a Individually, students match the questions with the answers. Don't check answers at this point.

b ▶09.16 Play Part 2 of the audio recording again for students to check their answers in 2a. Check answers as a class.

> **Answers**
> 1 c
> 2 a
> 3 b
> 4 d

c 💬 Drill the questions and answers before students work in pairs. Monitor and correct students' pronunciation as appropriate.

d 💬 In pairs, students practice helping each other choose clothes. Monitor, but don't interrupt fluency unless students make mistakes with the questions.

♀ FAST FINISHERS

Ask fast finishers to close their books and ask and answer the questions in 2a from memory, using their own ideas for the answers and changing the clothes, colors, and sizes.

3 LISTENING

a ▶ 09.17 Play Part 3 of the audio recording for students to answer the questions. Check answers as a class.

> **Answers**
> 1 Yes, she does.
> 2 He thinks it's too bright.

Audioscript (Part 3)

DANIELA James, that pink shirt looks really good on you! Do you like it?

JAMES Not really. I don't like bright colors.

D So you don't like the yellow or the purple either?

J No. What do you think of this outfit I'm holding in my hand?

D Blue shirt, khaki pants? That looks great!

J Those are mine! That's what I came in!

D I still like that pink shirt and the gray pants you have on. Do you want to buy them?

J There's no price on them. Excuse me, how much are these?

SALESPERSON The shirt is $49.99 and the pants are $74.50.

J OK. I'll take them. Can I pay by credit card?

S Yes, of course. Should I put the receipt in the bag?

J Yes – thanks. I feel like a flamingo.

D Camila will love them. Trust me.

b ▶ 09.17 Play Part 3 of the audio recording again for students to complete the receipt. Check that students understand that the total isn't included in the recording and they will only be able to figure out the correct answer if they write down the other numbers correctly. Check answers by copying the receipt onto the board and asking individual students to come up and complete it.

> **Answers**
> Shirt $49.99
> Pants $74.50
> Total $124.49

💡 EXTRA ACTIVITY

Give students a mathematical challenge. Tell students: *I went to a clothing store yesterday and I bought a shirt for $19.99, a pair of pants for $24.49, and some boots for $66.75. How much was the total?* Allow students to use their cell phones to figure out the answer if they have them ($111.23). Repeat with: *I bought a lot of new clothes yesterday. I got some socks that cost $6.99, two T-shirts that were $4.99 each, and a pair of shorts for my vacation. I paid $29.46. How much were the shorts?* ($12.49)

Students then work individually to prepare their own mathematical challenge. Monitor and check that students know the answer themselves. Put students into small groups to test each other.

4 USEFUL LANGUAGE Paying for clothes

a ▶ 09.18 Individually, students look at the sentences and try to find the mistakes. Play the recording for students to check their ideas. Check answers as a class.

> **Answers**
> 1 I'll take them.
> 2 How much ~~they are~~ are these?
> 3 Should I put the receipt ~~on~~ in the bag?

b Students complete the conversation, working individually. They then check in pairs. Check answers as a class.

> **Answers**
> 1 help   2 much   3 take   4 card

🔄 LOA TIP MONITORING

- Drill the conversation in Exercise 4b before continuing. Try drilling the conversation together with the class with you being the salesperson (A) and the class being the customer (B). Work on the customer's sentences, building them up word by word, starting at the end of each sentence, e.g., *sunglasses – these sunglasses – are these sunglasses – much are these sunglasses – How much are these sunglasses?*, until the class can say it together with correct pronunciation. Then, ask them the salesperson's first question: *Can I help you?* Elicit the response from the class all together. Repeat with the customer's second line and continue until you've built up the whole conversation.

- Provide appropriate models of connecting words, but don't actively draw students' attention to them at this point as they will study these in detail in the Pronunciation section.

c 💬 Write on the board: *B Yes, how much are these (sunglasses)? A They're ($29.99). B OK, I'll take them.* Ask students: *Is "sunglasses" singular or plural? What happens to the underlined words if we change "sunglasses" to "shirt"?* Check that students understand that these words will change to *is this / It's / it* when they use a singular noun. In pairs, students practice the conversations. Monitor and point out errors for students to self-correct.

5 CONVERSATION SKILLS
Saying something nice

a Read the sentences together and elicit suggestions for how to complete the sentences from the class.

> **Answers**
> 1 looks
> 2 looks

b Answer the questions as a class. Ask students: *Which words make it clear that the sentence is about something someone's wearing?* (on you)

> **Answers**
> a Sentence 1
> b Sentence 2

c 💬 Demonstrate the activity by paying two or three students compliments using the language from this unit, e.g., *Silvi, I love your ring. It looks really good on you. Marc, I really like your sneakers. They look fantastic!* Students then work in pairs, saying nice things about something their partner is wearing. Monitor and help with any vocabulary students need.

6 PRONUNCIATION Connecting words

a ▶ 09.19 Play the recording for students to listen to sentences 1–5 and see if there is a pause between the words in bold. Check the answer as a class.

Answer
No, there isn't.

b Read the explanations as a class. Drill each example.

> **📖 LANGUAGE NOTES**
>
> This section develops the work on connecting words started in Unit 8 and gives examples of two features common in connected speech. In sentences 1–5, students see how the consonant sound moves to the beginning of the second word when one word finishes with a consonant sound and the next word begins with a vowel sound. Some common linking sounds between vowels are: /j/ as in *I am* (individually /aɪ/ and /æm/, but together /aɪjæm/), and /w/ as in *go away* (individually /goʊ/ and /əˈweɪ/, but together /goʊwəˈweɪ/). One of the reasons students often have problems understanding spoken English is because they hear these sounds at the beginning of words and are therefore unable to recognize words in speech that they would normally recognize in writing.

c 💬🔊 Students work in pairs, practicing saying the sentences and giving replies. Monitor and correct students' pronunciation as appropriate.

7 SPEAKING

a Tell students that they can now practice choosing and paying for clothes. Check that students understand the dialogue map before they start. Give them a few minutes to write notes about what they want to say.

b 💬🔊 In pairs, students take turns being the salesperson and the customer. Monitor and praise students when they use the language from this lesson correctly.

c 💬🔊 Students work with different partners and practice more conversations, but using different clothes.

> **⊕ ADDITIONAL MATERIAL**
>
> Workbook 9C
>
> Unit Progress Test

9D SKILLS FOR WRITING
Thank you for the nice present

⚙ OPTIONAL LEAD-IN

Books closed. Draw a present with a ribbon around it on the board and write underneath it: *The perfect present for me is …*

Tell students: *The perfect present for me is something I can eat, with lots of sugar, and it certainly isn't healthy!* Elicit suggestions, e.g., *a box of chocolates, a really big cake*, etc. Then give students another example, e.g., *The perfect present for my sister is expensive jewelry!* Again, elicit ideas, e.g., *earrings, a ring, a necklace*, etc. Ask students to work individually and write two sentences like yours about perfect presents, one for themselves and one for someone else. In pairs or small groups, they then read each other their sentences and suggest appropriate presents.

1 LISTENING AND SPEAKING

↻ LOA TIP ELICITING

- Consider eliciting some of the vocabulary in 1a by miming rather than using the picture in the book. Books closed. Mime opening a present and showing a delighted face. Take the "present," e.g., some earrings, out of the "box" and "put them on." Point to them and ask students: *What are these?*

- As you elicit each word, drill it for correct pronunciation. Then, ask students *How do you spell "(word)"?* Gesture for them to write the word down. After eliciting all the vocabulary, check that students have spelled the words correctly by writing them on the board for them to check.

a 💬 Read the questions with students and then give them one minute to think about their answers. Discuss the questions as a class and find out which presents are popular and which aren't popular and why. If you used the optional lead-in, ask students if they think any of the presents mentioned are "perfect" presents.

b ▶ 09.20 In pairs, students look at the people and discuss which presents they think the people give. Play the recording for them to listen for general meaning and check their ideas. Check answers as a class.

Audioscript

BRENDAN I always give my girlfriend an expensive birthday present. I don't give her flowers or chocolates. I often give her jewelry, maybe a necklace or earrings. Or maybe a beautiful dress. She loves expensive clothes. But clothes are difficult because I don't know what she likes. So, she usually chooses them and then we buy them together.

BOB We don't buy presents. We give the children some cash and then they always buy their own presents. I think that's better because they know what they want. And then we do something fun together, maybe go out to eat or go to the movies.

FERNANDA We buy small birthday presents for the children – usually toys or clothes, something small, like a toy car or a T-shirt maybe. Some people buy things like a laptop or a bike, but I don't like giving expensive presents. I prefer to give small presents.

LEILA My husband doesn't think clothes or computers are important. He doesn't need many things, and he doesn't like spending money on himself. But he reads lots of books and he likes movies, – so for his birthday I usually buy him a book or a movie. He's very easy!

c ▶ 09.20 Students listen to the recording again for specific details and decide who the sentences are about. They compare in pairs. Check answers as a class.

Answers
2 Leila's husband
3 Fernanda's children
4 Brendan's girlfriend
5 Bob and his family

d 💬 Students talk about the questions in pairs or small groups. Monitor, but don't interrupt fluency.

⚙ FAST FINISHERS

Ask fast finishers to talk about situations where it is typical to give presents in their countries, e.g., birthdays, Mother's/Father's Day, Valentine's Day, when people get married, etc. and whether any specific presents are typical on those days.

2 READING

a Tell students it was Brendan's 30th birthday last week and Molly gave him a present. Individually, students then complete the thank-you email. Check answers as a class.

Answers
a 4
b 1
c 3
d 5
e 2

b Students read the email in 2a again and answer the questions. Check that they understand that the answer to question 2 isn't included directly in the email, so they have to understand it from the context. Check answers as a class.

> **Answers**
> 1 a
> 2 He says "Love" at the end of the email, which you use for someone you know very well.

c Students read Molly's email to Mr. Lewis and answer the questions. Check answers as a class.

> **Answers**
> 1 a
> 2 b

d Discuss the question as a class and check that students understand the differences between the two emails. Ask them: *Which email is formal and which is informal?* Check that they are clear that Brendan's email is informal while Molly's email is formal. Ask students: *Do you usually write formal or informal emails or both?*

> **Answers**
> 1 Molly's email is more formal than Brendan's in 2a. She says "Dear Mr. Lewis," not "Hi,"; "I just want to say thank you," not "Thanks very much,"; and she finishes with "Regards," not "Love."
> 2 It's different because they have a formal relationship – they're not friends.

3 WRITING SKILLS
Writing formal and informal emails

a Read the example with the class. Students work individually, adding one word to each sentence. They then check in pairs. Check answers as a class.

> **Answers**
> 2 …to say thank you very <u>much</u> for the …
> 3 Thanks so <u>much</u> for the …
> 4 Thank you <u>for</u> the …

b Answer the question as a class. Ask students which phrase makes the sentence sound more formal (*I'd just like to say …*), and ask students to find a similar phrase in Molly's email in 2c (*I just want to say …*).

> **Answer**
> Sentence 2 is more formal.

c Individually, students classify the phrases as informal (1) or formal (2). Check answers as a class.

> **Answers**
>
> | Beginning | Ending |
> |---|---|
> | 2 Hello, Mrs. Finch. | 1 Love, |
> | 1 Hi there! | 1 Thanks, |
> | 1 Hi Marie, | 2 Best wishes, |
> | 2 Dear Mr. Parker, | 2 Regards, |
> | | 1 See you, |

4 WRITING

a To make sure all students receive a "present," tell each student who they should choose a present for. Students then write their "presents" on pieces of paper and exchange them. Encourage them to say thank you briefly, e.g., *Oh thank you, it's just what I always wanted!* If you used the optional lead-in, ask students to try to remember their partner's perfect present.

b Students work individually to plan their emails. Monitor and help with vocabulary and give them ideas if necessary.

c Students write their thank-you emails, working individually. Remind students to use the informal phrases in 3c for beginning and ending their emails. If you're short of time, this exercise can be completed for homework. Students could then bring their thank-you emails to the next class.

d 💬 In pairs, students switch emails and check their partner's work. Tell them to check that their partner has used appropriate informal phrases in their email. They then give each other feedback. If they have made any mistakes with the informal phrases, or mistakes in other areas, they prepare a second draft of their email before giving it to you for correction.

e Tell students to imagine that the present was from someone they don't know well. Ask them to write a second version of their thank-you email. Elicit from the class that they need to use more formal phrases for the beginning, the sentence saying thank you, and the ending.

> ⊕ **ADDITIONAL MATERIAL**
> Workbook 9D

UNIT 9
Review and extension

1 GRAMMAR

a Highlight the example question and answer. Students then write questions and answers for the people in the picture. Monitor and help as necessary. Point out errors for students to self-correct. Check answers as a class.

> **Answers**
> 2 What's she doing? She's running.
> 3 What are they doing? They're doing yoga.
> 4 What's she doing? She's reading a newspaper.
> 5 What are they doing? They're playing soccer.
> 6 What's he doing? He's playing a guitar.

b Individually, students complete the conversation. Check answers as a class by asking individual students to write the correct answers on the board.

> **Answers**
> 1 are you doing
> 2 'm cooking
> 3 cook
> 4 'm making
> 5 make
> 6 put
> 7 'm adding
> 8 'm trying

2 VOCABULARY

a Read the first sentence and elicit the answer as an example. Students then read the sentences and identify the places. Check answers as a class.

> **Answers**
> 1 a drugstore
> 2 a clothing store / a department store
> 3 a fast food restaurant / a coffee shop
> 4 a bookstore
> 5 a coffee shop
> 6 a department store

b Individually, students look at the pictures and write the correct clothes words. Check answers and spelling as a class.

> **Answers**
> 1 scarf
> 2 shoes
> 3 gloves
> 4 boots
> 5 dress
> 6 raincoat

> 💡 **FAST FINISHERS**
> Ask fast finishers to write down all the other clothes words they remember from the unit, making sure they spell them correctly.

3 WORDPOWER *time*

a Tell students to close their books. Write the five verbs *find, save, spend, take,* and *waste* on the board and draw a large clock face next to the verbs. Ask students: *What word can go after all of these?* Elicit *time*. Students open their books, look at the sentences, and match the phrases with the meanings. Check answers as a class.

> **Answers**
> 1 b
> 2 d
> 3 a
> 4 e
> 5 c

> 💡 **EXTRA ACTIVITY**
> Books closed. Write sentences 1–5 on the board underneath the five verbs from 3a. Ask students to complete the sentences with the correct form of the verbs: *1 She _____ a lot of time with her brothers and sisters.* (spends) *2 It _____ time to check the prices online first.* (takes) *3 I can't always _____ time to do my homework.* (find) *4 Don't _____ time – your exams are next week.* (waste) *5 You can _____ time by taking the bus and not walking.* (save)

b Individually, students read the mini-conversations and answer the questions. They then compare in pairs. Check answers as a class. Ask students to think of other adjectives that can be used with *time* as well as *nice* and *good*, e.g., *fantastic, great,* and also to think of negative adjectives, e.g., *awful, terrible.*

> **Answers**
> Have a <u>nice</u> (good) time.
> … like doing in your <u>free</u> (extra) time?

c As an example, complete one or two of the sentences so that they are true for you. Students then complete the sentences with their own ideas. Monitor and point out errors for students to self-correct.

d 💬👎 In pairs, students tell each other their sentences and find out how similar they are.

≫ Photocopiable activities: Wordpower 9

> 🔄 **LOA REVIEW YOUR PROGRESS**
>
> Students look back through the unit, think about what they've studied, and decide how well they did. Students work on weak areas by using the appropriate sections of the Workbook and the Photocopiable activities.

UNIT 10 COMMUNICATION

🔄 UNIT OBJECTIVES

At the end of this unit, students will be able to:

- understand information, texts, and conversations about technology, languages, and communication habits
- talk about and compare different kinds of technology
- ask and answer questions about their own and other languages and about their communication habits
- understand conversations in which people ask for help
- ask for help and check instructions
- write a post on an online discussion board about something that annoys them and an appropriate reply to another student's post

UNIT CONTENTS

G GRAMMAR
- Comparative adjectives
- Superlative adjectives

V VOCABULARY
- IT collocations: *charge a phone/computer, check my email, click on a link, download a document/file, log in to a computer/ website, make calls, save a document/file, visit a website*
- High numbers
- Linking ideas with *also, too,* and *as well*
- Wordpower: *most*

P PRONUNCIATION
- *than* with comparative adjectives
- Word stress in superlative adjectives
- Main stress and intonation

C COMMUNICATION SKILLS
- Talking about different kinds of technology
- Comparing two pieces of similar technology
- Asking and answering questions about languages and language learning
- Asking for help and responding appropriately
- Using appropriate phrases to check instructions
- Writing a post about something that annoys you and writing a reply to someone else's post

GETTING STARTED

💡 OPTIONAL LEAD-IN

Books closed. Write these beginnings of sentences and questions on the left side of the board: *1 Can you call; 2 He'll; 3 This is; 4 Just; 5 Can you wait; 6 Is; 7 Here's my; 8 He's not; 9 Can he; 10 What do you think of.* Write these endings on the right side of the board, leaving the area in the middle clear: *a location. Come and meet me! b a minute? c this picture? d Dan there? e me back? f be back soon. g here right now. h my new phone number. i a minute. j call me back?*

Ask students to match the sentence halves. Then, they compare in pairs. Check answers by asking individual students to draw lines joining the two sentence halves on the board (1 e, 2 f, 3 h, 4 i, 5 b, 6 d, 7 a, 8 g, 9 j, 10 c).

Ask students: *Where do we use all these phrases?* (on the phone or in text messages). Tell students that some of the phrases are from text messages and some are from phone calls. Put students into pairs and ask them to classify the phrases. Check answers as a class (text messages: *3, 7, 10*; phone calls: *1, 2, 4, 5, 6, 8, 9*).

a 💬 Give students one minute to think about their answers to the questions before talking about the picture as a class.

b 💬 Individually, students decide which sentences are true for them. They then compare in pairs. Invite pairs to share their answers with the class and ask students if they think cell phones are good or bad when families are together.

💡 EXTRA ACTIVITY

Write other common kinds of communication on the board, e.g., *face-to-face, letters, emails, social media sites, instant messaging, blogs, video chats,* etc. Ask students to write three sentences about how they use some of these forms of communication. Some of the sentences should be true and some false, e.g., *I sometimes write letters to my grandparents because they don't use the Internet; I usually talk to my friends over texts,* etc. Monitor and point out errors for students to self-correct. In pairs or small groups, they then read aloud their sentences to each other and decide if they are true or false.

Exercises **a** and **b** can be prepared as homework before this lesson to give students time to look up unfamiliar vocabulary. Ask students to look at the picture and to prepare their answers to the questions as homework to talk about in the next class.

10A

THEY'RE MORE COMFORTABLE THAN EARBUDS

At the end of this lesson, students will be able to:

- read and understand a text comparing earbuds with headphones
- use comparative adjectives correctly
- understand a casual conversation that compares cell phones with landlines
- use a lexical set of IT collocations correctly
- compare two pieces of similar technology

⚲ OPTIONAL LEAD-IN

Books closed. Tell students they are going to have a test on technology words. Explain that you're going to read a definition for each word and they have to write down the word with the correct spelling. Read definitions 1–10: *1 You use this at a party so everyone can listen to music.* (speaker) *2 You use these to listen to music. You put them on your ears.* (headphones) *3 You use this small object on your arm to send messages and emails and use the Internet.* (smartwatch) *4 You can make phone calls, send messages and emails, and use the Internet with this small object.* (smartphone) *5 Families usually have one of these at home for working or playing games. It's pretty big.* (computer) *6 This object has numbers, symbols, and all the letters of the alphabet on it. You use it to write an email on the computer.* (keyboard) *7 When you travel a lot on business, you need this kind of computer so that you can work easily on the plane or train.* (laptop) *8 This is what photographers use to take pictures. They're sometimes very expensive.* (camera) *9 This is very useful when you need a copy of a document on paper.* (printer) *10 This is great for using the Internet or watching movies. It has a big screen, and you touch it to control it.* (tablet)

Check answers as a class and give one point for the correct word and an additional point for spelling it correctly. The student with the highest score is the winner.

1 READING

a 💬 In pairs, students ask and answer the questions. Invite pairs to share their answers with the class.

b Students read the posts quickly and find out what they talk about. Check the answer as a class.

Answers
1 Kyle, Emily, Alyssa
2 Kyle, Monica, Noah, Alyssa
3 Alyssa, Pedro, Monica, Noah
4 Monica, Noah

c Tell students to read the posts again in detail. Individually, students find the people. They then check in pairs. When checking answers, ask students to read the sections of the text which helped them find the answers.

Answers
1 in her pocket
2 in his bag
3 He likes good sound.
4 She loses things.
5 in the gym
6 in a case
7 They cover your ears.
8 He has small ears, so the earbuds fall out.

⚲ EXTRA ACTIVITY

Ask students to read the posts again and answer questions 1–4: *1 Why doesn't Monica like headphones?* (They're not comfortable if you're working out.) *2 Who thinks the sound is better with headphones but prefers earbuds?* (Monica) *3 Who prefers headphones?* (Kyle, Noah, Pedro) *4 Who prefers earbuds?* (Alyssa, Emily, Monica)

d 💬 Discuss the question as a class. Encourage students to justify their answers as much as possible.

2 GRAMMAR Comparative adjectives

a Books closed. On the board, write: *Earbuds are ... than headphones.* Point to the blank and ask students to complete the sentence trying to remember the posts from the previous page (*better, smaller*). Help students if they can't remember. Then, write: *Headphones are ... than earbuds.* Ask students to complete the sentence using what they remember from the posts on the previous page. (*bigger*) Say each adjective / comparative adjective pair, e.g., *small – smaller, big – bigger*, etc. and say *These are comparative adjectives.* Wipe the board before students work individually, looking at the posts and underlining the correct words to complete the sentences. Check answers as a class.

Answers
1 better
2 bigger
3 more expensive
4 smaller, cheaper, easier
   The adjectives tell us how earbuds and headphones are <u>different</u>.

b Individually, students underline the comparative adjectives and complete the rule. Check answers as a class.

Answers
Alyssa: better	Noah: more comfortable
Pedro: bigger	Monica: clearer
Kyle: more expensive	Noah: better
Emily: cheaper	Alyssa: smaller, cheaper, easier
Monica: smaller, lighter	

c Give students a few minutes to complete the rules and the examples. They then check in pairs. Check answers as a class.

Answers
1 *-er*; harder
2 *i*; -er; happier
3 *more*; more
4 better

◆ LOA TIP DRILLING

- Check that students have fully understood why we use comparative adjectives by asking them: *When we use comparative adjectives, how many things are we usually talking about?* (two) *Are the things exactly the same?* (no)

- After checking students have understood the use of comparative adjectives, double-check they are clear about the form by asking: *Can I say "my headphones are more big than my earbuds"?* (no) *Why not?* (Because "big" is a short adjective – the comparative is "bigger."); *Can I say "my laptop was expensiver than my tablet"?* (no) *Why not?* (Because "expensive" is a long adjective – the comparative is "more expensive."); *Can I say "my smartphone is gooder than my computer"?* (no) *Why not?* (Because "good" is an irregular adjective – the comparative is "better.")

d ▶️ **10.01** Students complete the sentences, working individually. Play the recording for students to listen and check. Check answers as a class.

> **Answers**
> 1 than
> 2 than

e ▶️ **10.01** **Pronunciation** Play the recording again for students to listen to the pronunciation of *than*. Check the answer as a class. Drill the sentences.

> **Answer**
> not stressed

👁 CAREFUL!

One of the most common mistakes with comparative adjectives is with the spelling. The spelling rules for comparative adjectives are highlighted in Grammar Focus 10A on SB p. 156. At this level, the most common mistakes are with double letters. Students may either not double the final consonant in comparative adjectives, e.g., ~~biger~~ (Correct form = *bigger*), or double the final consonant where it isn't necessary, e.g., ~~cheapper~~ (Correct form = *cheaper*). Students may also use *more* with one-syllable adjectives, which should form the comparative with *-er*, e.g., ~~more hard~~ (Correct form = *harder*) and ~~more light~~ (Correct form = *lighter*). They may also use both *more* and *-er* at the same time, e.g., ~~more heavier~~ (Correct form = *heavier*) and ~~more smaller~~ (Correct form = *smaller*).

After studying *more* for comparatives, students may then start to overuse it in sentences which require *very*, e.g., ~~... they are more expensive~~ (Correct form = *I don't have headphones because they are* **very** *expensive*).

f ≫ ▶️ **10.02** Students read the information in Grammar Focus 10A on SB p. 156. Play the recording where indicated and ask students to listen and repeat. Students then complete the exercises. Check answers as a class, making sure students are forming and spelling the comparative adjectives correctly. Tell students to go back to SB p. 101.

> **Answers (Grammar Focus 10A SB p. 157)**
>
> **a** 2 worse
> 3 cleaner
> 4 colder
> 5 more comfortable
> 6 more crowded
> 7 faster
> 8 fatter
> 9 better
> 10 more interesting
> 11 more modern
> 12 noisier
> 13 older
> 14 more popular
> 15 sadder
> 16 stranger
> 17 stronger
> 18 thinner
> 19 wetter
> 20 wider
>
> **b** 2 The movie is more interesting than the book.
> 3 Her children are noisier than my children.
> 4 She is a better cook than my dad.
> 5 Dubai is more modern than Dublin.
> 6 This hotel is more comfortable than the last hotel.
> 7 My friends are funnier than me.
>
> **c** 1 She's / is quicker
> 2 ~~good~~ better
> 3 ~~worser~~ worse
> 4 ~~prettyer~~ prettier
> 5 ~~weter~~ wetter
> 6 ~~more big~~ bigger
> 7 ~~most~~ more interesting
> 8 faster than mine

💡 EXTRA ACTIVITY

Draw two simple cars on the board, one a "high-end" expensive car, e.g., a Ferrari, and one a smaller, cheaper car, e.g., a Honda. Label them with the makes. Put students into pairs and give them one minute to compare the two cars in as many ways as possible. If you wish, write some adjectives as prompts down the side of the board, e.g., *comfortable*, *big/small*, *expensive/cheap*, *fast/slow*, etc. Ask some pairs to share their sentences with the class. Then, nominate a student to choose two things and to draw and label two simple pictures of them on the board, e.g., two stick people to represent two famous actors, two skylines to represent two cities, etc. Students work in pairs to compare the two things. In pairs or small groups, students can then choose two things to compare and continue the activity.

g ≫ Divide the class into pairs and assign A and B roles. Student As read the instructions and look at the picture on SB p. 134. Student Bs read the instructions and look at the picture on SB p. 137. Check that they understand that they first should ask and answer questions about the smartphones, and then they should compare them. Monitor, but don't interrupt fluency unless students make mistakes with comparative adjectives. Tell students to go back to SB p. 101.

💡 FAST FINISHERS

Ask fast finishers to write sentences to compare a piece of technology they have or use at home with a similar piece of technology in the classroom/school.

3 LISTENING

a ▶️ **10.03** Play the recording for students to listen for general meaning and answer the question. Check the answer as a class.

> **Answers**
> 1 He wants to give up his landline phone.
> 2 No, she doesn't.

Audioscript

GREG Your mom and I are thinking about giving up our landline.
RUBY Oh, OK.
G I don't really think I need a regular telephone any more.
R You never know …
G Well, I have a smartphone and I can do everything with it – go online, check my email, – and, obviously, make calls.
R But what happens if … if, I don't know, there's an emergency or something?
G I still have my cell phone for that.
R But what if you forget to charge it or something?
G I always charge my phone! I keep it plugged in.
R Or what if the power goes out? There are times when a landline is really useful.
G I thought you'd be happy for me to give up the landline. You never call me on it – you just text me.
R Yeah, I know, but … but if something really bad happened – like a big storm – often cell phones don't work. But landlines do – they're much safer.
G So you want me to keep the landline?
R Well, that's not what I'm saying – I just think you should … well, think about it.
G Oh, I have. And I've found out that with no landline, I'll save $50 a month.

b ▶ `10.03` Students listen to the recording again for specific details and complete the chart. Check answers as a class.

	good	bad
Landline phones	3	1
Cell phones	4	2

c 💬 Discuss the question as a class. Don't interrupt fluency, but write down any mistakes with comparative adjectives on the board. After the class discussion, ask students to correct any mistakes on the board.

4 VOCABULARY IT collocations

a Individually, students complete the phrases. Check that they understand that the number of lines indicates the number of missing letters. Check answers as a class.

> **Answers**
> 1 go
> 2 check
> 3 make

b Students match the verbs with the nouns, working individually. Make sure students understand that there are two possibilities for some of the verbs. They then check in pairs. Check answers as a class and point out the verbs which have two possibilities (*download, log in to, save,* and *charge.*). Drill all the possible collocations.

> **Answers**
> 1 b; c
> 2 e
> 3 a
> 4 a; f
> 5 b; c
> 6 d; f

c 💬 Students work in pairs or small groups, asking and answering questions using IT collocations. Monitor and check that they are using the vocabulary from this section correctly.

5 SPEAKING

a Individually, students decide if they want to talk about idea 1 (something new versus something old) or idea 2 (two similar things that they use).

b Give students a few minutes to prepare and write notes about the two things. Monitor and help as necessary.

c 💬 Students work in pairs, telling each other about the two things they chose and asking and answering each other's questions. As you monitor, don't interrupt fluency, but note any mistakes with comparative adjectives or the IT collocations. After the activity, write the mistakes on the board and ask students to correct them.

💡 FAST FINISHERS

Ask fast finishers to talk about two objects from the category in 5a that they didn't write notes about.

⊕ ADDITIONAL MATERIAL

Workbook 10A

Photocopiable activities: Grammar 10A, Vocabulary 10A, Pronunciation 10A

10B | WHAT'S THE MOST BEAUTIFUL LANGUAGE IN THE WORLD?

At the end of this lesson, students will be able to:

- understand a radio program in which an expert talks about languages
- use superlative adjectives correctly
- read and understand a text with unusual facts and figures about languages
- use high numbers correctly
- ask and answer questions about their own and other languages

♀ OPTIONAL LEAD-IN

Books closed. Organize a quiz to review some of the countries that students have seen in the class. Consider including some of the countries that students will need to complete question 3 in 1a and any additional countries that you know your students have problems spelling. To elicit the countries, either tell students the capital city (e.g., *Australia – Canberra, Canada – Ottawa, China – Beijing, France – Paris, Greece – Athens, Italy – Rome, Japan – Tokyo, Portugal - Lisbon, Saudi Arabia – Riyadh, Spain – Madrid, Switzerland – Bern*), or select a typical tourist picture for each country (e.g., the Sydney Opera House for Australia, the CN Tower for Canada) and show these to students. Students work in teams, writing down the names of each country without referring back to their books or their notes. Check answers as a class. Elicit the names of the countries and write them on the board for students to check their spelling. Give one point for identifying the country correctly and a bonus point for correct spelling. The team with the highest score is the winner.

1 LISTENING

a 💬 Students ask and answer the questions in pairs or small groups. If you used the optional lead-in, tell students that they can use the countries on the board to help them with question 3. Invite pairs or small groups to share their answers with the class and give students some of the suggested answers below to question 3, if you wish.

Suggested answers for 3
Navajo – the United States; Italian – Italy, southern Switzerland; English – the U.K., the U.S., Canada, Australia, New Zealand, South Africa, and former British territories; French – France, Belgium, Canada, Switzerland, and former French or Belgian territories in Africa; Arabic – North Africa and the Middle East; Quechua – Peru, Bolivia, Ecuador, Colombia, and Argentina; Japanese – Japan; Mandarin Chinese – northern and southwestern China; Portuguese – Portugal, Brazil, Mozambique, Angola, and former Portuguese territories throughout the world; Spanish – Spain and former Spanish territories in Latin America, the Caribbean, and Africa

b ▶ 10.04 Play the recording for students to listen for general meaning and check the languages that Professor Hunter talks about. You may wish to pre-teach the word *population* (the total number of people who live in a city, country, etc.). Check answers as a class.

Answers
Italian ✓, English ✓, Japanese ✓, Mandarin Chinese ✓, Navajo ✓, Spanish ✓

Audioscript

HOST Good evening, and welcome to the program. Today, we're talking to Professor Ryan Hunter. The professor is well known for his love of languages and has a new book in stores tomorrow. Professor, welcome!

PROFESSOR Thank you. It's great to be here!

H So let's start with my first question. Professor, in your opinion, what's the most beautiful language in the world?

P That's a very good question. Of course, there is no right or wrong answer here. I'm sure we all have our favorites. But for me, the answer is easy: Italian. It was the first language I learned. I still remember my teacher, Mrs. Monti. Mrs. Monti was the best teacher at my school and she started my love of languages. Now I can speak more than 20 languages well, but Italian is the most musical language I know. It's the language of opera and love.

H OK, next question. What's the most difficult language in the world?

P Hmm. That's an interesting question, too. It partly depends on your first language. For example, for a speaker of English, Japanese is very difficult, but for a speaker of Mandarin Chinese, it's much easier. However, a few years ago, we did a project at my university and decided that the hardest language to learn is Navajo, a Native American language from the United States. Last year, we did another project on the Internet to find the easiest language to learn. More than 3,000 people answered the question and the most popular answer was Spanish. So perhaps Spanish is the easiest language to learn. That's probably because it's not very different from many other European languages.

H And one final question, what's the most useful language to speak?

P That's easy – the language of the country where you live. But if you want to learn the most popular language in the world, then take lessons in Mandarin Chinese. More than 900 million people speak it. That's not a surprise, as China has the biggest population in the world. So with Mandarin Chinese, you can speak to about 14% of all the people in the world. That's pretty useful.

H That's very useful, indeed! Well, Professor Hunter, thanks for talking with us today. I'm sure our listeners enjoyed hearing your thoughts on language!

c ▶ 10.04 Individually, students match the sentences with the languages. Play the recording for students to listen and check. Check answers as a class.

Answers
1 Italian
2 Japanese
3 Spanish
4 Mandarin Chinese

d ▶ `10.04` Students listen to the recording again for specific details and answer the questions. They compare in pairs. Check answers as a class.

Answers
1 Italian
2 more than 20
3 in the United States
4 14%

e 💬 Individually, students choose one thing they found interesting and one thing they found surprising. They then compare in small groups or as a class.

2 GRAMMAR Superlative adjectives

a ▶ `10.05` Books closed. Copy the following chart onto the board:

adjectives	_____ adjectives	_____ adjectives
big	bigger	_____
easy	easier	_____
good	better	_____
hard	harder	_____
musical	more musical	_____

Point to the first column. Say *adjectives*. Point to the second column. Elicit and write the heading *comparative (adjectives)*. Then, point to the last column. Elicit and write the heading *superlative (adjectives)*. If necessary, say *the biggest* as an example. Elicit the superlative adjectives, write them in the third column, and drill them (*the biggest, the easiest, the best, the hardest, the most musical*). Students then open their books, look at the spelling of the superlative adjectives in the box, and complete the sentences. Play the recording for students to listen and check. Check answers as a class.

Answers
1 best
2 musical
3 hardest
4 easiest
5 biggest

b Individually, students read the sentences and order the languages from very easy to very difficult. They then check in pairs. Check answers as a class.

Answers
1 Spanish
2 French
3 Japanese
4 Navajo

c Discuss the question as a class. If you wish, extend the discussion by saying nationalities, e.g., *Japanese, German, Turkish*, etc., and asking students if they think their language is easy or difficult for those particular nationalities to learn.

d Give students a few minutes to complete the rules and the examples. They then check in pairs. Check answers as a class.

Answers
1 *-est*; smallest
2 *most*; most expensive
3 best

🎯 CAREFUL!

Student errors with superlative adjectives are generally similar to those with the comparative form. They may have problems with double letters, e.g., ~~bigest~~ (Correct form = *biggest*) and ~~cheappest~~ (Correct form = *cheapest*), or use *most* with one-syllable adjectives, e.g., ~~Navajo is the most hard language …~~ (Correct form = *Navajo is the **hardest** language to learn*). After studying both the comparative and superlative forms, students may then start to confuse the two forms, e.g., ~~This is the cheaper dictionary …~~ (Correct form = *This is the **cheapest** dictionary in the store*) and ~~He's the more intelligent person …~~ (Correct form = *He's the **most intelligent** person I know*). They may also have problems with word order when using *most*, e.g., ~~This is the laptop most practical when …~~ (Correct form = *This is **the most practical** laptop when you're traveling*). Sometimes students may have problems with word order and also confuse *more* and *most*, e.g., … ~~I like more my smartphone~~ (Correct form = *I like my smartphone, my laptop, and my tablet. But I like **my smartphone (the) most***).

e ≫ ▶ `10.06` Students read the information in Grammar Focus 10B on SB p. 156. Play the recording where indicated and ask students to listen and repeat. Students then complete the exercises. Check answers as a class, making sure students are forming and spelling the superlative adjectives correctly. Tell students to go back to SB p. 102.

Answers (Grammar Focus 10B SB p. 157)

a 2 the shortest 7 the friendliest 11 the safest
3 the funniest 8 the best 12 the most exciting
4 the driest 9 the biggest 13 the most tiring
5 the prettiest 10 the nicest 14 the hottest
6 the worst

b 2 The shortest 5 The fastest
3 the most popular; 6 the most important
   the most interesting 7 the best
4 The most useful 8 the worst

💡 FAST FINISHERS

Ask fast finishers to brainstorm other adjectives they know and write down the comparative and superlative forms of each one, e.g., *angry – angrier – the angriest*; *intelligent – more intelligent – the most intelligent*; etc.

f ▶ `10.07` **Pronunciation** Play the recording for students to listen to how the words are stressed.

g ▶ `10.08` **Pronunciation** Students listen to the questions and identify the main stress. Drill each word in 2f and the questions in 2g.

Answer
on the adjective

h 💬 In pairs or small groups, students ask and answer the questions in 2g. Monitor, but don't interrupt fluency unless students make mistakes with the form or pronunciation of the superlative adjectives.

3 READING

a 💬 Students ask and answer the questions in pairs or small groups. Invite pairs or small groups to share their answers with the class, but don't check the answer to question 3 at this point.

b Students read the text quickly and find out if their guesses in 3a were correct. Check the answer as a class.

Answer
It has interesting facts about languages and learning languages.

c Individually, students complete the text with the superlative forms of the adjectives in the box. Check answers and spelling by asking students to write the correct answers on the board.

Answers

1 the best	6 the heaviest
2 the fastest	7 the shortest
3 the most popular	8 the longest
4 most expensive	9 the most difficult
5 the biggest	10 the most difficult

d Tell students to read the text again in detail. Individually, students identify who or what the people are talking about. They then check in pairs. Check answers as a class.

Answers

1 Harold Williams
2 Quechua
3 Khmer
4 the *Oxford English Dictionary*
5 Fran Capo
6 English

e 💬 Discuss the questions as a class. Encourage students to justify their answers to question 1 as much as possible.

4 VOCABULARY High numbers

> **💡 EXTRA ACTIVITY**
>
> Review numbers 1–100. Put students into small groups and tell them to stand in a circle and try to count from 1–100 around the circle. Tell them that if they make a mistake or pause for more than three seconds, they have to start again. If you want to give your students an additional challenge, ask them to repeat the activity counting down from 100 or to add the word *beep* after every two numbers, i.e., *one, two, beep, three, four, beep*, etc.

a Individually, students find the numbers and write down what they refer to. Check answers by copying the chart onto the board and asking individual students to come up and complete it.

Answers

nine hundred million	people who speak Mandarin Chinese
six hundred and three	words Fran Capo can say in 54 seconds
six hundred thousand	words in the *Oxford English Dictionary*

b ⟫ ⏵10.09 Students complete the exercises in Vocabulary Focus 10B on p. 169. Check the answers to Exercise a as a class, play the recording for students to check their answers to Exercise b, and monitor Exercises c and d. Tell students to go back to SB p. 103.

Answers (Vocabulary Focus 10B SB p. 169)

a 1 d   2 g   3 a   4 f   5 c   6 e   7 j   8 i   9 h   10 b
b 2 two thousand <u>and</u> two
  3 –
  4 three hundred <u>and</u> eighty-one thousand two hundred <u>and</u> forty-five
  5 two million six hundred <u>and</u> seventy
  6 fifteen million six hundred <u>and</u> eighty thousand four hundred <u>and</u> thirty

> **💡 EXTRA ACTIVITY**
>
> Choose ten high numbers to say to the class for students to write down in numerals. Practice a variety of numbers, including examples with *hundred*, *thousand*, and *million*, and focus particularly on any that students have problems with. Read each number twice, making sure you say *and* in the correct position. Students then compare in pairs. Check answers by asking individual students to come up and write the numbers in numerals on the board as you say them. Drill the numbers.

c 💬 Students take turns writing down a high number for their partner to say. Monitor and check that students are using *and* in the correct position.

5 SPEAKING

a Individually, students complete the questions. Check answers and spelling by asking students to write the correct answers on the board. Drill the questions.

Answers

1 the nicest
2 the most beautiful
3 the best
4 the longest
5 the hardest
6 the most difficult
7 the most interesting

b 💬 In pairs or small groups, students ask and answer the questions. Monitor, but don't interrupt fluency unless students make mistakes with the content of this lesson.

> **🔄 LOA TIP MONITORING**
>
> - Give students a few minutes to think about their work in Lesson 10A on comparative adjectives and their work in Lesson 10B on superlative adjectives. Tell them to look back at the exercises and see where they made mistakes and where they did well. Ask them to identify one thing they were good at and one thing they need to improve.
>
> - Students take turns sharing the things they were good at and the things they need to improve with the class. Encourage them to explain why things were difficult for them, e.g., *It's difficult to remember when to use "more" and when to use "most." It's the same word in my language*, etc.

> **⊕ ADDITIONAL MATERIAL**
>
> Workbook 10B
>
> Photocopiable activities: Grammar 10B, Vocabulary 10B

10C

EVERYDAY ENGLISH
There's something I don't know how to do

At the end of this lesson, students will be able to:

- understand informal conversations in which people ask for help, respond appropriately, and check instructions
- use appropriate phrases for asking for help
- identify the main stress and intonation in questions asking for help
- use appropriate phrases to check they have understood instructions
- ask each other for help with a piece of new technology, respond appropriately, and check they have understood the instructions

💡 OPTIONAL LEAD-IN

Books closed. Write sentences 1–5 on the board: *1 I get a new cell phone every year. 2 I regularly use three or more social media sites. 3 When I buy a new gadget, I never read the instructions. 4 I have a computer, a laptop, a tablet, and a smartphone. 5 My friends always call me when they have problems with their gadgets.*

Put students into pairs or small groups to discuss how many of the sentences are true for them. Invite pairs or small groups to share their answers with the class and find out if all the sentences are true for any of the students. Tell students that these sentences are for people who use gadgets and technology a lot. Ask them to work in their pairs or small groups again and write five sentences for people who don't use gadgets and technology a lot, e.g., *I'm not on any social media. I always get the simplest kind of cell phone I can find.*, etc. Monitor and point out errors for students to self-correct. Ask students to share their sentences for people who don't like technology with the class.

1 LISTENING

a 💬 Read the questions with the class and give students one minute to think about their answers before they work in pairs. Monitor and invite pairs to share their answers with the class.

b ▶ 10.10 Point to the picture of Juan Pablo and ask: *Do you think Juan Pablo knows how to use his tablet? Why / Why not?* Then, play Part 1 of the audio recording for students to answer the questions. Check answers as a class.

Answers
1 The volume is too loud.
2 a game called Crazy Monkeys

Audioscript (Part 1)

JUAN PABLO Hana, you're just the person I need.

HANA Really?

JP Can you help me with my tablet?

H Yes, of course. What's wrong?

JP There's something I don't know how to do. Do you mind showing me?

H Not at all.

JP There's a problem with the volume.

H Is it not loud enough?

JP It's too loud. All the time. Can you take a look?

H Hmmm.

JP And I can't put it on silent – you know, for meetings.

JP That's…just a game I was…

H Crazy Monkeys! I love that one. Yeah, you don't want to hear *that* during a meeting.

JP No. No, you don't.

c ▶ 10.10 Play Part 1 of the audio recording again for students to answer the questions. They then check in pairs. Check answers as a class.

Answers
1 She doesn't mind helping him. / She's happy to help.
2 He doesn't want it to make noise during meetings.

2 USEFUL LANGUAGE Asking for help

a ▶ 10.11 Individually, students look at the different ways to ask for help and try to remember which ones Juan Pablo uses. Play the recording for students to listen and check. Check answers as a class.

Answers
2 Can you help me?
4 Do you mind showing me?

b ▶ 10.12 Tell students that some of the sentences have mistakes. They work individually to identify and correct the wrong sentences. Play the recording for students to listen and check. Check answers as a class.

Answers
1 ✓
2 Would you mind ~~tell~~ telling me?
3 ✓
4 Could you ~~showing~~ show me?
5 ✓

c Check that students understand that one answer matches both questions. Individually, students match the questions with the answers. Check answers as a class.

Answers
1 a; b
2 a; c

3 PRONUNCIATION
Main stress and intonation

a ▶ 10.11 Play the recording and highlight the main stress in the third question in the recording.

b Answer the question as a class.

Answer
the main verb

c ▶ 10.11 Play the recording again for students to decide if the intonation goes up or down. Highlight the intonation movement by writing the questions on the board and drawing a falling arrow over the end of each.

Answer
The intonation goes down.

LOA TIP ELICITING

- Drill the four questions in 2a before students work in pairs in 3d. Try focusing on the main stress in each phrase first before filling in the other words, e.g., *help – help me – Could – Could you – Could you help – help me – Could you help me?* If necessary, clap out the rhythm of the questions for them so that they can then apply the rhythm to the sentence, e.g., *Could you help me?* would be "clap clap CLAP clap."
- Show students the downward intonation movement at the end of the phrase using hand gestures to give them a visual reference.

d 💬 Drill the questions in 2b and 3a. Students then work in pairs, practicing saying the sentences. Monitor and correct students' pronunciation as appropriate.

e Individually, students think of a question to ask their partner for help with their studying, e.g., *Can you help me with the pronunciation of this word?* Monitor and point out errors for students to self-correct.

f 💬 Remind students to stress the main verb in their questions and to make sure the intonation goes down. In pairs, they practice asking for help and agreeing to help each other. Monitor and praise students with a smile or a nod when they pronounce the questions correctly.

4 LISTENING

a ▶10.13 Play Part 2 of the audio recording for students to answer the questions. They then check in pairs. Check answers as a class.

Answers
1 Yes, she does.   2 Yes, he does.

Audioscript (Part 2)

JUAN PABLO Wow. You're really good at Crazy Monkeys.
HANA Thanks.
JP But can you help me? With the volume?
H No problem! I fixed it already.
JP You did! Do you mind showing me how?
H Sure. First, you touch this icon here and open a new screen.
JP So first I touch this icon?
H Yes.
JP I open this screen – is that right?
H Yes, it is. Then touch this "Yes" box and move this slider.
JP I move the slider like this?
H Right.
JP That's it? That's so easy.
H Now no one can hear you playing Crazy Monkeys during the meeting.
JP Thanks! I mean, I never do that.

b ▶10.13 Students listen again for specific details. Play Part 2 of the audio recording again for students to put the things in order. Check answers as a class.

Answers
1 b Touch this icon.   3 d Touch the "Yes" box.
2 a Open a new screen.   4 c Move the slider.

5 CONVERSATION SKILLS
Checking instructions

a Individually, students read the sentences and decide who says them. Check answers as a class.

Answers
Juan Pablo says all three sentences.

b Answer the question as a class. Ask students: *What would you say to ask someone to repeat instructions?* Elicit some ideas for option b, e.g., *Sorry, I didn't understand. Could you repeat that, please?* or *Sorry, I don't understand you. Can you say that again?*

Answer
a He wants to be sure he understands the instructions.

c Elicit the correct answer from the class.

Answer
like this?

d Read the instructions with the class. Students then work individually and put them in a logical order. Check answers as a class.

Answers
1 c Touch the word "Open" here.
2 a And next, go to a new screen.
3 b And last, save the photos here.

e 💬 Put students into pairs to practice giving the instructions in 5d and checking that they understand them.

♀ EXTRA ACTIVITY

Ask students to work in pairs and use a piece of technology they have with them, e.g., a smartphone, a tablet, etc., and write a script for a conversation similar to the one with Juan Pablo and Hana in the audio. They should choose just one area they have a problem with for their conversation and include appropriate phrases for asking for help and checking instructions. Monitor and help as necessary. When students have prepared their scripts, give them time to rehearse and check that they are using correct stress and intonation. Correct students' pronunciation as appropriate. Pairs then take turns performing their conversations for the class, using the piece of technology as a prop.

6 SPEAKING

a–b ≫ Divide the class into pairs and assign A and B roles. Student As read the first card on SB p. 105 and Student Bs read the first card on SB p. 136. Students then role-play the conversation. Monitor, but don't interrupt fluency unless students make mistakes with the content of this lesson. Students then read the second card and role-play the second situation.

♀ FAST FINISHERS

Ask fast finishers to choose another object which they don't know how to use and invent a similar conversation.

⊕ ADDITIONAL MATERIAL

Workbook 10C

Photocopiable activities: Pronunciation 10C

Unit Progress Test

10D | SKILLS FOR WRITING
My friends send really funny texts

At the end of this lesson, students will be able to:

- understand text messages and people talking about what they use text messages for
- understand a post on an online discussion board and a series of responses agreeing and disagreeing
- link ideas using *also*, *too*, and *as well*
- write a post about something that annoys them and an appropriate reply to another student's post

---

♀ OPTIONAL LEAD-IN

Write on the board: *thx for the pic – LOL! pls send me + when u can xxx.*

Ask students: *Where do you sometimes see messages like these?* Elicit that they are used in text messages and instant messaging. Circle the abbreviations in the message, i.e., *thx, pic, LOL, pls, +, u, xxx*, and then put students into pairs to try and work out what the message means. Check answers as a class. (*Thanks* for the *picture* – (I was) *laughing out loud*! *Please* send me *more* when *you* can. *Kisses*.) Ask students if they know any other similar abbreviations, e.g., *PLZ* (please), *GR8* (great), *NP* (no problem), *TTYL* (talk to you later), etc.

1 SPEAKING AND LISTENING

a 💬 Read the questions with the students. Then, put them into pairs or small groups to ask and answer the questions together. Monitor and invite pairs to share their answers with the class.

b Individually, students match the texts with the pictures. They then compare in pairs and discuss where the people are and what they are doing. Check answers as a class. If you used the optional lead-in, ask students if the texts they send look more like the ones on the board or the ones in the Student's Book.

> **Answers**
> a 3 (She is at the airport and is texting her family to say she is going to be late.)
> b 2 (He is in Italy and is taking a picture of his meal.)
> c 4 (He is on a train and is texting someone to ask what is for dinner.)
> d 1 (They are waiting for someone and texting them.)

c ▶ 10.14 Play the recording for students to listen for general meaning and identify the texts. Check answers as a class.

> **Answers**
> Speaker 1 c
> Speaker 2 a
> Speaker 3 d

Audioscript

SPEAKER 1
I send text messages all the time, like to my parents to say when I'm coming home. I also chat on social media apps. I always have my phone with me so I can see what my friends are doing. It's really good to know what people are doing. I chat with everybody all the time and we send each other pictures.

SPEAKER 2
I only really send text messages when I'm traveling. I text my family to tell them when I arrive somewhere new or tell them when I'll be back. It's useful because I'm often away on business trips in other countries and it's cheaper than calling. But usually I don't send text messages. I prefer to talk to people on the phone. It's easier and you can say more.

SPEAKER 3
Of course I text more often than I call people. It's faster. For example, I usually send a text message if I'm meeting a friend somewhere so we can find each other.

d ▶ 10.14 Students listen to the recording again for specific details and complete the chart. They then compare in pairs. Check answers by copying the chart onto the board and asking individual students to come up and complete it.

> **Answers**
>
> | | Sends texts to | Prefers to | Why? |
> |---|---|---|---|
> | Speaker 1 | parents | send text messages; chat on social media apps | It's good to know what people are doing. |
> | Speaker 2 | family | talk on the phone | It's easier and you can say more on the phone. |
> | Speaker 3 | friends | send text messages | It's faster. |

e 💬 Students talk about the questions in pairs, small groups, or as a class. Invite students to share their answers with the class.

2 READING

a Individually, students read the posts on the discussion board quickly and check the people who sometimes get annoyed. You may wish to pre-teach the word *laugh* (v.) (to make a noise when something is funny). Check answers as a class.

> **Answers**
> ✓ Genji, ✓ Meepe, ✓ MadMax, ✓ AdamB, ✓ Lars2

b Tell students to read the posts again in detail. Students identify who thinks the things. After checking answers, ask students: *Which person are you like?*

> **Answers**
> 1 Lars2
> 2 Rainbows
> 3 AdamB/Lars2
> 4 Genji/Meepe/MadMax
> 5 MadMax/AdamB

c Students read the posts again and underline the adjectives. They then check in pairs. Check answers as a class.

> **Answers**
> important, useful, funny
> Negative: worst, annoying, rude

d Tell students that they need to find short phrases/sentences, not just individual words. Check answers as a class.

> **Answers**
> 1 Yes, I agree; Yes, you're right.
> 2 I don't agree (with you, Genji).

> ### 💡 FAST FINISHERS
>
> Ask fast finishers to write their own short responses to Genji's original post.

③ WRITING SKILLS
Linking ideas with *also*, *too*, and *as well*

a Tell students to close their books. Write the first sentence from 3a on the board, leaving a blank space in place of *also*. Point to the blank and ask students: *What's this word?* Elicit *also* and write it in the sentence. Ask students: *What kind of word is this?* and elicit *a word to link ideas* (an adverb). Students open their books, look at the sentences with *also*, and underline the correct answers. Check answers as a class.

> **Answers**
> 1 after
> 2 before
> 3 beginning

b Individually, students identify the words and phrases that mean the same as *also*. They then compare in pairs. Check answers as a class.

> **Answers**
> 1 too
> 2 as well
> They come at the end.

> ### 💡 EXTRA ACTIVITY
>
> Write sentences 1–5 on the board and ask students to decide if they are correct or not. Tell them to correct the wrong sentences. Tell them that there is more than one correct option to make correct sentences. *1 I can speak French and I can too speak German.* (✗ … I can (<u>also</u>) speak German (<u>too</u> / <u>as well</u>).) *2 Texting is really boring. Also, texts can be kind of confusing.* (✔) *3 I think Italian is the most beautiful language in the world, too.* (✔) *4 I have a laptop and a tablet also.* (✗ … and (<u>also</u>) a tablet (<u>too</u> / <u>as well</u>).) Check answers as a class.

c Check that students understand that they can link the ideas in the sentences with *also*, *too*, or *as well*, but tell them that they should use each linking word at least once. Students work individually, adding *also*, *too*, or *as well* to the sentences. Monitor and check that students are putting the linking words in the correct position.

> **Answers**
> 1 … and I (<u>also</u>) have a new laptop (<u>too</u> / <u>as well</u>).
> 2 … and we (<u>also</u>) took a street map (<u>too</u> / <u>as well</u>).
> 3 … and she (<u>also</u>) knows a lot about computers (<u>too</u> / <u>as well</u>).
> 4 (<u>Also,</u>) they have a large screen, so they are easy to read (<u>too</u> / <u>as well</u>).

④ WRITING AND SPEAKING

> ### 🔄 LOA TIP ELICITING
>
> - Monitor the Writing and Speaking section closely, making sure at all stages that students are completing the task correctly and are clear about what they have to do.
> - In 4a, monitor and help with vocabulary, and give students ideas if necessary. If students complete 4b and 4c in class, then monitor and note the kinds of mistakes they are making to see how well they have understood and can use the content of the unit. However, don't point out students' mistakes at this point as other students will do this in 4d. In the final speaking stage, listen for correct use of comparative and superlative adjectives, but don't interrupt fluency.

a Students work individually to plan a post about something that annoys them.

b If you're short on time, this exercise can be completed for homework. Students could then bring their posts to the next class.

c Students switch posts and write a comment agreeing or disagreeing with the original post and using *also*, *too*, or *as well* if possible. Again, if you're short on time, this exercise can be completed for homework. They then pass the original post and their comment on to a third student.

> ### 💡 FAST FINISHERS
>
> Ask fast finishers to pass the original post and their comment on to another fast finisher, who can then write an additional response both to the post and the comment.

d Students read both the original post and the comment and check the other students' work. Tell them to check that the other students have used *also*, *too*, or *as well* correctly. If there are any mistakes with the linking words, or mistakes in other areas, students prepare a second draft of their original post/comments before giving it to you for correction.

e 💬 Put students into small groups to compare their posts and discuss which they think is the most interesting. After correcting students' work, ask them to make a final version to share with other students. You may display the posts and comments around the classroom for other students to read and comment on further. Alternatively, if you and your students have the technology available, set up a class discussion board where students can display their posts and comment on each other's texts.

> ### ⊕ ADDITIONAL MATERIAL
>
> Workbook 10D

UNIT 10
Review and extension

1 GRAMMAR

a Individually, students complete the conversation. Check answers as a class and check students are spelling the comparative adjectives correctly.

> **Answers**
> 2 more powerful
> 3 bigger
> 4 more expensive
> 5 heavier
> 6 lighter
> 7 thinner
> 8 more practical
> 9 faster

b Check that students understand that they have to use one word from each box to complete the questions. Monitor and help as necessary. Point out errors for students to self-correct. Check answers as a class.

> **Answers**
> a the hottest place
> b the longest river
> c the most expensive hotel room
> d the best soccer player
> e the biggest country

2 VOCABULARY

a Students underline the correct words in each sentence. Check answers as a class.

> **Answers**
> 1 save
> 2 goes; website
> 3 log into; check
> 4 Click on; file

b Students write the numbers as words, working individually. Check answers and use of *and* as a class by asking students to write the correct answers on the board.

> **Answers**
> 1 fifty million
> 2 two thousand and three
> 3 two hundred and fifty-six
> 4 one thousand five hundred
> 5 two hundred thousand
> 6 two thousand six hundred and fifty-five

3 WORDPOWER *most*

a Books closed. Ask students the following questions and discuss them as a class: *What language do most of the people in your country speak? Do most of them understand English? In your opinion, what's the most beautiful language in the world?* After discussing the questions, ask them: *What word is in all three questions?* Elicit *most* and write it in a circle on the board. Students open their books, read the text, and answer the questions. Check answers as a class.

> **Answers**
> 1 Spanish, German, English, and Portuguese
> 2 writer – English – because she was at school in London and also because it's an international language and most people speak it; her mother – Spanish – she says it's the most beautiful language in the world

b Read the meanings with the students and discuss the first phrase (*Most of the people we know …* − meaning b) as an example. Students work individually, matching the phrases with *most* with the meanings. They then check in pairs. Check answers as a class.

> **Answers**
> a 4,6   b 1, 2, 3, 5

c Check that students understand that this question is referring to items 1 and 5 from the text in 3a. Answer the questions as a class.

> **Answers**
> a most people   b most of the people

d Individually, students complete the sentences with the words in the box. Check answers as a class.

> **Answers**
> 1 of the evening   2 people   3 of the way   4 of my friends

> ### 💡 EXTRA ACTIVITY
>
> Write sentence beginnings 1–4 and endings a–d on the board and ask students to match the sentence halves: *1 I do my homework most of; 2 I get up early most; 3 I think most of; 4 I love all my gadgets, but most of; a my friends speak English better than me.; b all, I love my smartphone.; c the time, but sometimes I forget.; d days, but not on the weekend.*
>
> Check answers as a class (1 c, 2 d, 3 a, 4 b). Tell students to use these as examples of the kind of sentences they should write in 3e.

e As an example, make sentences about your life using two of the phrases, e.g., *Most days I get up very early, but on weekends, I stay in bed until very late.* Students then write sentences about their lives. Monitor and point out errors for students to self-correct.

f 💬 In pairs, students tell each other their sentences and find out how similar they are. Encourage students to ask follow-up questions if possible.

≫ Photocopiable activities: Wordpower 10

> ### 🔄 LOA TIP MONITORING
>
> Students look back through the unit, think about what they've studied, and decide how well they did. Students work on weak areas by using the appropriate sections of the Workbook and the Photocopiable activities.

UNIT 11
ENTERTAINMENT

⟳ UNIT OBJECTIVES

At the end of this unit, students will be able to:

- understand information, texts, and conversations about actors, actresses, music, and movies
- ask for and give information about movies, TV shows, books, and music
- discuss things they've seen and places they've been to in their town or city
- understand conversations in which people express their opinions and agree or disagree
- use appropriate phrases to ask for, express, and respond to opinions
- write a review of a movie they've seen and structure it correctly

UNIT CONTENTS

G GRAMMAR
- Present perfect: affirmative
- Present perfect: negative and questions
- Present perfect or simple past

V VOCABULARY
- Irregular past participles: *been, bought, broken, caught, eaten, fallen, flown, forgotten, grown, had, heard, read /red/, seen, written*
- Music: *a band, classical, a DJ, a festival, folk, jazz, a musician, opera, an orchestra, pop, rock, a singer*
- Wordpower: Multi-word verbs: *call back, come over, fill out, grow up, lie down, try on*

P PRONUNCIATION
- Main stress in the present perfect
- Word stress in music words
- Main stress and intonation

C COMMUNICATION SKILLS
- Talking about actors, actresses, movies, TV shows, books, and music
- Talking about things you have and haven't seen and places you have and haven't been to in your town and city
- Using appropriate phrases to ask for and express opinions
- Responding to opinions with short phrases and questions
- Discussing movies that you've seen and enjoyed and movies you would like to see
- Writing a review of a movie you've seen

GETTING STARTED

♀ OPTIONAL LEAD-IN

Books closed. Write these jumbled phrases on the board and tell students they are all kinds of entertainment: *achwngti a ieovm* (watching a movie), *inogg ot a cerntco* (going to a concert), *gnsiee a yapl ta het heatert* (seeing a play at the theater). In pairs, students work out what the phrases are. Give students one minute to think of other common forms of entertainment, e.g., *watching a dance show, seeing a musical,* etc. Invite pairs to share their answers with the class and add their ideas to the board. Ask students: *Which of these are most popular in your country? Choose the top three.* Students work individually. Then, invite students to share their answers with the class.

---

a 💬🗨 Give students one minute to think about their answers to the questions before talking about the picture as a class. If you wish, ask students additional questions, e.g., *How old do you think the people are?* and *When and where do you think they took this photo?*

b 💬🗨 In pairs or small groups, students talk about what they like to watch with their friends. If you have a class with a variety of ages, try to mix older and younger students together, as it will give them more to talk about. Help with vocabulary and pronunciation, but don't interrupt fluency. Invite pairs to share their answers with the class and ask students to share the thing they enjoyed most.

♀ EXTRA ACTIVITY

Extend the discussion and get students to talk more about what other entertainment they enjoy with their friends. Write the following questions on the board and put students into small groups to discuss them: *Do you and your friends play any games when you're together? What is your favorite indoor game? And outdoors? What music do you enjoy listening to with your friends? Do you think your parents enjoy the same kinds of entertainment as you do? Why / Why not? What about your grandparents?*

Exercises **a** and **b** can be prepared as homework before this lesson to give students time to look up unfamiliar vocabulary. Ask students to look at the picture and to prepare their answers to the questions as homework to talk about in the next class.

11A | I'VE HEARD SHE'S A GOOD ACTRESS

At the end of this lesson, students will be able to:

- read and understand a text about three actresses
- use the present perfect to talk about experience
- understand a conversation about actresses and the movies they are in
- use a lexical set of irregular past participles correctly
- ask for and give information about popular movies, TV shows, and books

💡 OPTIONAL LEAD-IN

Write sentence beginnings 1–4 on the board: *1 Hugh Jackman and Nicole Kidman both lived …*; *2 Robert Downey Jr. and Sean Penn both went …*; *3 Ashton Kutcher and Charlize Theron were both …*; *4 Leslie Mann and Milla Jovovich are both …* . Put students into pairs or small groups and ask them to discuss possible ways to complete the sentences. Then, ask students to match sentence endings a–d to the actors: *a models before they became actors.*; *b in Australia.*; *c married to movie directors.*; *d to the same school.* Check answers as a class (1b Jackman was born in Australia. Kidman was born in Hawaii to Australian parents, but the family returned to Australia when Kidman was four years old. 2d They both went to Santa Monica High School in California, though at different times. 3a Kutcher modeled for Calvin Klein and Abercrombie & Fitch, and Theron was a model in Milan. 4c Mann is married to Judd Apatow and Jovovich is married to Paul W. S. Anderson.)

1 READING

a 💬 Look at the pictures as a class. In pairs, students then decide what they think the three actresses have in common.

📖 VOCABULARY SUPPORT

movie director (B1) – the person who tells the actors and actresses what to do in a movie

have something in common (B1) – to be the same for two or more people or things

b Tell students they should only read the fact files directly below each picture. Check the answer to 1a as a class.

> **Answer**
> b They all lived in Australia.

c 💬 Put students into pairs to guess the answers to the questions. You may wish to pre-teach the word *ice-skate* (v.) (to move across ice using special shoes) and *trapeze* (n.) (a short bar that hangs high in the air from two ropes that is used in a circus).

d Tell students to read the main part of the article *Film International* and check their answers to the questions in the quiz. Check answers as a class. Ask students: *Do you know any other movies that these actors are in?* If you wish, give students information from Culture Notes in the next column. You may wish to help students with words in the Vocabulary Support box.

> **Answers**
> 1 Rose Byrne
> 2 Mia Wasikowska
> 3 Mia Wasikowska
> 4 Margot Robbie
> 5 Rose Byrne
> 6 Margot Robbie

📖 VOCABULARY SUPPORT

act (B1) – to perform in a movie or a play

award (B2) – a prize someone is given for something special they have done

soap opera (B1) – a TV show with a story that continues for a very long time and is always about the same group of people

UNICEF – the United Nations Children's Fund, a charity that helps children in difficult situations around the world

🌍 CULTURE NOTES

Margot Robbie (b. 1990) starred in the 2019 movie *Once Upon a Time in Hollywood* and has appeared in many other movies, including *Bombshell* and *Focus*. In 2019, she was ranked among the world's highest paid actresses.

Rose Byrne (b. 1979) started making movies at the age of 15 when she appeared in *Dallas Doll*. Since then, she has made many movies, including *Insidious*, *Bridesmaids*, *X-Men: Apocalypse*, *Neighbors*, *Neighbors 2: Sorority Rising,* and *Instant Family.* She also co-starred alongside Glenn Close in all 59 episodes of the television series *Damages* from 2007 to 2012.

Mia Wasikowska (b. 1989) acted in the television drama *All Saints* in 2004 when she was 14. She became famous when she starred in Tim Burton's *Alice in Wonderland* in 2010. She has also starred in *The Kids Are All Right*, *Albert Nobbs*, *Stoker*, the 2011 film version of *Jane Eyre,* the 2014 film version of *Madame Bovary, Alice Through the Looking Glass,* and *Blackbird*.

💡 EXTRA ACTIVITY

Ask students to read the fact files and the article again and decide if sentences 1–4 are true or false: *1 Mia has never acted in the U.S.* (F – All three actresses work in Hollywood in the U.S.) *2 Mia is younger than Margot.* (F – Margot is the youngest of the three.) *3 Rose has acted in television.* (T) *4 Mia has won prizes for both acting and photography.* (T)

e 💬 Students talk about the questions in pairs or small groups.

2 GRAMMAR Present perfect: affirmative

a Books closed. Write on the board: *Marilyn Monroe …
(make) her first movie in 1947.* Ask students to complete
the sentence (*made*). Then, write on the board: *Sofia
Coppola … (make) a new movie right now.* Again, ask
students to complete the sentence (*is making*). Finally,
write: *Meryl Streep … (make) a lot of fantastic movies.*
Ask students to try to complete the sentence. They may
suggest using *makes* (simple present), but tell them that
a native speaker would use *has made.* Then, to elicit the
three tenses (simple past, present continuous, and present
perfect), point to each verb one after the other and ask:
What tense is this? Students then open their books and
complete the sentences. Check answers as a class.

> **Answers**
> 1 have acted   2 has worked   3 has directed

b Discuss the question as a class.

> **Answer**
> No, we don't.

c Individually, students complete the rule. Check answers
as a class. Ask students: *How do we form the past participle
of regular verbs?* (by adding *-ed* to the base form).

> **Answers**
> I / you / we / they + <u>have</u> ('ve)
> he / she / it + <u>has</u> ('s)

3 LISTENING

a ▶ 11.01 Students listen to the conversation for general
meaning and check the films Maggie and Stephen talk
about. Check answers as a class.

> **Answers**
> 1 No, they didn't. (Maggie got 1 and 5 wrong and Stephen got 2
> and 4 wrong.)
> 2 All except a *Bridesmaids*

Audioscript

STEPHEN How many quiz answers
did you get right?

MAGGIE All of them except for
numbers one and five.

S I got question two and four
wrong. How did you know
Margot Robbie learned to go on
a circus trapeze?

M I remembered she was in *The
Legend of Tarzan,* but I haven't
seen the movie. I've only seen
her in *I, Tonya.* Which of the
movies in the list have you seen?

S I've seen *Mary Queen of Scots.*
She's really good in it. I've never

seen any of Mia Wasikowska's
movies.

M Really? Try *Jane Eyre* – she's
great in that.

S OK. I read the book in college,
but I haven't seen the movie.
What about Rose Byrne? Have
you seen any of her movies?

M No, I haven't, but I've heard she's
a good actress.

S Yeah, she's really good. I've seen
her in a couple of *X-Men* movies.
She plays a CIA agent – she's
great.

---

b ▶ 11.01 Students listen to the recording again for
specific details and complete the chart. They then check
in pairs. Check answers as a class.

> **Answers**
>
> | | Rose Byrne | Mia Wasikowska | Margot Robbie |
> |---------|------------|----------------|---------------|
> | Maggie | | ✓ e | ✓ b |
> | Stephen | ✓ d | | ✓ c |

c Students try to remember what Maggie and Stephen
thought about the actors. Play the recording again if
necessary. Check answers as a class.

> **Answers**
> They thought they were good.

4 VOCABULARY Irregular past participles

a ▶ 11.02 Individually, students complete the sentences
with the words in the box. Play the recording for
students to listen and check. Check answers as a class.
Ask students: *How are these past participles different from
the examples in 2c?* (They are irregular so they don't end
in *-ed.*)

> **Answers**
> 1 seen
> 2 heard
> 3 read, seen
> No, they don't.

b ⟫ ▶ 11.03–11.04 Students complete the exercises in
Vocabulary Focus 11A on SB p. 170. Play the recording
for students to check their answers to Exercise a and
complete the Pronunciation activity. Check answers
to Exercise b as a class and monitor Exercise d. Tell
students to go back to SB p. 111.

> **Answers (Vocabulary Focus 11A SB p. 170)**
> **a** broken – break; read (/**red**/) – read (/**rid**/); been – be;
>   caught – catch; written – write; seen – see; had – have;
>   eaten – eat; bought – buy; heard – hear; flown – fly;
>   forgotten – forget; fallen – fall; grown – grow
> **b** 1 caught   5 been   9 seen   13 fallen
>   2 written   6 bought   10 heard   14 grown
>   3 eaten   7 forgotten / had 11 broken
>   4 flown   8 read   12 eaten
> **c** 2 girl, learn, nurse, German, work

> 💡 **FAST FINISHERS**
>
> Ask fast finishers to use the irregular verbs list on SB p. 129 and
> take turns testing each other on the past participle forms.

---

5 GRAMMAR
Present perfect: negative and questions

a ▶ 11.05 Students complete the sentences with the words
in the box. Play the recording for students to listen and
check. Check answers as a class.

> **Answers**
> 1 seen   2 never   3 ever

b Ask students to look at the position of *not, ever,* and *never*
in the examples in 5a. Complete the rules as a class.

> **Answers**
> 1 after   2 before

c ▶ 11.05 **Pronunciation** Play the recording for students to
listen again to the sentences in 5a. Check the answer by
writing the sentences on the board and underlining the
three past participles to indicate the main stress. Drill the
sentences.

> **Answer**
> the past participle

There are several common student mistakes with the present perfect. Students may simply avoid using the present perfect altogether and use the simple present instead, e.g., ~~I see all of ...~~ (Correct form = *I've seen* all of Brad Pitt's movies), or they may use the incorrect auxiliary verb, using has / hasn't instead of have / haven't or vice versa, e.g., ~~I hasn't been ...~~ (Correct form = *I haven't been* to the U.S.).

When using *ever* and *never*, students are also likely to make mistakes. They may try and use both words in the same sentence, e.g., ~~... I never ever see~~ (Correct form = *It is the best movie I **have ever seen***), or they may omit the auxiliary verb, e.g., ~~I never see a movie ...~~ (Correct form = *I've never seen a movie with Rose Byrne*). When forming a negative with *never*, they often include a negative auxiliary verb, e.g., ~~I never don't see a city ...~~ (Correct form = *I've never seen a city like it.*).

d ≫ ▶11.06 Students read the information in Grammar Focus 11A on SB p. 158. Play the recording where indicated and ask students to listen and repeat. Students then complete the exercises. Check answers as a class, making sure students are forming the present perfect and positioning *ever* and *never* correctly. Tell students to go back to SB p. 111.

Answers (Grammar Focus 11A SB p. 159)

a 2 written   5 brought   7 driven   9 run
  3 swum   6 done   8 ridden 10 been
  4 had
b 2 've visited / have visited
  3 hasn't borrowed
  4 've never eaten / have never eaten
  5 've walked / have walked
  6 's played / has played
  7 haven't done
  8 's had / has had
c 1 I've seen / I have seen; I've never seen / I have never seen
  2 Have you ever met; I've met / I have met; Has he visited; he's been / he has been

• Drill the two conversations in Exercise c in Grammar Focus 11A on SB p. 159 before continuing. Divide the class in half down the middle and tell the group on your left that they are A and the group on your right that they are B. Drill A's first question with the left-hand group and B's response with the right-hand group. Then, put the two lines together with the left-hand group asking and the right-hand group answering the first question all together. Repeat the process until students can perform the first conversation without you having to model the lines for them. Tell the groups to switch A and B roles before you work on the second conversation.

e ▶11.07 Students work individually, completing the conversation. Play the recording for students to listen and check. Check answers as a class. If you wish, give students information from Culture Notes in the next column.

Answers

1 Have you seen   4 Have you read
2 've read   5 've heard
3 haven't seen   6 Have they made

The movie *Crazy Rich Asians* is based on Kevin Kwan's 2013 best-selling novel. It's based on the writer's childhood in Singapore in a very rich family where they had their own cruise ships and private planes.

The movie also got a lot of attention because there are so many Asian American actors in it. There haven't been many opportunities in Hollywood for Asian American actors, and many people saw this movie as an opportunity for that to change.

6 SPEAKING

a Individually, students think of some popular movies, TV shows, and books and write six questions about them. Monitor and help with any vocabulary students might need and the titles in English if necessary. Point out any errors in the students' questions for them to self-correct before they start on the groupwork stage in 6b.

b 💬 Put students into small groups to ask and answer each other's questions. As you monitor, don't interrupt fluency, but note any mistakes with the present perfect. After the activity, write them on the board and ask students to correct them.

Ask each student to write down the other students' answers as they ask and answer the questions in 6b. They then summarize what they found out for the class. Demonstrate the activity by asking five students an example question, e.g., *Have you read all three of the* Crazy Rich Asians *books?* and pretending to write down their answers. Then, give the class a summary of what you learned, e.g., *There are five people in my group. Two of them have read all of the* Crazy Rich Asians *books.* Students then work individually and write summary statements for each of the six questions they asked in 6a. Monitor and point out errors for students to self-correct. Ask each student to read two or three of their summary statements to the class.

Workbook 11A

Photocopiable activities: Grammar 11A, Vocabulary 11A, Pronunciation 11A

11B

I BET YOU'VE NEVER BEEN TO THE OPERA

At the end of this lesson, students will be able to:
- read and understand a text about music in Buenos Aires
- use a lexical set of music words correctly
- understand a conversation in which people talk about places they've been to
- distinguish between the simple past to say when something happened and the present perfect to talk about past experiences
- talk about things they have and haven't seen and places they have and haven't been to in their town and city

💡 OPTIONAL LEAD-IN

Write the names of a number of famous sights in the city/country where you're teaching on the board, e.g., in Mexico City – *the Zócalo, the Frida Kahlo Museum, the Chapultepec Castle, the Palace of Fine Arts,* etc. Try to include two or three places connected with music and performing arts in the list. Write *Have you ever ... ?* on the board and put students into pairs to think of questions they would like to ask you about the places, e.g., *Have you ever visited the Chapultepec Castle? Have you ever seen an opera at the Palace of Fine Arts?,* etc. Monitor and point out errors for students to self-correct.

As a class, students take turns asking you their questions. Reply with *Yes, I have. / No, I haven't.* and then, if appropriate, give students a little bit of extra information using the simple past, e.g., *Have you ever visited the Frida Kahlo Museum? / Yes, I have. I went a few years ago. It's beautiful.* Don't draw students' attention to the use of the simple past or allow them to ask you additional follow-up questions at this point as they are likely to make mistakes with the tenses.

1 READING

a 💬🔊 Discuss the question as a class and elicit that the people are dancing the tango. Ask the students: *Which city is this?* Elicit *Buenos Aires.* Then ask students: *Have you ever been to Buenos Aires?* If any students answer *yes,* then ask them one or two follow-up questions using the simple past, e.g., *When did you go? Did you see people dancing in the street like this?* Monitor to see if they use the correct tenses in their answers. Don't, however, correct any grammatical mistakes at this point.

b Individually, students guess what they think the text is about. They then read the text quickly and find out if they were correct. Check the answer as a class.

> **Answer**
> 2 places to hear music

c Tell students to read the text again in detail and answer the questions. They compare in pairs. Check answers as a class. You may wish to help students with words in the Vocabulary Support box.

> **Answers**
> a San Telmo district   d Teatro Colón
> b Konex Cultural Center   e Jazz y Pop
> c The Roxy

📖 VOCABULARY SUPPORT

basement (B2) – part of a house or a building that is under the level of the street

district (B1) – a specific area of a town, city, or country

live /laɪv/ (B1) – not recorded in advance, something you watch or listen to while it is happening

season (B1) – a series of concerts, plays, etc. that all happen in the same place in a specific period of time

💡 EXTRA ACTIVITY

Write sentences 1–5 on the board. Ask students to read the text again and complete them with the names of the places.

1 In ... , you can have a coffee, listen to music, and go shopping. (San Telmo)
2 ... is very, very small, and they don't always need to pay the musicians. (Jazz y Pop)
3 At ... , there are two different areas for different kinds of music. (The Roxy)
4 You can see the best classical singers and musicians from around the world at the ... . (Teatro Colón)
5 The ... is a good place to go at the beginning of the week. (Konex Cultural Center)

d Tell students to read the text again in detail and answer the questions. They compare in pairs. Check answers as a class.

> **Answers**
> 1 Teatro Colón   3 very late – after 2 a.m.
> 2 Jazz y Pop   4 Students' own answers

e 💬🔊 Discuss the places students would and wouldn't like to go to as a class. Encourage students to justify their answers as much as possible.

2 VOCABULARY Music

a ▶️ 11.08 Students read the text again and underline more examples of kinds of music and people who play music. Play the recording for students to listen and check. Check answers as a class.

> **Answers**
> 1 kinds of music: classical music, opera, jazz, rock, pop, folk music, dance music
> 2 people who play music, sing, or dance: orchestras, musicians, bands, DJs, singers

b ▶️ 11.09 **Pronunciation** Look at the example with the class and then play the recording for students to circle the number of syllables and underline the stressed syllable. Check answers as a class. Drill each word.

> **Answers**
> 1 <u>dan</u>cer 2   2 mu<u>si</u>cian 3   3 <u>clas</u>sical 3   4 <u>or</u>chestra 3   5 <u>op</u>era 3

c ▶️ 11.10 Play the recording for students to listen to the pieces of music and match them with words from 2a. Check answers as a class.

> **Answers**
> 1 classical   2 rock   3 jazz   4 pop   5 opera

d 💬🔊 In pairs or small groups, students discuss the questions. Invite pairs to share their answers with the class. Find out which kinds of music are the most/least popular.

3 LISTENING

a ▶**11.11** Play the recording for students to listen for general meaning and list the places Max and Alana talk about. Check answers as a class.

Answers
Jazz y Pop, The Roxy, Teatro Colón
Alana has been to all three places; Max hasn't been to any of them.

Audioscript

MAX Hey, Alana, have you seen this article? It says Buenos Aires is one of the world's best cities for music. I didn't know that.

ALANA You didn't? There's so much good music here in Buenos Aires, Max!

M I haven't been to any of these places, and I've lived here for years. Like Jazz y Pop, it says it's a famous jazz club, but I've never heard of it. Have you ever been to Jazz y Pop?

A Yes, I went there two weeks ago. They had a really good band.

M Oh, OK. What about The Roxy? Have you been there?

A Yes, of course I have! We all went there for Antonia's birthday. We had a great time. We didn't leave until five in the morning. Didn't you come … ?

M Antonia's birthday? Hmm … Oh, I remember. I had to study, so I couldn't go. OK, well, I bet you've never been to the Teatro Colón.

A Yes, I have, actually. I went there last year. It was my dad's 50th birthday, so we went to the opera.

M Oh, cool. What did you see?

A I don't remember. Something by Mozart. I didn't like it very much.

M You've been everywhere …

A Yeah, well, you should go out more. You spend too much time studying. Look, it's a nice evening. Why don't we go down to San Telmo and sit in a café? We can watch the dancers …

M Hmm … well, I'd love to. I've never been there. But I have this essay to write …

b ▶**11.11** Students listen to the recording again for specific details and complete the chart. Check answers by copying the chart onto the board and asking individual students to come up and complete it.

Answers

Where?	When?	Did she like it?
1 Jazz y Pop	two weeks ago	yes
2 The Roxy	Antonia's birthday	yes
3 Teatro Colón	father's 50th birthday	no

4 GRAMMAR
Present perfect or simple past

a ▶**11.12** Individually, students match the questions with the answers. Play the recording for students to listen and check. Check answers as a class.

Answers
1 a   2 b   3 c

b Give students a few minutes to answer the questions. Check answers as a class.

Answers
1 b, d
2 a present perfect   b simple past
3 a present perfect   b simple past

🔁 **LOA TIP** CONCEPT CHECKING

- Check that students fully understand when we use the present perfect and when we use the simple past by asking them: *When we use the present perfect, which is more important – when the action happened or the experience?* (the experience) *Which words do we often use with the present perfect to mean "at any time in my life" and "at no time in my life"?* (ever and never) *Which tense do we use when we want to ask for more details about an experience?* (simple past).

- After checking that students have understood the uses of the present perfect and simple past, double-check they are clear about the form by asking them: *Which auxiliary do we use in simple past negatives, questions, and short answers?* (did/didn't) *What about with the present perfect?* (have/haven't).

👁 **CAREFUL!**

As well as the common student mistakes with the present perfect outlined in Lesson 11A, students are also likely to confuse the present perfect and simple past forms. They may use the simple past instead of the present perfect, e.g., ~~I didn't buy new clothes …~~ (Correct form = *I* **haven't bought** *new clothes this month for my vacation in Buenos Aires!*) or the present perfect instead of the simple past, e.g., ~~Last year I've been to …~~ (Correct form = *Last year, I* **went** *to The Roxy for my birthday.*).

c ▶▶ ▶**11.13** Students read the information in Grammar Focus 11B on SB p. 158. Play the recording where indicated and ask students to listen and repeat. Students then complete the exercises. Check answers as a class, making sure students are not confusing the present perfect or simple past forms and are using the correct auxiliary verbs. Tell students to go back to SB p. 113.

Answers (Grammar Focus 11B SB p. 159)
a 2 I've never seen   5 she's never won   7 've never eaten
   3 We went   6 We visited   8 Did he win
   4 Have you ever danced
b 2 c 3 e 4 h 5 a 6 d 7 f 8 b
c 2 have   6 I went   10 was   14 Did you go
   3 I've gone   7 Did you like 11 was   15 didn't
   4 I've gone   8 did   12 I've seen   16 I wanted
   5 I've gone   9 It was   13 she played 17 I finished

💡 **FAST FINISHERS**

Ask fast finishers to look at all the verbs in Exercises a–c and check that they know the base form, simple past, and past participle forms of each one. They can use the irregular verbs list on SB p. 129 to check their answers.

d ▶**11.14** Tell students to work individually and order the sentences to make a conversation. Play the recording for students to listen and check. Check answers as a class.

Answers and audioscript

A 1 Have you ever been to a music festival?

B 2 Yes, I have. I went to one last summer.

A 3 You did? Where was it?

B 4 It was in Rio de Janeiro – the Rock in Rio festival.

A 5 I've heard that's a great festival! Did you enjoy it?

B 6 Yes, we had a great time.

A 7 Oh, who did you go with?

B 8 I went with a group of friends from college.

e 💬 In pairs, students practice the conversation in 4d. Monitor and correct students' pronunciation as appropriate.

5 SPEAKING

a Individually, students think of two things they've seen or places they've been to in their town or city. Give them a few minutes to write notes. Monitor and help as necessary.

b Students think of two things they haven't seen or places they haven't been and write notes.

c 💬 Students work in pairs or small groups talking about the things and places they wrote notes about. Listen carefully to check that students are using the present perfect and the simple past forms correctly. When students make a mistake with the forms, try to catch their eye discreetly so that they can correct their mistake.

💡 FAST FINISHERS

Ask fast finishers to talk about things or places from the categories in 5a that they didn't write notes about, i.e., if they wrote notes about a concert and a play, they could talk about a music event, a movie, a club, etc.

⊕ ADDITIONAL MATERIAL

Workbook 11B

Photocopiable activities: Grammar 11B, Vocabulary 11B

11C

EVERYDAY ENGLISH
I thought they were really good

At the end of this lesson, students will be able to:

- understand informal conversations in which people ask for and express opinions and agree or disagree with one another
- use appropriate phrases to ask for and express opinions
- respond to opinions with short phrases and questions
- identify the main stress and intonation in short phrases and questions used to respond to opinions
- ask for, express, and respond to opinions about a concert and a restaurant

💡 OPTIONAL LEAD-IN

Books closed. Write these questions on the board: *When was the last time you went out in the evening? Where did you go? What did you do? Who did you go with? Did you have a good time? Why / Why not? How did you get home? How did you feel when you got home? Was it a typical night out for you? What is your idea of a perfect night out?* Put students into pairs or small groups to discuss the questions. Monitor and praise students who are able to express what they want to say, even if their English isn't perfect. Invite pairs or small groups to share their answers with the class, and discuss the last question to find out what students think would be a perfect night out.

1 LISTENING

a 💬 Students talk about the questions in pairs. Invite pairs to share their answers with the class and find out what the most popular kind of transportation is.

b 💬 Tell students to look at picture a and ask them to write down what they think Paul and Celia are doing.

c ▶ 11.15 Play Part 1 of the audio recording for students to check their answers in 1b. Students then choose the correct answers. Check answers as a class.

Answers
They are hailing a taxi.
1 on their way home
2 525 Washington Road

Audioscript (Part 1)

PAUL Taxi! ... 525 Washington Road, please.

DRIVER 525 Washington Road. You got it.

CELIA Ooh. It's nice to sit in quiet.

P So, what did you think of the concert? Did you enjoy it?

C Yeah, it was OK. I had fun. How about you?

P Yeah, me too. I really liked it. I didn't like the opening band, though.

C No, me neither.

P But I loved the last band – Atlantis.

C You did? I just thought they were kind of boring. All their songs sound the same.

P Do you think so? I thought they were really good.

C Yeah. They really only had one song.

P I thought they had a lot of great songs. Like "Have you ever been in love?" That's a good song!

C Mmm, maybe.

P Or, "I've never been to Vegas—"

C That's enough, honey.

P Another great song!

C Those were different songs? They sounded the same to me.

P OK, OK.

d ▶ 11.15 Play Part 1 of the audio recording again for students to answer the questions. Check answers as a class.

Answers
1 They have been at a concert.
2 No, they don't.

e ▶ 11.15 Individually, students read the sentences and decide who they correspond to. They then listen again for specific details. Play the audio recording again for students to listen and check. Check answers as a class.

> **Answers**
> 1 B 2 B 3 P 4 C

2 USEFUL LANGUAGE
Asking for and expressing opinions

a ▶ 11.16 Students put the conversation in the correct order. Play the recording for students to listen and check. Check answers as a class.

> **Answers**
> 1 d So, what did you think of the concert?
> 2 a Did you enjoy it?
> 3 e Yeah, it was OK.
> 4 f I had fun.
> 5 b How about you?
> 6 c Yeah, me too.

b 💬 In pairs, students practice the mini-conversation in 2a. Monitor and correct students' pronunciation as appropriate.

c Students match the opinions with the reasons, working individually. Check answers as a class.

> **Answers**
> 1 b 2 c 3 a

> **💡 EXTRA ACTIVITY**
>
> Books closed. Write these prompts on the board:
> *A* what / you / think / the concert? / So,
> *A* Did / it? / enjoy
> *B* it / OK. / Yeah,
> *B* fun. / I
> *A* Yeah, / too.
> Ask students to work in pairs and write the complete conversation. Remind them to think carefully about which tenses to use. Students then open their books, look at the Useful Language section, and check for any mistakes in their conversation. Check answers by eliciting a full version of the conversation and writing it on the board. Make sure students understand that more than one answer is possible. (Suggested answer: *A* So, what did you think of the concert? *A* Did you enjoy it? *B* Yeah, it was OK. *B* I had fun. *A* Yeah, me too.)

3 LISTENING

a ▶ 11.17 Point to picture b and elicit ideas from the class about what is happening. Play Part 2 of the audio recording for students to listen and check. Check the answer as a class.

> **Answer**
> They are playing pop / rock music.

> **Audioscript (Part 2)**
>
> **PAUL** Atlantis is one of my favorite bands right now. I have some of their songs on my phone. Here, listen.
> **CELIA** No, thanks. I've heard enough.
> **P** "Had a great time, we had a—"
> **C** OK, enough!!
> **P** All right, sorry.
> **C** I don't really like pop music in general.
> **P** Do you think they're a pop band? I think they're more like a rock band.
> **C** I just thought they were too loud.
> **P** Yeah, they were kind of loud.
> **C** Not as loud as you, though!
> **P** Hey!

4 CONVERSATION SKILLS
Responding to an opinion

a Ask students: *Do you think Celia and Paul like the same kind of music?* Encourage students to justify their ideas as much as possible. Point to the mini-conversations and ask students to decide if the replies mean the other person agrees or doesn't really agree. Check answers as a class.

> **Answers**
> 1 a 2 a 3 b 4 b 5 a

b Complete the chart as a class. Check that students have fully understood the use of the auxiliary verbs by writing these questions on the board and asking students to choose the correct answers: *Which auxiliary verbs do we use to respond to an opinion: do/did or have/had?* (do/did) *Do we use the same tense as the original sentence or a different one?* (the same tense).

> **Answers**
> 1 Did
> 2 Do

c 💬 Drill the mini-conversations in 4a. Students then work in pairs, practicing saying them. Monitor and correct students' pronunciation as appropriate.

> **💡 FAST FINISHERS**
>
> Ask fast finishers to close their books and invent similar mini-conversations without looking at the mini-conversations in 4a or the chart in 4b to help them.

5 PRONUNCIATION
Main stress and intonation

a ▶ 11.18 Play the recording and highlight that both words are stressed in each reply.

b ▶ 11.18 Play the recording again for students to answer the questions. They then check in pairs. Check answers as a class.

> **Answers**
> 1 up: 1, 2; down: 3, 4
> 2 b surprised

c ▶ 11.18 Play the recording again for students to listen and repeat. Drill each reply.

d 💬 Put students into pairs to practice responding to the opinions. Monitor and check that students are using the correct stress and intonation.

6 LISTENING

a ▶ 11.17 Play Part 2 of the audio recording again for students to check their answers. Check answers as a class.

> **Answers**
> 1 F (Atlantis is one of his favorite bands.)
> 2 T
> 3 F (She doesn't want to hear him sing.)
> 4 T
> 5 F (She thinks Atlantis was too loud.)

7 SPEAKING

a ⟫ Divide the class into pairs and assign A and B roles. Student As read the first card on SB p. 134 and Student Bs read the first card on SB p. 136. Students then role-play the conversation. Students then read the second card and role-play the second situation.

> ### 🔄 LOA TIP CONCEPT CHECKING
>
> • Monitor both the preparation stage and the speaking stage of the Speaking section closely. During the preparation stage, encourage students to think carefully about what they want to say before they start speaking so that they don't have to pause and ask you for vocabulary once they have started.
>
> • During the speaking stage, monitor and check that students are forming the short phrases and questions for responding to an opinion correctly and using the correct stress and intonation. When students make a mistake with the phrases or the pronunciation, try to catch their eye discreetly so that they can correct their mistake.
>
> • If students continue to form the phrases and questions incorrectly and aren't using correct stress and intonation, you may wish to check this again or ask them to do the activity in Workbook 11C.

> ### 💡 EXTRA ACTIVITY
>
> Ask students to work in pairs and give them one minute to think of as many things as they can that they have both seen and done, e.g., seen an opera, been to a comedy club, etc. Check that they understand that they should just make a list at this point, not discuss the things in any detail. When students have finished preparing their lists, tell them that now they should take turns discussing each item in turn using the useful language for asking for, expressing, and responding to opinions, e.g., **A** *We've both seen an opera. What did you think of it?* **B** *I didn't like it very much.* **A** *Me neither. I thought the singers were great, but I didn't like the story.*, etc. Monitor and praise students with a smile or a nod when they use the language from this lesson correctly and use appropriate stress and intonation in their replies.

> ### ⊕ ADDITIONAL MATERIAL
>
> Workbook 11C
>
> Photocopiable activities: Pronunciation 11C
>
> Unit Progress Test

11D SKILLS FOR WRITING
It was an interesting movie

At the end of this lesson, students will be able to:

• understand a conversation in which people discuss a movie they've both seen

• understand positive and negative reviews of a movie

• structure a review correctly and avoid repetition

• write a review of a movie they've seen and structure it correctly

> ### 💡 OPTIONAL LEAD-IN
>
> Before students arrive, write these questions on the board:
>
> *Which movie do you think …*
>
> *– is about a superhero?*
>
> *– tells an amazing story about one person's life?*
>
> *– is best for families?*
>
> *– looks most exciting?*
>
> *– is about people from another planet?*
>
> *– teenagers would enjoy?*
>
> *– is about the world in the past?*
>
> *– has a lot of special effects?*
>
> As students arrive, put them into pairs or small groups to look at the movie posters in Lesson 11D and answer the questions with the title of one or more of the movies. Tell them it doesn't matter if they haven't seen the movies because they can base their answers off what they can see in the posters. Invite students to share their answers with the class and give students information from Culture Notes on the next page, if you wish.

1 SPEAKING AND LISTENING

a 💬 Discuss the questions as a class and find out if they have ever watched a movie more than once. If you didn't use the optional lead-in, give students information from Culture Notes on the next page.

🌐 CULTURE NOTES

Captain America: *The First Avenger* (2011) is a superhero movie that tells the story of Steve Rogers, a man who volunteers in a secret government experiment that changes his body. He has to fight for his country against an evil secret Nazi organization. This movie is based on the Marvel Comics superhero Captain America.

Mary Poppins (1964) is a musical set in London about a nanny who changes the lives of the two children she cares for. Walt Disney Studios released *Mary Poppins Returns* in 2018, 54 years after the original. The original movie was so successful that Walt Disney was able to buy land in Orlando, Florida to build Disney World.

Men in Black (1997) is a science fiction movie starring Will Smith and Tommy Lee Jones. They are secret government agents who must save the world from alien invaders. The combination of science fiction and comedy made this movie a huge international success.

Forrest Gump (1994) tells the incredible story of a man who goes to fight in the Vietnam War, becomes a shrimp boat captain, and later a millionaire, although he has a mental disability. Tom Hanks won an Oscar for best actor for his role in this movie and has said it was his favorite movie to film.

Star Wars: *Episode IV – A New Hope* (1977) is the first in a widely successful series. Young Luke Skywalker has to save Princess Leia from Darth Vader and the evil Galactic Empire. The Star Wars franchise became an international phenomenon with nine movies, the final one released in 2019.

Pirates of the Caribbean: *The Curse of the Black Pearl* (2003) stars Johnny Depp as the pirate Captain Jack Sparrow who has to stop a ship of pirates and save the love of his life from his old associates who have taken her.

b ▶ **11.19** Tell students that they are going to listen to Ron and Melissa talking, but that they are not talking about any of the movies on SB pp. 116–117. Play the recording for students to listen for general meaning and answer the questions. Check answers as a class.

Answers
1 *Skyfall*
2 Ron liked it, but Melissa didn't.

Audioscript

MELISSA Have you seen the James Bond movie *Skyfall*?

RON Yes, have you?

M Yes, I watched it with my brother last night. Pretty bad, isn't it?

R Oh, I don't agree. I really enjoyed it.

M Well, I thought it was boring. James Bond movies are always the same. James Bond is cool, he goes to some beautiful country, and he meets a beautiful girl. The bad guys all die at the end. You always know what's going to happen. Of course the special effects were great, but that's about all.

R Well, it's not meant to be too serious, you know. I thought it was fun. I liked it.

M Did you really?

R Yes, I did. I thought it was exciting. It was great to watch, the actors were great, and James Bond was fantastic. In fact, I'm going to watch it again this weekend. Do you want to come over and watch it with me?

M What, again? No thanks, once was enough. I'm going to the movie theater to see the latest superhero movie.

c ▶ **11.19** Students listen to the recording again for specific details and decide who the sentences correspond to. They then check in pairs. Check answers as a class.

Answers
1 M 2 R 3 M 4 R

d Individually, students choose two movies, one they've seen and one they haven't seen, and write notes. Monitor and help with vocabulary if necessary.

💡 EXTRA ACTIVITY

Write jumbled questions/responses 1–6 on the board. Ask students to put them in order:
1 *you / so / do / think ?* (Do you think so?)
2 *enjoy / it / you / did ?* (Did you enjoy it?)
3 *agree / really / don't / I* (I don't really agree.)
4 *very much / like / it / I / didn't* (I didn't like it very much.)
5 *a / director / fantastic / he's / think / I* (I think he's a fantastic director.)
6 *story / thought the / I / good, / was pretty / actors were / awful / but the* (I thought the story was pretty good, but the actors were awful.)
Check answers as a class. Remind students to use appropriate phrases for asking for, expressing, and responding to opinions in their discussion in the next exercise.

e 💬 In small groups, students discuss the questions. Monitor and check that students are using the language for expressing opinions correctly.

2 READING

a Point to the photo of Ashley on SB p. 116 and tell students that they are going to read her review of *Roma*. Individually, students read the review quickly and find out if it's positive or negative. Check the answer as a class.

Answer
positive

b Tell students to read the review again in detail and answer the questions. They then check in pairs. Check answers as a class.

Answers
1 twice
2 *Possible answers:* He's a Mexican movie director; he directed Roma; he grew up in Mexico City.
3 *Possible answers:* She was the best; she's a great actress; she was unknown; she plays the role of a maid.

c Point to the photo of Oscar on SB p. 117 and his review. Students read it quickly to find out if it's positive or negative. Check the answer as a class.

Answer
negative

d Students read Oscar's review again in detail and answer the questions. They then check in pairs. Check answers as a class.

Answers
1 A friend recommended it.
2 Good: the acting
Bad: the story is boring; nothing exciting happens.

e Point to the photo of Anna on SB p. 117 and her review. Students read it quickly to find out if it's positive or negative. Check the answer as a class.

Answer
mainly positive

f Students read Anna's review again in detail and answer the questions. After checking answers, ask any students who have seen Roma if they agree with Ashley's, Oscar's, or Anna's opinion.

Answers
1 at a friend's house
2 *Possible answers:* It's a sad movie; it's in black and white; the maid comes from a village.

3 WRITING SKILLS Structuring a review

a Look at the two reviews with the class and check that students understand that the numbers 1–6 appear in both Ashley's and Oscar's reviews. Read the example and show students how this question is answered in sentence 4 of both reviews. Students then work individually, identifying the sentences. Check answers as a class.

Answers
b 1 c 2 d 6 e 3 f 5

b Individually, students look at Anna's review again and compare it to Ashley's and Oscar's reviews. Check the answer as a class.

Answer
No. She talks about the movie (f) and then about the actors (a).

c Read the first comment and elicit the answer as an example. Individually, students match the other comments with the questions in 3a. They then check in pairs. Check answers as a class.

Answers
1 c	5 e
2 b	6 d
3 c	7 c
4 a	8 f

d Individually, students read the sentences and compare them with the ones in the reviews. Check answers as a class.

Answers
1 The review uses *it*.
2 The review uses *she* and *her*.
3 The review uses *it*.

e 💬🗨 In pairs, students discuss the questions. Invite pairs to share their answers with the class and ask students: *Why do the reviews use "it," "this movie," and "the movie"?* Check that students understand that it isn't good style to keep repeating words and names in English.

Answers
1 Once, at the beginning.
2 They use *it*, *the movie*, and *this movie*.

💡 FAST FINISHERS

Ask fast finishers to read the three reviews again and find *good* and its comparative and superlative forms. They then underline all the other adjectives in the reviews and list their comparative and superlative forms.

4 WRITING AND SPEAKING

🔄 LOA TIP CONCEPT CHECKING

- If students need more support, demonstrate 4a and 4b (writing notes and the review) by eliciting notes and writing them onto the board for questions a–f in 3a. Then, work as a class to build the notes into a model review so that students fully understand the process.

- Use questions a–f in 3a to write short notes down the left-hand side of the board. For example, choose a movie together and ask the class: *When did you see the movie?* Suggest that you saw it together as a class last week (note down: *last week, as a class*). Then ask: *Did you like it?* (e.g., *teacher – great, student – terrible!*). Continue with the other questions.

- Elicit complete sentences from the class, helping the students by using the notes on the board, the comments in 3b, and Ashley's, Oscar's, and Anna's reviews in 2a, 2c, and 2e. Write the review on the right-hand side of the board, e.g., *I went to see* The Hobbit *last week with my class. The teacher told us it was great, but I thought it was terrible! … .* Tell students to use exactly the same process to prepare their reviews.

a Students work individually to plan a review of a movie they've seen. Monitor and help with vocabulary and give students ideas if necessary. Check that students know the English title of the movie they have chosen.

b If you're short of time, this exercise can be completed for homework. Students could then bring their reviews to the next class.

c In pairs, students switch reviews and check their partner's work. Tell them to check their partner has answered all six questions in 3a and has not repeated the name of the movie or the names of the actors too often. They then give each other feedback. If they have made any mistakes with the structure or in other areas, they prepare a second draft of their review before giving it to you for correction.

d 💬🗨 Put students into small groups to read each other's reviews and discuss which movies they would like to see. If you wish, if you and your students have the technology available, set up a class blog where students can post their reviews and respond to each other's opinions.

⊕ ADDITIONAL MATERIAL
Workbook 11D

UNIT 11
Review and extension

1 VOCABULARY

a Students underline the correct word in each sentence. Check answers as a class.

Answers

1 classical	4 pop
2 rock	5 musician
3 orchestra	6 opera

b Students write the past participle of each verb. They check their answers by looking at the irregular verbs list on SB p. 129.

Answers

1 been	5 read (/**red**/)
2 done	6 seen
3 gone	7 won
4 heard	8 written

> ### ♀ FAST FINISHERS
>
> Ask fast finishers to look at the verbs in 1b again and check the ones that have the same form for the simple past and the past participle. For the ones that are different, students write down the simple past form, too.

2 GRAMMAR

a Students write the sentences and questions. Check answers as a class by asking individual students to write the correct answers on the board.

Answers

1 I've been / I have been to South Africa twice.
2 She's met / She has met a lot of famous actors.
3 Have you seen the latest James Bond movie?
4 He hasn't / has not worked in an office before.
5 We've / We have never won the lottery.
6 Have they read all the Harry Potter books?
7 I haven't / have not heard a lot of jazz music.

b Individually, students read the sentences and correct the verb form in the ones that are wrong. Check answers as a class.

Answers

1 ✓	5 ✓
2 He read	6 ✓
3 I've never seen	7 I haven't read / I've never read
4 They won	

c Complete the first item as an example with the class. Check that students understand that they can use the present perfect or the simple past and so need to think carefully about the meaning. Check answers as a class. Drill the conversation.

Answers

1 Have you been	4 went	7 did
2 've been	5 did you stay	8 was
3 've never been	6 wasn't	9 Have you ever tried

3 WORDPOWER Multi-word verbs

a Tell students to close their books. Write the following incomplete sentences 1–3 on the board: *1 I come … Brazil. 2 She sometimes wakes … very late. 3 We went … to a restaurant for dinner last night.* Point to the three blanks and ask students about each missing word. Write *from, up,* and *out* on the board in each sentence. Then, circle the multi-word verb in each sentence (*come from, wakes up, went out*) and ask students: *What kind of words are these?* Elicit/Teach *multi-word verbs.* (You could also point out the alternative term, *phrasal verbs,* which students may already know.) Students open their books, look at the sentences, and match them to make conversations. Check answers as a class.

Answers

1 c   2 e   3 b   4 f   5 a   6 d

b Individually, students match the multi-word verbs with the meanings. They then check in pairs. Check answers as a class.

Answers

1 call back
2 try on
3 fill out
4 lie down
5 come over
6 grow up

c Students complete the sentences with the correct form of a multi-word verb from 3a. Check answers as a class.

Answers

1 try (things) on
2 fill (it) out
3 grew up
4 called (me) back
5 lie down
6 came over

> ### ♀ EXTRA ACTIVITY
>
> Write example answers a–f below to questions 1–6 in 3d on the board. Ask students to match them to the questions and complete the answers before they ask and answer the questions in pairs: *a No. I always _____ people _____ when they leave a message. (2 call … back) b Yes, I often _____ _____ after lunch and sleep for twenty minutes. (6 lie down) c I _____ _____ a form last week because I need a new passport. (5 filled out) d They never _____ _____ – they live far away! (1 come over) e No, I can't _____ them _____ because I buy everything on the Internet. (4 try … on) f I _____ _____ in a little town in the mountains in Colorado. (3 grew up)*

d 💬🔊 In pairs, students ask and answer the questions. Monitor, but don't interrupt fluency unless students make mistakes with the phrasal verbs.

≫ Photocopiable activities: Wordpower 11

> ### ⟲ LOA REVIEW YOUR PROGRESS
>
> Students look back through the unit, think about what they've studied, and decide how well they did. Students work on weak areas by using the appropriate sections of the Workbook and the Photocopiable activities.

UNIT **12**
TRAVEL

GETTING STARTED

♀ OPTIONAL LEAD-IN

Use a "live listening" to introduce the topic of travel. Choose a picture with friends or family on vacation to show the class. Find out about the people and vacation in the picture, or make up your own ideas, e.g., *These are my friends Sarah and Russell. They are in Iceland.*, etc. Alternatively, use a picture of yourself on vacation. Write questions 1–3 on the board: *1 Where are the people? 2 Who are they? 3 What did they do while they were on vacation?* Project your picture on the board, or print it out to show the class, and tell students about it. Students listen, answer the questions on the board, and note any other information you give. They then check in pairs and ask you to confirm any information they are not sure about.

a 💬🔊 Give students one minute to think about their answers to the questions before talking about the picture as a class. If you wish, give students information from Culture Notes below and ask students if they would like to go on vacation to Egypt.

🌍 CULTURE NOTES

This picture shows the Giza pyramid complex in Egypt, also called the Giza Necropolis. All the pyramids were built in the Fourth Dynasty of the Old Kingdom of Ancient Egypt. The Great Pyramid (the largest in the photo) is the oldest of the Seven Wonders of the World and the only one still in existence. It's 147 meters high and made up of an estimated 2.3 million stone blocks, each weighing approximately 2.5 to 15 tons.

These pyramids are located approximately nine kilometers west of the Nile River in the city of Giza and about 13 kilometers southwest of Cairo.

b 💬🔊 Read the questions with students before they ask and answer them. If they wish, they can show each other pictures of friends and family, vacations, etc. on their cell phones if they have them. Invite students to share their answers with the class and find out what students do with their photographs after they've taken them, e.g., make albums, share them on social media, etc.

♀ EXTRA ACTIVITY

Give students time for a "long turn" at this point (see the extra activity after 3d on p. 32.). Ask students to choose a picture they have taken that is special to them and that they are happy to share with the class. If you used the optional lead-in, tell students that you want them to talk about their picture in the same way. If students don't have a suitable picture on their phone, ask them to prepare their notes for homework and bring the picture to the next class. Tell students to write notes about it, but not to write complete sentences. Monitor and help students write their notes if necessary. Ask students to speak to the class one by one about their picture and show it to the class. Remind students not to look at their notes too much while they are speaking. After each long turn, allow two or three students to ask the speaker questions based on their talk.

Exercises **a** and **b** can be prepared as homework before this lesson to give students time to look up unfamiliar vocabulary. Ask students to look at the picture and to prepare their answers to the questions as homework to talk about in the next class.

12A | WHAT ARE YOU GOING TO DO?

At the end of this lesson, students will be able to:

- use a lexical set of geography words correctly
- read and understand a text about working vacations
- understand a conversation in which people talk about their vacation plans
- use *be going to* to describe future plans
- ask for and give information about a working vacation

♀ OPTIONAL LEAD-IN

Write *Vacations* on the board and underneath, write question beginnings 1–4 and endings a–d: *1 Where do you like 2 What time of year 3 Where do you 4 Who do you usually; a do you like going away? b go on vacation with? c going on vacation? d like staying?* Leave a small space, then write question beginnings 5–8 and endings e–h: *5 Where and when 6 How long did 7 What did 8 Was it a typical; e you stay? f vacation for you? g you do? h was your last vacation?*

Check that students understand that 1–4 match with a–d, and 5–8 match with e–h. Individually, they match the beginnings and endings. Check answers as a class (1c, 2a, 3d, 4b, 5h, 6e, 7g, 8f).

Put students into pairs to ask and answer the questions. Finally, point to questions 1–4 and ask: *Are these questions about the past, present, or future?* Elicit that they use the simple present to talk about general preferences. Then, point to questions 5–8 and repeat the question. Elicit that they use the simple past to ask about a specific vacation in the past. Tell students that Lesson 12A is about the future.

d ≫ ◐ **12.02** Students complete the exercises in Vocabulary Focus 12A on SB p. 170. Play the recording for students to complete the Pronunciation activity. Monitor Exercise d and check other answers as a class. Tell students to go back to SB p. 120.

Answers (Vocabulary Focus 12A SB p. 170)
a a coast b jungle c hill d countryside e woods f fields
b jungle; countryside
c 1 field (It's not water.)
    2 hill (It's not trees.)
    3 mountain (It's not connected to the ocean.)

♀ FAST FINISHERS

Ask fast finishers to write sentences about the geography of the place where they live, using the emails in Vocabulary Focus 12A, Exercise a as model.

1 VOCABULARY Geography

a Ask students to cover the words and see how many of the things in the pictures they know. Individually, students then match the words with the pictures.

b ◐ **12.01** **Pronunciation** Play the recording for students to listen and check their answers to 1a. Then, read the questions with the class and, if necessary, play the recording again. Check answers as a class. Drill each word.

Answers
a 1 d 2 g 3 b 4 j 5 f 6 a 7 e 8 h 9 i 10 c
b 1 lake; beach 2 the first syllable

♀ EXTRA ACTIVITY

Put students into pairs. Explain that you're going to say ten places in the world and students have to write which part of the world they are in. Teach/Elicit *Antarctica*, if necessary. Allow students to refer to SB p. 162 if necessary.
1 Mount Everest – the world's tallest mountain (Asia)
2 the Nile River – the world's longest river (Africa) *3 the Amazon Rainforest – the world's biggest rainforest* (South America)
4 the Sahara Desert – the world's biggest sand desert (Africa)
5 Lake Superior – the world's biggest lake (North America)
6 Praia do Cassino Beach – the world's longest beach (South America) *7 the Lambert Glacier –the world's biggest glacier* (Antarctica) *8 Angel Falls – the world's tallest waterfall* (South America) *9 Greenland – the world's biggest island* (geographically North America, politically Europe) *10 the Taiga forest – the world's biggest forest* (North America, Europe, and Asia).
Check answers as a class and award one point for each correct answer. The pair with the highest score is the winner.

c 💬📲 In pairs, students ask and answer the questions. Monitor, but don't interrupt fluency unless students make mistakes with the pronunciation of the geography words.

2 READING

a 💬📲 Read the question and the ideas with students and check that they understand the vocabulary. In pairs, they discuss what's important for them when they're on vacation. Ask pairs to share their answers with the class.

b Students read the website quickly and find out which ideas from 2a it mentions. Check answers as a class.

Answers
- meet new people
- do a lot of sightseeing
- understand a new culture
- try a new sport
- eat local food

c Tell students to read the website again in detail. Individually, students identify which jobs would be appropriate for the different profiles. Encourage students to guess the meaning of any new words from the context. However, you may wish to help students with words in the Vocabulary Support box. Check answers as a class.

Answers
- swimming and dancing – job 2
- drawing – job 3
- outdoor sports – job 1

📖 VOCABULARY SUPPORT

accommodations (B1) – the place where you live or sleep
kayaking – an activity using a small, narrow boat usually for only one person
local (B1) – from or in the area near you
scenery (B1) – beautiful, natural views out in the countryside

d 💬📲 In pairs, students talk about whether they would like to do any of these jobs and decide which would be the most and least hard work. Ask students to share their answers with the class. Encourage them to justify their answers as much as possible.

3 LISTENING

a ▶️12.03 Play the recording for students to listen for general meaning and answer the question. Check the answers as a class.

> **Answer**
> Emily – vacation 3
> Chloe – vacation 2

Audioscript

CONVERSATION 1

ZOE So, about next year – what are you going to do?

EMILY I finally decided yesterday.

Z And?

E Well, I don't really want to continue studying. I'd like to do some traveling. So, I'm not going to go to college next year.

Z Go traveling? Nice idea – but that costs a lot of money.

E I've saved a bit of money. But you don't need a lot. Look. I found this website Work Around the World.

Z OK …

E Well, you can go places and get free food and accommodations – you just have to do a little work.

Z I don't know … I heard you work really hard on those things.

E But look at this one. I'm going to email and ask about it. It looks so beautiful there close to the mountains and I love drawing and things, so it's perfect.

Z But what about … what about all our friends? I mean, college starts next year.

E I know. Sorry. It starts for everyone, but not for me.

CONVERSATION 2

CHLOE I want to do something different for a while. I'm going to quit this job.

FRANK Get a new one?

C No, I want to go away and have some fun.

F Ah, so a vacation.

C Yes, a very long vacation. Look at this website …

F Work Around the World vacations …

C There are some interesting things on it.

F … free accommodation and food … But no pay.

C No, but it doesn't matter. Look at this job I read about. I'm going to find out more about it. It's in such an amazing place. I can go to the beach every day.

F It says you have to spend a lot of time with children. Do you even like children?

C Yeah – I love them.

F And do you know how to teach?

C I'm sure I can learn.

b ▶️12.03 Students listen to the recording again for specific details and answer the questions. They then compare in pairs. Check answers as a class.

> **Answers**
> **CONVERSATION 1**
> 1 She doesn't really want to continue studying and she'd like to do some traveling.
> 2 She likes the free food and accommodations. It's close to the mountains and she can draw.
> 3 She wants Emily to go to college at the same time as her and their friends.
>
> **CONVERSATION 2**
> 1 She wants to do something different for a while.
> 2 It's in an amazing place and she can go to the beach every day.
> 3 He doesn't think it's a good job for Chloe because she doesn't know how to teach.

⬤ EXTRA ACTIVITY

Play the recording again for students to decide if sentences 1–6 are true or false: *1 Emily isn't sure if she wants to go on a Work Around the World vacation.* (F – She decided yesterday.) *2 She has a lot of money to take with her.* (F – She's saved a little money, but she doesn't need a lot.) *3 Zoe thinks you have to do a lot of work on these vacations.* (T) *4 Chloe only wants to go away for a couple of weeks.* (F – She wants a very long vacation.) *5 She's sure she wants to go to Mexico.* (F – She wants to find out more about it.) *6 Frank doesn't like the idea that there isn't any pay.* (T)

c 💬 Students work in pairs or small groups, answering the questions. Invite students to share their answers with the class.

4 GRAMMAR *be going to*

a ▶️12.04 Books closed. Write the incomplete sentences on the board and ask students to complete them as a class. Students open their books. Play the recording for students to listen and check. Check answers as a class. Drill the sentences.

> **Answers**
> 1 going
> 2 going

b Ask students to look at the examples of *be going to* in 4a. Check the answer as a class.

> **Answer**
> a future plan

c ▶️12.05 Individually, students complete the sentences with the affirmative, negative, and question forms of *be going to*. Play the recording for students to listen and check. Check answers as a class by asking individual students to write the correct answers on the board.

> **Answers**
> + 'm going to find out
> – 'm not going to go
> ? are you going to do

d ▶️12.05 **Pronunciation** Play the recording for students to answer the question. Check the answer as a class. Drill the sentences.

> **Answer**
> the main verb

👁 CAREFUL!

There are several common student mistakes with *be going to*. They may omit part of the construction, possibly *going*, e.g., ~~How are you to get to the airport?~~ (Correct form = *How are you **going to get** to the airport?*) or possibly the auxiliary *is/are*, e.g., ~~We going to go to the beach~~ (Correct form = *We **are going** to go to the beach on the train*).

Students may also make mistakes with the base form and use the *to* + verb + *-ing*, e.g., ~~I'm going to wearing my …~~ (Correct form = *I'm **going to wear** my new shorts tomorrow*). Sometimes students will use *go to* instead of *be going to*, e.g., ~~I'm happy that I go to Finland~~ (Correct form = *I'm happy that **I'm going** to Finland*) or use *will go* in places where *be going to* is required, e.g., ~~I bought new boots because I will go hiking on vacation~~ (Correct form = *… I bought new boots because **I'm going to** go hiking on vacation*).

e ⟫ ▶ `12.06` Students read the information in Grammar Focus 12A on SB p. 160. Play the recording where indicated and ask students to listen and repeat. Students then complete the exercises. Check answers as a class, making sure students are forming the sentences with *be going to* correctly. Tell students to go back to SB p. 121.

Answers (Grammar Focus 12A SB p. 161)

a 2 h 3 g 4 b 5 c 6 d 7 a 8 f

b 2 is going to get
 3 're going to do
 4 're not going to stay / aren't going to stay
 5 are going to buy
 6 'm going to go
 7 's not going to go / isn't going to go
 8 're not going to visit / aren't going to visit
 9 're going to stay

> 💡 **FAST FINISHERS**
>
> Ask fast finishers to rewrite the affirmative sentences in Grammar Focus 12A, Exercise b in the negative and vice versa, e.g., *1 I'm not going to travel to South America.*

f ▶ `12.07` Students work individually, completing the conversation. Play the recording for students to listen and check. Check answers as a class.

Answers

1 'm going to spend
2 going to go
3 'm going to travel
4 are you going to do
5 'm not going to do
6 'm going to look

5 SPEAKING

> 🔄 **LOA TIP** ELICITING
>
> • If you think students need more support before completing the Communication activity, elicit a second model conversation from the class like the one in 4f. Write the following notes on the board in the same style as the ones on SB pp. 135 and 137.
>
>
>
> | Notes ⊕ |
> | --- |
> | **Where:** Africa |
> | **Why:** *see the desert and the Nile River* |
> | **How long:** *seven weeks* |
> | **Possible jobs:** *teaching in a local school, building basic houses* |
> | **Before trip:** *buy a new camera* |
> | **After trip:** *write a blog and share pictures* |
>
> • Tell students: *I'm going to spend seven weeks traveling and working this summer.* Point to the word *Where* in the notes and elicit the question: *Where are you going to go?* Answer the question and then point to *Why* to elicit the next question and so on until you've elicited all the questions that students will need to complete the task.

a 💬 In pairs, students answer the question. Ask students to share their answers with the class and find out which of the three vacations is most popular.

b ⟫ Tell students that they can now practice using all the language from the lesson with a partner. Divide the class into pairs and assign A and B roles (Student As go to SB p. 135 and Student Bs go to SB p. 137). Students read the information about their working vacations and write questions they can ask their partner. Monitor and point out errors in the questions for students to self-correct before they work in pairs, asking each other about their vacations. Monitor, but don't interrupt fluency unless students make mistakes with the content of this lesson. Tell students to go back to SB p. 121.

> ⊕ **ADDITIONAL MATERIAL**
>
> Workbook 12A
>
> Photocopiable activities: Grammar 12A, Vocabulary 12A

12B YOU SHOULD LIVE LIKE THE LOCAL PEOPLE

☉ OPTIONAL LEAD-IN

Organize a "grammar auction" (see p. 152) to study areas of grammar that you know students find problematic. Prepare 15 sentences containing items of grammar and/or vocabulary from the course. Some of them should be correct, e.g., *That was the best vacation I have ever had!,* and some of them incorrect, e.g., *I haven't never been to Egypt, but I really want to.* Write the sentences on the board. Put students into small groups, tell them they have $100, and explain that they need to buy the correct sentences. Students work in their groups, discussing which sentences they want to buy. Don't help and don't allow students to look at their notes or the Student's Book.

Run the auction, selling each sentence to the group that offers the most money. After all the sentences have been sold, reveal which are correct and which are incorrect and ask students to correct the mistakes. The winning group is the one with the most correct sentences.

1 READING

a 🗨️ In pairs, students ask and answer the questions. Ask students to share their answers with the class and find out some of the places where students would like to live.

b Students read the texts quickly and match the people with the pictures. Check answers as a class.

> **Answers**
> a Troy
> b Kirsten
> c Liona
> d Avery

c Tell students to read the texts again in detail. Students identify who wrote each sentence. When checking answers, ask students to read the section of the text which helped them to find the answer.

> **Answers**
> 1 A 2 OK 3 T 4 A 5 OK

☉ EXTRA ACTIVITY

Ask students to read the texts again and answer questions 1–6:
1 How old was Troy when he moved to Portugal? (He was 39.)
2 How many jobs does Troy have? (two – He's an English teacher and a DJ.) *3 How many different countries did Oliver and Kirsten visit before they arrived in Egypt?* (They visited seven countries.)
4 Which other countries do they want to live in? (They want to live in Ecuador and South Africa.) *5 When did Avery start her very long vacation?* (She started after she finished college.) *6 When did she decide to take a class to become a diving teacher?* (when she was in Australia)

d 🗨️ Discuss the question as a class. Encourage students to justify their answers as much as possible.

2 VOCABULARY Travel collocations

a Books closed. Write *do y_ _ _* and *c_ _ _ _ on a link* on the board. Point to the first missing word and mime a yoga pose. Ask students what the word is (*yoga*). Repeat the process by miming looking at a computer screen and clicking the mouse to elicit *click*. Remind students that *do yoga* is from the set of Sports and exercise collocations in Lesson 8A and *click on a link* is from the set of IT collocations in Lesson 10A. Explain to students that a collocation is two or more words which we often use together. Tell them that now they are going to see a set of travel collocations. Individually, students match the pairs of verbs with the words/phrases in the box, using the texts for help. Check answers as a class.

> **Answers**
> 1 plans   4 a vacation
> 2 abroad   5 a hotel
> 3 home   6 a bag

b ▶️ 12.08 Students complete the sentences, working individually. Play the recording for students to listen and check. Check answers as a class.

> **Answers**
> 1 plan   4 pack
> 2 travel   5 go back
> 3 book   6 make

c 🗨️ In pairs or small groups, students talk about which speakers they agree with. Encourage them to change the sentences that they don't agree with so that they are true for them, e.g., *I never plan my vacations carefully. I like to find things out when I'm there.*

3 GRAMMAR should / shouldn't

a Books closed. On the board, write: *You should try to make friends with people from the country.* Ask students: *Who said this?* (Kirsten). Then, draw ≠ on the board and write *You shouldn't try to make friends with people from the country.* Next, ask students which sentence they agree with. Ask: *Are these sentences giving advice or giving information?* (giving advice). *Which words tell us that this is advice? (should / shouldn't).* Circle *should / shouldn't* on the board and tell students to underline the correct words in the sentences in the Student's Book. Check answers as a class.

> **Answers**
> 1 should   2 shouldn't   3 should

b Complete the rules as a class.

> **Answers**
> b it's a good idea
> b the base form

c ▶️**12.09** **Pronunciation** Play the recording for students to listen and answer the questions. Check that they understand that the letter *l* is an example of a silent letter, like the ones they saw in Lesson 9B. Drill the sentences.

Answers
1 no 2 good

👁 CAREFUL!

Students often make mistakes with *should* and may use *do*, *can*, or *may* instead, e.g., ~~What do I pack to go on vacation?~~ (Correct form = *What **should** I pack to go on vacation?*) or ~~You may take a class to learn to dive~~ (Correct form = *You **should** take a class to learn to dive*). They may also use *should* in contexts where it's not correct, most commonly confusing it with *would*, e.g., ~~It should be nice to travel abroad~~ (Correct form = *It **would** be nice to travel abroad*).

There are also several mistakes that students make with the negative form, *shouldn't*. Students often confuse the meaning of *don't have to* (= you don't need to do it, but you can do it if you want) with *shouldn't* (= I think it's a bad idea), e.g., ~~You don't have to stay in that hotel; it's horrible~~ (Correct form = *You **shouldn't** stay in that hotel; it's horrible*), or ~~You shouldn't know how to dive…~~ (Correct form = *You **don't have to** know how to dive; it's a beginners' course*). Students may also forget that *shouldn't* is negative and may make mistakes with *some/any/no* and similar words, e.g., ~~You shouldn't tell no one about the party~~ (Correct form = *You shouldn't tell **anyone** about the party*).

d ≫ ▶️**12.10** Students read the information in Grammar Focus 12B on SB p. 160. Play the recording where indicated and ask students to listen and repeat. Students then complete the exercises. Check answers as a class, making sure students are using the base form after *should / shouldn't*. After students complete the Grammar Focus activities, ask them: *Is "should/shouldn't" easy or difficult?* Elicit an indication of their confidence level. Tell students to go back to SB p. 123.

Answers (Grammar Focus 12B SB p. 161)
a 2 should drink 4 shouldn't drive 6 should come 8 should say
   3 shouldn't bring 5 should take 7 shouldn't pay
b 2 Should we go to a museum? 6 What time should we arrive?
   3 What clothes should I wear? 7 Where should we stay?
   4 Should I come back later? 8 Who should we ask for advice?
   5 Should we eat the local food?
c/d You ~~don't should~~ shouldn't book before you go.
   ~~I should go~~ Should I go to Bangkok?
   You should ~~to~~ go to Bangkok for a few days, …
   What ~~do I should do~~ should I do on an island?
   You ~~should not to~~ shouldn't worry about money on vacation!

e Students work individually, adding *should* or *shouldn't* and changing the verbs in blue as necessary. They then check in pairs. Check answers as a class.

Answers
1 You should go out and meet people.
2 You should try to visit a new place every weekend. You shouldn't wait until the last few weeks of your stay.
3 You should read about the country before you go there.
4 You shouldn't get mad when things go wrong.
5 You should remember that things work differently in other countries.

💡 FAST FINISHERS

Ask fast finishers to invent more sentences with *should* or *shouldn't* to add to the advice about living abroad in 3e.

4 LISTENING AND SPEAKING

a 💬 Give students one minute to read the comments and think what the people mean. They then discuss in pairs or small groups whether they are the same. Discuss the questions as a class and find out what kind of people your students are.

b 💬 Individually, students read the texts again quickly and decide which things they think Troy and Avery like. They then compare in pairs.

c ▶️**12.11** Play the recording for students to listen and check their answers in 4b. Then, check answers as a class.

Answers
T = big cities, cafés, shopping, noise, dancing, music
A = sports, the country, the ocean, beaches

Audioscript

TROY I grew up in Toronto and I've always lived in big cities. I love cities – I like going to cafés and I love shopping. Every city's different. I've been to London, Paris, Tokyo, Buenos Aires, Lisbon … and I love them all. I'm never very happy in the countryside. There's nothing to do there. I like people and noise.
In my free time, I listen to music a lot – mainly dance music, but I like rock music, too. I don't play any sports; I've never really liked sports, … well, I like dancing, but that's not really a sport, is it?

AVERY I think I've always been an active person. I loved sports at school. And I love water sports of all kinds. I go swimming, surfing, I love being in the water. I spend a lot of time on beaches; it's great to be by the ocean. I'm not really a "city person." I don't really like big cities and I'm not interested in shopping. I only go shopping if I need to buy something, not for fun. And I never go to museums or concerts. I feel happier in the countryside … or on a beach by the ocean somewhere. I live in Jamaica now, and that's fine because it has beautiful beaches.

💡 EXTRA ACTIVITY

Use one of the monologues in 4c as the basis of a dictation activity. Ask students which person they found easier to understand and then tell them that they are going to write down exactly what that person said. Remind them that Troy/Avery speak pretty quickly, so they aren't going to have time to write everything down the first time, but they should listen carefully and write down the most important words they hear, e.g., with Troy, they might write down *grew up, Toronto, always lived, cities* for the first line. Play the recording twice without stopping. Then, put students into small groups and ask them to compare the words they wrote down and put them together to make the full text. Play the recording as many times as necessary, but don't break it down into sentences. Each time, students compare their ideas in their groups and try to put together a bit more of the text. Remind them to use the vocabulary and grammar they already know to help them. Check answers by asking students to come up and write the text on the board one sentence at a time. Play the recording after students write each sentence to correct any mistakes on the board.

d 💬 In pairs or small groups, students talk about where Troy and Avery should and shouldn't go and what they should and shouldn't do in their countries and give reasons, e.g., *Troy should spend some time in Madrid. It's a really exciting city.*

145

- Monitor both the controlled practice in 4d and the freer practice in 4e and 4f closely, but adjust the way you give feedback in the two stages. During the more controlled practice in 4d, you could choose not to interrupt fluency, but write down any mistakes with *should / shouldn't* and then, after the activity, write these on the board and ask students to correct them. This method of monitoring and correction is best suited to hesitant speakers, who may become even more hesitant if they are constantly interrupted. Alternatively, if your students are more confident speakers, you may prefer to gently interrupt them as they are speaking so that they can self-correct.

- During 4e and 4f, allow students to focus more on fluency, so don't interrupt them or note mistakes for later correction. However, monitor the activity closely and be available to help students if necessary. When students make a mistake with the content of this lesson, i.e., *should / shouldn't*, try to catch their eyes discreetly so that they can correct their mistakes.

e 💬 Regroup students and put them into pairs, preferably with a student they don't know very well. They then find out what their partner likes and doesn't like doing on vacation.

f 💬 Students use the information they learned in 4e to give their partner advice about what they should and shouldn't do in a city they know.

⊕ **ADDITIONAL MATERIAL**

Workbook 12B

Photocopiable activities: Grammar 12B, Vocabulary 12B

12C

EVERYDAY ENGLISH
Is breakfast included?

1 LISTENING

a 💬 Students talk about the questions in pairs. Ask students to share their answers with the class and find out where most students prefer to stay. Encourage students to justify their answers as much as possible.

b ▶ 12.12 Play Part 1 of the audio recording for students to answer the questions. Check answers as a class.

> **Answers**
> 1 Julia won a contest.
> 2 No, they can't.

Audioscript (Part 1)

JULIA Wow! Diego, guess what?
DIEGO What?
J I won a contest!
D You did? Julia, that's great! What's the prize?
J A weekend for two in Las Vegas. Airfare, hotel, tickets to a show ...
D Really? That's amazing! We could go in June to celebrate our fifth wedding anniversary!
J No, we have to fly the Friday after next.

D So, that's the 20th?
J Yes.
D Oh. We're going camping that weekend ...
J But we go camping all the time.
D That's true. OK, let's do it. We're going to Vegas!

At the end of this lesson, students will be able to:

- understand informal conversations in which people show surprise, and use appropriate phrases for showing surprise themselves
- understand conversations in which people check in at a hotel and ask for tourist information
- pronounce consonant clusters with /t/ correctly
- use appropriate phrases for checking in at a hotel and asking for tourist information
- maintain a polite conversation with a hotel receptionist

c ▶ 12.12 Students listen again for specific details. Play Part 1 of the audio recording again for students to complete the email. Check answers as a class.

> **Answers**
> 1 Julia
> 2 two
> 3 Las Vegas
> 4 Friday
> 5 20th

2 CONVERSATION SKILLS
Showing surprise

a Ask students to read the conversation and underline the two ways that Diego shows surprise. Check answers as a class.

> **Answers**
> You did?
> Really?

b Answer the question as a class. Check that students understand that *Really?* can be used to reply to any news.

> **Answer**
> Really?

c ▶12.13 Write on the board: ***A** I love studying English.* ***B** You do?* Ask students: *What's the subject in the sentence?* (I) and *What's the subject in the question?* (you). Then ask: *How do we form the short question to show surprise?* Elicit that we change *I* to *you* and use the same auxiliary we would use to form a normal question. Individually, students match the sentences with the questions. Play the recording for students to listen and check. Check answers as a class.

> **Answers**
> 1 c
> 2 a
> 3 d
> 4 b

d ▶12.13 **Pronunciation** Repeat the recording for students to listen to the intonation movement in the questions. Check the answer as a class.

> **Answer**
> The intonation goes up a lot.

e Individually, students think of two surprising things to tell a partner. Check that they understand that they can invent things if they wish.

f 💬 Students work in pairs, taking turns telling each other their surprising things and responding appropriately. Monitor and make sure students are not only using *Really?*, but are also using the more complex short question forms.

> ♀ **FAST FINISHERS**
>
> Ask fast finishers to make sentences about other people and change the short questions in 2c as necessary, e.g., ***A** Our teacher is going to quit his job next month and travel around the world.* ***B** He is?*

3 LISTENING

a ▶12.14 Point to the picture at the bottom of the page and ask students: *Where is this?* (a hotel reception). Elicit ideas for what they think Julia and Diego's hotel is like and if they think they'll like it. Play Part 2 of the audio recording for students to listen to the conversation for general meaning and check their ideas. Check the answer as a class.

> **Answer**
> Julia and Diego don't like the hotel. It's kind of gross, and it's old.

> **Audioscript (Part 2)**
>
> **DIEGO** This is the prize? This place is kind of gross.
> **JULIA** Shhh!
> **RECEPTIONIST** Good evening.
> **J** Hello. We have a reservation for Torres.
> **R** Yes, I see a reservation for Mr. and Mrs. Torres for three nights. Here's your keycard. That's room 312 – a double room on the third floor. Turn left as you come out of the elevator.
> **D** I'm not getting on that old elevator.
> **J** Diego! Is breakfast included?
> **R** Yes, it's from 7:00 a.m. until 10:00 a.m. in the dining room – just over there.
> **J** Great – thank you. And what time is checkout?
> **R** Checkout is at 11:00 a.m.
> **J** Thanks.
> **D** We're checking out long before 11 a.m., believe me.

b ▶12.14 Students listen again for specific details. Play Part 2 of the audio recording again for students to complete the guest information card. Check answers as a class by asking individual students to write the correct answers on the board.

> **Answers**
> 1 312   2 7:00 a.m.   3 10:00 a.m.   4 11:00 a.m.

4 USEFUL LANGUAGE
Checking in at a hotel

a Individually, students read the useful expressions and try to remember which two expressions Julia used. If necessary, play Part 2 of the audio recording again. Check answers as a class.

> **Answers**
> 3 Is breakfast included?   5 What time is checkout?

b Answer the question as a class.

> **Answers**
> 2 Is there a parking lot?   4 Is there Wi-Fi in the room?
> 3 Is breakfast included?   6 Is there a safe in the room?

c ▶12.15 Individually, students complete the conversation. They then check in pairs. Play the recording for students to listen and check. Check answers as a class.

> **Answers**
> 1 have a reservation for a double room for two nights
> 2 breakfast included
> 3 there Wi-Fi in the room
> 4 time is checkout

> 🗘 **LOA TIP DRILLING**
>
> • Drill the conversation in 4c before continuing. Try drilling the conversation together as a class, you taking the part of the receptionist and the class taking the part of the guest. Work on the guest's sentences, building them up using any of the techniques you've previously used, e.g., backward drilling (see notes to Lesson 2C, p. 26), drilling in small chunks (see notes to Lesson 6C, p. 73), focusing on the main stress (see notes to Lesson 10C, p. 124).
>
> • Remind students of the importance of both stress and intonation. If necessary, clap out the rhythm of the guest's sentences so that they can then copy it themselves. You can also show students the intonation changes in the conversation using hand gestures to give them a visual reference.

5 PRONUNCIATION Consonant clusters

a ▶ **12.16** Play the recording and highlight the consonant clusters with /t/ for students.

b ▶ **12.17** Students listen to the sentences and underline the consonant clusters with /t/. They check in pairs. Then, check answers as a class. Drill the consonant clusters.

> **Answers**
> 1 ne<u>xt</u>
> 2 touri<u>st</u>
> 3 le<u>ft</u>
> 4 ticke<u>ts</u>

c 💬 In pairs, students practice conversations at a hotel reception. Monitor and correct students' pronunciation as appropriate.

6 LISTENING

a ▶ **12.18** Tell students that Julia and Diego want to go on a bus tour. Students listen to Part 3 for specific details. Play the audio recording for students to complete the information. Check answers as a class.

> **Answers**
> 1 outside the hotel
> 2 $25
> 3 the hotel lobby
> 4 credit card

Audioscript (Part 3)

DIEGO Now this is a real hotel.
JULIA It's so beautiful! I'm glad we changed hotels. Let's go see the city!
RECEPTIONIST Good morning.
D Can you help us? Is there a city bus tour we can go on?
R Yes, there is. It leaves from just outside the hotel.
D And how much is it for a ticket?
R It's $25.
D Can we buy tickets here in the hotel lobby?
R Yes, you can.
D And can we pay with a credit card?
R No problem.
D OK. We'll take two tickets, please.
J Vegas, here we come!

---

b 💬 In pairs, students answer the questions. Check answers as a class. Ask students: *Do you think Julia and Diego are happy to be in Las Vegas together?*

> **Answers**
> 1 They didn't like the first hotel.
> 2 Students' own answers

7 USEFUL LANGUAGE
Asking for tourist information

a ▶ **12.19** Individually, students match the beginnings with the endings of the questions. Play the recording for students to listen and check. Check answers as a class. Drill the questions.

> **Answers**
> 1 c (Can you help us?)
> 2 d (Is there a city bus tour we can go on?)
> 3 a (How much is it for a ticket?)
> 4 e (Can we buy tickets here in the hotel lobby?)
> 5 b (We'll take two tickets, please.)

b Students answer the questions, working individually. Check answers as a class and elicit possible alternative questions for 2d in Exercise 7a.

> **Answers**
> 1 no
> 2 You have to change 2d.
> 3 Is there a museum tour I can go on? / Is there a museum I can visit?

> 💡 **EXTRA ACTIVITY**
>
> Before students practice the conversation in 7c, put them into pairs to brainstorm other questions that could be useful at a Tourist Information Office, e.g., *Do you have a map of the city, please? Can you recommend a good restaurant near here? What time does the museum open/close? Are there any other interesting things to see and do here?* Point out errors for students to self-correct. Invite pairs to share their questions with the class and write them on the board.

---

c 💬 In pairs, students practice conversations at a tourist information office. Monitor and check that students are using the questions in 7a correctly.

8 SPEAKING

a ≫ Divide the class into pairs and assign A and B roles. Student As read the first card on SB p. 135 and Student Bs read the first card on SB p. 137. Students then role-play the conversation. Students then read the second card and role-play the second conversation. Monitor, but don't interrupt fluency unless students make mistakes with the content of this lesson.

> ⊕ **ADDITIONAL MATERIAL**
>
> Workbook 12C
>
> Photocopiable activities: Pronunciation (x2) 12C
>
> Unit Progress Test

SKILLS FOR WRITING

You should go to Stanley Park

ⓥ OPTIONAL LEAD-IN

Books closed. On the board, write: *Visiting [city]? Take our advice!* Use the name of the city where you're teaching. Give students some examples of things people should do and things they shouldn't do when visiting the city, e.g., *You should go and have coffee at the Hotel Villa Magna – it's beautiful inside. You shouldn't walk down streets late at night because it can be dangerous.* Put students into pairs and give them a few minutes to write as many sentences with *should/shouldn't* as possible. Monitor and point out errors for students to self-correct, and make sure they are using the base form of the verb after *should/shouldn't*. Put pairs together to make groups of four and ask students to share their ideas.

Ask students: *When you travel to a city, how do you usually get information about the place?* Elicit ideas, e.g., from a guidebook, online, by talking to friends, by going to a Tourist Information Office, etc.

1 SPEAKING AND LISTENING

a 💬 Individually, students choose an answer to the question. They then discuss in pairs and explain why. Ask pairs to share their answers with the class.

b 💬 Discuss the questions as a class and find out if any students have visited Vancouver. Elicit students' ideas about what they can see in the pictures, but don't tell them if they are correct.

ⓥ EXTRA ACTIVITY

⏵ 12.20 Books closed. Before students listen for specific details in 1c, write questions 1–3 on the board: *1 What's the relationship between the two speakers?* (They are coworkers.) *2 Why is the man happy?* (He's decided to go on vacation.) *3 Where's he going to go?* (He's going to go to Vancouver in Canada.) Play the recording for students to listen for general meaning and answer the gist questions. Check answers as a class.

c ⏵ 12.20 Play the recording for students to listen for specific details and choose the correct answers. They compare in pairs. Check answers as a class.

Answers
1 online
2 week
3 hostel
4 next
5 Tiffany

Audioscript

ZACH Hey, Tiffany! Here's your coffee.

TIFFANY Thanks, Zach. When's our next meeting?

Z In half an hour.

T Good – time to take a break. You're looking happy today.

Z Well, yeah, I feel happy.

T Oh – good news?

Z Well, yeah, I just booked my next vacation. There was a sale online.

T Exciting! Where are you going to go?

Z To Vancouver – for a week with my brother.

T Oh, great. Is it your first time in Canada?

Z Yes, it is – can't wait to go! We're going to stay in Vancouver, but we also plan to visit places in British Columbia.

T Oh, yeah, I've heard it's really beautiful.

Z I found tickets online at a really good price.

T Lucky you!

Z Yes, and we're going to stay in this cool hostel with free Wi-Fi, a kitchen, and these incredible sleeping pods – very private. And it's not expensive at all.

T So when are you going to go?

Z At the end of next month.

T Early fall? OK, I think the weather is still good then.

Z That's right.

T I actually have a friend, Nicole, who lives in Vancouver. You can email her for information so you can plan your vacation. She won't mind helping you. I'll send you her email address.

Z Thanks!

d 💬 Put students into pairs to brainstorm questions to ask Nicole. Ask students to share their questions with the class and write them on the board.

2 READING

a Students read the email quickly and identify the topic that Nicole doesn't talk about. Check the answer as a class. Ask students to look at their questions from 1d again and ask: *Which of your questions did Nicole answer?*

> **Answer**
> b the hostel

b Tell students to read the email again in detail. Individually, students complete the chart. Check answers by copying the chart onto the board and asking individual students to come up and complete it.

Answers

Place to visit	Reason to visit
Gastown	historic & [1]modern stores & [2]restaurants
Stanley Park	forests & [3]beaches & a big [4]aquarium
Vancouver Island	interesting history & [5]culture

ⓥ FAST FINISHERS

Ask fast finishers to read Nicole's email again and try to work out exactly what Zach said to her in his email, e.g., *I'm going to spend some time in your hometown. Can you help me plan my vacation? What are the top three tourist things to do in Vancouver?*

3 WRITING SKILLS Paragraph writing

a Look at the email from Nicole again and check that students understand they need to use the numbers 1–17 to indicate which sentences go in each paragraph. Students then work individually, dividing the email into four paragraphs. Check answers as a class.

> **Answers**
> Paragraph 1: sentences 1 to 3
> Paragraph 2: sentences 4 to 12
> Paragraph 3: sentences 13 to 15
> Paragraph 4: sentences 16 to 17

b Individually, students look at Paragraph 2 and underline the linking words. They then check in pairs. Check answers as a class.

> **Answers**
> First, second, Finally

💡 EXTRA ACTIVITY

Write jumbled sentences 1–3 on the board. Ask students to put them in order and identify the city (Rome):
1 visit / Piazza Navona / should / you / first (First, you should visit Piazza Navona.)
2 the Vatican Museums / to / should / second / go / you (Second, you should go to the Vatican Museums.)
3 should / see / you / the Colosseum / finally (Finally, you should see the Colosseum.)
Individually, students then choose another city and write three similar sentences about that city using *first*, *second*, and *finally*. Monitor and point out errors for students to self-correct. Put students into pairs or small groups to read each other their sentences and guess the cities.

---

c Students read Alice's email for general meaning and answer the questions. Check answers as a class.

> **Answers**
> 1 She's going to visit your hometown.
> 2 She wants to know some interesting things to see and some interesting sports activities to do.

d Students look at the email again and divide it into three paragraphs. When checking answers, ask students what each paragraph is about (*Paragraph 1: Alice introduces herself and explains why she is writing; Paragraph 2: Alice asks about things to see and do; Paragraph 3: Alice finishes her email*).

> **Answers**
> Paragraph 1: sentences 1 and 2
> Paragraph 2: sentences 3 to 6
> Paragraph 3: sentence 7

🔄 LOA TIP REVIEW AND REFLECT

- Before students start on the writing task, ask them to look back through the eleven pieces of writing they've done and note any mistakes they have made more than once. These might be grammar, vocabulary, or spelling errors. Monitor and take the opportunity to point out to students any mistakes you know that they often make in their writing.

- Ask: *How many emails have you written in the D lessons in the Student's Book?* (three – an email invitation in Lesson 3D; an email to a homestay family in Lesson 7D; an email to say thank you in Lesson 9D). Then ask: *How well did you do them? Do you feel confident writing friendly, informal emails?* Elicit an indication of their confidence level.

- Remind students that this is the last piece of writing they are going to do in the class, so it is an excellent opportunity to show how much they have learned. When correcting students' emails in 4c, you might like to write a comment on them to highlight how much students have progressed and improved during the course, e.g., *In Lesson 3D, you could only use the present tense in your email, but now you can use the past and the future. Good progress!*

---

4 WRITING

a Students plan their emails, working individually. Monitor and help with vocabulary and give students ideas if necessary. Read the checklist with students before they start writing their emails.

b Individually, students write their emails. If you're short of time, this exercise can be completed for homework. Students could then bring their emails to the next class.

c Remind students of the importance of checking their work carefully before handing it in. In pairs, students switch emails and check that their partners can answer yes to all three questions. They then give each other feedback. If they have made any mistakes with the paragraphs or the linking words, or mistakes in any other areas, they prepare a second draft of their emails before giving them to you for correction.

⊕ ADDITIONAL MATERIAL

Workbook 12D

UNIT 12
Review and extension

1 GRAMMAR

a Students complete the sentences with the correct form of *be going to* and a verb from the box. Check answers as a class.

> **Answers**
> 1 's going to have   3 'm going to wear
> 2 're going to move   4 's going to travel

b Highlight the example question. Students then complete the conversation. Check answers as a class.

> **Answers**
> 2 I'm going to go to New York.
> 3 What are you going to do there?
> 4 Are you going to stay with him?
> 5 he's going to find me a job.
> 6 How long are you going to stay?
> 7 I'm not going to book my flight back.

c Individually, students complete the text. They then check in pairs. Check answers as a class.

> **Answers**
> 1 you shouldn't   3 You should   5 you should
> 2 you should   4 you shouldn't

2 VOCABULARY

a Students underline the correct word in each sentence. Check answers as a class.

> **Answers**
> 1 island; beach   4 waterfalls
> 2 Desert   5 mountains; glacier
> 3 rainforest

b Individually, students put the words in the correct order to make questions. Check answers as a class. Drill the questions.

> **Answers**
> 1 Have you ever lived abroad?
> 2 Have you planned your next vacation?
> 3 When did you last stay in a hotel?
> 4 Do you always pack your own bags for a vacation?
> 5 Are you staying home this weekend?

c 💬 Students ask and answer the questions in 2b in pairs or small groups.

3 WORDPOWER *take*

a Tell students to close their books. Create a blank word map on the board by drawing a small circle in the middle and adding six lines. At the end of the lines, write: *the number 23, care, five minutes, the first left, your suitcase for you,* and *one three times a day before meals.* Ask students: *What word can go before all of these?* Elicit *take* and write it in the circle. Students open their books, look at the phrases in context, and match them with the pictures. Check answers as a class and elicit what the people are talking about.

> **Answers**
> 1 d 2 a 3 f 4 c 5 b 6 e

b ▶12.21 Individually, students match the sentences with the uses of *take*. Play the recording for students to listen and check. Check answers as a class.

> **Answers**
> a 4 b 3 c 2 d 1 e 6 f 5

Audioscript

CONVERSATION 1
MAN 1 Excuse me. How can I get to the train station?
MAN 2 The best way is by bus. You can take the number 23. It's just over there.
M1 Oh, OK, thank you.

CONVERSATION 2
BOY OK, I'm off on my bike. See you in a bit.
WOMAN 1 OK. Don't go on the main road. And please take care!
B Don't worry. … Look, Mom. No hands!

CONVERSATION 3
WOMAN 2 Excuse me, could I ask you a few questions? It will only take five minutes.
MAN 3 Um, I don't really have time.
W2 Just five minutes.
M3 Well, OK, if it's really just a few questions …

CONVERSATION 4
MAN 4 Excuse me, is there an ATM near here?

WOMAN 3 Um, yes. Go down this road. Then you take the first left. There's a bank on the next corner.
W4 So down here, then left.
W3 That's right.
M4 Thanks.

CONVERSATION 5
MAN 5 Mrs. Green?
WOMAN 4 Yes, hello.
M5 Hello. I'm Mark Thompson. Very nice to meet you. Let me take your suitcase for you.
W4 Oh, thank you.
M5 The car's right over there. I hope you had a good flight?
W4 Yes, thank you, it was fine …

CONVERSATION 6
WOMAN 5 OK, here you are, this is for the pills. Take one three times a day before meals.
WOMAN 6 Thank you.
W5 And if you aren't better in a week, come and see me again.

---

c Students complete the sentences, working individually. Check answers as a class.

> **Answers**
> 1 take hours   4 take the first left
> 2 take a taxi   5 take my laptop
> 3 take care   6 take my medicine

> 💡 **EXTRA ACTIVITY**
>
> Ask students to copy and extend the word map on the board, adding in the new expressions in 3c, i.e., *hours* (next to *five minutes*), *a taxi* (next to *the number 23*), *my laptop* (next to *suitcase for you*) and *my medicine* (next to *one three times a day*). Then, ask them to add to the word map any other expressions with *take* they can think of, e.g., *take a moment, take an aspirin, take the train*, etc.

d Put students into pairs to choose two of the uses of *take* and write a conversation. Monitor and point out errors for students to self-correct.

e 💬 In pairs, students practice their conversations. Monitor and correct students' pronunciation as appropriate. Pairs then take turns performing their conversations for the class.

≫ Photocopiable activities: Wordpower 12

> 🔄 **LOA REVIEW YOUR PROGRESS**
>
> Students look back through the unit, think about what they've studied, and decide how well they did. Students work on weak areas by using the appropriate sections of the Workbook and the Photocopiable activities.

TEACHING PLUS

Ideas for pre-teaching vocabulary

Before reading and listening tasks, it's often necessary to make sure students understand a few key words. This is called "pre-teaching." There are a number of ways to do this. Here are some ideas:

Give a definition: Use a short sentence to explain the meaning of a word. You could use the definitions given in the Vocabulary Support boxes throughout the Teacher's Notes. You could also use a learner dictionary to find on-level definitions, e.g., *dive – to swim underwater, usually with breathing equipment* (from *Cambridge Essential American English Dictionary*, Second Edition).

Draw/Show a picture or object: One of the easiest ways to teach students new words is to draw a picture on the board or show a picture on an interactive whiteboard, computer, or tablet. Using (or drawing) funny and/or interesting pictures is a good way to ensure students remember the new words, e.g., to teach the word *dive*, you could find a picture of a diver with a big shark behind him.

Act it out: With lower-level students, it can be useful to show the word by acting it out, rather than giving definitions which may use above-level vocabulary.

Elicit it: Elicitation allows you to check which words students may already know. Don't tell them the word you want to teach. Elicit it by asking questions or saying open-ended sentences, e.g., *What is the activity when we swim under the ocean and look at fish?* or *When we swim underwater and look at fish, we … ?* (dive).

Fill-in the blanks: It's useful for students to see the word in a sentence to understand the context. Write a sentence with a blank on the board (this can be one from the text), e.g., *Cristina _____ in the ocean every summer. She loves to see the beautiful fish under the water* (dives). Allow students to guess what word goes in the blank, but don't confirm if they're right or wrong. After they read the text, they can guess again. Then, confirm their answer.

Discussion questions: With more confident students, you can write discussion questions containing the new words on the board. Then, give students one or two example answers to these questions. Students try to guess the meaning. Give more example answers, if necessary. You may then wish to allow students to ask and answer these questions for themselves.

Pre-teaching for listening: You can use any of the above ideas or others you may have to teach new words before students listen. It may also be useful to model the pronunciation of the words so students are used to hearing how they sound. This is particularly useful when a word has an unfamiliar spelling rule. If you don't want to model the word, it can be useful to write the word in IPA on the board (you can find this in all dictionaries).

Extra activities – how to …

Bingo
Use: to review numbers, times, prices, years, etc.
Dynamic: whole class
Procedure:
- Decide what kind of numbers you want to review, e.g., *times*, and write 25 of these numbers on the board in numerals, e.g., 10:20, 11:30, 4:55, etc.
- Ask students to draw a bingo grid with four columns and two rows. Tell them to complete it with eight times from the board.
- Play the game as a class. Read aloud the numbers on the board in random order, taking note of the ones you read aloud.
- Students cross out the numbers on their grid as they hear them. The first student to cross out all their numbers calls out "Bingo!" Check that the numbers they crossed out were ones you read aloud, then announce that they're the winner.
- Depending on the kind of numbers you have chosen to review, you may wish to adjust the difficulty of the activity. For example, if you are working with numbers 1–100, include some pairs of numbers that you know often cause students problems, e.g., 14 and 40, or 16 and 17, etc. With times, you can have students write out the numbers, e.g., ten twenty, eleven thirty, or with *o'clock*, e.g., twenty after ten, a quarter to eleven, five to five, etc.

Spelling competition
Use: to review general vocabulary and reinforce the alphabet
Dynamic: whole class
Procedure:
- Ask all the students to stand. Nominate a student and give them a word to spell aloud by asking: *How do you spell "(word)"?* Nominate students one by one and ask each one to spell a word, e.g., *Hello, book, open.* Choose students at random to prevent students from feeling stressed as they see their turn approaching.
- When a student makes a mistake, they are eliminated and have to sit down. Move on to the next student with the same word until someone spells it correctly.
- Gradually increase the length and difficulty of the words, e.g., *yellow, question, police officer*, leaving words you know students often have problems spelling until later in the activity.
- Eliminated students listen to the words and try to write them down before the nominated student completes the word. They then check their own spelling by listening to the student. The winner of the game is the last student standing.

Grammar auction
Use: to review a specific grammar area or general grammar
Dynamic: whole class (in teams)
Procedure:
- Prepare 10 to 15 sentences containing either items of grammar from the unit you're currently working on or areas of grammar you know students find problematic. Some of them should be correct and some incorrect.
- Write the sentences on the board and explain what an auction is (when you sell something to the person who offers the most money).

- Put students into small groups and tell them they have $100 and need to buy the correct sentences. In their groups, students discuss which sentences they think are correct and decide which to buy and how much they are prepared to pay for each. Don't help or allow students to look at their notes or the Student's Book.
- Take the role of auctioneer and sell each sentence to the group that offers the most money. Keep track of how much each group has spent. Remind students that once they have spent all their money, they can't buy any more sentences, so they shouldn't spend too much too soon.
- After all the sentences have been sold, go through them one at a time, revealing which are correct and which are incorrect. Ask students to correct the mistakes. The winning group is the one that has bought the most correct sentences. If it's a draw, then the group with the most money left wins.

Guess who?

Use: to practice question forms: simple present, present continuous, simple past, etc.
Dynamic: whole class (with optional group/pair extension)
Procedure:

- Tell students that you are thinking of a person and that they have to guess who it is by asking *yes/no* questions. If you wish to practice a specific grammar area, you might tell students that this person is living (for present tenses), dead (for past tenses), etc. Alternatively, you can use this activity to practice question forms in general by not specifying anything about the person.
- Put students into pairs or small groups to brainstorm possible questions. Specify a total number of questions, between five and ten, for the class to try to guess who you're thinking of. Students then take turns asking you some of the questions they thought of. Make sure you reply only with *yes* or *no* (NOT *Yes, he/she is*) in order not to give away if the person is a man or a woman.
- Students win if they guess the person within the specified number of questions. The teacher wins if students can't guess the person.
- Continue the game either as a class, by asking a student to choose a person and take over for you at the front of the class, or by putting students into pairs or small groups to play.

Memory game

Use: to review a specific lexical set, e.g. common objects, clothes, food
Dynamic: whole class
Procedure:

- Before the class, decide which lexical set you want to test students on and collect ten objects to take into class, e.g., for *clothes*, some earrings, a raincoat, a scarf, etc. Alternatively, source pictures of these items if you do not have the objects themselves readily available.
- Show each object to the class and elicit the word for it before putting it out of sight, either in a bag or a box or simply behind your desk. Don't allow students to take notes at this point.
- When you've shown students all the objects, put them into pairs and give them three minutes to write down as many of the ten objects as they can remember. Ask them to do so by using the grammar you'd like students to use in their replies, e.g., *What objects do I have?* (to elicit answers with *have*), *What objects are there in the box?* (*there is / there are*), *What objects did I show you?* (simple past), etc.
- Check answers as a class. Pairs win one point for every object they remember correctly. The pair with the most points wins.

Listing game

Use: to review a specific lexical set, e.g., food, common objects, etc.
Dynamic: groups
Procedure:

- Before the class, decide which lexical set you're going to test students on and decide the best sentence to lead in to this. If, for example, you want to review food, you can say: *I went to the store and I bought … .* However, if students haven't seen the simple past yet, you could adapt the game to review common objects: *In my bag, I have …,* etc.
- Demonstrate the activity with the lead-in sentence and then the first item, e.g., *In my bag, I have a pen.* Gesture to a student to repeat your sentence and add an item, e.g., *In my bag, I have a pen and a notebook.* They nominate the next student who repeats the sentence and adds another item, and so on until the list is too long to remember.
- Put students into groups of three to five to play together. Depending on your students, you may wish to adjust the difficulty of the activity. For example, ask students to include the number of each item, e.g., *… three textbooks, a notebook, and five pens.* Or if students have studied quantifiers, you can suggest they use these in their answers, e.g., *… some textbooks, a notebook, and a lot of pens.*

Backs to the board

Use: to review a specific lexical set or general vocabulary
Dynamic: whole class (in teams)
Procedure:

- Put students into small groups of four to five. If possible, mix more and less confident students so no group is noticeably stronger or weaker than another.
- Tell students in each group to sit close together, leaving space between the groups so they can't easily hear one another. Tell one student in each group to sit with their back to the board and the others to sit so that they can see the board.
- Explain that you're going to write a word or phrase on the board and that the students who can see the board have to communicate the meaning to the student who can't. They can use any method to do this, such as drawing pictures, miming, using synonyms, providing simple explanations, etc. However, use of a language other than English will mean they are disqualified.
- When the student(s) with their back(s) to the board think they know the word, they raise their hand(s). Ask the first student to raise their hand for the word, and, if they're correct, award their group a point. If they aren't, the other teams continue. Any student who shouts out the answer is also disqualified.
- The winning group is the one who has the most points at the end of the game.

Tennis

Use: to review specific word pairs, e.g., opposite adjectives, simple past / past participle forms, collocations
Dynamic: pairs
Procedure:

- Explain which lexical set you're going to work on, e.g., *adjectives.* Demonstrate the activity by asking a confident student to help you. Say an adjective, e.g., *old,* and ask the student to respond with the opposite, i.e., *new.* The student continues with a different adjective and you respond with its opposite.
- Tell students that, just like in a real game of tennis, it's important not to pause for a long time. If one of the students pauses too long between items, they lose that round, e.g., in **A** *old* **B** *new* – *good* **A** *bad* – *big* **B** *ummm ahhh … small,* **B** would lose.
- Put students into pairs to play together. Tell them they should continue for as long as possible. If one student loses the round, they start again.

Acknowledgments

Author

The authors and publishers acknowledge the following sources of copyright material and are grateful for the permissions granted. While every effort has been made, it has not always been possible to identify the sources of all the material used, or to trace all copyright holders. If any omissions are brought to our notice, we will be happy to include the appropriate acknowledgments on reprinting and in the next update to the digital edition, as applicable.

Screenshots are taken from Student's Book and Documentary videos.

Typeset by QBS Learning.

Corpus

Development of this publication has made use of the Cambridge English Corpus (CEC). The CEC is a computer database of contemporary spoken and written English, which currently stands at over one billion words. It includes British English, American English, and other varieties of English. It also includes the Cambridge Learner Corpus, developed in collaboration with the University of Cambridge ESOL Examinations. Cambridge University Press has built up the CEC to provide evidence about language use that helps us to produce better language teaching materials.

English Profile

This product is informed by English Vocabulary Profile, built as part of English Profile, a collaborative program designed to enhance the learning, teaching, and assessment of English worldwide. Its main funding partners are Cambridge University Press and Cambridge Assessment English, and its aim is to create a "profile" for English, linked to the Common European Framework of Reference for Languages (CEFR). English Profile outcomes, such as the English Vocabulary Profile, will provide detailed information about the language that learners can be expected to demonstrate at each CEFR level, offering a clear benchmark for learners' proficiency. For more information, please visit www.englishprofile.org.

CALD

The Cambridge Advanced Learner's Dictionary is the world's most widely used dictionary for learners of English. Including all the words and phrases that learners are likely to come across, it also has easy-to-understand definitions and example sentences to show how the word is used in context. The Cambridge Advanced Learner's Dictionary is available online at dictionary.cambridge.org.

This page is intentionally left blank.

This page is intentionally left blank.

This page is intentionally left blank.

This page is intentionally left blank.

This page is intentionally left blank.

This page is intentionally left blank.